D1131088

Waiting for Elijah

Waiting for Elijah DISCARD

A History of the Megiddo Mission

GARI-ANNE PATZWALD

The University of Tennessee Press   Knoxville

Copyright © 2002 by The University of Tennessee Press / Knoxville.
All Rights Reserved. Manufactured in the United States of America.
First Edition.

This book is printed on acid-free paper.

Library of Congress Cataloging-in-Publication Data

Patzwald, Gari-Anne.

Waiting for Elijah : a history of the Megiddo Mission / Gari

Anne Patzwald. — 1st ed.

p. cm.

Includes bibliographical references (p.   ) and index.

ISBN 1-57233-209-3 (cl.: alk. paper)

1. Megiddo Mission Church (Rochester, N.Y.)—History.

2. Rochester (N.Y.)—Church history.   I. Title.

BX9999.R66P38 2003

286.6'3—dc21   2002009063

To my teachers, mentors, and friends from the State University
of New York at Geneseo

Charles Randall ("Randy") Bailey, Susan Bailey, Kathryn J. Beck,
William R. Cook, Valentin H. Rabe, Richard V. Salisbury, and
Laureen A. Sherner

Contents

Illustrations

Foreword

Over the past several decades, scholarly interest in those religious communities that claim to have recaptured biblical truth and practice has mushroomed. Much of that interest has centered on groups with roots in the teachings of Barton W. Stone and Alexander Campbell, now often called the Stone-Campbell movement to distinguish these clusters of Christian believers from others who also claim to replicate biblical precept and practice. Such claims to absolute truth, while long a part of American religious life, have proved somewhat fragile. Any deviation from the truth, however minor, becomes something like a virus that invades the body of believers with a dangerous infection that must be countered and, if possible, destroyed. If such efforts fail, the only choice is to separate from the infected body and form a new religious community where, one hopes, truth will again flourish.

The Megiddo Mission Church, which in Patzwald's careful study receives its first sustained analytical treatment, is one such religious movement. Emerging from the teachings of L. T. Nichols when he was living in Oregon just after the Civil War, the Megiddo Mission Church (first called the Christian Brethren) has ties to the Restorationist impulse going back to Stone and Campbell. But by the time Nichols formulated his own theology, there had already been numerous separations of one group from another in an effort to capture and preserve the pure truth. Nichols himself had some associations with the Christadelphians, a small religious movement started in Virginia in the 1840s by British immigrant and physician John Thomas, who had himself separated from Alexander Campbell's movement after spending some time editing and writing for Campbellite periodicals.

Nichols and Thomas, like the early Campbellites, had a disdain for denominational structures, especially those controlled by clergy. Indeed, both believed that centuries of domination by clergy had almost fatally corrupted Christianity so that they must separate from others to recapture what they believed to be the essence of biblical teaching. Both hesitated to take a distinctive name for their adherents, insisting that the biblical record eschewed such trappings of denominationalism—but note the similarity between Nichols's early use of Christian Brethren and Thomas's Christadelphians (literally brothers of Christ). Both also shared an enduring preoccupation with the Second Coming of Christ and things eschatological, a fascination that had become muted among the Campbellites as generations passed.

But Nichols and his followers soon took a path that diverged from that of the Christadelphians and became a separate strand of the larger Restorationist-Adventist families. Patzwald does an admirable job unfolding the belief system that developed from Nichols's interpretation of Scripture, especially those passages that asserted the Hebrew prophet Elijah would return in bodily form prior to the second advent of Christ and the final culmination of history. The return of Elijah cemented Nichols's sense of religious kinship with the Hebrew tradition where waiting for Elijah's return marks the messianic hope embedded in the Passover Seder celebration, including setting a place at the table for Elijah. Woven into this idiosyncratic eschatological expectation are notions of sin, ideas about immortality, questions about the divinity of Christ, and challenges to orthodox Trinitarian thinking that make the Megiddo Mission Church unique among American religious groups and fascinating to study.

Nichols never attracted a large following—at its peak the Megiddo Mission Church numbered only a few hundred—but he was ahead of his time in the techniques he used to promote his vision of religious truth. Like others, Nichols worked the revival and camp meeting circuit when possible, sometimes organizing devotees into a paradelike cadre that marched through town literally drumming up interest. But most extraordinary was the use of a river steamer, the mission ship *Megiddo,* that sailed the Mississippi River system, docking at ports along the way, in the opening years of the twentieth century. Later, after the group coalesced in the Rochester, New York, area and the automobile became fashionable, a Megiddo gospel car became an alternative to the river steamer for a time. Nichols knew continuity of leadership was essential to preserving the pure truth, and he designated convert Maud Hembree, a one-time Roman Catholic and longtime associate, as his successor. Thus the Megiddo Mission Church offers a new lens through which to look at the role of women in American religious life in an age when most Christian groups denied women positions of leadership and formal authority.

Probably no larger today than a century ago, the Megiddo Mission Church remains based in Rochester, there maintaining its own version of Christian truth, down to a rather unorthodox understanding of Christmas and other festivals, and also keeping basic materials in print. The faithful remain alert for the signs of Elijah's return, eager to herald the return of Christ and the vindication that will come to the faithful when history draws to a close.

It is easy to overlook groups like the Megiddo Mission Church if for no other reason than because numerically it has always been small. Yet with the Megiddos, as with others, we have a rich opportunity to see not only the diversity that has marked the Restorationist movement but also the inner dynamics by which a small group, intent on avoiding bureaucracy and just as intent on remaining separate from a corrupt Christianity, has developed mechanisms for survival. In other words, we can learn much about the dynamics of small religious movements from the story of the Megiddo Mission Church.

In addition, Patzwald offers a model for how to go about fleshing out a group that has remained marginal if not elusive. She has tracked down not only the writings of L. T. Nichols, Maud Hembree, and some other key Megiddo Mission advocates but also a dazzling array of newspaper accounts that follow the group's movement from Oregon to the Midwest, along the Mississippi, and then to Rochester. In these journeys the group attracted attention and frequently found itself at the center of controversy. Patzwald also learned about the movement from contemporary followers, giving her account the flavor of a detailed and complex anthropological study of a tribal civilization. Patzwald has also probed the relevant sociological and historical literature, analyses of alternative religions, and materials regarding new religious movements to gather interpretive constructs that enable her to get a critical focus on the Megiddo Mission Church.

Readers will come away from this study with a deeper appreciation of Restorationist currents in American religious life and a better understanding of how to study what some have called the perfectly stable sectarian group, one that has never taken the time-honored path of moving from the margins and into a structured denomination. Patzwald brings to life the Megiddo Mission Church as it awaits Elijah's return to inaugurate the culmination of history itself.

Charles H. Lippy

LeRoy A. Martin Distinguished
Professor of Religious Studies
The University of Tennessee
at Chattanooga

Preface

When I was about eleven years old, one summer afternoon, I rode my bicycle from my home on a residential street on the southwest side of Rochester, New York, to Thurston Road, a nearby street occupied by a combination of homes and businesses. Among the businesses with particular appeal to me and my friends were an ice cream parlor/candy store, a bakery, and a five-and-dime store where one could really buy things for a nickel.

As I walked my bicycle along Thurston Road, I glanced over at the complex of buildings, the entrance to which was marked by a large arch with a banner heading that read "Megiddo Mission" and a periodically changed Bible verse underneath in large white letters. That particular day, a group of women had a large piece of fabric, perhaps a carpet, spread out on tables on the lawn, and they were obviously engaged in a sewing project. In spite of the warm weather, the women were dressed in high-necked, long-sleeved dresses that had hemlines down to their shoe tops. I tried not to stare, but it was not easy; the women of the Megiddo Mission were always somewhat of a curiosity. I admit that I was somewhat suspicious, if not afraid, of the strangely dressed women, although I had often seen them stop on the street for friendly conversation with other women attired in what we would call normal clothes.

In 1995, when searching for a subject for a graduate project at Lexington Theological Seminary, I turned my curiosity about the Megiddos into a thesis that has now become this book. Coincidentally, as I began my research, I discovered that the Megiddo Church evolved out of the same tradition as the Christian Church (Disciples of Christ), the denomination with which the seminary is affiliated.

The purpose of this book is to help readers understand the Megiddo Church, an association of dedicated people who have elected to separate themselves from the mainstream of American society because they believe they are called to an exceptional way of living in order to achieve their goal of eternal life. The book is arranged in a chronological-topical manner, with subjects being discussed in their entirety as they arise in the chronology. An appendix features a member's diary kept during a ministry that the church conducted on the Mississippi and Ohio Rivers. This boat ministry has to some degree shaped if not the actual history of the Megiddo Church at least the way that members perceive their history. The diary not only describes the ministry but also gives a sense of the dedication and faith that have undergirded the church throughout its history.

Writing a history of the Megiddo Church has been a challenge. As member Margaret Tremblay noted, the church is looking forward to the coming return of Christ and has little interest preserving mementos of its past, a contention confirmed by historian Richard T. Hughes, who noted in *The Primitive Church in the Modern World* (Urbana: University of Illinois Press, 1995) that a central theme in the Restorationist tradition, the tradition out of which the Megiddo Church developed, is "a rejection of any sense of history." Personal papers and church records are not routinely retained, and I have been very dependent on newspaper accounts for the early history of the church. Newspapers, of course, focus on newsworthy events and, especially in the late nineteenth century, when even fairly small communities had more than one newspaper, have tended to put the most sensational slant possible on events in order to sell papers. One needs to remember that while some members of the church have been involved in activities that came to the attention of the press, the vast majority have led lives of dedicated Christian service well removed from the media spotlight.

I have many people to thank for helping me find information. The Megiddo Church has been generous in sharing its few records as well as manuscript items, scrapbooks, and literature produced by the church and its founder, L. T. Nichols, beginning with published camp meeting minutes from 1882.

It would have been impossible to produce this book without the cooperation, assistance, and hospitality of the members of the Megiddo Church. Deserving of special note are Pastor Ruth Sisson, who answered my constant questions; former pastor Newton H. Payne, whose wisdom, recollections, insights, and interest in saving the photographic records of the church helped the church's past come alive for me; Margaret Tremblay, who assisted with photographs and whose enthusiasm for the church and its doctrines is infectious; and Elva and Shirley Byers, Alice Cummings, Clifford and Donna Ruth Mathias, and David and Marie Sutton, who shared memories and perceptions.

Much of the research outside the church involved finding newspaper articles, some public records, files kept by historical societies, information compiled by genealogists, and even a seminary student research paper. For helping me locate and use these materials, I would like to thank Jennifer Blacke, a professional researcher who located most of the resources I needed for the Oregon part of the story and who saved me immeasurable time and effort; Owen J. Nichols, who provided genealogical information about the family of the church's founder; and Idella M. Conwell of the Dodge County (Minnesota) Historical Society. Joan Marie Meyering, who is also doing research on the Megiddo

Church, shared information she had found and put me in touch with a former member of the mission, who provided helpful information and insights. Several librarians have been most helpful, including Janet Timberlake, interlibrary loan librarian at Lexington Theological Seminary; Wayne Arnold of the Local History Division of the Rochester Public Library; Sue Rhee of Northwest Christian College; Lotte Larsen of Western Oregon University; and Peggy Rawlings of the Barry (Illinois) Public Library. Special thanks to Dorothy James of the B. L. Fisher Library at Asbury Theological Seminary for her skillful acquiring of numerous reels of newspapers on microfilm and many obscure books and pamphlets.

I have made extensive use of newspapers on microfilm from the Illinois Historical Society, the Minnesota Historical Society, the State Historical Society of Iowa, the University of Kentucky, and Rochester Public Library. Tom Flynn provided me with access to photographs in the collection of the Gannet Rochester Newspapers. Jim Lutzweiler was kind enough to give me the hard copies of more than seventy years of the *Megiddo Message* after he completed the microfiche edition. Richard Kostlevy assisted with the illustrations, and Jeanne Sturgill provided computer support.

Finally, I would like to thank my advisor Philip E. Dare of Lexington Theological Seminary for advice and encouragement; Rochester genealogist and historian Karen E. Dau for casting a critical eye on the manuscript and making helpful suggestions; Professor Madeleine Duntley of the College of Wooster for showing me new possibilities for my manuscript; church historian William Kostlevy of Asbury Theological Seminary for assisting at all points in the preparation of the manuscript; Charles H. Lippy, who clarified some elusive elements of Christadelphian doctrine and practice; Joyce Harrison, acquisitions editor of the University of Tennessee Press; those who reviewed my manuscript for the press for many helpful suggestions; and my colleagues at the University of Kentucky for their flexibility in allowing me to adjust my schedule to accommodate my research needs.

All possible efforts have been made to present the Megiddos' history and doctrines as accurately as possible given the limited resources available. I take full responsibility for any inadvertent errors.

Introduction

The Restorationist movement in Protestantism arose in the United States about the beginning of the nineteenth century with the goal of restoring the New Testament church. Its most influential early manifestations were a group headed by Barton Stone that separated from the Presbyterian Church in Kentucky in 1803 and the followers of Alexander Campbell, known as Campbellites, who left the Presbyterian Church in 1808. These groups united in 1831, adopting the names Christian Church and Disciples of Christ.

The Restorationists looked to biblical authority for direction, but as children of the Enlightenment, they took a rationalist approach to Scripture, and since the reason applied to the biblical text by individuals was informed by their own experiences and exposures, divisions soon developed. These divisions spawned various sects and denominations, the most notable of which is the Churches of Christ. One smaller Restorationist denomination, the Christadelphians, followers of former Campbellite John Thomas, included Wisconsin Civil War veteran, entrepreneur, and itinerant preacher L. T. Nichols, who would come into conflict with Thomas's successors and organize his followers into what would eventually become the Megiddo Church.

While the roots of his theology lay in biblical authority and in the writings of John Thomas, Nichols added several elements of nineteenth-century American thought and culture to produce a remarkably vital and enduring small sect. Among these were the redefinition of gender roles and sexuality, patriotism, perfectionism, and communitarianism, which he tempered with elements of middle-class capitalism.

While most of the Restorationist denominations either became locked into a system of ceremonial practices (for example, the weekly celebration of communion) or adopted creedal statements that made change difficult, the Megiddos, under Nichols's direction, retained a commitment to biblical authority and reason, and the church remained open to new insights into the meaning of Scripture and accepted the possibility that old meanings could be found wanting. New interpretations and emphases have allowed the church to respond with surprising dynamism to changes both within the group and in American society. However, evidence that elements of the Restorationist tradition have persisted in its theology is the selection of its multipart Bible study series, "Understanding the Bible," as a text for the Barton W. Stone School of Divinity, a distance-learning program operated by the Evangelical Christian Church (Disciples of Christ), a group that seeks to restore the church of Campbell and Stone.[1]

Since 1880, the key to Megiddo orthodoxy has been the doing of so-called good works, which includes everything they see the Scriptures as directing them to do. This has manifested itself most obviously in their efforts to spread their message. Nichols employed a variety of promotional techniques to draw attention to his teachings and to his church: public debate, public lectures on controversial topics (for example, the springtime celebration of Christmas) or topics of popular interest (for example, temperance), camp meetings, tent revivals, a uniformed band, newspapers, pamphlets, and, in spite of an aversion to popular entertainment, a bandwagon and a religious version of the show-boat. Nichols's followers have expanded on his creativity through the use of automobiles (especially a slogan-covered gospel car), door-to-door evangelism, a magazine, tracts, advertising in popular magazines, a book publication to coincide with public interest in the millennium, and use of the Internet.

No discussion of the Megiddo Church would be complete without a consideration of whether or not it is a communal society. Most of the members of the Megiddo Church live in or near a complex of cream-colored frame buildings behind a green arch on Thurston Road in Rochester, New York, and at first glance the members appear to comprise a communal society. However, for the Megiddos, the suggestion that they are a communal society is treated as an accusation—one that they have been fighting since the early years of their existence in Oregon.[2]

Throughout its history, America has been viewed as a promised land, a place where utopian dreams can be fulfilled. While most of these dreams involved individual effort, thousands of people envisioned spiritual salvation or economic prosperity through communal effort. Consequently, communal societies of three main types—religious, social, and economic—proliferated. Most were short-lived and little-noticed; a few were long-lived and noteworthy.

In an era in which communal societies such as the Shakers are the subject of considerable curiosity and often admiration, it may be difficult to understand the reasons behind the Megiddos' vehement denial that they are communitarian. To do so, one must understand the way in which such groups were viewed when the Megiddos evolved into a distinctive religious body.

According to Philip Jenkins, "though controversy had always surrounded marginal religious groups," it was during the 1870s and 1880s, the very time when the Megiddos were developing their separate identity, that "an accumulation of scandals and exposés led to a public reaction against fringe religious groups." Communal groups, who usually eschewed contact with the wider society, were particularly vulnerable to attack in the press and were often the subjects of sensational news stories, which focused on their peculiarities, especially unusual sexual practices (such as among the Shakers and in the Oneida Community), or abusive or exploitive leaders (for example, Frank Sandford of Shiloh or John Alexander Dowie of Zion). These exposés occasionally even led to attempts to legislate restrictions on the groups' activities. Consequently, the designation "communal" or "communitarian" came to have a negative connotation.[3]

In addition, the cooperative economic aspects of communal societies were in conflict with the individualistic entrepreneurial atmosphere of the Gilded Age into which the Megiddos' founder fit so well. In the twentieth century, the aversion to designation as a communal society has been reinforced for the patriotic Megiddos by the association of community of goods with Soviet communism and with the controversial hippie communes that arose in the 1960s.

Whether or not the Megiddos constitute a communal society may well depend on one's definition of the term *communitarian*. In the strictest sense of the usual economic definition of a communal society, they are not a communal society because they do not practice community of goods. However, there may be more than one definition of a communal society. In the preface to *America's Communal Utopias,* Donald E. Pitzer recounts the response of Madeline Roemig, a descendant of members of the Amana Colony of Iowa, to Pitzer's contention that the Colony ceased to be communal in 1932 when it abandoned community of goods. Roemig countered, "We are still a community. We still share common concerns. We still care deeply for one another. We still practice the faith of our religious movement. We still worship together."[4] Perhaps what constitutes a communal society depends on what one requires the members have in common. Or perhaps it is in the eye of the participant rather than the eye of the beholder.

While L. T. Nichols eschewed community of goods, he developed a system for the financial support of the church that has virtually assured its endurance. By helping his followers prosper economically through a form of cooperative middle-class capitalism, which often involved investment in real estate, and encouraging tithing, Nichols created the foundation for the development of a stable financial base for the church. This base was enhanced through the church's doctrine, which discouraged childbearing, resulting in substantial amounts of property being willed to the church by childless members.

In an age when communal societies are considered by at least one expert to have been successful if they lasted past the first generation, Nichols managed to create an organization that has most of the characteristics of a communal society but which, by maintaining a commitment to the concept of private property, has managed to avoid the pitfall at the root of the failures of many if not most communal societies—the stifling of individual initiative. As one newspaper reporter described the group that became the Megiddos, "They are alert to a community of interest, but they do not seek to destroy competition." Furthermore, in discouraging childbearing the Megiddos avoided the problem identified by Dolores Hayden: "by the third or fourth generation, members of even the most stable experimental societies usually grow restless and choose to rejoin the outside world." Although there are second-generation members, including current pastor Ruth Sisson, the Megiddos have depended on converts to replenish their numbers and, consequently, first-generation members have always constituted most of the membership. As a result, the semicommunitarian Megiddo Church is well into its second century.[5]

In his seminal work *Religious Outsiders and the Making of Americans,* R. Laurence Moore wrote that "the American religious system may be said to be 'working' only when it is creating cracks within denominations, when it is producing novelty, even when it is fueling antagonisms. These things are not things which, properly understood, are going on at the edges or fringes of American life. They are what give energy to church life and substance to the claim that Americans are the most religious people on the face of the earth."[6] If Moore is correct, as long as there are sects like the Megiddos, religion will remain one of the most dynamic threads in the fabric of America.

Finally, although the Megiddo Church or Megiddo Mission is included in several lists of so-called cults, primarily lists on the World Wide Web, I have elected to avoid using the term. The word *cult* is often used by scholars to signify groups with distinctive doctrines or practices that look for authority to a person who either claims a special relationship with a higher power or to whom special powers or insights are attributed.[7] Under this definition the Megiddo Church would qualify. However, in popular usage, the term *cult* has become a largely pejorative term used to designate any religious group with which the user of the word strongly disagrees. Consequently, the word *cult* has become virtually useless for describing a religious group of any kind.[8]

1

A New Faith on a New Frontier

Beginning in the 1920s, classified and display advertisements heralding the imminent coming of Elijah in preparation for the return of Christ began to appear in publications in the midwestern United States. Later, the campaign that produced the advertisements was expanded to include national publications and the advertisements became familiar to readers of magazines as diverse as *The Christian Herald, Prevention, Saturday Review,* and *Psychology Today,* which published the following classified advertisement in its December 1983 issue:

> FREE BOOK. Prophet Elijah Coming Before Christ.
> Megiddo Mission, Dept. 60, 481 Thurston Road,
> Rochester, N.Y. 14619.

These advertisements were placed by a small sect firmly rooted in the Restorationist tradition of Alexander Campbell and his followers, the Campbellites, or Disciples of Christ. Since 1880, the dedicated Christians who became the Megiddo Mission, and now the Megiddo Church, have spread their message throughout the United States and English-speaking Canada and occasionally outside North America, not only through advertisements and the mails but also via gospel boats, a gospel car, automobiles, bicycles and motorcycles, and, more recently, the Internet.

The Megiddo Mission grew out of the ministry of Civil War veteran, farmer, inventor, and minister L. T. Nichols. L. T.'s father, Lemuel Truesdale Nichols, was born in the so-called burned-over district of upstate New York. Over a period of several decades, he followed the frontier and eventually settled in the Pacific Northwest. Before 1834, Lemuel Nichols moved to Michigan, where he married Emeline Dunbar, another native New Yorker. The couple relocated to the South Bend area of northern Indiana, where, on October 1, 1844, their third child, a son, was born and given his father's initials, L. T., instead of a name.[1]

Sometime after L. T.'s birth, the family moved to Indianapolis, where another son was born. In 1849, they continued their westward migration, relocating to a farm near Lomira, Dodge County, Wisconsin, about eighty miles northwest of Milwaukee.[2]

The Wisconsin in which the Nicholses settled had recently experienced phenomenal growth, with the population quintupling between 1842 and 1847, and had been admitted to the Union in 1848. By 1850, the population numbered 305,390, most of whom lived in the southeastern quarter of the state and about 80 percent of whom were engaged in farming. The population of the state tended to be settled in ethnic enclaves, and the 1850 census indicates that in one Dodge County community, seventy-eight of eighty-one families had roots in New York or New England. Following the political and social unrest of 1848 in Europe, there was an influx of immigrants to Wisconsin, and the Lomira population became increasingly German over the next several decades.[3]

In 1849, economic development was just beginning in Wisconsin and transportation was rudimentary. There were few navigable waterways, and although the railroad was first extended into the state in 1849, it was many years before rail service was widely available. Roads were few and many were impassible in some seasons of the year, but the road between Milwaukee and Fond du Lac, the nearest city of any size to the Nicholses' farm, did allow for thrice-weekly stagecoach service by 1850.[4]

Like most newcomers, the Nicholses probably chose Wisconsin because excellent farmland was available at cheap prices, but living on the primitive land was not an easy task. The first white settler had arrived in Lomira only five years before, and the immediate area was still sparsely populated, so assistance and supplies were not conveniently available.

Typical of the area, the farm on which the Nicholses settled was heavily wooded, providing material for the crude log house in which the family initially lived. The house had no fireplace, making it necessary to cook outside. Nichols remembered that "the wild Indians were all around us in the daytime; and bears, wildcats, panthers, and deer around us at night." He frequently told of going out in the dark to fetch wood and seeing the eyes of wild animals observing him from among the surrounding trees.[5]

Most of what little is known about L. T. Nichols's early life is drawn largely from materials compiled into a biography, originally titled *The Life and Work of the Rev. L. T. Nichols,* a revised version of which is published by the Megiddo

Church under the title *An Honest Man: The Life and Work of L. T. Nichols.* The manuscript was assembled in the early 1940s by E. C. Branham, a member of the mission, from references in Nichols's sermons and from recollections of members of the mission who had known Nichols and his family. Since Nichols's youngest sister, Ella, was alive at the time and was a member of the mission, it is possible she contributed to the book and reviewed its contents for accuracy. The volume was published in 1944 to coincide with the centennial of Nichols's birth. Parts of the book have also been published in the church's magazine, the *Megiddo Message.*[6]

L. T. Nichols, circa 1890. Courtesy Megiddo Church, Rochester, N.Y.

The source of L. T. Nichols's religious education is uncertain, and there may have been several elements that contributed to it. According to *An Honest Man,* he received his initial religious instruction from his mother, who was "of the Christian or 'Campbellite' persuasion." He also may have attended a Sunday school class of unknown theological orientation held in a local schoolhouse. There is some suggestion he attended Methodist services in his youth. In sermons he preached late in his life, he mentioned having attended a Christmas celebration at a Methodist church, and he made reference to a statement contained in "the old Methodist Catechism away back when I was a boy."[7] Whatever the roots of his religious views, even as a child, Nichols began to have doubts about the religious truths his elders taught him. Increasingly into adolescence, he sought his own truth through careful study of the Bible.

According to *An Honest Man,* life was not easy for the young L. T. Nichols. His father became an invalid and Nichols became responsible for much of the work on the family farm. In what time he had away from physical labors, he studied Scripture. As a result, he gained a local reputation as a budding religious scholar and preacher, a reputation that apparently made him an object of ridicule among his schoolmates. By the age of thirteen, Nichols's interest in religion earned him the sobriquet "the boy preacher." A mission member recalled Nichols and his mother telling how he would take his Bible to school with him and try to interest his classmates in Bible study at lunchtime and during recess. At age eleven, he vowed to refrain from tobacco, alcohol, and the use of profanity, and he promised never to commit an immoral act, a pledge that may well have been influenced by his parents, or at least by his mother, who had been affiliated with a chapter of the Washingtonian Temperance Society in Goshen, Indiana, about the time of L. T. Nichols's birth.[8]

On October 6, 1864, L. T. Nichols was drafted into the U.S. Army. The draft had been instituted in 1862 when the realities of war reduced the number of volunteers and Wisconsin had become unable to meet its quota of soldiers through voluntary means. While the draft was accepted by most Wisconsinites, it met with some resistance, especially among German immigrants, many of whom had come to the United States to escape conscription in their native countries. There were antidraft demonstrations in Milwaukee, and rioting broke out in Port Washington in Ozaukee County, which resulted in considerable property damage and the dispatch of troops to quell the disturbance. In Dodge County, where Nichols lived, one of the enrolling officers was murdered and there was a demonstration by two or three hundred Germans, most of them armed. As a consequence of these actions and of the sense among the volunteers that the draftees were unpatriotic and cowardly, the volunteers by 1863 had developed a low opinion of conscripts and treated them with disdain. "From the time they were mustered in the draftees were under armed guard and the guards were under orders to shoot anyone who tried to escape. . . . Upon their arrival in Madison the conscripts were first imprisoned in the stockaded 'bull pen' within the camp . . . under constant surveillance from an elevated walkway."[9] A statement by Nichols that he was "held in the army, taken to Fond du Lac, from there to Madison; was waiting in suspense and was taken into camp and evil entreated for 8 months" suggests that he may have been among those to suffer the consequences of the earlier draft resistance.[10]

In Madison, Nichols was stationed at Camp Randall. For the newly drafted soldier, the camp was often an unwelcoming environment. It had been constructed in 1861 on the state fairgrounds to the west of the city, and by the time L. T. Nichols arrived there in 1864, housing for the troops was a conglomerate of converted stables, barracks of varying quality, and tents. After three years of constant trampling by drilling troops, the ground was devoid of vegetation and was either dusty or muddy depending on the weather.

The moral atmosphere was lax. Although there were some Good Templars and other temperance advocates among the soldiers at Camp Randall, most of the soldiers drank alcohol and smoked tobacco. Many played cards and engaged in other forms of gambling.[11] However, there were also regimental chaplains and regular religious services.

Nichols joined the army reluctantly, believing it was wrong to kill even in wartime. It is not certain how he developed his pacifist views. According to *An Honest Man,* it was through his study of Scripture, but it may also be evidence of his ties to the Campbellites. Although pacifism was certainly not universal among Campbellites, almost all of the early leaders of the movement, including Campbell himself, counseled their followers to refrain from participation in the military in the Civil War. Some southern members of the Christian Church even petitioned Jefferson Davis and were granted exemption from service in the Confederate army. Mennonite theologian John Howard Yoder noted that many Disciples held to pacifism during the Civil War "with more vigor" than some of the traditionally pacifist Mennonites.[12]

Under the Act of February 24, 1864, the U.S. government recognized as conscientious objectors "members of religious denominations, who shall by oath or affirmation declare that they are conscientiously opposed to the bearing of arms, and who are prohibited from doing so by the rules and articles of faith and practice of said denominations." The secretary of war was directed to assign them to noncombatant duties in hospitals or to providing services to freedmen.[13] However, according to *An Honest Man,* Nichols had difficulty establishing his status as a conscientious objector. This was probably because he was not affiliated with a religious body or because the body with which he was affiliated was not recognized as exempt from combat duty. Apparently, Nichols's difficulties were fairly short-lived. By February 1865, while his regiment had been sent to the Louisville, Kentucky, area, he had been assigned to duty as a nurse in the post hospital in Madison.

Nichols stated in a sermon illustration that he was "Superintendent . . . of the largest Post hospital in the State where I lived. I had entire charge of everything; nothing could be bought without an order from me." However, Nichols's military record contains no indication that he held a supervisory position, and it is unlikely he did so due to his young age, low rank, and lack of experience. Supervisory personnel were usually men with some military or medical experience who were assigned to the hospital and were not subject to transfer. On the other hand, nurses were drawn from the ranks and were often soldiers in the later stages of convalescence. In most cases, these nurses "lacked training and few showed natural aptitude. And they were nearly always called back to their regiments as soon as they had learned enough to be of any use." Because Nichols had a strong work ethic and was in the unique position of being unlikely to be transferred, it is possible he was assigned the duties of a ward master, supervising patient care and cleaning on a hospital ward, and as such he may have had responsibility for procuring supplies for the ward. There is also the possibility that because the camp was sparsely populated toward the end of the war, he may have been given responsibilities beyond those a nurse would have had had there been more experienced soldiers available. Whatever his position, Nichols served in the hospital until his separation from the service in May 1865.[14]

It should be noted here that much of the material in *An Honest Man* was drawn from Nichols's sermons and that may affect the content and character of the information. Autobiographical accounts in sermons are usually designed to illustrate points, and ministers have always been given a certain latitude to alter, embellish, or dramatize life events to make them fit the requirements of the message. Consequently, while it is likely that the essential facts of incidents recounted by Nichols in his sermons are accurate, details may have been altered to enhance the ability of the events to illustrate his points.

It is evident that Nichols's military service was a watershed event in his life, and he told many stories of his military service. For example, according to the stories, patients at the hospital where he served entrusted their money to him for safekeeping, and, even though he had no medical training, he "even devised improved methods of treatment for the sick." None of these stories can be verified due to a paucity of sources, but what is known about Nichols from the accounts of people who knew him and his subsequent demonstrated inventiveness lend them an air of plausibility. Regardless of their accuracy, the stories are important to the members of the church both because of what they say about Nichols and because, given the American romantic fascination with the Civil War, they are useful in conveying Nichols's qualities to outsiders.[15]

Upon separation from the service, Nichols returned to Dodge County and to his wife, Harriet Eliza Griffis Nichols, a school classmate whom he had married on October 15, 1864. He purchased a farm near Fond du Lac, Wisconsin, and, in addition to farming, developed and maintained a preaching circuit that took him to the nearby towns and cities of Oshkosh, Berlin, Green Bay, and Ripon.

According to historian Whitney R. Cross, the religious fervor that earned western New York the designation "the burned-over district" had died out by the middle of the nineteenth century, partly as a result of the decline of agrarian culture in the region. The focus of religious enthusiasm then transferred to parts of the Midwest, such as southern Wisconsin, where agrarian culture survived. Here, "new religious phenomena, somewhat similar to those experienced [in western New York] before 1850, later developed under conditions at least slightly reminiscent of western New York in the period of its spiritual experiments."[16] In such an environment, it is likely that Nichols found a receptive audience for his ministry.

By 1868, Nichols had become acquainted with the Christadelphians, a small religious body that rejected tradition and sought to recover the essence of biblical teaching and the characteristics of the early church through direct study of Scripture. The Christadelphians had grown out of the Campbellites, who encouraged a strong sense of community, practiced adult believers' baptism, and observed the Lord's Supper weekly, as do the Disciples of Christ today.

John Thomas, founder of the Christadelphians, was a physician who was born in England but immigrated to America in 1830, where he joined the Campbellites. After a falling out with Alexander Campbell, he embarked on an independent preaching ministry, touring the United States and speaking on the eschatological significance of past and current events based on examination of the Old Testament, primarily the book of Daniel, and the New Testament book of Revelation.

Initially, Thomas's followers were not organized into a denomination, but during the Civil War, in an attempt to gain conscientious objector status for his followers, Thomas adopted the name "Christadelphian." Thomas's efforts were successful in the parts of the South where his adherents were exempted from military service but came too late in the war to help the brethren in the North.[17]

Nichols's contact with the Christadelphians may have been through his mother's affiliation with the Campbellites since Thomas had drawn many of his followers from among his former associates; or, Nichols may have encountered them in the army during the Civil War. However he found them, in 1866 or 1868 Nichols went to Milwaukee to hear Thomas preach. Recalling the trip in an 1882 sermon, he noted that he had been "much rejoiced to hear [Thomas] talk about, and expound the truth."[18]

Wisconsin was part of the frontier when the Nichols family first moved there, but by 1871, the frontier had moved further west.[19] Like many others, members of the Nichols family, including Lemuel Truesdale, L. T. and his wife, and L. T.'s brother, George, resumed the family's westward migration. They left Wisconsin for Kansas in 1871 as part of a group of sixty-one families from the Ripon, Wisconsin, area called "the Northwestern Association," or "Northwest Colony," who founded the city of Russell, Kansas. The three Nichols men signed the articles of association and purchased property. For unknown reasons, the Nicholses did not remain in Kansas long and returned to Wisconsin during the first half of 1872.[20]

The Nicholses' return to Wisconsin was short-lived and in 1874, L. T. and Harriet Nichols moved to a large farm near McMinnville, Yamhill County,

Oregon. Accompanying them from Wisconsin were some of L. T. Nichols's followers, including his parents; his sister, Ella; and several members of his wife's family. There L. T. Nichols continued to farm; he also sold sewing machines and invented and manufactured agricultural implements and continued his religious activities.

The Megiddo Church regards the frontier as a place with "a special purpose in the plan of God; [because] it proved to be the forum where true religion could . . . be proclaimed," and, indeed, there were many factors at work on the frontier that would have made it a fertile ground for evangelization. In his study of Sublimity, Oregon, a community southeast of McMinnville on the other side of the Willamette Valley, Dean May noted that in the post–Civil War period, the scattered nature of the population made it difficult to develop churches. Religious services were often held in buildings built for other purposes, such as schoolhouses. In his study of Middleton, Idaho, May suggests that church development in the West may have been affected by the fact that people on the frontier were long separated from their former churches, and when they came together to form new churches, at least in the Boise Valley, they were not seeking "a replication of the Baptist congregations these folks had left in the Midwest or Old South" but were instead open to new ideas and forms. Consequently, the Pacific Northwest may have seemed to Nichols to be fertile ground for his ministry.[21] It is interesting to note that in a conversation in 1997, Joan Marie Salzmann (Meyering), author of an article on the Oregon Christadelphians that appeared in the March/April 1997 issue of the genealogy magazine *Heritage Quest,* equated the Megiddos with religious cults currently of concern in Oregon.

By 1877, Nichols had established a firm connection with the Christadelphians, and he may well have thought that he could draw converts from among those with similar beliefs who were affiliated with the Christian Church already established in the McMinnville area. As it happened, he attracted not only Disciples but also people from a variety of religious backgrounds.

As he began to acquire followers, Nichols sent the British Christadelphians lists of people he had baptized. These lists were printed in *The Christadelphian* magazine and gave the names and previous religious affiliations of the converts. In addition to Campbellites, those baptized included Methodists, Adventists, Baptists, and Spiritualists. One William Green is listed as having been an "infidel."[22] Men and women appear to have joined the group in about equal numbers, which was typical of Christadelphian churches. Several members were single women, in spite of the fact that "Christadelphianism has no distinctive appeal to women. It offers them no important roles in the movement, and in general favours no form of feminism."[23]

Census records indicate that Nichols drew his followers mainly from among fellow farmers and farmworkers and their families. A few tradesmen, including a carpenter, a bricklayer, a gardener, and two blacksmiths, were also among the members, as were two merchants and one doctor. These members were quite different from the British Christadelphians, who, according to Bryan Wilson, were "from among the very poorest members of the community—often labourers and manual workers."[24]

In spite of their differences, Americans and British were both attracted to the Christadelphians because of their powerful apocalyptic message, initially evident in the writings of John Thomas. While the apocalyptic promise of improved status following the Second Coming appealed to disadvantaged people like the British Christadelphians, other forces were operating to make apocalyptic attractive to the new settlers in the West. Inspired by Manifest Destiny, the idea that American civilization was destined to spread across the country to the Pacific Coast, settlers left stable environments and institutions and moved West. Buoyed by high hopes, these pioneers often found only hard work, uncertainty, and isolation in the West. These people were ripe for the apocalyptic message of the Christadelphians because, as Charles Lippy noted, "the social fluidity of westward expansion" and other forces operating in the latter half of the nineteenth century "all left a feeling of personal and social dislocation among large numbers of Americans," and "strong interest in apocalypticism comes during times of social instability or transition . . . when once-operative norms and standards no longer regulate or explain behavior . . . These conditions created a setting which charismatic prophets found ripe for harvesting followers."[25]

In rural Yamhill County, Nichols and his followers founded a Christadelphian church, or "ecclesia," that initially met in the Nicholses' home or the homes of other members.[26] Eventually they built a large church on property owned by one of the members. The congregation grew to about fifty members in the immediate vicinity who were joined by others from more distant places for an annual three-week camp meeting, begun in 1878.

It is surprising that Nichols chose the camp meeting as a vehicle for gathering followers. In spite of the important role Barton W. Stone (1772–1844), of the Disciples of Christ, played in the early history of the camp meeting, in the popular mind of the 1880s the meeting was associated with two important elements of American Protestantism that were anathema to Nichols—the holiness movement and revivalism. The holiness movement institutionalized the camp meeting through its National Campmeeting Association for the Promotion of Holiness, and camp meetings were often where large groups of people obtained the experience that characterized the movement—entire sanctification, an instantaneous assurance of salvation that was in direct opposition to Nichols's doctrine of a gradual progression toward salvation through a lifetime of good works. Camp meetings were also associated with revivals, the emotionalism of which was offensive to rational Restorationists like Nichols. Nevertheless, Nichols gathered his followers annually for meetings largely devoted to his preaching on matters of doctrine and lifestyle with lesser amounts of time devoted to communion, the reading of correspondence, and an occasional debate.[27]

Throughout the latter half of the nineteenth century, public religious debates were popular, serving not only as sources of edification but also as entertainment. Debates were particularly popular in the Restorationist tradition because of its rationalist orientation. Alexander Campbell believed that "orderly discussion on clearly stated propositions was one of the ways that biblical truth might be advanced," and beginning in 1820, over a twenty-three year period, he participated in five highly publicized debates, including one with the Roman Catholic archbishop of Cincinnati, John B. Purcell, and what was perhaps his most famous debate, one with Robert Owen (1771–1858), the Scottish utopian visionary who founded a short-lived colony devoted to the advancement of learning at New Harmony, Indiana.[28]

In the tradition of Alexander Campbell, L. T. Nichols became a frequent debater. His most noteworthy debate in Oregon was with Thomas Campbell, president of Monmouth College, a Disciples of Christ institution in Monmouth, Oregon; editor of the *Pacific Christian Messenger;* and a student of Alexander Campbell. The debate was announced several weeks in advance in Campbell's publication, and a large crowd assembled in Carlton, Oregon, for its start at 10:00 A.M. on June 27, 1877. The debate lasted four hours a day for three days and addressed two topics: the existence of heaven and the destination of the soul after death. People came from as far away as one hundred miles, brought their lunches, and stayed all day. Following the debate, as was true with most religious debates of the day, both sides claimed victory. The *Pacific Christian Messenger* stated in its July 12, 1877, issue that "we have heard of no one who was convinced by Mr. Nichols." Nichols, on the other hand, reported to *The Christadelphian,* the British Christadelphian publication, that he "had a three days' discussion with a prominent Campbellite advocate, resulting in obedience to the faith on the part of a number."[29]

Among those attracted to the debate between Campbell and Nichols was Mrs. Maud Hembree, a homemaker from the McMinnville area. Sarah Maud Galloway Hembree was born in Amity, Oregon, in 1853. She was raised a devout Roman Catholic and was an unlikely person to become a follower of L. T. Nichols; however, his presentation at the debate convinced her, and she quickly became one of his most devoted disciples and a leader among the Christadelphians.[30]

About 1878, L. T. Nichols became involved in a controversy that divided Christadelphians in both the United States and England. Known as the "Renunciationist" or "Free Life" controversy, it arose among Christadelphians in England in the early 1870s and quickly spread to North America. According to the orthodox Christadelphian position, Christ was human, and, although he himself did not sin, he had inherited Adam's sinful nature. According to the Renunciationists, since Jesus was the son of God, he was not under Adamic condemnation and, consequently, his death was not an atonement for the sins of others.[31]

Nichols adopted the Renunciationist position, which he explained in an 1881 pamphlet titled *Adam before He Sinned.* In the pamphlet, Nichols stated that God was the father of Jesus, and "as God cannot be the father of any when under condemnation, as stated in John 3, 18, he that believeth on him is NOT condemned, we must conclude that Christ was not under wrath or condemnation." In the pamphlet, Nichols was openly critical of both John Thomas and his successor as de facto leader of the Christadelphians, Robert Roberts, citing their views on the atonement as unscriptural. He rejected the notion that Christ ever sinned or that he took human sins upon himself and died to atone for them. Instead, he contended that Christ died as an example of total obedience to God, the type of obedience that would be required for anyone to become one of the 144,000 who would be saved at the judgment.[32] The idea that Jesus died to show obedience carried the Christadelphian emphasis on works as a demonstration of faith to its logical conclusion in Jesus' ultimate act of obedience.

Nichols's position on the Renunciationist controversy was a significant factor in a split among his followers. About 1879, nine people led by W. L. Skeels and H. C. Plummer separated from the Nichols group and relocated to Scholl's Ferry, Oregon, from where they wrote letters to *The Christadelphian* criticizing Nichols and defending their position. At the same time, the distribution of a Nichols pamphlet entitled "Christadelphian Synopsis of the Truth" angered readers of *The Christadelphian,* one of whom complained that it contained "a great deal that no Christadelphian can endorse [and] a great deal that is quite subversive of the one faith for which we contend and which we hold."[33] The criticism would have no effect on Nichols, and a later edition of the "Synopsis of Truth" would become a standard of orthodoxy in the Megiddo Church.

Nichols's response to his rejection reflects the way in which the history of Christianity has been viewed by many Restorationist groups. The Restorationist movement has been affected in varying degrees by dispensationalism, the belief that God has periodically changed his method of dealing with humankind and that these changes are discernible through careful study of Scripture. The roots of dispensationalism are ancient, but the beginning of modern dispensationalism is attributed to John Nelson Darby (1800–1882), who was the first to create a concrete system of periods, or dispensations. Darby's thought was institutionalized by C. I. Scofield in his popular reference Bible. There has been considerable disagreement among individuals and groups as to how many dispensations there have been or will be.

In the Restorationist movement there were dispensationalist elements from the very beginning. In 1813, Alexander Campbell preached a controversial sermon in which he identified a sharp distinction between the law of Moses in the Old Testament and the New Testament covenant introduced by Christ, which essentially superceded the Mosaic law. This belief became common to the Disciples of Christ, the Christadelphians, and the Megiddos.[34] In addition to the break between the Old and New Testament periods, the Christadelphians identified another break at the end of the Apostolic Age, when the last of Jesus' apostles died. This break did not affect the practice of the Disciples and the Christadelphians, who continued to attempt to recover the practices of the early church, such as water baptism and weekly communion, but it would allow Nichols's followers to begin to move in a direction that would separate them from their Restorationist roots.

The sense that there were concrete breaks in Christian history primed Nichols to attach great significance to a major doctrinal change he initiated in 1880 when he claimed to have been led by his study of the Bible to discover the true route to salvation. As Nichols later stated it, "We see that in 1880 was the first time since the Apostasy, that any one has become a bearer of the truth in its entirety as it is in Jesus. The little flock that are here assembled are the first that fully believed that we must understand every commandment and principle of truth before baptism would do any good, and that after coming out of the water every commandment must be lived up to, and a growth must be effected, so that we would have a perfect character, even live without sin."[35]

"The Apostasy," or, as the Megiddos usually call it, the "Great Apostasy" (a term also used by Alexander Campbell), was to Restorationists, including Nichols and his followers, the period during which the true message of Christ was lost. According to Richard T. Hughes, "Restorationism . . . assumes that at some point in Christian history a fall or apostasy occurred. Without a fall, a loss, or an apostasy, the notion of restoration is simply unintelligible."[36]

According to the Megiddos, the Great Apostasy was forecast in the Bible in the book of Daniel and by Jesus and Paul in the books of Matthew and Timothy respectively. It was caused by several factors, including the withdrawal of the Holy Spirit at the end of the Apostolic Age; the association of Christians with people from outside the church; the church's relaxation of standards in order to attract more adherents; weakness in the face of persecution; the influence of other religions (particularly gnosticism); and Greek philosophy. The Megiddos have focused particularly on Greek philosophy as "the greatest single cause of the apostasy." Frequently referring to the writings of the German Lutheran church historian Johann Lorenz von Mosheim (1694–1755) and to *The Decline and Fall of the Roman Empire* by Edward Gibbon (1737–1794), the Megiddos have attributed "contamination of the Christian faith" to its coming "more and more into the hands of the educated and cultured part of Roman society . . . men whose training had been grounded in . . . Greek philosophy."[37] The most serious result of the influence of Greek philosophy was the introduction of new doctrines that could not be supported by Scripture: the Trinity, the immortal soul, and the man-god nature of Christ.

For the Megiddos, the apostasy began with the death of the last apostle and increased during the post-apostolic period, fueled by the establishment of state religion, the development of a church hierarchy, and, particularly, the rise of the papacy. Eventually, the apostasy was complete and there was no one in the world for 1,260 years (a length of time determined through the study of

Daniel and Revelation) who understood the truth of the Scriptures until L. T. Nichols discovered it in 1880.

The truth that Nichols discovered from his reading of Scripture, which ended the Great Apostasy and which he subsequently began to preach, called on his followers to strive for salvation through lives of perfection achieved through the meticulous study of the Bible and adherence to its mandates. By doing this, they could be among "only 144,000 kings [who] would reign with Jesus." As part of his discovery of the truth in 1880, Nichols also claimed to have begun the cleansing of the sanctuary predicted in Dan. 8:14. Nichols's statements echo the words of many preachers of perfectionism, a doctrine that had considerable influence on American religious thought in the second half of the nineteenth century and the early twentieth century.

Perfectionism had its roots in the teachings of John Wesley, which stated that following conversion the believer needed to undergo a second experience, usually called "entire sanctification," that eradicated original sin and made it possible for the believer to lead a life free from sin. The perfectionist doctrine was essentially lost to Methodism but was recovered in the middle of the nineteenth century and eventually institutionalized in the camp meeting and in holiness denominations such as the Salvation Army and the Church of the Nazarene.[38] However, the influence of perfectionist thinking was not limited to the holiness movement, and the Restorationist movement was not without its perfectionist elements. Richard T. Hughes noted that "Christian primitivism was sometimes related to the more traditional form of perfectionism which focused on individual sanctification, but the common thread that bound all primitivists together was a mutual striving to live and move in a perfect church, patterned after an apostolic mode."[39] Nichols seems to have combined the two currents of perfectionist thought. While he rejected both the experiential and individualistic aspects of the holiness movement and the Campbellite attempt to recover the practices of the primitive church, he sought to form a church composed of individuals who were becoming perfect through strict adherence to the tenets of Scripture.

Nichols's new doctrines were in conflict with Christadelphian belief and practice and exacerbated the already strained relations between Nichols and his co-religionists. Still adhering to many ideas that were also held by the Christadelphians, Nichols began to call his followers "True Christadelphians," while he continued to hold out hope that he could bring other Christadelphians to see the truth as he saw it.

Nichols further distanced himself from the Christadelphians when, about 1881, he produced his own Bible chronology, a plan based on Scripture for determining the date for the Second Coming of Christ. This chronology was in keeping with Christadelphian tradition, as an apocalyptic vision had been a major theme of John Thomas's preaching and his primary written work, *Elpis Israel,* published in several editions beginning in 1847. Thomas had also published his own chronology, titled *Chronikon Hebraikon or the Chronology of the Scriptures* (1865), in which he predicted the return of Christ in 1868. While Nichols's chronology bore many similarities to that of Thomas, it differed at key points, allowing Nichols to arrive at a different conclusion as to when Christ would return. Nichols predicted that Christ would probably return no sooner than the end of 1891 and not later than 1896. He allowed that there was "a bare possibility" that, depending on the interpretation of a passage in the book of Micah, the Lord might not come until the end of 1896 at the earliest and no later than 1901.

In his chronology, the first edition of which was published about 1882, Nichols was openly critical of John Thomas and Robert Roberts. While the chronology itself would have angered the Christadelphians, who were still defending Thomas's chronology as essentially correct even though the concluding date had been wrong, Nichols's criticisms of Thomas in particular would have been even more disturbing. With no central organization, the Christadelphians were very dependent on the writings and person of John Thomas for what sense of unity they had, and Nichols's questioning of the accuracy of Thomas's calculations would have created a further breach between him and the Christadelphian leadership.[40]

A point related to the Second Coming on which Nichols also came to disagree with the Christadelphians was the position of Israel in the end time scenario. The Christadelphians believe that only they, who have "become Jews in a higher sense," and the Jews in Palestine will be resurrected when Christ returns. Like many other apocalyptic groups, the Christadelphians also believe that the Jews must occupy Palestine as a prerequisite for the Second Coming. In 1875, in an apparent effort to help set the stage for the Second Coming, Christadelphians began to provide financial support for the resettlement of Jews in Palestine, and they still evince a strong interest in affairs in the Middle East.

Nichols's position on Israel was not in total disagreement with that of the Christadelphians. He identified his followers as "Spiritual Israel" or "Jews indeed" for purposes of salvation, but, unlike the Christadelphians, he excluded the actual Jews in Palestine from the resurrection. He did note, however, that "the Jews must go back to their land . . . [they] must be gathered back into the land of Canaan with their great wealth before Russia marches her hosts into the holy land to take the spoil." He further noted that Christadelphian leader Robert Roberts should be able to "see that things in the east are not ready for the Lord to come yet. There is more entire work to be done in the holy land." In other words, even though the Jews would not be among those resurrected, they needed to return to the Holy Land for the realization of events prophesied in Scripture to occur before the Second Coming of Christ. In contrast, Nichols's successor as leader of the Megiddos, Maud Hembree, apparently did not view the return of the Jews to Palestine as necessary but stated in her book *The Known Bible and Its Defense* (1934) that although the Megiddos would prefer to see Palestine inhabited by Jews because, "as a rule, Jews are industrious and progressive, and they would manage its affairs so that it would soon present a very different aspect from the desolation of past centuries"; still, "the nation bringing forth fruits of righteousness to whom the Kingdom shall be given, will be spiritual Israel, those worthy of the name. They shall inherit 'the Homeland' for an eternal inheritance."[41]

In dissenting from the Christadelphian leadership, Nichols was not unusual. The rise of dissenting leaders was common in American religious denominations. In a work that focused on larger denominations than the Christadelphians, Nathan Hatch contended that the democratic nature of American society made it difficult for denominations to prevent the rise of "powerful, self-made leaders." This would have been particularly the case for a denomination that was as loosely organized as the Christadelphians. According to Hatch, these leaders "called their followers back to the first principles of the movement and noted how far the current generation had fallen. Their language and tone matched that of their audience and of its local concerns. In these respects they competed far more effectively than could far-away and cosmopolitan leaders."[42]

Nichols had more than local ambitions for his message. In order to disseminate his teachings, he began to devote his time to preaching and writing and to the distribution of tracts and pamphlets that stated his views and critiqued the Christadelphian leadership. In the pamphlet *Adam before He Sinned,* Nichols wrote that he intended to start for the East Coast in November or December of 1881 and from there go to England. He said he would "like to have all who can see the truth and are interested in it write to me, so that I will know best what point to stop at." Nichols and his wife, using the $1,100 he had made from farming that year, went on the missionary trip, even though Nichols expected to "meet with much opposition, especially in England." It is likely that it was on this trip that Nichols first visited an interested reader in Barry, a small community in western Illinois, who had acquired some of his publications in 1880 and who had written to him. In Barry, Nichols planted a congregation, giving the first indication that he was considering expanding his ministry on an organized basis outside of Oregon. The Barry and Oregon ecclesias carried on an active correspondence, with Reverend Nichols reading letters from the Barry ecclesia to his congregation and presumably the Barry congregation sharing letters from Oregon with each other.[43]

On the same trip that took him to Barry, he also visited Indiana and Ohio, returning via San Francisco, where he purchased a printing press with which to continue his publication ministry independent of the Christadelphians, who had previously printed his materials. His sister, Ella Skeels, and her husband, Henry, operated the small hand press, and Nichols "found names here and there and sent the pamphlets off."[44]

Much of what is known about the doctrines that Nichols was preaching while he was in Oregon is the result of the survival of a six-volume printed pamphlet series. These documents, more than five hundred pages long, contain Nichols's account of the True Christadelphians' 1882 camp meeting, including the contents of the messages he delivered. It is evident from the series that Nichols had great respect for John Thomas and was influenced by him. Nichols wrote that Knox, Wesley, and Campbell "have all in their places brought out some truth, each progressing a little, and Dr. Thomas progressed farther than the rest," but he criticized Robert Roberts and his cohorts because "they are governed by Dr. Thomas. They go just as far as the Dr. and no farther . . . They stand upon the Dr's works; and they will not move one iota from what the Dr. has said, it matters not how plain the word of the Lord states to the contrary." Consequently, significant parts of the pamphlets are devoted to identifying points on which the True Christadelphians' interpretation of Scripture disagrees with that of the Christadelphian leadership, and there are even personal attacks on Roberts. Nichols was likely to have been convincing in his attacks on the Christadelphians since most, if not all, of what his followers knew about the Christadelphian leadership came from his sermons and writings, and he was probably the only one in the congregation who had had any direct contact with Thomas.[45]

Nichols retained one Christadelphian doctrine that drew local attention in Oregon and earned Nichols's followers the epithet "Soul Sleepers." Stated simply, the doctrine of soul sleep holds that when people die, they do not go immediately to heaven (or hell) as most Christians believe, but they fall into an unconscious sleep in their graves in which they are unaware of anything. The Megiddos and the Christadelphians believe that humans are fully mortal—that is, that there is no such thing as an immortal soul—and that the dead are truly dead until the return of Christ, when all who have faithfully served Christ in their lifetimes will rise. Those who did not serve Christ will remain asleep in their graves forever. This belief is also held by other groups, most notably Seventh-Day Adventists.[46]

Anti-Catholicism, which, if Nichols did not acquire from Thomas and the Christadelphians, he at least shared with them, is also clearly expressed in the camp meeting minutes. A chart included in the text of his Bible chronology demonstrates how the name of the Roman Catholic church, in the form of "Lateinos," adds up to 666, a number with eschatological significance for many Adventists, and Nichols identifies the pope as the beast of Revelation.[47]

Nichols came to disagree with Thomas on the role of women in the church. Thomas was strongly opposed to women in public ministry and wrote the following:

> We hear much in some parts of the world of the political rights and equality of women and of their preaching and teaching in public assemblies. We need wonder at nothing which emanates from the unenlightened mind of sinful flesh. There is no absurdity too monstrous to be sanctified by unspiritualized animal intellect. Men do not think according to God's thinking, and therefore they run the most unscriptural conceits; among which may be enumerated the political and social equality of women. . . . [Women] would be guilty of indiscretion, presumption, and rebellion

against God's law, in assuming equality of rank, equality of rights, and authority over man, which is implied in teaching and preaching. It is the old ambition of the sex to be equal to the god . . . Preaching and lecturing, women are but species of actresses, who exhibit upon the boards for the amusement of sinful and foolish men. . . . A man should never permit the words of a woman to intervene between him and the laws of God. This is the rock upon which myriads have made shipwreck of the faith. Adam sinned in consequence of listening to Eve's silvery discourse. No temptation has proved more irresistible to the flesh than the enticing words of woman's lips.[48]

There is no concrete evidence that Nichols ever addressed the issue of women's ministry with the Christadelphian leadership. However, the Megiddo Church owns a copy of Robert Roberts's 1880 book *Seasons of Conflict at the Table of the Lord,* which possibly belonged to Nichols. There are a number of marked passages with which Nichols would have disagreed, including a statement about women keeping silent in church. This may indicate that Nichols at least recognized this as a point on which Roberts needed additional light.[49]

In spite of the Christadelphian teaching in opposition to women in ministry, early in their association Nichols recognized Maud Hembree's gifts for public ministry. He welcomed her participation in the debate with a holiness preacher at the 1882 camp meeting, where she, "with sword in hand, entered the field and [did] valiantly for the truth, driving the opposor at every move, holding her ground, and proving her position," and, further, she "spoke at some length with love, but with boldness."[50]

Undoubtedly, in selecting Maud Hembree for leadership, L. T. Nichols was at least indirectly influenced by the feminist currents in American society at the time, mediated through the religious groups that had already allowed women to assume positions of leadership. Among the most notable of these groups were those in the holiness movement, including the Wesleyan Church, Free Methodist Church, and the Salvation Army, all of which allowed women to occupy positions of responsibility.[51]

The opportunities presented to women in the holiness movement extended beyond preaching and evangelism to administration of church agencies, educational institutions, parachurch mission and reform agencies such as the Woman's Christian Temperance Union (WCTU), and social service institutions such as orphanages, rescue missions, and homes for unwed mothers. As a natural consequence of these opportunities, women in many holiness denominations eventually moved into the secular sphere, primarily in developing helping professions such as nursing and social work. The small size of the Megiddo Mission and the limitation of its mission programs to door-to-door and print evangelism, coupled with the closed nature of the mission's semicommunitarian lifestyle, have allowed the mission to maintain a somewhat conservative view of the roles of women. In spite of its having had two women pastors, in

1958, when the mission adopted its constitution and bylaws, article 4 stated that the board of trustees would consist of six members, "four male and two female." In 1980, that article was changed to make the board consist of six members "without regard to sex."[52] Even today, when their pastor is a professional woman who owns a graphic arts business, the women of the Megiddo Church still dress much as they did a century ago and are all accomplished homemakers who during evening meetings work on traditional women's sewing and handwork projects. As an article in the November 1998 issue of the *Megiddo Message* noted, "modern women in their striving for equal rights have many times overstepped reasonable and realistic limits. God designed the two sexes with different built-in capabilities, and certainly there are tasks more appropriate for men, others more appropriate for women."[53]

There is no evidence that Nichols's views on woman's role in the church was a major focus of his differences with the Christadelphian leadership. It is evident, though, that during the period from 1878 to 1883, L. T. Nichols formulated a number of doctrines based on his reading of Scripture that increasingly separated him from the Christadelphians. Meanwhile, he was building a small body of dedicated followers and was laying the groundwork for an expansion of his ministry.

2

Despised and Rejected

In urging historians to undertake the study of American religious history, Frederick Jackson Turner noted that "the multiplication of rival churches in the little frontier towns had deep and lasting social effects."[1] In light of this assertion, it is not surprising to find that in addition to the controversies within the Christadelphian movement, doctrines expounded by Nichols and the resulting practices of his followers excited considerable controversy in the McMinnville area.

The practices that met with the strongest opposition were two that were not part of the Christadelphian tradition—the holy kiss and marital purity. The holy kiss is mentioned in several places in the writings of the Apostle Paul in the New Testament, and it has been practiced by many Christian groups over the centuries. According to one author, "no ordinance of God commanded to be observed in [the] church is stated in the New Testament in plainer terms or with more authority than that of the Christian greeting, termed a holy kiss or kiss of charity."[2] The kiss is traditionally performed by the touching of lips between members of the same sex. However, Nichols saw no place in Scripture where the kiss was so limited, and, therefore, he advocated the practice of the holy kiss between men and women.

It is unknown how Nichols came to emphasize the holy kiss, which, along with several other practices of the primitive church, had been rejected by Alexander Campbell as nonessential. He may have encountered it in the writings of William Thurman, to whom Nichols referred in his *Bible Chronology*. Thurman was a German Baptist Brethren with close ties to Christadelphians in Virginia, whose predictions of several dates for the return of Christ attracted interest in the nineteenth century. In addition to his writings on eschatology, Thurman also promoted the holy kiss along with other practices common among members of his denomination.[3]

The decision to practice the holy kiss was based on Nichols's belief that members of his congregation constituted a new family, the members of which were bound to show each other love and affection, and that salvation was based on the doing of good works. All true Christians should "do ALL, not just part but ALL things that Christ commanded his servants to do." He looked to the apostle Paul, "the example to us Gentiles," for direction and noted that Paul "did not hesitate to show his affection to the family of the Lord to which he belonged. . . . [and] was not ashamed to greet his brethren with a holy kiss, neither did he hesitate or refuse to receive the same." Nichols criticized "the men of the nineteenth century," and Robert Roberts and his followers in particular, for scoffing at the practice of the holy kiss.[4]

The practice of the holy kiss scandalized the McMinnville community and resulted in a virulent attack on Nichols and the Christadelphians by a contributor to the local newspaper, the *Yamhill County Reporter*, who stated the following:

> It appears that Bro. Nichols has been looked upon by his people "as one sent from God to lead them out of the bondage of Egypt and over the desert into the promised land;" have faithfully followed him in all his wanderings, and have kept all his commandments without an objection or murmur until he commanded that all the brethren should salute one another with the holy kiss. Then those that had wives and daughters in the Church began to murmur and say that they thought Bro. Nichols had misconstrued the testimonies, and had not rightly divined the truth. Some of the Elders and those that are mighty in the scriptures went and advised with Bro. Nichols, saying: We believe that thou art pure at heart and meaneth not to kiss the sisters more than the brothers from impure motives; but we think that thou art mistaken in the meaning of the word of truth. We think that when the Scriptures sayeth 'Salute the brethren with an holy kiss' that meaneth the brethren only, and not the sisters.[5]

Some of the male Christadelphians and the male family members of women affiliated with the Christadelphians demanded that Nichols defend his position on the holy kiss, which he did at a four-hour meeting that attracted an overflow crowd to a local schoolhouse on August 4, 1878. Using Rom. 16:16, Nichols justified the practice of the holy kiss as he encouraged it. Members of the crowd adjourned to a nearby home where the discussion lasted into the

evening, apparently with nothing being resolved. Finally, "the sheep were separated from the goats; those willing to receive the 'holy kiss' passed to the right
and saluted Bro. Nichols, and those of a contrary will passed to the left." The
writer concluded, "As to the propriety of this indiscriminate bestowal of a deli-
cate and sacred token among the motley assemblage, we fear Bro. N. will fail to
persuade many people to believe in it. Let your readers judge for themselves."[6]

That the holy kiss was a divisive issue among the Christadelphians in Oregon is evident from an item dated September 21, 1878, in the North Yamhill
news section of the *Yamhill County Reporter:* "the Christadelphians had
another 'set to' at the Mercer school house . . . yesterday. The impression is that
Nichols will take the greater portion of the congregation with him, 'bus' or 'no
bus.'" The holy kiss may also have contributed to the later split, noted above,
since Rev. H. C. Plummer, who would become a leader of the group that left
with the split, argued with Nichols at the Mercer School, claiming to represent
"that part of the congregation who were not in favor of kissing the sisters."[7]

The practice of the holy kiss proved embarrassing to families in the community whose female relatives had joined the Christadelphians. Nichols was
apparently accused of practicing free love, and the local newspaper implied
Nichols had other than a platonic interest in the women and young girls in his
congregation. According to the *Reporter,* "It was observed that in practicing the
holy kiss, Bro. Nichols was chaste enough with the old and ugly sisters, but the
young, good looking ones always received a vigorous hug and a lingering on
the kiss that looked altogether too carnal, and in some cases, where the sister
was buxom, smacked decidedly of the lascivious."[8]

In addition to the holy kiss, marital purity also became an important issue
among Nichols's followers and their families. The late eighteenth century and
the nineteenth century were periods of sexual experimentation among American religious communities, as demonstrated by the system of complex marriage
adopted by the Oneida Community, various groups that practiced free love, the
polygamy of the Mormons, and the strict separation of the sexes among the
Shakers.[9] Nichols advocated a less well-known variation on relations between
the sexes—marital purity. In its most common manifestation, this doctrine
stated that married couples should refrain from all sexual relations, except for
the purpose of procreation. The doctrine was a product of several currents that
affected nineteenth-century society: the health reform movement; perfectionism; the women's movement; the social purity teachings of organizations such
as the WCTU; and the moral teachings of the holiness movement. The health
reform movement's most noted spokesman, Sylvester Graham, believed sex
was debilitating and that even sex within marriage should be limited to one act
per month, while the WCTU attacked the double standard of sexual behavior
and advocated holding men to the same high standard of sexual purity as that
to which women were held. However, it was in the holiness movement that
marital purity was promoted in its purist form. It was in this form that Nichols

advocated total abstinence from sexual activity, believing that "that man or woman who is gratifying . . . lust, either in marriage relation or any other way, is still living to their lust; and have not as yet become clothed with the mind of Christ." In this environment, the exchange of the holy kiss between members of the different sexes may have served as public statement that the members of the True Christadelphians had truly overcome the lusts of the flesh.[10]

Nichols also admonished his congregation to follow certain lifestyle rules that attracted attention in the community and even caused dissension within households. He told his followers they must separate themselves from the world, including all people who did not believe as they did. This caused many members to limit or avoid contact with even their closest relatives. In the same vein, he advocated having nothing to do with governments, including holding office and serving on juries. He was also opposed to secret societies. He told his followers to refrain from the use of the "nasty weed" tobacco; coffee and tea, which people only used to "gratify their lust"; and "cinnamons and spices," which were "neither nutritious or beneficial" but only served to "burn up the stomach" and hinder digestion. He preached against personal adornment in the form of fancy clothes and jewelry. When asked what a woman should do if removing "superfluities" from dresses spoiled the clothing, Nichols said that the woman should leave the decorations on the dresses but "wear them out at home at the wash tub, and every day work" to prove that she did not take pride in her clothing. Home decorations, including pictures, and fancy trappings on horses or carriages were also forbidden. He told his congregation to stop "joking" and not allow their children to "joke and carouse around."[11]

Nichols came out strongly against the public school for four reasons: it was a "worldly institution"; teachers and school officials were required to swear oaths, a practice Nichols believed was forbidden by Scripture; school was "a place where more iniquity is learned than any other place that people send their children"; and in school children were encouraged to read books that contained "lies of the deepest dye."[12]

Nichols's negative attitude toward public education should not be taken as an indication he was opposed to learning. Nichols's writings are peppered with references to various texts he used to complement his study of Scripture and Christadelphian literature. In addition to the aforementioned writings of Mosheim, these include the *Encyclopedia Britannica;* Gibbons's *Decline and Fall of the Roman Empire;* writings of the early historian Josephus; the Hebrew lexicon of Heinrich Gesenius; *Young's Concordance;* a history of the Reformation by d'Aubigné; and "Jones' *Church History,*" probably *The History of the Christian Church from the Birth of Christ to the Eighteenth Century* by William Jones (1762–1846). Nichols extolled the efficacy of reading "histories, [and] volumes of instruction on almost every topic." He claimed that "the pages of history" were as familiar to him as the pages of the Bible and that, "once read, their thoughts are forever impressed on my mind." He also read magazines such as *Literary Digest* and *Scientific American.*[13]

Nichols announced at the 1882 camp meeting that the program committee had "seen fit to arrange to have a meeting for all the brethren to bring up, in the spirit of meekness, any thing that any one has done that looked wrong, and have it (in the spirit of Christ) investigated." He proposed having such meetings often and offered himself as the subject for criticism, inviting the brethren to point out anything in him that appeared to be deficient. He admonished his followers to "ever be willing to receive rebukes in love, humility, kindness, and thankfulness."[14] This practice, which is known as "mutual correction" or "mutual criticism," was practiced by a number of groups in the nineteenth and early twentieth centuries, most notably John Humphrey Noyes's Oneida Community. Lawrence Foster has suggested that at Oneida the practice acted as a form of social control and it probably had a similar function among the True Christadelphians. It also encouraged correct behavior and helped maintain orthodoxy.[15]

Although he extolled the virtues of reading edifying works, Nichols was vehemently opposed to reading newspapers. He attributed this to the fact that people who read them were wasting their time with the "gossip of the world." However, the ill treatment he received from the local press may have been a contributing factor. According to Philip Jenkins, "during the latter years of the nineteenth century, the climate for . . . new sects became chillier as the news media became more sensational in tone, finding rich material in the religious fringe." Chains as prominent as Hearst and Pulitzer found new religious movements fodder for a public hungry for sensationalized accounts of the unfamiliar and "all the emerging movements faced deep hostility from the media and other critics, who now lumped new creeds together under the suspicious title of 'cults.'" Since adherence to the strict dictates of the True Christadelphians required obvious changes in lifestyle and considerable sacrifice, it is not surprising that the sect came to the attention of the local media.[16]

According to the *Yamhill County Reporter,* Nichols's teachings attracted "mostly ignorant, soft-headed women," and the few men who joined "dropped the business when they saw the drift of his teachings." Several men who joined the True Christadelphians did leave, but it is unclear whether they did so because of opposition to Nichols's teachings or because of social pressure exerted by such occurrences as the negative articles in the newspaper. In some households, spouses found themselves in disagreement on matters critical to domestic peace, largely due to Nichols's teachings.[17] The result in at least two cases was divorce.

Charles N. Buckingham, a forty-eight-year-old farmer from Yamhill County, sued his wife, Adeline, for divorce, complaining that "about January 1st 1882 she left my bed without cause, [and] she refuses to live with me as my wife." The suit noted that it was after "she had become under the influence of

one L. T. Nichols, that she commenced this conduct and kept it up." Buckingham
stated:

> It was in May . . . she left me in my home with my two younger children to
> attend a camp meeting about five miles from my house; she was gone
> nearly three weeks and was only at home twice or not to exceed three
> times [during] that time, she was gone nine days at a stretch. . . .
>
> Last September without my consent she left our home and children
> and was gone for four or five days. We knew nothing about where she had
> been until she had come back. We afterwards learned from other parties
> she had gone over to Nicholas's [sic] or in that neighborhood.[18]

Mrs. Buckingham would not cook pork or use lard; she would not "touch
a shirt that has sleeve buttons or shirt studs"; and she would not allow her children to attend school or read newspapers. She removed decorations from her
house and refused to accompany her husband anywhere. She even refused to
attend her mother's funeral or burial, even though her mother was buried
within sight of the Buckingham house.

The holy kiss also figured in Buckingham's suit. He stated that "Nichols has
kissed her frequently as well as other men." He had been informed by his wife
and by "other good authority" that "she has practiced this kissing for this past
three years" and that the kissing had always been done in his absence.

Charles Buckingham claimed that before his wife came under the influence
of Nichols, she had been "as good a wife as any man had in Oregon" and that
they had lived "happily and pleasantly together." He testified that he attributed
all his troubles to L. T. Nichols and noted that Nichols had caused trouble in
other families. Among the other families was that of J. L. Hembree, who had
sued his wife, Maud, for divorce on October 5, 1882.

In Hembree's suit, his attorney, W. D. Fenton, stated that Maud Hembree,

> unmindful of her marriage vow, on or about September 1st 1880, com-
> menced a course of cruel and inhuman indiscreet and personal indignities
> against and towards [her husband] . . . which have rendered and do now
> render life burdensome to him . . .
>
> The said Defendant . . . was guilty of lewd and familiar conduct
> towards one L. T. Nichols and other men to this Plaintiff unknown and she
> has frequently and without Plaintiffs knowledge or consent kissed said
> L. T. Nichols and other men and thusly exposed herself and this Plaintiff
> and their . . . family to disgrace and shame, and such conduct is a great
> personal indignity to this Plaintiff, in this, that said Defendant is caused to
> be charged by the public as an adulteress but that this Plaintiff does not so
> charge . . . not knowing.[19]

Hembree, a thirty-seven-year-old farmer from Yamhill County, testified, in
much the same manner as Buckingham, that his wife had left his bed "without
any cause" and refused to live with him "as my wife." She was also absent from

home for three weeks to attend a camp meeting, only returning home once during the three weeks. He further accused his wife of having gone to town without telling him and leaving her two children, who were sick with whooping cough, at home unattended.

Like Mrs. Buckingham, Maud Hembree refused to touch shirts with sleeve buttons or studs or to use lard. She also refused to pick up the family's mail at the post office or to have anything to do with newspapers. Maud Hembree's brother William Galloway testified that she refused to visit her aged father because she considered him "a man of the world . . . and will associate with no one out of her own sect." She refused to ride with her sister who was wearing

Maud Hembree, circa 1900. Courtesy Megiddo Church, Rochester, N.Y.

a collar with ruffles on it. She destroyed all photographs of her relatives and friends and would not allow pictures in her house. "She will leave home under any condition of weather and walk five miles and return and pack her children in a storm to attend one of their prayer meetings." Further, she said she would "forsake her family and every thing" for her faith. William Galloway testified that it had been suggested to Maud Hembree that she might be sent to an asylum. In response, she declared that all the members of her faith would be "ready to go for their faith."

With regard to the holy kiss, Hembree testified that he had seen her kiss "a man by the name of Skeels" at a camp meeting and that he had been informed that she had kissed L. T. Nichols. S. J. Ely, apparently a former member of the True Christadelphians, testified that he had seen Maud Hembree and L. T. Nichols kiss each other at general gatherings or meetings and that kissing was "a common practice with these people and is done according to their religious beliefs."

In the nineteenth century no-fault divorce was unknown and divorce suits were virtually always adversarial in nature. It is clear that L. T. Nichols believed that divorce was forbidden by Scripture and that his followers would not institute divorce proceedings and would probably not defend themselves in a divorce suit. Without testimony from the wives in the divorce cases, it is impossible to determine how both parties felt about each other and their marriage. Evidence from later in Maud Hembree's life suggests that the contention surrounding her religious activities may not have been the only source of discord in the Hembree marriage. According to people who knew Maud Hembree in the years immediately preceding her death, she was referring to her husband when she stated in a sermon in 1933 that she "knew a man who was cruel to animals; he would strike the horse, and I could never bear to see animals mistreated. I used to tell him to take the animal out and kill it if it was of no value, but not to torture it. The Lord would not torture anything. . . . But this man would not stop torturing the animals, so when I saw it coming I got out of the way and controlled my temper. It would have done no good to get angry, and would only have been worse for me. I always got away from the danger." [20]

In the twentieth century, one could gain a better sense of where to place blame in a divorce by observing who gained custody of children, but in the United States in the nineteenth century, although custody was awarded to women three times more often than it was awarded to men, "child custody decisions were erratic." Economic factors often affected child custody since "alimony awards were often small, one-time sums" and many women had difficulty earning money with which to support children. [21]

Maud Hembree was known among members of the Megiddo Mission for her special interest in the children of church members. Having to leave her children was probably a very heavy price for her to pay for taking to heart Jesus' contention that "anyone who prefers son or daughter to me is not worthy of me. Anyone who does not take his cross and follow in my footsteps is not worthy of me" (Matt. 10:37–38). It may have been a response to the loss of her children that caused Maud Hembree to take permanent responsibility for Maggie Millican, a blind member of one of the Oregon True Christadelphian families. According to members of the church, Reverend Hembree avoided physical contact with the children of the mission because it brought back sad memories of her lost years with her own children.

When Nichols accepted, or if he encouraged, women leaving their husbands, he was further distancing himself from Christadelphian orthodoxy, for, as John Thomas had stated, "Christian women should not copy after the god-aspiring Eve, but after Sarah, the faithful mother of Israel, who submitted herself in all things to Abraham. . . . Nor should their obedience be restricted to Christian husbands only. They should also obey them 'without the word'; that is, those who have not submitted to it, in order that they may be won over to the faith when they behold the chaste and respectful behaviour of their wives, produced by a belief of the truth." [22]

In addition to the controversies over the holy kiss and the disruption of family relations, there were also accusations in the *Yamhill County Reporter* that Nichols was taking financial advantage of his followers. According to the newspaper, Mrs. Frank Martin, a member of the True Christadelphians, had considerable property of her own and had inherited more when her husband died.

> Soon after Mr. Martin's death, Nichols, who had an eye to business, managed to get complete control of Mrs. M. and the result was soon apparent: She . . . declared her property belonged to the Lord, which was readily understood to be equivalent to saying that it belonged to Nichols. About the same time rumor had it that all Christadelphians were ordered to turn their property into cash, and gather together in one community. Mrs. Martin's children and her mother . . . all used their best efforts to change the lady's mind, but to no purpose. She remained fixed. Then, her oldest son, William, returned and he and James [a younger son] stood guard over their mother's home and fairly drove Nichols and his dupes off by force and threats.[23]

The financial basis of Nichols's ministry is not evident from existing records. His basic income from farming was supplemented by sales of sewing machines, which, according to *An Honest Man,* were quite expensive; this probably limited the number of sales he made. It is impossible to tell what income he might have had from inventions. He did not patent any inventions while he lived in Oregon, but he may have manufactured versions of products that were patented later. It is possible that his ministry started with an infusion of cash from the sale of real estate. A deed indicates that L. T. and Harriet E. Nichols purchased a large tract of land in 1875 for the sum of $12,750. In addition, Nichols's father had at least been prosperous enough to retire from farming before the family moved to Kansas, and L. T. Nichols may have inherited additional property when the elder Nichols died in 1876. Records show that in

1875 and 1877 the Nicholses sold pieces of their property to relatives and associates.[24] However, even with all of these possible sources of income, L. T.
Nichols was never more than a prosperous small farmer, and it is unlikely that
the family resources would have supported a ministry that included the purchase of a printing press, substantial time spent away from the farm during the
growing season while Nichols was engaged in debates and conducted the camp
meeting, travels to meet with the Christadelphians in distant places, and, perhaps, evangelistic trips elsewhere.[25] Consequently, it is almost certain that
Nichols's ministry received some support from his followers, probably both in
terms of labor to operate his farm while he engaged in his ministry and direct
financial contributions. The contributions, however, could not have been exces-
sively large, as most of the True Christadelphians who can be identified in the
1880 census were either farmwives with limited access to money or small farmers like Nichols, most with families to support.

In concluding the 1882 camp meeting, Nichols evinced neither surprise
nor dismay at the way the community responded to his ministry. In fact, he
claimed his followers should be pleased "to be numbered with those that are
having all manner of evil said against them FALSELY for Christ's sake." He said that
he rejoiced "exceedingly" to be among the "despised and rejected of men," a
reference to Isa. 53:3. Further, he stated that he would "rather have curses, evil
speeches and persecutions of the world and obtain God's approval, accompanied with the promised blessing, than to have the good-will, company and fair
speeches of the world and the Lord's disapproval, . . . accompanied with his
curses." He went on to remind his followers and critics that he did not compel
anyone to listen to him or follow his teachings, but that all did so of their own
free will. Responding to the specific charge that he had divided families, Nichols
stated that he was not to blame if wives adopted plain dress, refused to accompany their husbands to places of "worldly amusement" or to places where they
could not talk about salvation. He said that the Bible was actually responsible
and that he was only the instrument of God who had revealed the true meaning of the Scriptures. He admonished his congregation to continue to follow
the teachings of Scripture in spite of the "waves of persecution that are to roll
over and drench every true follower of Jesus." [26]

The True Christadelphian camp meeting was held on or near Mrs. Martin's
property, and it is highly likely that Mrs. Martin also provided financial support
to the ministry, which may have been a source of animosity between Nichols
and other members of the Martin family.[27] Whatever the reason for the conflict,
matters turned violent on June 10, 1883. As Nichols arrived at church, an
unknown assailant pursued him on horseback and shot him in the back of the
hip. Nichols was wounded, but a local physician removed the bullet. After a
period of convalescence, Nichols recovered. The Martins denied involvement
in the shooting and no one was ever convicted of the crime, but the *Yamhill
County Reporter* attributed the crime to James Martin and stated that "while
everyone regrets the necessity of using the pistol . . . the Martin boys have the

sympathy of nearly all the country." The failure to prosecute Martin is not surprising if the rest of McMinnville shared the views of the *Reporter* editor that "shooting a human being is deplorable in most cases, but the regret in this case is that the ball didn't take a more fatal course." The writer went on to say that since there were no laws to protect a family from "scoundrels" such as Nichols, "every man must be a law unto himself." He proposed that if Nichols had been driven out of the community or "strung up to the first tree . . . several families now separated might be still living happily together."[28]

The newspaper reported on June 28, 1883, that "the Nichols church" and the small row of houses used for the camp meeting had been burned on the night of June 20. The perpetrators were unknown, but the editor stated it had possibly been done by someone "who thought the best way to get rid of noxious animals was to destroy their dens."

Following Nichols's recovery from his wounds, he and some of his followers left Oregon and began a national search for a new location. After rejecting sites in Texas and Kentucky, Nichols returned to the upper Midwest, settling at Ellington in Dodge County, Minnesota.

3

A Church of Their Own

The Founding of the Christian Brethren

It is uncertain why Nichols chose Dodge County, Minnesota, as a location for his new church. However, it could well have been because he already had contacts there among people from Dodge County, Wisconsin, who had been early settlers of the Minnesota county of same name. One of these settlers was Mary J. Morehouse, who had been a schoolmate of Nichols. At the age of twenty-four she moved to Minnesota, where she married Levi M. Morehouse of Owatonna, in Steele County, just over the county line from Dodge County.[1]

It is evidence of Nichols's influence on his followers and the power of his message that he and his family were accompanied east by several members of the True Christadelphians. It is difficult to determine what drew Nichols's followers to him and his message. With the exception of the diary kept from 1901 to 1903 by Mary Lee, a longtime member of the church, all other writings by his followers that directly concerned Nichols were prepared as memorials to him and focus on him specifically. L. T. Nichols does typify a kind of charismatic leader with an apocalyptic vision who arose in the United States in the nineteenth century. As Nathan Hatch has noted, while in the eighteenth century millennial speculation was the purview of an educated theological elite, in the nineteenth century, "American popular culture allowed self-educated people to espouse millennial hopes, hopes rife with the conviction that a *novus ordo seculorum* was unfolding."[2]

Since Nichols drew his followers from among people whose origins were probably similar to his, his lifestyle likely resonated with his followers, who could readily identify with him and feel that he understood their lives. Nichols was proud of his humble origins and lack of formal education. Concerning his youth, he wrote the following:

> I remembered the words of the celebrated Edward Everett. . . "of the great benefactors of our race, the men who by wonderful inventions, remarkable discoveries, and extraordinary improvements, have conferred the greatest benefit on the human race, the most eminent service to their fellow men—by far the greatest part have been men of humble origin, narrow fortunes, small advantages, and self-taught. Whoever has learned to read, possesses the key of knowledge, and can, whenever he pleases, not only unlock the portals of her temples, but penetrate to the inmost halls and most sacred cabinets." If I could but learn to read aright I could grasp the key of knowledge that would open the door to the store-house of truth.[3]

Nichols sought to convince his followers that they, like him, could understand the meaning of even the most apparently obscure passages of Scripture. He constantly displayed confidence in each listener's ability to understand by encouraging everyone to compare his words to the passages he cited to determine if they were true. Thus, the congregation became assured that the entire Bible was subject to discernment, although not without diligent study and effort.

The possibility of gaining access to the gnosis, or secret knowledge, that had escaped the more highly educated, who were also likely to be wealthier and more powerful, raised the self-esteem of those who heard Nichols's message, endearing him to them and creating an allegiance to him similar to that engendered in their followers by other nineteenth-century American religious leaders, such as Mormon founder Joseph Smith and Adventist William Miller. While Nichols never claimed to be a prophet and often emphasized his simple beginnings, he was not reticent when it came to describing the importance of his discovery of the biblical truth that forms the basis for the Megiddo Church. As he stated in his *Bible Chronology,* "no one prior to 1880 ever taught that we must be cleansed and become pure even as Christ is pure. No one prior to that time since the Apostasy [*sic*] ever taught that 'EVERY MAN that hath this hope in him PURIFIETH HIMSELF EVEN AS HE (Christ) IS PURE.'"[4] Because his contribution is based on claims of superior learning rather than on special powers or a special relationship with God, Nichols fits the model of what religious historian J. Gordon Melton sees as a typical leader of a new religion, one who is "'charismatic' only in a weaker sense of having been the discoverer of new truth or insight as a result of their hard work and/or specialized research."[5]

The relocation of his followers to Minnesota reinforces the sense that unlike the British Christadelphians, the True Christadelphians were primarily middle class. It is unlikely that lower-class people would have had the resources to pay for transportation and the costs of setting themselves up in farming or business in Minnesota.

At the same time that Nichols relocated to Minnesota, plans were put in motion to add additional sheep to the flock. Maud Hembree moved to Barry, Illinois, to become pastor of the fledgling congregation there. Hembree was accompanied by others from the Oregon community, including her blind companion Maggie Millican.[6]

In Minnesota, Nichols limited his farming and devoted most of his time to preaching and writing. Minnesota was a more settled area than Oregon had been when Nichols began his ministry there, and the social dislocation that had drawn people to his ministry in the West was not evident here. Since much of the attraction of the True Christadelphians rested on Nichols's personal claims to be the first person since the Apostasy to have "become a bearer of truth in its entirety as it is in Jesus," it is not surprising that even the modest success he had among people outside the small community of believers who relocated with him was slow in coming.[7]

Nichols continued to publish and distribute his tracts and pamphlets and to engage in public debate. Among the topics on which he was most interested

Rev. Maud Hembree's congregation at Barry, Illinois, circa 1900. Courtesy Megiddo Church, Rochester, N.Y.

in debating was the Sabbath. Nichols believed, as the Megiddos do today, that the biblical mandate to keep the Sabbath applied only to ancient Israel and that the day to keep holy is any day that the laws of the government under which one is living, in this case the United States, designate as the day of rest. There was an active Seventh-Day Adventist church in Owatonna, and Nichols challenged Adventists to debate him on the topic of the Sabbath. In the November 9, 1888, edition of the *Owatonna People's Press,* a notice appeared: "L. T. Nichols of Claremont, a preacher of the Christadelphian sect, challenges any of the Seventh Day Adventist ministers in the world to bring text of Scriptures to prove that Saturday is the Biblical Sabbath. If they can, let them come out in a friendly discussion. Mr. Nichols may be addressed at 108 Second Street SE, Minneapolis, Minn. or at Claremont, Minn." It is not known whether anyone responded to the challenge.

Nichols debated the local Baptist minister H. C. First in Barry, Illinois, when he visited there in 1888. In September of 1890, the *People's Press* in Owatonna, Minnesota, announced a public debate between Nichols and W. F. Jamieson, "of Des Moines, Iowa, the champion Infidel lecturer of the United States," to be held in Kasson, Minnesota, for eight evenings beginning September 25. The subjects to be debated were the origins, authority, and morality of the Bible.[8]

The Jamieson-Nichols debate was reported in some detail by the *Dodge County Republican,* which described the participants as "able men; learned in history and Bible lore, and gifted orators. Both of mature age, and profound reasoners; firm in their different positions and graceful and gentlemanly in their manners." The article further stated that they "appeared to confirm an emphatic sentence in the bill that announced the debate: 'A battle of words between giant intellects.'"

The debate was well attended, especially on the final evening, when "the house was more densely packed than on any previous night." The *Republican* reporter was unable to determine who won the debate, as "people differed as to which was the victorious disputant . . . prior opinions and prejudices" affecting the opinions of many. The reporter, however, apparently sided with Nichols, who was "a man of the world who would not willingly see destroyed the only existing guarantee of progress and civilization, simply because they cannot fully comprehend it [the Bible] in all its beauties and usefulness."[9]

In the fall of 1891, Nichols debated Spiritualist Moses Hull, one of the more interesting characters on what amounted to a debate circuit. Nichols may have gone into the debate with Hull with more than usual high hopes of winning over his opponent as Hull had changed his religious orientation several times. In the early 1850s, he had joined the United Brethren only to be converted to Seventh-Day Adventism in 1857. He became a popular Adventist preacher and staunch opponent of Spiritualism, whose meetings attracted large crowds. In 1862, in a moment that was very rare in the annals of religious debate, he admitted to having lost a debate with a Spiritualist opponent and declared himself converted to Spiritualism. He briefly recanted and returned to the Seventh-Day Adventists, but in September of 1863, he left the Adventists for good and became a prominent Spiritualist, traveling with his wife, Mattie, as a platform speaker on behalf of his newfound faith. According to the *Life and Work of the Rev. L. T. Nichols,* Hull told Nichols that if he died before Nichols, he would appear to Nichols to prove that "the dead are alive and conscious." *Life and Work* claims that "a short time afterward, Prof. Hull was killed in an accident" and that to date nothing had been heard from him. In actuality, Hull, who was born in 1835 or 1836, died—or "passed to the Spirit World," as the Spiritualists would have it—in 1907. Like Nichols, Hull also debated W. F. Jamieson.[10]

In 1891, at Davenport, Iowa, Nichols engaged in a debate with Thomas Williams, a Christadelphian minister who was the "unofficial leader of the Christadelphians in the United States and Canada."[11] Williams was born near Swansea, Wales, and as an adolescent became a follower of John Thomas. In 1872, he immigrated to the United States, settling at Riverside, Iowa. He traveled widely and became a popular debater and defender of Christadelphian orthodoxy with a major focus on the Renunciationist controversy.

In 1892, the Nichols-Williams debate was reported at length in *The Advocate* (or *Christadelphian Advocate*), of which Williams was editor.[12] Williams stated that at Davenport,

> Mr. N., in his boastful manner, announced that it was his intention to visit all the ecclesias he could; and try to turn them to his theories; also that he was going to demand another discussion with us, when a large assembly of Christadelphians could be present. Since the debate, however, we have not heard of his visiting any of the ecclesias; neither have we heard a word about another discussion. He seems to have disappeared from view, at least so far as Christadelphians are concerned; and this fact would seem to make it unnecessary for us to notice his books now.

However, Williams noted, "some have expressed a desire to see the fallacy of his position exposed . . . [and] the books do create confusions in the mind of some." Williams attacked Nichols's publications, starting with the pamphlets he had issued in Oregon, "in which his [Nichols's] name figured beyond all limits of modesty." He faulted Nichols for his "blind, venomous and reckless attack upon Dr. Thomas and Brother Roberts." This would seem to indicate that Nichols's publications were being distributed among Christadelphians and that there was some concern they could be influential.[13]

Williams seemed particularly concerned about two pamphlets, one titled *Try the Spirits* and the other *Adam before He Sinned,* the latter of which, as previously noted, supported the Renunciationist position. He discussed several specific points addressed in the pamphlets and went to great lengths to refute Nichols's arguments. At one point, when Nichols appeared to be in the right when discussing a statement from an article that appeared in the *Chris-*

tadelphian in 1880, Williams wrote that Nichols's statement "would not be worth noticing"

> were it not that it shows the kind of a man this piece of human vanity is. One seeking the truth and disposed and able to be reasonable would have known that the quotation given was either a slip of the pen or a typographical error; and he would have had sufficient respect for himself not to condescend to ridicule the writer on what was so palpably clear he did not intend to say. Such a meanness as would take advantage of such a case is really distressing when seen in any way associated with things pertaining to the Bible.[14]

In 1891, accompanied by his wife, Nichols returned to England, where Christadelphianism had had much more success than in America. He intended to meet with the Christadelphians and attempt to resolve his differences with them. According to *An Honest Man,* in England Nichols debated a Christadelphian named Martin and then Christadelphian leader Robert Roberts. In the debate, Roberts "found the evidence too powerful and became nervous. At last, in desperation he tried to flee by way of a door leading from the rostrum. The door opened outward, but Roberts, in his confusion, kept trying to pull it inward, to the amusement of his audience. A number of converts were made and baptized in the sea."[15]

In spite of what appeared to be local success, Nichols's attempt to bring the British Christadelphians to his point of view failed, and, according to Thomas Williams, the trip would have gone unnoticed had Nichols not "announced to the world in a country town paper that he . . . had concluded to abandon the name Christadelphian."[16] Indeed, about this time Nichols's Christadelphians became the "Christian Brethren," the new name being a translation of the word *Christadelphian.*[17]

Nichols apparently remained known in Christadelphian circles for some time after he separated from the denomination. In a 1903 address to British Christadelphians, Thomas Williams referred to Nichols by last name as part of a list of people who held a view on Adamic condemnation he opposed. One may probably conclude that he assumed his audience would know about whom he was speaking.

Nichols's separation from the Christadelphians was not unusual for the Restorationist movement, a tradition which, according to J. H. Garrison, has "a morbid fondness for controversy" and has experienced many divisions. Christadelphianism itself owes its existence as a separate denomination to John Thomas's split from the Campbellites. In his book *Sects and Society,* Bryan R. Wilson notes that power struggles among leaders of the Christadelphian church have been frequent. According to Wilson, Christadelphianism may have attracted "a particularly contentious individual," especially in earlier generations, and "clashes of personality, perhaps specifically concerned with the

ambition to lead, appear to have been the basis of most schism in Christadelphianism."[18] Although Thomas Williams suggested that Nichols was attempting to assume control of the Christadelphians, nothing in Nichols's extant
writing confirms this. However, it is clear that he was, at the very least, trying
to bring the most important Christadelphian leaders into his sphere of
influence.

Following his trip to England, Nichols changed more than the name of the
church. Relieved of any self-imposed obligation to adhere to the teachings of
John Thomas, Nichols retained those Christadelphian teachings that he found
to be compatible with Scripture and rejected those that were not. Nichols's
ministry clearly turned in a direction that made reconciliation with the Christadelphians virtually impossible. The newly renamed Christian Brethren refo-
cused their Restorationist orientation away from the practices of the early
church and toward the directives of Scripture. The most important change was
one that represented a clear break with Restorationism. About 1893, the
Brethren stopped practicing water baptism. For the Christadelphians, water
baptism was, and still is, an initiation rite performed as the culmination of a
period of intense study. It signifies that the person undergoing baptism has
gained sufficient understanding of Scripture to be accepted for membership.[19]
The Brethren determined that water baptism was a practice restricted to the
Apostolic Age, and while baptism was still experienced, it was a personal "baptism into [Christ's] death" and a total turning away from sin rather than a public ritual.[20]

When they rejected water baptism, the Brethren removed the rite of passage into membership in the ecclesia and made baptism no longer the test of
whether or not one was truly of the faith. The Brethren would not again have
readily identifiable specific membership requirements until 1958, when the
Megiddo Mission adopted a constitution stating that its membership consists of
"such persons as accept and sincerely endeavor to practice . . . the doctrines
which the members of this Church accept as derived from the Holy Scriptures,
to which we subscribe as our rule of faith and practice." These doctrines are
"those set forth in the SYNOPSIS OF THE PRINCIPLES OF TRUTH OF THE MEGIDDO CHURCH,
dated West Concord, Minnesota, December 1890, and as edited; and those proclaimed by our Founder since the publication of said synopsis." In order to
become a member, a person must have attended church for one year. Voting on
church matters is restricted to members who have been active for two years,
and there is a specific rite of induction into full fellowship, a provision for
removing members for "persistent absence," and an associate membership for
"persons living at a distance" who maintain contact through correspondence.[21]

In spite of his problems within the Christadelphian community, Nichols's
ministry in Minnesota does not seem to have been as controversial as his ministry in Oregon.[22] However, Nichols did have at least one confrontation with a
member of the press. As early as 1886 Nichols had been giving lectures in Owatonna on such topics as the Sabbath and prophecy. In 1887, he announced in
the local newspapers that beginning on December 2 he was going to give "a

course of Bible lectures" at the Opera House. In one of the lectures he apparently referred to his belief that children are not saved because salvation is earned and children have not had time to earn their salvation. As Nichols wrote while in Oregon, "God never intended to save infants: as we are only babes when we come out of the water; without character. We must grow until the full stature of Christ. We must become full grown men and women." Nichols's lecture angered B. E. Darby, the editor of the *Owatonna People's Press*. Darby had lost two children, most recently his three-year-old daughter, Fanny, who died of scarlet fever just two weeks before Nichols's lecture. The two men got into a "heated argument" that was reported in the *Owatonna Journal and Herald*. The editor of the *Journal and Herald* noted that "the trouble is that the elect of Elder Nichols are so select and limited in number, that, should the children be saved, there would be no room left for the cranks." He advised editor Darby "to search the Scriptures for himself and especially study the text: 'Answer a fool according to his folly.'" [23]

The fate of dead children was of particular concern in the nineteenth century, when disease took large numbers of infants. In response, most Protestant churches came to hold the position that children who died would be given special consideration because of their innocence and would be granted salvation. Consequently, the issue of the salvation of children was of constant concern to people who encountered Nichols's teachings, particularly if they were parents of young children. In spite of the possibility of its position alienating potential followers, the church continued to hold firmly to what it saw as a Bible-based position that "all who do spurn His warnings shall not be given another chance when this present life is over," and that "inasmuch as young children or infants are not capable of discerning between good and evil they are not responsible for what they have done or not done. They are neither consigned to punishment nor taken to glory. They are not subject to a resurrection and judgment . . . but the tender mercy of our heavenly Father permits them dreamless sleep."

In the 1960s that position was modified somewhat when pastor Kenneth Flowerday wrote the following based on a passage in the book of John: "'If any man will do his [God's] will, he shall know of the doctrine . . . ,' no child will die in infancy if at maturity it would do God's will." Since that time, the position has undergone further modification and, according to minister Ruth Sisson, the Megiddos now believe that children will probably be given additional time after the return of Christ to prove their worthiness. [24]

Tempering the view that children cannot earn salvation was the denial of the existence of hell. During the second half of the nineteenth century, concerns arose about the fate of the unrepentant dead, particularly in light of the large number of casualties resulting from the Civil War. Many a wife, mother, father, or sibling feared that an unrepentant loved one had gone to hell, where he would experience eternal punishment. Consequently, much to the annoyance of members of the clergy who believed only the fear of hell brought people to repentance, many people were attracted to religions and sects that denied the existence of hell. The most popular of these religious groups were the Universalists, who believed that all would be saved. The Christian Brethren fell into a second category. They believed that while the unrighteous dead would not be granted eternal life, they would simply not be raised from the dead and their eternal punishment would take the form of unconscious sleep and eternal separation from God. This was very comforting to many people, including one woman with whom the Brethren came into contact in Iowa:

> a Mrs. Borden, after hearing Bro. Nichols' sermons, called . . . to express her profound thanks for being enlightened on the subject of "Hell." She had an only son who died suddenly, and her minister told her, her son was in hell because he had not joined the church. She was beside herself with grief and worry because she was convinced her poor boy was suffering in Hell. After explaining to her the Truth on the subject, she felt much relieved and grateful for the help and enlightenment. She showed her thankfulness by furnishing the Mission with green vegetables such as lettuce; also butter and milk, all free of cost, which was provided from the store the family were operating.[25]

Apparently, editor Darby came to terms with the unusual beliefs of the Christadelphians and by 1891 was able to report positively on their activities. In its January 30, 1891, edition, the *People's Press* carried an account of a "revival" among the Christadelphians in Owatonna, "occasioned by the visit of Mr. Nichols, from Ellington, and a young man who has been drawn over from London, England, by his interest in their remarkable views on Bible teachings. . . . Quite a goodly number of people were present [and] . . . they certainly showed considerable interest in the proceedings." The Englishman spoke on the Second Coming and Nichols concluded the meeting by showing "the unscripturalness of some of the doctrines . . . of certain ones of the audience tinged with adventism."[26]

At some point Nichols changed his stance in opposition to newspapers. At least as early as 1888 he began to use the newspapers to announce his lectures, and in July 1893, when the local newspaper, the *West Concord People*, was served with a legal judgment and had its office seized, the editor "secured" type from L. T. Nichols and published the paper.[27] This change of opinion was fortunate because the Brethren would become increasingly dependent on newspapers to publicize their meetings.

Minnesota in the 1880s was a center of wheat farming in the United States, and it became a center for the development of agricultural implements that were part of what William E. Lass calls "the leavening in the rapid growth of Minnesota's industries." In order to support himself, his wife, and his ministry, Nichols turned his efforts to inventions. In 1885, he patented a farm gate; in 1886, an improved horse hitch and a railroad car coupling; in 1890, a fire escape; in 1891, a bailing press; in 1893, a "rotating measuring-vessel" for sacking grain; and in 1897, with H. E. Skeels, a hay loader.[28] The bailing press was probably his most successful invention. The *Owatonna Journal* reported the following:

> Mr. L. T. Nichols, of Dodge County, had his lightening hay press in operation during our county fair last week. Mr. Nichols claims that it presses hay the tightest and fastest of any press in the world, making a bale of 100 pounds per minute. Since the fair, we learn that Mr. N has made a contract with the Diamond Feed Mill Mfg. Company giving it the privilege of the exclusive sale and manufacture of the machine in the United States. They will begin manufacturing the machine at once, as they have several orders for their fall work.

In 1894, the Owatonna *People's Press* noted that Z. A. Bryant, a follower of Nichols from Oregon who lived in Claremont, a community near Ellington, was running the "celebrated Diamond hay press built in Winona." According to a 1908 Winona, Minnesota, city directory, the New Winona Manufacturing Company manufactured Diamond grinding mills as well as other agricultural equipment, including hay presses, and they were probably the manufacturers of Nichols's Diamond hay press, which Bryant was using.[29]

Nichols's interest in science and invention was not unusual for someone also interested in the millennial texts of the Bible. In the same way he applied himself to solving practical problems through his inventions, he applied himself to discovering the process of history from the time of Adam to the coming return of Christ and beyond. In doing so, he placed himself in the same category with many others of a more scientific or practical bent who have tried to answer the same questions. John Thomas was a physician, while scientists Isaac Newton and Joseph Priestly and, more recently, NASA engineer Edgar Whisenant, author of the best-selling *Eighty-eight Reasons Why the Rapture Will Be in 1988,* all dabbled in the apocalyptic.[30]

Nichols's inventions provided a financial base that did not require the attention of a farm. This was important for Nichols as his ministry expanded. About 1890, a congregation was planted at Davenport, Iowa. The following year, a church was built at Ellington, and a congregation that eventually grew to include thirty families was planted at Minneapolis. Sometime before 1893, an ecclesia was planted in nearby Owatonna. There are also suggestions that Nichols may have had followers in other communities. A Davenport, Iowa, newspaper reported that a Chicago newspaper had published an article about a congregation of Brethren in Kewaunee, Illinois. About the same time, another Davenport newspaper reported that some of the members of the Davenport ecclesia had relocated to Iowa from Ohio.[31] It is also possible that there were attempts to plant ecclesias in Texas. Maud Hembree did missionary work in Texas in 1890, visiting the family of Ethel Morrison, who eventually joined the church. L. T. Nichols preached in the Vernon, Texas, area sometime later.[32]

Although the camp meeting had been one of the focal points of the ministry in Oregon, the True Christadelphians did not establish one in Minnesota.

In its place, visits to the churches by L. T. Nichols and Maud Hembree became the principal means of maintaining orthodoxy. Nichols visited the Owatonna, Davenport, Barry, and Minneapolis ecclesias, and Hembree preached in Owatonna and Minneapolis.[33]

Little is known about any of the ecclesias Nichols planted except those in Davenport and Minneapolis. The Owatonna ecclesia is mentioned in local newspapers, which indicate that by June of 1893 it was at least large enough to warrant obtaining a room in a local hotel building for its two Sunday services. That the congregation was growing is indicated by an item at the beginning of the following month announcing that Maud Hembree was coming from Barry to hold services and to baptize new members by immersion in the Straight River.[34]

The origins of the Davenport, Iowa, congregation are uncertain. Like the Barry congregation, it may have been the result of contacts L. T. Nichols made through his travels and tracts while located in Oregon. Whatever its origins, early in its existence the mainstays of the congregation became Nichols's old teacher from Wisconsin, Mary Eastman Lee, and her husband, M. G. Lee.

M. G. Lee was born in Rush, New York, in 1820. He began his business career as a farmer raising broom corn. Because it was difficult to take his corn to market, he began to manufacture the brooms himself, selling them in the vicinity of Rush, which is in Monroe County, the county seat of which is Rochester. In 1866, Lee moved to Davenport, Iowa, where he sold sewing and knitting machines. In 1870, he established a broom manufacturing business, the

Mary Eastman Lee and M. G. Lee. Courtesy Megiddo Church, Rochester, N.Y.

Lee Broom and Duster Company in Davenport. Where and how he met Mary Eastman is not known, but at the time of their marriage in Chicago in 1888, he was recently widowed, having been married for forty-six years to his first wife, who died in 1887. Although he was a successful businessman, according to an obituary in the *Davenport Democrat,* he "did not mingle with people in society, or take any interest in the Business Men's association, or other organizations of that kind, and lived much within himself." Lee retired from the broom business in 1894.[35]

The Davenport church apparently attracted little or no public attention until 1899 when it received considerable negative publicity in the local press. It is difficult to determine how much of the information from the newspaper reports is true. The largest amount of material is contained in a rather sensational series of articles that appeared in the *Davenport Daily Republican* between February 25 and May 14. The articles, however, are based on a limited number of unnamed sources, bring up the same charges repeatedly, and demonstrate a misunderstanding or misrepresentation of known beliefs of the Brethren. For example, without ever having met Nichols, the reporter accused him of being "knavish or insane" and of having the hypnotic powers of the fictional Svengali.[36]

The Davenport controversy first came to light when an article appeared in the *Davenport Daily Republican* promoting a forthcoming report based on the results of a two-week investigation of a group called the Brethren in Christ (a translation of *Christadelphian*) and their leader, Nichols, whose work had resulted in "unbalanced minds and wrecked lives." The following day, the paper printed an article about a woman (subsequently identified as Mrs. John C. Snyder) who had "nearly lost her reason on account of the things Nichols has said to her." The article claimed that the woman had questioned her husband about his relationship with two women associated with the Brethren (later identified as the British-born Smith sisters Tirzah and Margaret). According to the article, when the husband reported his wife's concerns to L. T. Nichols, the woman was subjected to "whipping," a term the reporter used for the practice of mutual correction. The result was considerable mental anguish for the woman, who had since left the Brethren.

With regard to Nichols, the *Daily Republican* stated, "L. T. Nichols . . . in the opinion of a religious sect in this city and in several other places, is the earthly representative of the Almighty. Only by coming to Nichols and believing in all he says, and doing everything he suggests, can one save his soul from perdition. The few who will enter Heaven would not have been privileged to do so, if this Minnesota man had never been born. Nichols can do no wrong. There is no appeal from his decisions. God has commissioned him to organize the Kingdom of Heaven on this earth and it will be transferred into eternity, bag and baggage, just as Nichols organized it."[37]

The *Davenport Daily Leader* took a slightly milder tone when reporting on the Brethren but still referred to "some queer practices" of the group.

According to that newspaper, the group, which numbered ten or twelve members, but had been larger, worshiped in members' homes. The paper further stated that the intention of the group was to live in community as one family with a single elder at the head, and while they had not been able to carry out this plan because they were "so scattered and numerically weak," at any time the elder might require the members to sell their property. Further accusations alleged that L. T. Nichols and the church were one and the same and that Nichols lived "in affluence and that he has on several occasions traveled to Europe." In an effort to be fair, the paper noted that "many people do this [travel to Europe] and that of itself is not so material."

Another peculiarity was the alleged belief that the marriage relationship was immoral unless both parties were members of the church. Children of members were not allowed to associate with other children and did not attend school. One couple was alleged to be living in "mortal fear of being expelled from the church" because they would not disown their grown daughters who had left the Brethren. The *Daily Leader* had its own version of the Snyder controversy that was very similar to that of the other paper but phrased in less definite terms.

> Still another, and a very distressing case, if the facts are true, was brought to light through the efforts of Police Matron Hill. According to her informant, and there is every reason to believe that the party telling her knew whereof the utterances were made, the wife of a member of [*sic*] professed believer in the sect, she herself being also a believer, complained to her husband that his attentions to certain unmarried female members, who since that time have been called to other fields of labor, were rather marked. This he reported to Elder Nichols and a decree was issued that this complaining wife should be subjected to castigation for an extended period and that at each of the meetings of the congregation she is now compelled to undergo severe diciplining [*sic*]. It did not end here . . . but the decree has been issued for the husband to dispose of their property, goods and chattels, leave his wife and report for duty to the locality where the females who were the subject of the complaint are now located.

It was further reported that the wife was suffering from extreme mental anguish and "fears are expressed as to the result on her mind." The *Daily Leader* tempered its story by noting that the residents of the area in which the Brethren lived were "considerably stirred over the matter," but since the members did not associate with people outside the group, it was "a hard matter to get direct information."[38]

The day after the initial report on the Brethren appeared, the *Daily Leader* printed a statement by C. R. Lee that attacked Mrs. Snyder and addressed accusations that had been made against the group. Lee stated, "The Christian brethren of this city have been deeply grieved over the false, malicious, evil and untrue statements made by Mrs. John Snyder as to her treatment by the

Brethren, and by Brother Nichols on his recent visit to this city. . . . These are uniformly false and are the results of an inherited natural jealousy, a disposition that at times makes her subject to hysterical fits and a mania which makes her act like an insane person, whose foolish talk should have no weight upon the mind of any sensible individual."[39]

Apparently, the *Daily Leader,* and even the *Daily Republican,* had declined to publish the most outrageous accusation against Nichols—that he had ordered Mrs. Snyder to take her four children and jump into the Mississippi River and drown herself. Lee assured readers that "six reputable citizens acquainted with the facts and who heard every word spoken by Mr. Nichols at the time" would confirm that he had given no such order. Further, Lee contended that Mrs. Snyder had stated to neighbors and to Police Matron Hill that she was not jealous of the Smith sisters but that she had objected to her husband's plans to move to Minnesota, where they would have been located near the sisters. Lee concluded by noting that in the three years since he had moved to Davenport, Mr. Snyder had had to get his own meals, clean house, and do the laundry, suggesting that Mrs. Snyder was a poor housewife. On the same day that Lee's letter appeared in the *Daily Leader,* the *Daily Republican* published an article stating "Chief of Police Martens follows the expose of Elder Nichols with the order that he be arrested if he ever makes his appearance in this city."[40]

In a further effort at damage control, M. G. and Mary Eastman Lee invited reporters to their home to learn about the Brethren's doctrines and beliefs. Representatives of several newspapers attended the meeting, which the reporter from the *Daily Leader* called "interesting." At the meeting, John Snyder confirmed most of the information that had appeared in C. R. Lee's statement the day before. Then he addressed the issues of his wife's housekeeping skills and the Smith sisters, who are referred to by the newspapers as "the Bicycle Sisters" because of their penchant for riding their bicycles around Davenport while dressed in what the populace apparently considered odd attire. He stated that it was not true that his wife had been unable to perform her household duties for the previous year. In fact, he noted that the house had been better kept during that period because other women in the ecclesia had helped his wife improve her housekeeping skills. He attributed her jealousy of the Smith sisters to "their evident superiority in housework" and further stated that they were "intimate friends of our family and assisted and instructed" his wife in "many things."

Mary Lee then took the floor. She denied that Mrs. Snyder had been castigated for forty days as had apparently been asserted, stating that the punishment had "only lasted one third of the time of the meeting" and that Mrs. Snyder was no longer a member of the Brethren "and so far as the organization is concerned can do as she pleases."

Mrs. Lee further denied accusations that the Brethren "taught free lovism." Addressing the contention that Nichols ordered John C. Snyder to leave his wife and move to where the Smith sisters had moved in Minnesota, Lee stated firmly that the Brethren did not believe in separation of husband and wife except on the grounds of adultery. Referring to the Smith sisters by the newspaper's designation as the "Bicycle Sisters, " she said that "they are a couple of nice young ladies who worked at Kuhnen's cigar factory until the health of one of them gave way," after which they went to live on their sister's farm in Minnesota.

On the education of children, Lee said that the Brethren's children were not sent to school "simply to avoid their children from coming in contact with children of people of the world." Instead, they were taught by private teachers who were not members of the church and they were doing well academically.

Mrs. Lee concluded her remarks with a brief description of the Brethren's beliefs about the fate of the dead and establishment of heaven on earth. There followed a question-and-answer period during which the reporter for the *Republican* asked, "Is Nichols infallible and appointed by God?" M. G. Lee answered that Nichols was a minister and "Nichols cannot work miracles. He is not a Moses or an Elijah. He belongs rather to the category of Luther, Calvin, and Knox. We are no more saved through Nichols than a Presbyterian is saved through Knox." The *Daily Leader* reporter noted that "several members of the association were present and they did not impress one with the idea that there was anything abnormally wrong. Husbands and wives seem to be happy."

Much of the meeting between the Brethren and the Davenport press dealt with the suggestion that the Brethren were a communal society whose members intended to hold goods in common. Mary Lee denied that the Brethren were communitarian and stated that there was not a common purse. Furthermore, she said that L. T. Nichols had discouraged the members from relocating to Minnesota to avoid any appearance that "he was after the money of his people." [41]

While the meeting at the Lee home was reported in a manner generally favorable to the Brethren in both the *Leader* and the *Republican,* and the former let the matter drop, the *Republican* continued to print negative articles. The *Republican* reporter had particular difficulty with the practice of mutual correction, which he blamed for Mrs. Snyder's problems. He portrayed the process as proceeding in only one direction, with graphic depictions of Nichols pointing out the faults of his followers while being unable to accept criticism himself. One article stated, "The members of the church are ranged around a room, and the leader standing in the center of the floor, extends a bony finger at first one and then another making criticisms on their conduct and lack of spiritual strength. Nichols has made a business of finding fault for a quarter of a century and he is an adept at it." Another article reported that when a former member attempted to turn the tables and subject Nichols to criticism, Nichols told him to shut his mouth. When he persisted in his criticism, Nichols ordered him to take his hat and leave. The man was subsequently disfellowshipped from the church, for which he was "heartily glad." [42]

Apparently, the public controversy and the complaints to authorities made the Brethren feel unwelcome in Davenport. A Davenport newspaper reported the following at the time of M. G. Lee's death in 1901:

> Several years ago, Mr. Lee became estranged from this city because of the unfriendly attitude that most of its people and especially the police force and authorities, took regarding the religious sect known as the Brethren in Christ, or Christadelphians, with whom he was intimately associated, and the incidents that attended the visits of Elder Nichols here, from time to time, culminated in so much unpleasant notoriety for the sect that its members gathered up bodily and moved from the city to Barry [Illinois] where they founded a sort of "heaven" and lived undisturbed in the practice of their peculiar beliefs.[43]

Some members moved to Minnesota, including Thomas Philips.

In spite of the threats, there is no evidence that Nichols was ever arrested in Davenport. It is possible that the members of the ecclesia left before he had an opportunity to visit again, or, more probably, as the *Daily Leader* stated, although the Brethren's practices had been reported to the police, there was "nothing of which the police can take cognizance."[44]

If the people of Davenport thought they had heard the last of the controversy surrounding the Christian Brethren when they left in 1899, they were mistaken. The following year, M. G. Lee deeded substantial real estate holdings in Davenport over to his wife "for $1 and love and affection." In response, his children filed a lawsuit seeking to have M. G. Lee declared to be of unsound mind and incompetent to administer his property. The principal complaint of the suit was that the Brethren, probably in the form of Mary Lee, were influencing Lee to use his wealth to support their ministry.[45]

The September 6, 1900, *Barry Adage* reported that when the lawyers for M. G. Lee's children tried to get testimony in Chicago, where Lee had apparently had business connections, that Lee was of unsound mind, they could find no one to testify to that effect. The writer stated that "the trial in Davenport will prove that the father has more good sense than the son, judging from the latter's attempt to get possession of his father's property and money."

The court ruled in favor of M. G. Lee, but the case was appealed. It was still pending when M. G. Lee died in April 1901, making the case moot because it was now impossible to assess Lee's mental state. However, the family continued to pursue the case. A favorable ruling would have increased their chances of success in their new lawsuit, which was filed to contest Lee's will.

Shortly after M. G. Lee's death, Mary Lee filed seven real estate deeds in Davenport showing that in the previous year she had sold some of the property in Davenport that Lee had transferred to her. Lee's children, including a daughter who had been living with M. G. and Mary Lee, contested the deeds, claiming that they were the principal rightful heirs and that Mrs. Lee was entitled to only one-third of the estate. The children further claimed that Lee had been incompetent to sign the deeds over to his wife "by reason of old age and physical and mental debility" and that Mary Lee, and others to whom she and M. G. Lee had sold some of the property, had exercised "undue influence" over their father. The children's case was weakened by the previous court ruling, which found M. G. Lee to be mentally competent, and the Iowa courts referred the case to Pike County, Illinois, where Lee died. It would be several years before the suit was settled and all parties received proceeds from M. G. Lee's estate.[46]

Information about the Christian Brethren's Minneapolis ecclesia appears in the minutes of its business meetings from 1894 to 1901 in a logbook located at the Megiddo Church Home. The minutes indicate that as of August 26, 1894, there were forty-two current and/or former members of the ecclesia. The ecclesia was highly organized and formed committees for even the most minor functions, such as welcoming visitors from England. Women had voting rights in the business meetings and served on committees.

On January 27, 1895, L. T. Nichols met with the leaders of the ecclesia to develop a "plan of the financial administration of all the ecclesias of America," a clear indication that he had left the Christadelphians and formed his own small quasi-denomination. The intent of the financial system was to "adopt a systematic mode of giving to the support of the poor and that the work of the Lord might be done in an orderly way, each member of the body giving as the Lord hath prospered him." The plan of administration designated Nichols as president and Henry Skeels as secretary, with a member of the Owatonna ecclesia as treasurer and three members of the Ellington ecclesia as other administrators. Each ecclesia was directed to appoint a subcommittee to act in conjunction with the administrator. It is unclear exactly how the financial aid system operated, but the Minneapolis ecclesia was engaged in helping financially disadvantaged members. At the January 1896 meeting it was reported that the Davenport ecclesia had sent the Minneapolis ecclesia forty dollars to support its poor relief program.[47]

The ecclesias corresponded with one another. In Minneapolis, at first, individual members were responsible for maintaining the contacts, but eventually, as with most things that the ecclesia did, a committee was appointed to handle the correspondence. For an unspecified reason, the committee was disbanded at the following meeting.

Music was an important part of the worship experience in the Minneapolis ecclesia. There were Sunday evening meetings to practice singing and frequent meetings just for singing. The ecclesia had an organist and used at least three different hymnals. Apparently, there was some controversy about which hymnal to use, and it was decided that the person leading the worship service could choose the hymnal.[48]

Initially, the ecclesia held afternoon services, perhaps because another church used the meeting room in the morning.[49] Eventually, they held a morning worship service on Sundays, with Sunday school in the afternoons and an evening service on Wednesdays. The business meeting was originally held late on Sundays but was moved to mornings in 1895 on those Sundays when there "was no reproof to be given." This last statement suggests that the practice of mutual correction had been institutionalized by the time the churches were established.

The Minneapolis ecclesia originally met in an upstairs room of the Labor Temple. However, the November 24, 1900, minutes reported that four trustees had been appointed for the Christian Brethren Church at 112 Second Street, S. E., and that it had been decided that the Minneapolis brethren would bear the entire cost of the church. A stove purchased for heating and the pulpit in the upstairs meeting room were donated to the Owatonna ecclesia.[50]

In keeping with the Christian Brethren's aversion to public education, the Minnesota ecclesia appointed a committee to investigate the possibility of establishing a school for its children. However, the committee reported at the September 25, 1895, meeting that "due to the financial condition of the brethren," it was decided that the four children of the ecclesia should be educated at home. A standing committee was appointed to oversee the education of the children.

It is difficult to determine the financial status of the Minneapolis ecclesia and its members. The members were prosperous enough to make regular contributions to the ecclesia, support their relief work, and pay for hall rental, a janitor, and, eventually, a church building. However, at the May 1896 meeting, for unknown reasons that may have had nothing to do with finances, it was decided to allow children to contribute to the church.[51] That the church members may have been prosperous is indicated by their willingness to commit themselves in August 1896 to raising one thousand dollars to help cover the cost of L. T. Nichols's trip "to England and to visit the different ecclesias so that they may receive more spiritual help." A Brother Leonard was "empowered to write to England and find out how much they will raise toward getting Bro. Nichols there, money to be pledged now, but paid while he is there." It is not clear from the minutes whether the English pledge was to be part of the thousand dollars the ecclesia planned to raise. It is also not clear whether the English brethren were considered to comprise an ecclesia. Nichols had made a number of converts on his 1891 visit to the British Isles. In 1899, a group of these converts immigrated to the United States and joined the Minneapolis ecclesia.[52]

At least one family from Minneapolis moved to Ellington to be near Nichols. E. A. Flowerday was born in England and immigrated to the United States, where he married May Adeline Brown of East Toledo, Ohio. The young couple lived on the frontier, while E. A. Flowerday worked in railroad construction in Montana before relocating to Minneapolis. He worked as a painter and handyman in the Ellington area.[53]

E. A. Flowerday's son Kenneth, who was five years old when his family moved next door to Nichols in Ellington, provided some of the few glimpses available of the human side of L. T. Nichols. According to Flowerday, a number of celebrations were part of the yearly activities of the church, some in Nichols's honor and others simply festive occasions. Nearly all were kept secret from Nichols until the actual time of the program because

> he enjoyed surprises, and especially he enjoyed prying into surprises others were trying to keep from him. From paper and card-board Father was making some display articles for one of these occasions. My younger sister, five years old, was told to watch lest Brother N. might "smell a rat" and come over. He did. My sister would not let him in at the kitchen door. Later he tried to get her to tell him what was being made. She was adamant, she had been told not to tell. Bro. N. commended her for doing what she was told.

According to Flowerday, Nichols liked to use life situations to teach object lessons to the children. One day, Flowerday's older sister was wearing a new pair of shoes of which she was most proud. Every so often, she would hold her feet out in front of her and display the shoes to those around her. Noticing this, Nichols asked Mrs. Flowerday to remove the new shoes and put older shoes on the child as a lesson in humility.

When Kenneth Flowerday was a teenager, Nichols's cook removed the pulp and juice from some oranges by making a hole in one end of the oranges. Nichols took the oranges and set them on a plate with the hole end down. He then sent the plate of oranges to the Flowerday house. Everyone was surprised when they picked up the fruit and it was very light. On being queried, Nichols said he wanted to impress on the Flowerdays the folly of living only for the present, because, "like the empty orange skin, it looked whole but lacked substance."[54]

L. T. and Harriet Nichols spent part of the winter of 1893–94 in Florida in an effort to improve Harriet's health. In February 1894, while staying in St. Augustine, they sent a letter to the churches that has today become a treasured document to church members. The letter, known as "A General Letter to All the Churches," has been published as a pamphlet. Part of the letter is written as rhyming verse, presaging the later use of poetry in the worship and literature of the church, and this portion has been printed separately as "Virtues of the General Letter." The letter is often mentioned in sermons and even in conversation among members. It has been read in worship services and reprinted in the *Megiddo Message*. In 1962, a high school student from central New York whose family later moved to Rochester to join the church, wrote to the *Message* from her second period study hall to report that at breakfast a member of her family had read "a few of the virtues of the General Letter," and she observed that "they certainly cover every phase of the Christian life and the best way to perfect our characters."[55]

As the high school student suggested, the letter is a blueprint for salvation. As such, the letter serves as a guide for members of the church, and it is assumed that all members are familiar with its contents. The letter reinforces Nichols's constant theme of the imminence of the return of Christ and cautions its readers to "remember, when the day comes, there will be no appeal, the decision will be final." It then gives guidelines for the study of Scripture:

> No one should endeavor to establish a notion or theory, but should go to the Record and always be guided by the plain evidence. No application of any text should be made that is in any way out of harmony with the general teachings of the oracles of God.
>
> . . . seeing there is a possibility of some giving a solution of the hard things in the Word which will prove their ruin, would it not be far better to go very slow in reference to such things, where there is no plain solution? . . . There are many things contained in the law of Moses that are typical of heavenly things, of which it is hard to give a correct solution or right application; so also there are a great many symbols, parables, visions, etc. which are the same. A great amount of study, as well as some natural ability, is required to enable us to give a proper scriptural application.[56]

The letter goes on to advise "the Brotherhood" not to waste precious time poring over "the puzzling texts of the Bible" but to devote their efforts to searching out the plain demands of the Word and comparing their conduct to it.

Nichols exhorts his readers "to go to work in real earnestness and purify" themselves because they can "become pure and holy in all things 'even as he [Christ] is pure.'" Lest the readers of the letter have any doubts as to what comprises the means to purity and salvation, Nichols admonishes them to remember that it is what they actually do in obedience to Scripture that will count in their favor at the judgment. He then lists specific acts and attitudes that will help them toward their goal:

> . . . reading, *daily* reading of the Word; careful meditation; prayerful self-criticism; humble confession of faults; chaste conversation, coupled with fear; godly example in every day life; heartfelt, sincere exhortations; rebuking in love; watchfulness for each other's welfare; fervent desire to do right; deep sense of self-respect; an abhorrence of evil; purity of motives; kindness of word and purpose; unbiased judgment; love unfeigned; courtesy to all; stability of character; uprightness in dealings; fervency of spirit; diligency in business; reverence for superiors; truthfulness in telling; holiness in conversation; cleanliness of person; loving the right, hating the wrong; true godly sorrow when we have done wrong; aiding the needy; chastening the guilty; upholding the righteous; crucifying all flesh that tempts to do wrong.
>
> . . . rejoice with the lowly; weep with the truly penitent; give the water of life to the thirsty, and bread to the hungry; ever be merciful; dare always to do right; be thankful for favors; never find unnecessary fault; live unto God, and not unto men; never be weary, but walk in the light;

> do unto others as we would have them do to us; be easily entreated;
> throw all stubbornness away; have no relish for error.[57]

Nichols left his followers with little time for frivolous activity or thought if they were to heed his prescription for eternal life. At the same time, he set challenging goals that still shape the lives of the Megiddos and make them a body of believers, all of whom are willing to make the sacrifices necessary to live up to the very high standards of conduct described in the letter.

By 1897, Harriet Nichols apparently recovered her health and the Nicholses traveled to Europe, presumably using the money raised by the ecclesias. They visited England, France, Germany, Switzerland, and Italy. Nichols preached in London and other locations in England and in Wales, probably at Swansea.

The Christian Brethren retained Nichols's strong focus on eschatology. The Minneapolis ecclesia sold Christian Brethren literature, including the *Fifth Pamphlet* of the minutes from the Oregon camp meeting, which is primarily made up of Nichols's Bible chronology.[58] The sermon topics for the Minneapolis ecclesia printed in the newspaper strongly emphasize the end times, the Second Coming of Christ, and the establishment of his kingdom on earth: "Christ the Future King of the World, with 144,000 to Rule with Him," "The Kingdom of God to Be Composed of Kings and Subjects, Laws and Territory," and "The World That God So Loved and the Present Evil World."[59]

In 1899, Nichols produced a new version of the *Bible Chronology*. In it, he noted that "it is now 1899 and it is plain to be seen that some of the links need altering, although you will see that the points we shall alter are in the main but just what we formerly told you might be."[60] Like their founder, the Megiddos accept the possibility that inaccurate interpretations can be made and later corrected.

The new chronology still contained Nichols's claim to be the first since the Apostasy to be "the bearer of truth in its entirety" and to have begun the cleansing of the spiritual Sanctuary. The only change in this claim is that, instead of identifying only 1880 as the time of the change, he identifies the period from 1880 to 1883 and possibly to 1887 as the period of the discovery. Pastor Ruth Sisson of the Megiddo Church believes that Nichols may have added the later dates because he did not consider the truth fully developed until he had made additional discoveries through his reading of Scripture.[61]

In the new chronology, Nichols proceeded to recalculate the time for the return of Christ, setting it between 1901 and 1909, with the Millennium, or thousand-year reign of Christ, to begin forty years later. The new chronology still contained references to the inaccuracies in the works of John Thomas and Robert Roberts and to the Christadelphians. At the end of the pamphlet, Nichols exhorted "ye professed Christadelphians" to "throw away Dr. Thomas' failures, come out in the fear of God and accept the truth upon the subject we have brought before you." This indicates that in spite of the degree to which Nichols had distanced himself and his followers from their former coreligionists, he still had hopes of influencing them.[62]

4

Sailing into the Millennium

In a sermon preached in February 1900, L. T. Nichols admonished his followers, "I tell you, beloved brethren, you are loving those who are not serving the Lord, and . . . the wrath is coming if you help the ungodly, or love those who hate the Lord." He further proclaimed, "I have left all my brothers and sisters behind— all who would not fear God and work righteousness," obviously suggesting that his listeners should do the same. By the following year, he had become convinced that his followers could only avoid the influences of the ungodly and pursue perfection by living apart from the rest of the world.[1] At the same time that he feared the results of his followers' contact with nonbelievers, he felt a need to take his message to a wider geographical area. As he would later write, "Looking at the world around us and seeing how few were keeping His commandments, how few were looking for His coming, and how few were ready to receive Him, we felt constrained to start out upon this, our mission work at any cost."[2] To address these seemingly contradictory needs, Nichols abandoned spreading the gospel through planting churches and conceived of the idea of a gospel boat on the Mississippi River as a place where, as one member later put it, "the gathering together and sounding of the midnight cry could be accomplished at one and the selfsame time."[3] It is evidence of the strength of Nichols's eschatological vision that he would abandon what appears to have been a growing quasi-denomination to gather his followers for the uncertain future of the boat ministry.

The idea for the boat ministry probably derived either directly or indirectly from passages of Scripture, particularly from the book of Daniel, that contain references to water. Nichols placed great emphasis on this in his *Bible Chronology:*

> Then I, Daniel looked, and behold! There stood other two; the one on this side, of the bank upon the river (or waters of life) and the other on that side, (or on the other side) of the bank on the river, or waters of life. We ask, what does the river represent? It can be none other than the waters of life. David tells us (Psalms 1:1,4) "Blessed is the man that walketh not in the counsel of the ungodly, nor standeth in the way of sinners. . . . But his delight is in the law of the Lord, and in his law doth he meditate day and night. And he shall be like a tree planted by the rivers of water, that bringeth forth his fruit in his season; his leaf shall not wither, and whatsoever he doeth shall prosper." Jesus settles this beyond all dispute. (John 4:14). "Whosoever drinketh of the water that I shall give him shall never thirst, but the water I shall give him, shall be in him as a well (or flowing stream) of water, springing up into everlasting life." This River of water must be the waters of life or the words that Jesus spake which we must all drink of, in order to be saved. And if we receive the truth, we are said to be planted upon the bank of the waters of life.

Nichols further wrote that "the waters of life is the pure stream of truth, and the ones who are upon it are the children of God." [4]

Nichols may also have gotten the idea for the boat ministry from other similar ventures. The *Megiddo* was not the only mission boat to operate during the later nineteenth and early twentieth centuries. In fact, the *Megiddo* was not even the first missionary boat to navigate the Mississippi and Ohio Rivers. At least two others had preceded it. From about 1885 until sometime after 1902, Free Methodist I. R. B. Arnold and his wife had operated two different boats, one dubbed "the floating chapel." More famous was the ministry of George T. Clayton of the Church of God (Anderson), who bought a sunken barge at Pittsburgh, refloated it, christened it the *Floating Bethel,* and spent the fall and winter of 1893 and 1894 on the rivers. While both ministries were conducted on the Mississippi and Ohio River systems, neither was as ambitious as the Megiddo—these ships were unpowered craft that needed to be towed from place to place, and neither ever had more than a dozen missionaries on board.

It is highly possible that the well-read Nichols had some knowledge of the *Floating Bethel.* The boat would have been known in the cities along the Mississippi, many of them the same cities Nichols and his boat would later visit, such as St. Louis, Missouri, and Evansville, Indiana. The boat was also the subject of an article in a popular national publication. [5]

Nichols may have undertaken the boat ministry with some sense of urgency. The eight-year period in which he had predicted that Christ would return had already begun. In preparation for the new ministry, Nichols gathered his follow-ers in Minneapolis beginning about April 1901. At that time, the Minneapolis ecclesia abruptly ceased keeping minutes, and Nichols and William Pickering began selling their property in Ellington. The April 18 edition of the *Barry Breeze* announced that Mrs. Maud Hembree "offers her house on the north-west part of the city for sale." Apparently, it sold quickly, as the May 2 edition of the *Breeze* announced that Mrs. Hembree and Miss Millican were offering their household goods at a private sale.[6]

Among the preparations made in Minneapolis was the acquisition of musi-cal instruments and the training of a band. Nichols purchased the instruments and personally undertook the drilling of the members "for many hours in the evening and sometimes through the day, giving them intensive training with all the instruments individually and collectively."[7]

Using his own money and perhaps funds contributed by others who sold their properties to join the mission, Nichols commissioned the construction of the boat at Clinton, Iowa. At a cost of about $22,000, it was, according to the *Quincy Whig,* "the largest steamboat that has been seen on the upper Missisipi [*sic*] for several years." It was a "large three-deck steamboat, dimensions 205 feet overall . . . with two engines each of 125 h.p. The boat . . . had 52 state-rooms, a complete machine shop for manufacturing and repair work, a carpen-ter shop and a flour mill. It was steam heated throughout, lighted by acetylene gas and fitted in every way for safety and comfort." It also had sanitary plumb-ing and "a touch of luxury . . . here and there."[8]

In her 1946 history of Clinton County, Iowa, Estelle Le Prevost Youle noted that the Megiddo left Lyons, Iowa, to make "a competitive run against the show-boats," and in many ways, including design and decoration, the boat resembled the entertainment palaces plying the Mississippi and Ohio Rivers at the time, a fact that was probably not lost on the entrepreneurial Nichols. The ship was painted various colors over the more than two years it was on the rivers. At one time it was a patriotic red, white, and blue, but at its height it was red and white with "pretentious" black smokestacks. Suspended between the smokestacks was a banner proclaiming "United We Stand," while arching over the bow of the boat was another banner that read "In God We Trust." Beneath the latter was a "galvanized iron Bible, three feet by two feet," which was open to Psalm 117. The psalm was printed in black letters on a white background. The name of the boat was painted on the pilot house.[9]

The *Megiddo,* which means "a place of troops," was launched on Octo-ber 24, 1901, amid great fanfare. According to the *Clinton Advertiser,* crowds began to assemble long before the scheduled time of the launching, and there were eventually "several hundred people of all classes, including the pastors of many churches." To begin the ceremonies, the uniformed Brethren band, led by L. T. Nichols, marched onto the levee and to the water's edge while alternately playing and singing missionary hymns. "A large number" of the Brethren marched with them. Nichols prayed, the band played "Nearer My God to Thee," and the other Brethren sang. Nichols then delivered an address describing the proposed work of the mission. The hymn "There's Sunshine in My Soul Today" followed, and the service concluded with a benediction by Nichols, after which the Brethren marched in order back to their quarters.[10] Thirty families, comprising ninety individuals, boarded the ship when it left Clinton. Included were members of at least the Ellington, Minneapolis, and Barry ecclesias.[11] Among the passengers were seventeen children.

Because the *Megiddo* was launched late in the sailing season, it was necessary to make special arrangements for the locks at Keokuk, Iowa, to be kept open an extra two weeks for the ship to pass. As a consequence, the ship left Clinton without work on it being completed. Painting and carpentry continued as the vessel proceeded south down the river. The ship made stops at Rock Island, Illinois, Dubuque, Iowa, and St. Louis before proceeding to Memphis, arriving on December 23, 1901, and remaining for the winter while the Brethren finished work on the boat. Leaving Memphis on March 27, 1902, the *Megiddo* returned to St. Louis, arriving April 8 and remaining for two weeks. Throughout the 1902 navigation season, the boat traveled up and down the Mississippi and Cumberland Rivers, making stops at ports in five states.

Although the Christian Brethren community was characterized by a high degree of cooperation, the Brethren were still strongly committed to the concept of private property. Consequently, even on the *Megiddo* each family had its own living quarters, dining facilities, and storage lockers. Each living area measured at least nine feet by twelve feet with eight-foot-high ceilings; families with children had additional space. According to a Clarksville, Tennessee, newspaper, "each room was made like a home in miniature. It was carpeted. Lace curtains

The gospel boat *Megiddo* at about the time of its launch in October 1901. Courtesy Murphy Library, University of Wisconsin–La Crosse.

were put upon the windows. . . . The furniture in each is different, the carpets, the hangings, the pictures." A reporter for the *Saint Paul Pioneer Press* noted that not all of the boat's residents were treated equally. Captain Nichols had "the biggest state room, the biggest arm chair, and the biggest mahogony [*sic*] bedstead."

Each family had its own cool cellar in the hold of the boat, a separate area in the community refrigerator, and a separate flour box. Each flour box had two doors; one dispensed wheat flour, the other, buckwheat flour. Women cooked for their own families, and as many as thirty meals were prepared at one time in the ship's sixteen-by-thirty-foot kitchen, which featured a "great brick range which stretches for twenty feet or more" and kitchen utensils that covered the walls. Each family had space in the cupboards that lined the dining room walls to store tableware and additional provisions. There was also a laundry room with a line of washtubs, an adjacent room for drying and ironing, and a sewing room.[12]

The ship had its own one-room school with the usual desks and maps. According to one student, L. T. Nichols took a keen interest in the school and would make occasional visits to address the students and monitor their progress. Because he wanted to encourage the students, he would occasionally devote evening gatherings to giving the children "exercises in mental arithmetic and spelling lessons." Similar public demonstrations of educational accomplishments would become characteristic of Megiddo education.[13]

In the center of the main deck was an assembly room/chapel that measured twenty by thirty-six feet and seated 120 people. This was used for community gatherings, including nightly services. The room was decorated with Scripture passages, scenes from the book of Revelation, and a large Bible chronology wall chart titled "From Adam to Eternity." It was also equipped with a piano and cabinet organ. A small barge pulled behind the ship provided each family with storage space for fresh fruits and vegetables and carried a carpenter's bench. The Cloverport, Kentucky, newspaper described the entire boat as "a model of convenience and economized space."[14]

Each family paid rent for its quarters and paid for food purchased in bulk by Nichols, who had assumed the title of captain. According to Maud Hembree, "We have poor and well-to-do on board . . . The well-to-do can afford the time required for the [mission] work. The poor work and support themselves . . . We apply the principle that he who eats must work."[15]

Wherever the boat went, some of the men on board sought work, which, an Owensboro, Kentucky, newspaper reported, they would have no difficulty in finding, as they "are all excellent workmen and sober and gentlemanly men." Among the men of the *Megiddo* were "a first class tailor, clerks, paper hangers, painters, sign painters, machinists, carpenters, teamsters, masons, plasterers, bricklayers, landscapers, and men who can do all general work." However, the men were generally employed "for short intervals where [work] could be obtained and fitted in with the regular activities," and it is unlikely that such work was a major source of income for the men of the *Megiddo*.[16]

The women were responsible for cleaning, sewing, laundry, and other household tasks. Even the young boys helped by carrying water onto the deck in sprinkling cans to put out burning embers that fell on the deck from the smokestacks. The boys also went ashore two or three times a day to get fresh water for cooking and drinking.[17]

The *Megiddo* was equipped with a machine shop and lathe, "where the community [made] windmills, acetylene lighting plants and other articles invented by Mr. Nichols." According to the *Saint Paul Pioneer Press,* the shop provided paid employment for some of the Brethren. The items made in the shop were sold to support the mission. A handbill featuring a photograph of the ship announced the following:

Mission Ship Megiddo.
L. T. Nichols, Manager.

A large three-decked steamer, 250 horse power. The only large Gospel Ship in the World. Over 80 workers aboard. We manufacture Acetyline Gasometers and Wind Mills. Are agents for a first class Automobile. Please send us an order, and help on the good work.
Send all orders to
L. T. Nichols, Mission Ship *Megiddo*

A Minneapolis address was given.[18]

An additional source of income was developed when

a sister in the group had made a shawl and conceived the idea of selling it, the returns to be used for the advancement and spreading of the Truth. From a meager start, a handful of yarn was made into a shawl, the payments of which were used to purchase ten times the original quantity to be made into more articles, and so on. The work grew until actually whole carloads of yarn were brought to the boat and unloaded. Everyone who even made a pretension of knowing how to use the crochet hooks became absorbed in the work. Even the 10 and 12 year old boys learned to crochet some of the simpler things. Most of the articles were shawls, which were white with pink or blue borders; also small children's wear such as bootees, and other small items. This line of work was begun before the boat was in the making, while a small nucleus were at Minneapolis, waiting for it to be built at Lyons, Iowa.

While on the boat, the finished products were taken out for display to the public in their homes, on the street, stores, farms, etc. Most everyone who saw them were so charmed with the wide variety of articles, it was difficult for them to decide which one they preferred. This difficulty was overcome somewhat by Bro. Nichols naively advising the sisters to take only one or two samples at a time with them.[19]

Payment was received in both kind and cash. At one place on Island 40, near Memphis, Tennessee, a farmer's wife was so "enthused" over her purchases that she and her husband gave the missionaries thirty bushels of turnips. According to a St. Paul newspaper, the goods that the women produced "they find in great demand to sell readily." It was estimated that the knitting industry netted approximately $1,000, a substantial sum at the time.[20]

Wherever the *Megiddo* sailed it aroused great interest and curiosity. Newspapers carried stories about the gospel boat, its passengers, and their message. The Brethren were able to capitalize on this curiosity, supplementing their income by accepting a free-will offering of twenty-five cents a person for tours of the boat. The offer's free-will status was questioned by one reporter, who wrote that "the dwellers by the sea . . . are not to enjoy all the wonders of the 'ship' as so many pearls cast free before swine. Above the red striped stage plank creaks this warning to the wind, 'Leave a free will offering of 25 cents before being shown the boat.'" Clergy were invited to tour free. The boat was a popular attraction in the many smaller communities such as Owensboro, Kentucky, where "scores of people" visited it and presumably paid their quarters for the tour.[21]

Even though the members onboard had abandoned their homes on land, many continued to be property owners. According to the *Saint Paul Pioneer Press,* "Farmers, mechanics, honest townsfolk, simple and sincere, . . . have sold their lands and their houses and their kine to labor in the vineyard of the Lord. But they have invested in real estate." According to one of the sailors, when the *Megiddo* sailed to St. Paul in 1902, it was not only to spread the gospel but also "to find a cool place for the summer and look after our investments." The article indicates that two-thirds of the residents of the boat derived their income from real estate. The *Pioneer Press* reporter apparently saw these investments as an inappropriate way for the members of the mission

The mission boat *Megiddo* at Paducah, Kentucky, December 1903, at the end of the boat ministry. Courtesy Megiddo Church, Rochester, N.Y.

to support their ministry, noting that the men on the boat who did factory work were those whose "mansions are in the skies and not in Minneapolis." [22]

During the winter spent in Nashville, the members added to their real estate holdings. Arriving in Nashville in December 1902, the mission band initially intended to stay only until March or April, making repairs and improvements on the boat. The *Nashville Banner* reported on March 9, 1903, that "the mission people have their steamer nearly completed, and will in a few weeks leave Nashville for other parts." However, a month later, the Brethren were still in Nashville when the *Banner* reported that "the mission boat was staying a little longer to enable some of the brethren who had had a little money in the bank, where it only drew 3 per cent, to build some cottages. They had bought a piece of land for that purpose, and hoped they would have success with their venture and get more for their money so that they could devote their time more fully to religious work." [23]

According to the *Cincinnati Enquirer,* "At Nashville the crusaders own 35 houses. Only three of these belong to Captain Nichols. Twenty-two three-room cottages were built in 14 hours each by the 40 men in the party. . . . The Captain, who stood all the expenses of building them, deeded these houses over to his men . . . The rent now accruing goes to the individual to whom the house belongs. He applies it at will to the crusade work." [24]

One drawback of real estate ownership was the attention that the property required. Mary Eastman Lee reported that in August 1902 "all who have means are investing in real estate and the brothers are busy fixing up the houses." Later she noted that one of the men had stayed behind when the boat left Minneapolis so that he could finish work on a house he and another member owned. During most of the period of the boat ministry, Mrs. Lee proved to be an unwilling landlord. She experienced constant frustration in her attempts to settle her late husband's estate and divest herself of her real estate holdings. Her efforts entailed considerable correspondence, a stop at Davenport, Iowa, and a trip to Barry, Illinois. On October 31, 1902, she wrote that she had filled out papers, "which if properly signed will settle this worrisome will business," but nearly a month later she found that it was "no nearer a settlement than before." [25]

Nichols was, as his title indicated, captain of the boat. According to Maud Hembree, "the community is not a corporation," and "the voice of Mr. Nichols is law as to the management of the boat." Nichols "attempted to realize on board his boat the ideal state for which he looked when Christ would return to earth." Consequently, he and his followers modeled the ideal community, placing an emphasis on working and living together in a spirit of cooperation. It was even reported that among the children in the school "no cross words, no quarrels, mar the peace." [26]

At each stop in their travels, the Brethren held meetings. Weather was often a factor in determining where the meetings would be held. If the weather was pleasant, the Brethren pitched their forty-by-eighty-foot tent in a prominent place, usually as close to the river as possible. The boys were allowed to help prepare the meeting site, and this became one of their favorite activities. First, they helped clean up the lot by raking up the tall grass the men had cut with scythes. Then they helped set up the tent, placed the chairs, and operated the acetylene lights. There was a platform set up in the front of the tent for the speaker, the band, and the choir. In front of the platform a long bench was placed for the children so their parents, who were usually in the band or choir, could watch them.

If the weather was unpleasant, it often caused considerable difficulty in using the tent. In June 1902, the Brethren were holding meetings at Clinton, Iowa, when a sudden storm came up that not only blew down the tent but also broke the stern line of the boat. And in Cincinnati in November 1903, it was too cold to hold services in the tent. It was also often difficult for the Brethren to find a lot near the boat landing large enough for the tent, making it necessary to pitch it several blocks away. This was not only inconvenient but also posed some danger for the women, who had to walk through the rough quarters near the river as they returned from evening meetings. Fortunately, the Brethren were frequently offered a church, court house, or opera house in which to meet. The facilities were usually rent free, but there was sometimes a small charge (around one or two dollars) for gas to provide lighting.[27]

One of the more unusual venues to shelter meetings was a rink used for the winter ice sport of curling. The Brethren used the rink on a visit to Winona, Minnesota, in June 1902. The Winona newspaper noted, "Usually through the summer the windows and doors of this structure are tightly boarded up, but the boards have now been removed and the windows covered with mosquito netting. . . . The roof has also been repaired, making it tight in wet weather." To use the rink, the Brethren made an extra entrance and constructed a platform on which to hold the services. The rink was wired for electricity which the Brethren arranged to use.[28]

Sometime in 1902, the Brethren were fortunate enough to come to the attention of Capt. Thomas Ryman. A native of Nashville, Ryman had purchased his first steamboat at the age of twenty-four, just after the Civil War. His business prospered and eventually consisted of thirty boats that carried goods between ports in Tennessee, Kentucky, and Indiana. Sometime shortly before 1891, Ryman was converted to Christianity by Sam Jones (1847–1906), an Alabama-born Methodist minister and popular revivalist whose homespun style had gained him wide appeal throughout the North and South beginning in the early 1880s. As a result of this conversion, Ryman had developed an interest in religion that made him receptive to the *Megiddo* and its occupants.

In December 1902, when the boat was moored at Paducah, Kentucky, Nichols was notified of Ryman's interest. On the evening of December 9, Ryman came aboard the boat. "Word had been sent in for the band to be ready to play for the Captain and his friend [a river pilot who accompanied him]. When all was in readiness, Bro. Nichols brought the guests in and the band played 'Wyoming' first; then 'Sunshine in the Soul.' Captain Ryman was completely taken with the band's performance. He sat enjoying everything with tears flowing down his cheeks." [29]

To show his appreciation to Sam Jones, Ryman oversaw the building of the Union Tabernacle in Nashville, a large revival hall financed with Ryman's own money and with donations from local churches and wealthy individuals. The hall opened in 1891, and when the Brethren wintered in Nashville in 1902–3, Ryman arranged for them to have free access to it for weekly services.[30]

When the Brethren arrived in Nashville, they found that Captain Ryman had arranged for Bible verses on "great, eye-catching placards, placed high and commanding the notice of all who passed by; and not just a few, but a great number of them." Ryman and his family also received Captain and Mrs. Nichols and Maud Hembree for Christmas dinner and the mission reciprocated by hosting the Rymans, including their two daughters, on New Year's Day in 1903. About 1910, some canvassers from the mission encountered one of the Ryman daughters in Chattanooga, Tennessee, and she told them that she remembered the visit to the boat and still had the pieces she and her sister recited at the time.[31]

The tabernacle was used for both religious meetings and popular entertainment and was a focal point for public activities in Nashville. For example,

The Union Tabernacle, later Ryman Auditorium, where L. T. Nichols preached in the winter of 1902-3. Courtesy Tennessee State Library and Archives.

during the period in which the Megiddo band was located in Nashville, newspapers reported numerous events that occurred at the tabernacle, including a visit by Salvation Army founder Gen. William Booth, which attracted some of the most prominent citizens of Nashville. As a consequence of the tabernacle's prominent location, the band's meetings drew considerable attention to the mission, and it quickly became an integral part of the city's religious scene. Beginning in February 1903, and continuing until the boat left in May, the *Nashville Banner* printed summaries of Captain Nichols's Sunday afternoon messages in its Monday editions. As the weather improved, meetings moved outdoors and were held in the public square. Evening meetings were also held in the public square or on the boat when weather prevented outdoor meetings.[32]

In addition to the use of the tabernacle, Ryman made other significant contributions to the mission. After visiting the boat, he gave the missionaries one hundred dollars. Just before Christmas in 1902, he gave them a most important gift—"a beautiful, practically new band-wagon, well-built of the best material, with lovely plush-covered seats. It's capacity was for about 40 persons, with the organ at one end." A bandwagon was not a new idea to the Brethren. When the boat was launched, a Clinton, Iowa, newspaper noted that "a fine band will be carried constantly and the band wagon will be drawn by an automobile through the streets of the cities." However, possibly due to the lack of a "great barge" Nichols had planned to have constructed, which would have been able to transport the bandwagon and automobile, the plan was not realized. Consequently, the Brethren band had to march through towns and cities on foot to publicize meetings, a tiring task for people who still had to do their daily chores and participate in evening meetings. With the bandwagon, beginning in the spring of 1903, upon arrival in a new port, if it were possible to borrow the use of some horses for an hour or two, the band would travel the main streets of the town in their wagon with signs attached to the side telling where and when meetings were to be held. The band played music as the wagon proceeded slowly along the main streets, and occasionally handbills were distributed from the wagon. "Such an appeal drew many, if not hundreds of people to the meetings."[33]

The bandwagon also parked in front of meeting sites before services began, and the eighteen-member band would give a concert. The band members were "dressed in an attractive gray uniform and the lady members of the band in white." The uniforms were decorated with red and blue braid and the men's uniforms had a star and crescent emblem on the chest. The emblem had "no special significance."[34]

The services consisted of songs, prayers, Scripture readings, and sermons by either L. T. Nichols or Maud Hembree. At five feet, nine inches, Nichols was not exceptionally tall, but he was apparently an imposing figure and had a stage presence. He had pale blue eyes and curly, graying brown hair. The *Saint Paul Pioneer Press* described him as "a keen-eyed, farmerlike man, kindly and cravatless," while a Henderson, Kentucky, newspaper described him as "a man of striking personality" and noted that "his manner and delivery is so intense and forceful that it is impossible not to be impressed by it." The same newspaper noted that he "holds himself prepared to answer any and every objection." The *Evansville Courier* reported that "there is never a dull moment in Mr. Nichols' lecture, his originality and fund of stories and reminiscences being inexhaustible." Although hardly an objective observer, Kenneth Flowerday wrote over half a century later that "Brother Nichols was a powerful and magnetic speaker, and having the real truth of God's Word to proclaim to the people, he would often hold his audience spellbound by his eloquence and logical arguments. Even now I can picture his towering form addressing the crowds in the brightly lighted tent, in the park on a warm summer afternoon, or from the rostrum of the large tabernacle at Nashville, Tennessee."[35]

As a woman preacher and "the woman lieutenant of Mr. Nichols," Maud Hembree excited considerable interest. Beginning around the middle of the nineteenth century, a significant number of women began functioning as preachers, many in small Protestant bodies, but at the time Maud Hembree began her public ministry, they were more common in the Northeast in denominations with roots in New England, such as the Universalists, Unitarians, Wesleyan Methodists, and denominations in the holiness tradition. They were unusual in the Mississippi and Ohio River valleys, although there were some women clergy affiliated with the Cumberland Presbyterian Church in the area.[36]

Although the Megiddos have frequently been called upon to defend their position on women in ministry, they have never had any problem with the concept, largely due to their tendency to interpret many Scripture passages

The Megiddo Mission bandwagon with L. T. Nichols, Rochester, N.Y., circa 1910. Courtesy Megiddo Church, Rochester, N.Y.

symbolically. For example, in an admonition in 1 Tim. 2:12 in which it would appear to say that women should not exercise authority over men, the Megiddos interpret "women" as signifying "all prospective heirs of salvation" and the "man" as signifying Christ. Consequently, the passage is viewed as having nothing to do with the roles of individual women in the church. Regarding the passage in 1 Corinthians that would seem to forbid women speaking in church, the Megiddos see the writer as referring only to speaking in unknown tongues.[37]

Mrs. Hembree was described as "a cheerful, serene-faced matron of middle age" who still retained her "youthful beauty" and, as "the lady preacher of considerable fame, who by her ability and saintly character, has been made a great blessing to the many hundreds who have heard her." Further, she was "a pleasant, earnest woman" and "a fine speaker and wonderfully well read in the Bible." A reporter for the *Nashville Banner* found Mrs. Hembree's "clear distinct language a pleasure to listen to." One newspaper even reported that she "made a spirited talk, and quoted the scriptures even more fluently than the captain."[38]

The services were well attended, often overflowing the capacity of the large tent, and the press reported Captain Nichols's messages at length. He spoke on a wide range of subjects, most of them relating to the impending Second Coming of Christ, or the coming Kingdom of God on earth and the importance of preparing for it through the study of Scripture and the living of the perfect life. In addition to regular services, Nichols sometimes gave temperance lectures.

L. T. Nichols, circa 1900. Courtesy Megiddo Church, Rochester, N.Y.

The Christian Brethren also held evening services on the boat, which were often attended by people other than the Brethren. Further, Nichols invited "anyone wishing to ask Bible questions" to board the boat to talk with him.[39] In addition to the services, the Brethren also sold booklets and pamphlets either door to door or at the meetings. Some of the pamphlets were printed before the start of the boat ministry; others were printed during the years on the boat.[40]

Nichols emphasized that the role of the mission was "to stir up Christian people to a more Godly life." It is clear that early in the boat ministry the Brethren had some interest in forming local groups of believers that would meet together much like a church. However, by 1903, probably as a result of difficulty keeping converts true to Brethren beliefs once the boat had left, and contrary to Nichols's preaching of exclusiveness that had caused so much controversy in Oregon, he was reported as saying that "he did not want one church member to leave his church but to become a better man and a better woman, to lead a purer and holy life."[41] In fact, he extended "a loving invitation to all ministers, and lovers of truth to join hands with us, and with us lift up the glorious banner of truth, upon whose folds shall appear no conflicting creeds. . . . Then we can bravely face the hosts of sin, all speaking the same things, perfectly joined together in the same mind and the same judgement."[42]

That most local clergy did not feel threatened by the boat ministry is attested to by the fact that the mission was often allowed, or even invited, to hold meetings in local churches. For example, on both of the mission's visits to Paducah, Kentucky, they held their meetings in the Second Presbyterian Church. Local ministers were occasionally curious enough about the Brethren to hold individual conferences with Captain Nichols. In October 1902, while the boat was moored at Clinton, Iowa, a Baptist minister went aboard to talk with Brother Nichols, as did a Methodist minister from Jennings, Trimble County, Kentucky, in 1903.[43]

However, not everyone was friendly to the Brethren's mission, and the Brethren occasionally found themselves at odds with ministers and local authorities. In April 1902, the Brethren docked at Alton, Illinois, where they excited the usual interest from a local newspaper that described the boat and its occupants and announced that the Brethren would pitch their tent and hold revivals. During the meetings, which drew large crowds, Nichols "aroused the ire of many of the church people and the preachers who have been pursuing the paths to a better life which they have seen marked out by the Scriptures as they understand it." Specifically, Nichols said that the local preachers had been "teaching untruths" and that the minds of the people were "being filled with untruths and fiction." Rev. G. W. Shepherd, pastor of the First Methodist Church, announced that he would "try to puncture some of the arguments of the Brethren." According to Mary Lee, Shepherd advertised in the paper "to puncture Bro N's bicycle, but got all the wind knocked out of his own." The story was picked up by newspapers in St. Louis, which is just across the Mississippi River from Alton. One St. Louis paper reported that Alton city officials had notified Nichols "that he must be good to the Alton ministers, must give them their amount of praise or the lines of the Megiddo will be cut and she will be compelled to steam to other quarters." Five days later, the same paper reported that the Alton chief of police would "ask Elder Nichols and his co-workers in Alton to leave the city. The chief contends that the religious controversy has caused such dissension that the matter ought to be stopped." The following day, after two weeks of meetings, the Brethren left Alton. The meetings had not been without success, however, as according to the *Alton Weekly Telegraph,* "Elder Nichols' private secretary said that they had made many converts" and would maintain "an organization" there.[44]

In November 1902, the Brethren returned to Alton and could hardly have been surprised to find themselves unwelcome. The harbormaster imposed a fee of three dollars per day for the *Megiddo* to dock at the wharf and notified Nichols that they could not hold services in Alton. Nichols appealed to the mayor, who agreed with the harbormaster, arguing that since the Brethren charged admission for tours of the boat, the boat fell into the same category as a showboat and hence had to pay the wharfage. Further, he agreed that the Brethren should be denied permission to hold meetings in Alton because when they had been there in April they "had stirred up so much ill-feeling by criticizing other churches."

In addition to being unwelcome in Alton, Nichols found that the group of followers he had left had "made a radical departure from [his] teachings by organizing a Bible class of a different belief." At a meeting on the *Megiddo* to which Nichols had invited the Bible class, he "launched forth at them a stream of abuse and both by innuendo and direct charges . . . accused them of many offenses against him. He abused city officials without stint and became very personal in his remarks. . . . The Elder even went so far as to cast reflections on the character of some of the teachers" from Zion's Watch Tower (later part of Jehovah's Witnesses) who had come to Alton to hold meetings. This may have been the group that influenced the followers Nichols left in Alton. The day following the stormy meeting, the *Megiddo* weighed anchor and left Alton. According to the *Weekly Telegraph,* Nichols declared that the people of Alton were very "inhospitable and intolerant."[45]

During the earlier visit to Alton the plan to construct a barge to be pulled by the *Megiddo* was still alive. The *Weekly Telegraph* reported that the Brethren "would build a large barge or floating convention hall" that would be "enclosed, fitted with a pulpit, chairs, etc.," making it unnecessary to pitch the tent at every stop. In July, the *Saint Paul Pioneer Press* described plans for "a big barge," the upper deck of which would contain a spacious chapel and a factory below, to be built the following winter in Tennessee. In November, the *Alton Daily Telegraph* stated that Nichols would "probably build a new cabin boat with one hundred state-rooms, to be towed by the *Megiddo* and to accommodate new recruits to the Christian Brethren who can provide money to support themselves." Perhaps Nichols felt the need to provide accommodations for converts so that they would not fall away as they had at Alton. While it is highly likely that the inventive Nichols would have considered the addition of such a large barge to the boat, it would have been unwieldy, especially on the Ohio River, and there is no evidence that there was ever any attempt to construct it.[46]

In 1903, when the boat was moored at Evansville, Indiana, another minister who disagreed with Nichols, Rev. J. T. Davis, pastor of the First Christian Church, challenged Nichols to a public debate. The challenge was published in the *Evansville Courier,* and the following day's edition of the *Courier* reported that Nichols had accepted. The debate was scheduled for the next evening but was canceled due to the illness of Davis's wife. However, the following evening, at the tent meeting, as Nichols finished his sermon, a local businessman arose and announced that Reverend Davis was present and that he would speak, if Nichols would agree, which he did. Davis spoke at length and concluded by stating that "if his argument was not good enough, the church had some very learned men and that one to whom he referred as 'a big gun' might be imported from California to answer the arguments of Mr. Nichols."

In reply, Nichols stated that Davis "had not made an argument worthy of reply" and that he "would very much like to meet one of the leading men of the church, as he much preferred arguing with the best informed men of any organization." Then Nichols became personal when he noted that "the knots behind Mr. Davis's ears, referring to the bumps of combativeness, were probably not very greatly developed or he would not have rushed into the discussion unprepared." With that, the people began to clap and talk, and Nichols "picked up his song book and started to lead in a song," but the crowd was too restless and finally he gave up trying to get their attention and turned and walked up the aisle.

When Nichols got outside the tent, several men tried to argue with him. It looked "like the wind-up of a ward political gathering where some candidate and his adherents had lost their all and were making strenuous efforts to get even. . . . In the discussion someone said something about someone else being a liar and the hubbub was started." Someone who was obviously unfamiliar with the fine points of phrenology confronted Nichols and shouted, "What do you mean by saying that Mr. Davis had knots behind his ears?" The man shook his fist at Nichols but did not attack him. Nichols attempted to explain but could not be heard above the commotion and shouted questions.

While the crowd challenged Nichols, Reverend Davis left the scene and the Brethren "busied themselves closing the tent for the night" and "took no part in it whatever." The *Courier* reported that the members of the band said that only once before in their three years of travel had they had such an experience, probably a reference to Alton.[47]

While the *Megiddo* was docked at Evansville, a group of four or five ladies, "obviously belonging to some religious sect," who were attending a convention in the city visited the boat and spoke with Nichols, who explained to them the Brethren's beliefs about the necessity of good works in order to achieve salvation. "It was soon perceived that this form of doctrine was displeasing to them for they thought they were already saved. . . . So the interview was soon brought to a close and they left. Upon reaching the gang plank, the leader of the group, a militant type of person, grasped her skirt and shook it vigorously, all the rest following suit; at the same time they were cutting capers and shaking their feet to make sure no dust was left thereon. This performance greatly amused Bro. Nichols and several others who had been watching them." [48]

Reverend Davis and the group of female visitors were apparently not representative of the population of Evansville, and there was enough interest for the Brethren to hold meetings for two weeks. According to Kenneth Flowerday, the meetings were "well attended, the people showing considerable interest," at least "in a superficial way." [49]

Other controversies arose that were not directly related to Nichols's preaching. Reminiscent of the experience in Oregon, during a stop at St. Paul, Minnesota, in 1902, Nichols found himself involved in a divorce suit in which E. F. Maxwell, a former member of the Christian Brethren, accused Nichols of having alienated his wife's affections and asked $10,000 in compensation. The suit resulted in an unflattering article in the *Minneapolis Times* in which an unidentified disaffected member of the Brethren was quoted:

> He [Nichols] didn't want us to have any mind of our own about anything. We had to ask him if we could do this—just like children. Even when we women folks wanted a new dress we had to ask him how many breadths we could put in the skirt. Our rules of living were very strict. We couldn't eat pie or cake nor drink tea or coffee. We were forbidden to wear ruffles on our dresses or trimmings on our hats and we couldn't entertain friends— not even our relatives—unless it was upon a matter of business. We couldn't visit people unless we talked about the bible all the time. We had to have the plainest kind of furnishings; if we had lace curtains they must not fall below the window sill because that would be an extravagance. When we disobeyed any of the rules we were called up in meeting and publicly reprimanded. [50]

The article noted that the Maxwells had been part of the party aboard the *Megiddo,* but Mr. Maxwell had left the boat and returned to Minneapolis. Mrs. Maxwell, "considering her religious vows of more importance than hymeneal vows," remained on the boat. The article concluded with a simple statement that the lawsuit had been settled out of court. [51]

Another controversy, this one quite minor, erupted on the front page of the *Barry Adage* in July 1902. Under the headline "Is Not a Loving Mother," the paper printed what were purported to be the contents of a letter from the daughter of former Barry resident and *Megiddo* missionary Laura Suiter to a friend in Barry. The letter referred to the Brethren as the "awfulest pack of people that I ever heard of" and went on to say that the writer was much happier living with her grandparents: "They are good to us. We haven't got any whippings since we have been here, and when we were at home we were just beat and cuffed around all the time." The child further accused her mother of having written relatives in Oregon indicating that the children were with her on the boat when they were actually with their grandparents. The child concluded, "It nearly kills me some times to think I have such a mother. It would have been a relief to me if she was dead and had always been good to me." The paper went on to mention "that man Snider, who deserted his wife and children," and noted it had been said that Ellis Greene and his wife, Barry residents who were also on the *Megiddo,* had also deserted their children and one of their sons was in St. Louis staying with relatives.[52]

A few weeks later, Mrs. Suiter wrote from St. Paul in response to the *Adage* article. Suiter stated firmly that the statements attributed to her daughter were "false from beginning to end" and that she had made every effort to keep her children with her as long as possible. She then gave a brief account of the events that led up to her placing her children with their grandparents. Suiter's husband had died twelve years before, and after his funeral expenses were paid she had been left with "nothing to live on." She and her children went to live with her mother, who supported them for nine years. Her mother became ill and could not keep the children anymore, as they "were getting unmanageable and annoyed her, and they needed the care of a man over them." At that point, Laura Suiter contacted the grandparents, who agreed to take the children. "They wanted to go, so I did what seemed to be the only thing to do under the circumstances."[53]

In general, the mission on the *Megiddo* was considered by its participants to have been successful, but the operation of the boat required considerable effort that took time away from the ministry. In her diary of her life on the *Megiddo,* Mary Lee reported several incidents of delays due to boiler problems and weather. In June 1902, the Brethren arrived at Burlington, Iowa, for what was, according to a newspaper report, supposed to be a visit of several weeks, only to find that there was no room at the wharf, which was occupied by "regular steamers and wood boats." They were ordered by the managers to move on.[54]

The following year, while on the Ohio River, the Brethren experienced a number of problems. The boat had particular difficulty navigating on the Ohio River, suggesting the possibility that the original plan had been to stay on the Mississippi.[55] When the boat docked at Owensboro, Kentucky, the hull of the barge was "broken" in the course of landing, resulting in an entire day spent in repairs. Then a planned two-week visit to Owensboro had to be cut to less than a week when the river level fell rapidly and it became necessary to get the boat to a place above Louisville, where the water was deeper, in order to continue to Cincinnati.

The trip back to Paducah, Kentucky, from Cincinnati was plagued with navigational problems. After passing Evansville, the boat became wedged on a sandbar, due, according to the *Paducah News-Democrat,* to the "incompetency of an Evansville pilot." While stuck on the sandbar, the boat was vulnerable to damage from floating ice, "which came down upon it in vast sheets, then acres in extent." Under the direction of Captain Nichols, the men barricaded the boat and soon positioned it so that the ice could not reach it. It was deemed advisable to remove the women and children from the boat, so the Shawneetown

(Illinois) Hotel was rented and the towboat *Conveyor* ferried the women and children to the town. After four days of hard labor, the boat was again floated and continued its trip downriver under the direction of the same pilot, only to become stuck on another sandbar a half mile from the first. "Captain Nichols then gave the pilot sixty seconds in which to get off the boat." He then telephoned to Paducah for another pilot, who successfully brought the boat to its destination.[56]

While at Paducah, Nichols announced his intention to try to find a buyer for the boat. "After two years of river work, he thinks now he would like to transfer his labors to inland towns." The exact reasons for Nichols's decision to abandon the river ministry are not given in the press. The low water in the river, the geographical limitations imposed on the ministry by the need to stay on the river, his own failing health, and other difficulties related to the community's mobile lifestyle are likely to have led Captain Nichols to decide that it would be impractical to continue the river ministry. Circumstances such as the legal controversy and consequent bad publicity at Minneapolis and the difficulties at Alton, coupled with the lack of interest in several communities, may have contributed to the decision. It may also have been influenced by increasing difficulty in obtaining the free newspaper publicity on which the Brethren depended to publicize their arrivals in various cities. As the boat became less of a novelty, it became less newsworthy. For example, when it arrived in St. Louis in 1903, the boat was still front-page news but only warranted a brief article noting that it had arrived and that services would be held if an appropriate place could be secured. The writer noted that it was unnecessary to describe the boat, as it had been adequately described during previous visits. The arrival of the boat in Cincinnati in November 1903 coincided with an important local election, which limited the amount of attention Cincinnati newspapers paid to the Brethren.[57]

Whatever the reasons, the decision was obviously sudden. Nichols indicated a willingness to continue the ministry on the Tennessee River for the winter if a buyer could not be found for the boat; however, a buyer was found and the ship was refitted by members of the Christian Brethren and sold to the Chattanooga & Tennessee River Packet Company in Paducah in December 1903.[58]

The boat ministry was to be an enduring memory to many who encountered the *Megiddo*. For years to come, the mission received letters from people who remembered it. For example, in 1918, a Miss Leonard wrote from St. Louis to order Megiddo publications and noted that her parents visited the boat while it was docked in Alton, Illinois, and that they later spent a night on board the boat at St. Louis.[59]

During the course of the boat ministry, the Brethren lost up to a quarter of their members while gaining few longtime adherents, but the ministry is still viewed as a golden age in the church largely due to the impact it had on the life of Kenneth Flowerday, who eventually became pastor and who kept the memory of the *Megiddo* alive in writing and oral presentations until his death in 1985. The boat ministry has also been an enduring source of media interest.[60]

5

"Peculiar Religious Views"

L. T. Nichols decided to relocate his ministry to Rochester, New York. The city was selected because, according to John Cass, whom Nichols had sent on ahead to secure temporary quarters, Nichols's "work was accomplished in the South and West [and] he determined to come North." Cass stated that after Nichols had made several trips to New York State and visited some of the larger cities, he had decided that Rochester was centrally located and a good place from which "persons can travel in all directions at less expense than from other cities in the state."[1]

As the principal city in the burned-over district, Rochester, New York, holds a prominent place in American religious history. It was the site of a famous revival held by Charles Finney in 1830 and 1831, a site of Millerite activity in the 1840s, and home to the Fox sisters, whose spirit rappings are credited with beginning modern interest in Spiritualism. A number of reform movements with strong Protestant ties, such as abolitionism and temperance, also had roots in the Rochester area. Former slave and abolitionist Frederick Douglass lived in Rochester, where he published his newspaper, the *North Star,* from 1847 to 1860, and Frances Willard, founder of the Woman's Christian Temperance Union, was born in nearby Churchville and frequently visited the active temperance community in Rochester. Probably as a consequence of this history, Rochester by 1900 was home to more than one hundred churches affiliated with a variety of denominations, including the mainline Protestant denominations such as Methodists, Presbyterians, and Episcopalians, as well as more marginal groups such as Seventh-Day Adventists, Spiritualists, and even a small congregation of Christadelphians founded in 1870.[2]

Rochesterians even took a certain pride in their special role in American religious history. As one newspaper stated, "Rochester is noted for being in the advance guard on all social and religious problems, with many leaders, able and willing to cast aside the shackles that error of past generations have bound around them, and advance the line of intellectual thought, casting behind them all that cannot be proven before the 'bar of reason and evidence.'"[3]

In this religious milieu, one might assume that the local press would be indifferent to the arrival of yet another small religious denomination, but even as Captain Nichols and about sixty of his followers left Paducah by train for Rochester on January 25, 1904, a Rochester newspaper was announcing the impending arrival of these "queer" but "sincere" people "who are coming to Rochester . . . to conduct a gospel campaign throughout New York and nearby states." The Brethren arrived in Rochester on January 27 and rented a large house on the city's near east side as a temporary headquarters. Four railroad carloads of furniture and other belongings arrived a few days later.[4]

In the months following their arrival in Rochester, the Brethren were objects of curiosity, and local newspapers devoted considerable space to descriptions of Captain Nichols and his followers and to reports of the activities of the mission. Captain Nichols was described as having "a strong, bearded face, a forceful style of address and the air of a man whose life has been given to much meditation." He was further described as "an interesting character, bearing all the earmarks of a Westerner who has lived with real men for a lifetime. He is tall and serious in aspect; his voice is soft but its tones leave no doubt that it can command attention when he wishes to catch the ears of a congregation or audience. His manner is direct, though not brusque, and altogether there is something of sincerity about the man that convinces his listener of the genuineness of his convictions and the sincerity of his purpose." The same article reported that Nichols was treated more like a brother than the leader of the community and that his followers were all "fond of him and look up to him as one who has their best interests at heart." An article in the *Rochester Herald* referred to his "magnetic leadership." "Rev. Mrs." Maud Hembree was described as "a gifted lecturer and of a scholarly nature." The members of the mission were also viewed in very positive terms. One newspaper referred to them as "a very desirable class of citizens . . . thrifty and kind-hearted and imbued with strong religious convictions."[5]

The economic prosperity of the mission was frequently commented upon and exaggerated in the local press. One reporter attributed this to L. T. Nichols's "abundant means." Another article identified Nichols as "an able business man and man of affairs who . . . has accumulated sufficient means to enable him to devote his life to the cause he so firmly believes in." Further, "some of the Brethren are well supplied with this world's goods and have no need to work." Mention was made of the fact that the community economized through the purchase of items in quantity at wholesale prices and through mutual aid. It was further noted that "not a single member is poor, and some have savings tucked away for a rainy day. They never buy anything on credit since it is against the rules."[6]

In order that the members of the mission might live in proximity to one another and support each other in their mission efforts, L. T. Nichols purchased five acres of land at the corner of Thurston Road and Sawyer Street on the southwest edge of Rochester, just inside the city limits. At the time of the purchase, the lot contained a large house and two smaller residences to which the Brethren quickly added a three-story building containing twenty-one rooms and another nine-room residence.[7]

The Megiddo Mission immediately became a visible part of the religious milieu in Rochester. During the summer after their arrival, the Brethren built a new bandwagon and purchased a larger tent, which they pitched at a street corner a little more than a mile from their headquarters. Later they moved the tent to the north side of the city and held services in the residential and recreation areas along the shore of Lake Ontario, to which the streetcar company provided free transportation. When the weather became too cold for tent meetings, services were held in local churches and auditoriums. Early in 1905, the mission rented Plymouth Church, which was located about halfway between the mission headquarters and the center of the city, where services were much the same as they had been on the *Megiddo*, with band music, singing, preaching by Captain Nichols or Reverend Hembree, and calls for

L. T. Nichols and members of the Megiddo Mission on the lawn of the mission property on Thurston Road, Rochester, New York, circa 1910. Courtesy Megiddo Church, Rochester, N.Y.

commitment to reformed lives. The services were very popular and reported regularly in the local newspapers.[8]

One reporter noted that the mission differed from other bodies in that it did not solicit contributions. The mission did not take up collections at public services, a practice that dated as far back as the boat ministry and probably was a remnant of the days when the ministry was associated with the Christadelphians, some of whose ecclesias also do not collect offerings from nonmembers. According to pastor Ruth Sisson, the rationale behind not taking up an offering when guests are present is that they "have a principle not to request money from non-members, or to do something that would make them feel obligated to support us."[9]

The ministry of the Megiddo Mission was financed through "a tithing system, adopted by the organization after their location in Rochester [which was] effective and satisfactory in financing the work of spreading the news of the Kingdom, affording all an opportunity to assist, while causing no hardship to any," and through donations and contributions from members and friends of the mission. Tithe money was not then, and is not now, "used to pay the minister, organist, choir or band. . . . All workers give their services absolutely free." In an article in the *Megiddo Message* in 1936, the janitor was identified as the only paid staff member. As the mission expanded, it began to receive donations from distant readers of the *Megiddo Message* and members of ecclesias outside Rochester who mailed their tithes to the mission. One follower in Canada even willed a substantial amount of real estate to the mission, which it subsequently sold.[10]

While tithing is important, the Megiddos believe that one should pay one's debts first before paying tithes. Kenneth Flowerday noted, "Our honored founder, Rev. L. T. Nichols, was aware that among his followers were some who were just about able to make ends meet financially without that additional 10% drain on their meager income. Hence, he would not accept tithes from any member if that member were in debt—that is, if he owed a grocery bill, or a doctor bill, or his house rent was not paid, etc. (A mortgage on a home, a farm, or a business, could not be considered a debt, but rather an investment.)"[11]

In Rochester, Nichols continued to address the lifestyle issues that had concerned him since the beginning of his ministry. He attacked the "lovers of pleasure" and castigated churches for encouraging gambling through such activities as euchre parties in church basements and even in the parsonage, which he said were no better than visiting a gambling establishment to play poker. He railed against amusement parks, circuses, museums, theaters, and Sunday baseball. He called novel reading "a great evil" because it caused the Bible to "lie neglected . . . while novels are flooding the land." He prided himself on never having read a novel.[12]

Many of the doctrines Nichols preached were not unfamiliar to Rochesterians; others were. A Rochester newspaper reporter probably summed up the public's response to Nichols's preaching when, in an article on the mission's first

Rochester tent meeting, he wrote, "There is much good counsel in the address given by Mr. Nichols between fragments of his somewhat startling beliefs."[13]

In 1905, L. T. Nichols began to preach a doctrine that would distinguish the Megiddo Mission from other religious groups and would become an important element in the mission's outreach: Based on his reading of Mal. 4:5–6 and Matt. 17:11, Nichols declared that the prophet Elijah would come to prepare the world for Christ's return.

The Malachi passage, which reads, "Behold, I will send you Elijah, the prophet before the coming of the great and terrible day of the Lord. And he shall turn the heart of the fathers to the children and the heart of the children to their fathers, lest I come and smite the earth with a curse," reflects a Jewish tradition based on 2 Kings 2:11, which says that the prophet Elijah did not die but was carried in a chariot of fire on a whirlwind into heaven. According to theologian Aharon Wiener, the reference to the future appearance of Elijah in the book of Malachi, which was written several hundred years after 2 Kings, indicates that there was an "obvious assumption that his contemporaries did not consider Elijah to have died in the conventional sense."[14] As a result, Elijah remained a significant figure in the period between Old and New Testament times. He is mentioned often in the Apocrypha, a series of books written during the intertestamental period, some of which are included in some Bibles. One of the apocryphal books even contains a prophecy that those who have been taken up into heaven and have not died shall appear before the Messiah.[15]

The idea that Elijah will come before the Messiah is reinforced in Matt. 17:11, where Jesus states that "Elijah is indeed coming and will restore all things." He goes on in the next verse to state that "Elijah has already come," and, based on other references in the Gospels (for example, Luke 1:16–17 and Mark 1:2–4), most biblical scholars believe that in the Matthew passage Jesus is referring to John the Baptist, even though in John 1:21, John the Baptist denies being Elijah. Nichols was aware of this interpretation and stated that Jesus had clearly identified the prophet Elijah as the one who would come and that John the Baptist was not the prophet but was merely doing as he was supposed to do according to Luke 1:17, working "with the spirit and power of Elijah."[16]

The idea of Elijah's return was not unique to Nichols. In fact, Christadelphian founder John Thomas predicted that Elijah would return as a messenger to the Jews and "restore all things" before Christ appeared to the ten tribes in Egypt.[17] However, Nichols's view of the role of Elijah was different from Thomas in that he did not see Elijah's mission as limited to the Jews in the Holy Land.

The Bible chronology Nichols published in 1899 contains no references to Elijah, suggesting that Nichols's emphasis on the teaching regarding Elijah was probably a response to the considerable publicity given to contemporaries of Nichols who also anticipated the coming of Elijah, particularly John Alexander Dowie. Dowie (1847–1907) was a Scottish-born evangelist, reformer, and faith healer who immigrated to the United States in 1888. He became a popular lecturer and founder of the Christian Catholic Church and of Zion, Illinois, an intentional community that operated as a theocracy with Dowie as its autocratic leader. Dowie was the subject of considerable interest on the part of the press when, in 1900, he declared himself to be the prophet Elijah. Nichols, who had been aware of Dowie at least as early as 1903 when he publicly criticized Dowie's belief in faith healing, rejected Dowie's contention, stating that "John Alexander Dowie's claim to be Elijah is so void of common sense and out of harmony with the prophetic word, that we shall not spend any time endeavoring to refute such folly. Suffice to say, he in no way fills the bill."[18]

Dowie was not the only person who claimed to be Elijah. A contemporary of Nichols and Dowie, Frank Sandford (1862–1948), controversial founder of the Shiloh Community in Durham, New Hampshire, also declared himself to be Elijah. Nichols was aware of that claim and mentioned Sandford in passing in a sermon in 1906. Coincidentally, like L. T. Nichols, Sandford took his evangelistic campaign on the water, on an oceangoing campaign. Unfortunately, Sandford did not show the concern for his followers that Nichols did, and several of them died of lack of food and water on the journey. As a consequence, Sandford was convicted of manslaughter and sentenced to ten years in federal prison.[19]

In Nichols's view, neither Dowie nor Sandford could have been Elijah because Nichols expected not a new Elijah but the return of the original Old Testament figure, Elijah the Tishbite, who Nichols believed to be waiting on another planet for the appropriate moment to return. According to Nichols, when Elijah returns, the world will be "in darkness and need to be sobered up, need waking out of [its] dreamy condition." In his writings and in public lectures, which were covered by the local press, Nichols stated that responsibility for awakening the world would fall to the Megiddo band, or "Megiddoites," now comprised of all the righteous from "Abel down," who will assist by carrying the message of the impending return of Christ throughout the earth. In order to do this, the Megiddoites will, as the Bible says, be able to "mount up like eagles" (Isa. 40:31), having been given an understanding of "the law of repulsion," which permits eagles and other birds to "ascend with as much ease as they can descend." There will be a time "when the earth will resound from its remotest ends the high praises of Jehovah in accents sweet and tones so grand for his wonderful and marvelous works accomplished through the instrumentality of Elijah and the Megiddo band moving with the freedom of the wind, whether on water or on earth as it is done in heaven." Then, "when the people of Rochester, and all great cities behold these swift messengers navigating the air with the ease and grace of angels, see them quietly light and begin to proclaim the message to the dark, unenlightened world, they will then do as the Lord says they will do, 'Lift up their eyes round about and see.'"[20]

More recent Megiddo publications about the coming of Elijah do not assign special responsibilities to the Megiddos, but they are more specific regarding what Elijah's duties will be. Most importantly, he will raise the righteous dead, as this will be necessary "if the dead and living are to be caught up together to meet the Lord in the air" before he descends to the earth. Elijah will also restore things that were withdrawn at the end of the Apostolic Age: the power of the Holy Spirit, the healing of the sick, and the opening of the eyes of the blind.

In Rochester, expectation was especially high when Nichols announced that he anticipated Elijah would appear in 1908 and that the thousand-year reign of Christ would begin about 1941. At the end of 1911, Nichols produced a third edition of the *Bible Chronology* with substantial changes from the 1899 edition (for example, there were now nine links in the chronology instead of fifteen). The year 1909 having passed, the new edition, which included a substantial section on Elijah that had not appeared in the 1899 edition, predicted that Christ would come 1,912 years after his birth. Since the church's calculation of Christ's birth was probably off by four, six, or eleven years, according to Nichols, the exact date of Christ's return was still uncertain, but the beginning of the millennium would be forty years later, and that would still fit within most of the period indicated in the 1899 chronology.[21]

While Nichols's preaching on the coming of Elijah drew considerable attention to the mission, it was his unique position regarding the proper celebration of Christmas that sparked the greatest interest among Rochesterians. Charles H. Lippy has identified the American celebration of Christmas not only as a prime example of the way Americans privatized religion to fit their individual lifestyles but also as a point at which the church, in setting the date of Christmas to coincide with a pagan holiday, early compromised with culture.[22] Consequently, it is not surprising that L. T. Nichols and the Megiddos focused their attention on this holiday, which had already by the end of the nineteenth century lost much of its religious significance in the United States.

In a masterful stroke of again reinventing the mission, gaining attention, and at the same time calling Rochesterians to a return to biblical orthodoxy, in February 1906, L. T. Nichols produced a pamphlet titled *True Christmas and New Year's,* which heralded the event that would firmly establish the uniqueness of the Megiddo Mission and its beliefs in the minds of the Rochester community—the springtime celebration of Christmas. In his pamphlet, Nichols stated positively that the birth of Christ occurred in the spring of the year. To support this contention, he cited passages of Scripture that indicated the shepherds, who play a critical role in the Christmas narrative, were in the fields, a place where they would not have been in December. Consequently, he declared that Christmas should be celebrated in the spring, and he had harsh words for those who celebrated Christmas in December. He stated that December 25 was set apart by the apostate church to coincide with the heathen feast of Saturnalia and that all who celebrated it as the anniversary of the Lord's birth were "paying tribute to a heathen feast and Pagan god." [23]

It is uncertain exactly how Nichols came to the conclusion that Christ was born in the spring, but the idea that Christ was born in some month other than December was certainly not new. In 1833, Bible commentator Adam

Clarke, citing the same reason later cited by Nichols, asserted that Christ was born sometime between Passover, which occurred in the spring, and October. Clarke went on to list various theologians throughout the history of the Christian church who had held that Christ's birth did not occur in December.[24] Since Nichols consulted theological sources other than the Bible, it is possible that he encountered the idea of a date other than December 25 for Christmas in the course of his reading.

The Brethren originally celebrated Christmas in December. The minutes of the Minnesota ecclesia reported plans for December Christmas celebrations between 1894 and 1897; and an entry in the diary that Mary Lee kept aboard the *Megiddo* contains an account of a December celebration of Christmas in 1902 while the boat was docked at Nashville. In the latter celebration, L. T. Nichols appears to have assumed the traditional role of Santa Claus, judging the merits of each child that would determine both the child's place at the table for Christmas dinner and the gifts he or she would receive. Less than a year later, by the end of 1903, Nichols came to the conclusion that Christmas was not to be celebrated in December but in the spring, and he made a public declaration of this change in a sermon preached at the Second Presbyterian Church in Paducah, Kentucky, in December.[25]

Nichols did not reject the idea that Christmas should be celebrated, as some groups have, most notably the Jehovah's Witnesses. In fact, he declared that "if ever there was a person whose birthday should be known and celebrated" it was Christ. However, he did have serious reservations about the way Christmas was celebrated in America. In his tract, he noted that having the date wrong was less important than the fact that most Christians had "made themselves much more abominable in the sight of God by accepting and putting into practice the low and groveling way and manner of Pagans in celebrating . . . Christmas day." He was especially critical of the materialism involved in the Christmas celebration, probably because Nichols attributed his early doubts of the truth of what his elders taught him to an event that occurred during a childhood Christmas celebration.

In 1854, when Nichols was ten, his mother took him to a Christmas celebration at a local church, promising him a gift from Santa Claus. The boy was excited, hoping for something like a shiny apple from the jolly old elf. "After awhile 'Santa Claus' came down the chimney and went around distributing the presents; and when he was cutting up some of his antics he stumbled and off fell his false face and his old wig, and well, I was met with astonishment—I saw it was old Deacon Graves, a member of the church and a deacon!"[26] The boy was disillusioned.

Concerning Santa Claus, Nichols wrote:

> Just think of trying to make children believe there is an old, heinous looking Santa Claus that crawls down the chimney, loaded with all manner of useless toys, hangs up stockings, filling them with different kinds of presents, and then to think that thousands, yea millions of dollars [are] spent every year

on their pseudo Christmas day, for jumping jacks, hobby horses, air guns, and a thousand other useless things of no real work or lasting value . . . [when] the poor are crying for the necessities of life in nearly every hamlet and city of our land.[27]

Because Christ's birth began a new era, Nichols also believed that "Christ's birth must inevitably have been on New Year's Day." Therefore, Christmas and New Year's occurred on the same day. Citing the biblical Hebrew calendar, Nichols determined that Christmas began on the first day of the Hebrew month of Abib, which started on the first new moon after the vernal equinox. Consequently, True Christmas and New Year's occur on different dates each year depending on the date of the new moon.[28]

With much advance publicity in the local press, the Megiddo Mission held its first public celebration of True Christmas on March 25, 1906, in their rented church in Rochester with about five hundred people present. The decorations emphasized the themes of spring and new birth. The women and children of the church had spent the three months prior to the celebration making more than ten thousand paper flowers and twenty thousand paper leaves. The church was decorated with "vast numbers of artificial flowers," including "roses, tulips, chrysanthemums, lilies, hyacinths and other flowers" that adorned the pillars in the church. There were also "rose bushes and Easter lilies, pinks and

An early Abib celebration. Courtesy Megiddo Church, Rochester, N.Y.

carnations arranged in a very attractive manner." "On an arch 30 feet above the platform embellished with lilies, carnations, and roses, are inscribed the words, 'Christmas Greeting to All.'" Another poster read "The Bible Proves Christmas & New Years to be March 25, 1906." [29] These decorations set the tone for decorations for subsequent celebrations of True Christmas.

The evening service began with a "triumphal march" of the orchestra and children around the church. The women and girls were dressed in white with pink sashes; the men in black, with roses on their lapels. The program featured a dialogue between Maud Hembree and the children of the mission with the youngest child, who was four years old, reciting the names of the books of the Bible. Reverend Nichols delivered a lengthy sermon giving the history of the development of the celebration of Christmas and explaining the biblical basis for his contention that Christmas should be celebrated in the spring.[30]

Following the Christmas celebration, the church hosted a dinner at which all—whether members, guests, or curious visitors—were welcome. About four hundred people attended the dinner in 1906. The hall in which it was held was decorated with paper flowers and leaves, and the mission orchestra provided dinner music. Reverend Nichols announced that leftover food would be given to the "deserving poor," but, Nichols added, "Don't come if you are wasting your money on tobacco or liquor. A man or woman who can afford to buy tobacco or liquor is lots richer than I am." [31]

In 1911, at the largest of the banquets, more than one thousand people were served in shifts between noon and midnight. Following the death of L. T. Nichols in February of 1912, the dinner was eliminated from the celebration, but it was revived in 1917, with a charge of fifty cents for adults and twenty-five cents for children. By the 1940s, the meal was served by the men of the church. The attendance at the dinner in 1943 was 165; in 1954, when a particularly large number of visitors attended Abib activities, almost 240 attended the dinner.[32]

The celebration of True Christmas was covered yearly by the Rochester press until the 1960s. When the Megiddos first celebrated True Christmas, the *Rochester Herald* had a less than positive view of the proceedings, announcing in a 1909 headline "Strange Religious Sect Will Celebrate Christ's Birth." The accompanying article noted that "Captain Nichols has been proclaiming his peculiar religious views." [33] However, over the years newspaper coverage of True Christmas has been at least neutral and usually positive, often including such things as the names and home cities of out-of-town guests. In 1928, the church presented a True Christmas program on Rochester radio station WHEC, sponsored by the Ludwig Music Company. The following year, there was an abbreviated version of the program on the same station.[34]

Early celebrations of True Christmas, and of other holidays, included edifying dialogues and small skits. The Megiddos are opposed to attendance at plays and other public amusements, so it is somewhat surprising that about 1930, under the leadership of Percy Thatcher, an avid writer who would later become pastor of the church, elaborate dramas for both adults and children began to be

Church drama, circa 1940. Courtesy Megiddo Church, Rochester, N.Y.

Bible drama, circa 2000. Courtesy Megiddo Church, Rochester, N.Y.

part of the celebration. The sanctuary of the church, which the Megiddos built and occupied in 1908, was constructed in such a way that there was room for the band, which was then, and still is, an integral part of Megiddo worship. This allowed ample space for the dramatic presentations performed by separate men's and women's groups or by groups of both sexes. Particularly in the 1930s, these presentations often involved elaborate costumes and sets. In 1934, the *Message* reported that "Brother Thatcher's productions need no comment. They are full of lively interest from beginning to end, and portray great spiritual truths in a forcible, realistic manner. The amount of work required to produce such a program can be realized only by those who do it." In 1998, Newton Payne, the retired pastor of the church who made his living as an electrician, was still complaining about the difficulties he had meeting Reverend Thatcher's demands for lighting to do justice to his plays, and Reverend Thatcher had died in 1958. The Abib services required so much preparation that Sunday school was even canceled in order to allow sufficient time to rehearse.[35]

Unlike the Christmas celebrations of most Christian churches, the Megiddo celebration is usually not focused on the Christmas story but often relates to other Bible stories or to religious issues that have no direct connection with Christmas. For example, the program for True Christmas in 1929 featured debates staged by the men's class on the topics "Is the Bible in Conflict with Science as to the Creation and Age of the Earth?" and "Is the Rib Story of Genesis True?"[36] By focusing on current issues or common questions, the Christmas program serves not only as a celebration of Christ's birth but also as an opportunity for the Church to present its teachings other than True Christmas to guests and visitors. Members also participate in the program by writing and reading poetry and giving recitations. Plays, poems, and other Abib writings are often printed in the *Megiddo Message* for the edification of those who cannot attend the services in Rochester.

Music is an important aspect of the Abib celebration. The music of True Christmas has included pieces composed especially for the Abib holiday by members of the church as well as traditional carols, many with words altered to fit the season. For example, the second verse of the True Christmas version of "Silent Night" reads as follows:

> Silent Night, Starry Night
> Abib moon, fair and bright
> Verdure clad the hillside round
> Grazing flocks in pasture bound
> Earth in beauty aglow
> Earth in beauty aglow

The April 27, 1930, issue of the *Megiddo Message* contains what is probably the most complete account of an Abib celebration to be published. The celebration described contains virtually all of the elements that have comprised the Abib services since the 1930s when multi-act dramas began to be featured in

Megiddo celebrations. It also demonstrates the way in which holiday celebrations are used in the Megiddo Church to encourage and teach and to reinforce church doctrines that may have little or nothing to do with the holiday itself.

Abib Celebration at Megiddo

Christmas at Megiddo! Only those who have a part in it can realize the extent and magnitude of the preparation made for the celebration of this glorious festival. And only those who hear and see can appreciate it all. No previous celebration has equaled the one just past. For weeks beforehand one brother was engaged in scene painting and decorating, while many others did their share in other lines. A large sign across the entire width of the church just above the curtain in front of the rostrum announced to the onlooker, "Unto you is born this day in the city of David a Saviour, which is Christ the Lord." Scripture mottoes outlined with small colored electric lights hung between the windows. . . .

Pots of tulips and other early flowers and ferns banked the space in front of the platform. A hanging basket and a window box adorned each window.

With weeks of intensive preparation and rehearsal in the past, Christmas found everyone looking eagerly forward to, and earnestly hoping for, a successful finale.

On Sunday evening, March 30, the three-act drama, "Pilgrims of Light," with a cast of 45 characters, was presented by the men of the Mission to a large audience. The church was packed to its utmost capacity and many were unable to gain an entrance. Rows of chairs were placed in the aisles and extra seats built in specially for the occasion. The fact that a large number stood in the back of the church and in the vestibule during the entire two and one-half hour program and gave individual attention, testified to the interest manifested.

Because so many were anxious to hear this very interesting and instructive service, the entire program was repeated on Sunday evening, April 6.

For the benefit of the many readers of the *Message* who could not be present, we print a short description of both dramas.

"Pilgrims of Light" is based upon the story of the three sons of Senior Wakefield. The Wakefields were one of the oldest, most influential and religious families of Whitehall, England; the Senior Wakefield being a wealthy merchant. The sons, Jeffrey, Homer, and Ariel were very devout students of the Bible and often amazed the community by their courage in defending it; being always true to their convictions, yet always seeking a better knowledge of its divine truths. The family were very devoted to each other, the circle never having been broken except by the mother's death. The father's grief can therefore be imagined when shortly after this event the sons besought the father to give them that portion of goods which should fall to them, hoping by this means to make a trip around the world in search of truth on certain great religious questions which they longed to know.

To their urgent request the father at last consented, but invited the family pastor to attend the farewell dinner given for the sons, hoping that some word might be spoken to turn them from their decision.

The first scene opens with the father, the sons, and the minister gathered around the table, with heads bowed in thanks, while a harpist and flute player sit by who furnish soft music for the occasion. Two butlers in uniform wait upon the table. During the course of the dinner, the minister, aided by the father, tries to dissuade the sons from their purpose. Finding his efforts in vain because of previous failures to answer their questions on the Bible, the minister indignantly leaves the dinner table. A touching scene is the last "good-nights" between father and sons.

Whitehall gives them a spectacular farewell, with a business men's parade headed by a band and ended with a group of small boys, Ariel's Sunday-school class. Small banners were carried by the men upon each of which was a single word. These when grouped read: "We hope our loss is your gain"; "Be sure to keep a diary"; "Good bye, Whitehall." The sons' part was represented by the words: "Truth is the gem for which we seek"; "We want facts"; etc.

In their travels they meet a rabbi who seeks to convince them of God's special favor to the Jews and tries to secure a contribution for the homeland or the synagogue. His false claims and solicitations are thwarted by the appearance of the Pilgrim of Light.

In act two, the fallacy of healing disease and relieving pain through the mind by the assistance of a Christian Science healer is forcibly demonstrated, resulting in the exposure of the would-be healer and setting forth the truth on this very important subject. The rescuer in this case also proves to be the Pilgrim of Light.

A sudden death by a live wire and two prisoners awaiting execution provide ample opportunity for demonstration of Bible truth concerning absolution of sins and pardon for the same at the last moment of life. In both cases, Pilgrims of Light appear upon the scene with Bible testimony to show the absurdity of such practices.

The religious fervor of the young Wakefields upon hearing truth set forth by Pilgrims of Light in a street meeting brings them into disfavor with the over-zealous bishops of a foreign king. Arrested by his officers, they are summoned before him with three Pilgrims, who make a stirring appeal to the king in music, song, and oratory, whereupon they are released by the king and given a safe conduct from the country. Being rewarded in their search for truth, they return to the father's home where they are met by their old pastor and a brother minister. These, however, fade from the picture upon the appearance of the Pilgrims of Light, seven in number, who come by request of the Wakefield brothers and are welcomed by the father as the benefactors of his sons in their search for Truth.

The ladies' program on Monday evening, March 31, also brought out a full house and was well received by the audience. Fifteen young ladies and matrons composed the cast which presented "The Better Part," a four-act religious drama in which Mrs. Jameson, a wealthy widow and mother of a very irreligious and heedless daughter, residing on Perplexity Ave., Dread City, is in despair because of the wild life and aviation activities of Gertrude. A devout Fundamentalist, she sees the religious training given her daughter flouted after a college career. Gertrude persists in carrying out her designs in spite of her mother's pleadings and is seriously injured in her first solo flight.

A nurse is employed who brings some new religious ideas into the family. A young missionary calls who brings the mother a ray of hope. Solicitous for her daughter's welfare, she later writes a letter to the young missionary, inviting her and her friends to visit them. College friends are also invited, by Gertrude's request.

Mrs. Osmond and daughter Betty, with three other young ladies from the "Maranatha Missionary Society," respond to the call. They meet Gertrude and her friends, some of whom have imbibed atheism as against theological dogmas. Also Miss Wilson, the nurse, who proves a valuable ally because of truths received from "Maranatha" literature. A lively discussion ensues in which the Atheists, Modernists, Spiritualists, and a minister's wife, are routed by the "Sword of the Spirit" in the hands of its defenders. Miss Kennedy, a teacher who is introduced to assist the cause of atheism through her historical knowledge, proves a happy surprise and a staunch defender of the "old-time religion" of Jesus, the Apostles, and Prophets. She, too, has come into possession of valuable Bible truth through the efforts of the "Maranatha Missionary Society."

Mrs. Jameson and Priscilla Jones, one of the girls from Inflation College, see the error of their religious views and decide to serve God in the true way. Gertrude leaves home for larger opportunities in aviation. A telegram brings tragic news of her death in her burning plane. After the death of her daughter, Mrs. Jameson adopts Priscilla and together they become adherents of the new faith, which is the "old-time-religion," and change their abode from Dread City to Truth Center.

At a welcome surprise in their new home by some of the girls of the "Maranatha Society," a letter is read from the girl—formerly an atheist—of Inflation College in which she admits the influence of the Bible discussion she had heard several years previously and expresses heartfelt thanks for the help she has received through the influence of Priscilla's life and the light from "Maranatha" literature. She also draws a striking contrast between the lives and endings of the two girls, Gertrude and Priscilla; that of Priscilla being the happy beginning of a glorious end, due to her wise selection of "the better part."[37]

The sermon by Rev. M. Hembree on Sunday, March 30, on the subject of Christmas, was heard by a full house and the evidence given was absolute and convincing. No one hearing it could honestly find any excuse for ever again celebrating the old pagan feast day, the 25th of December.

The Megiddos do not have Christmas trees nor do they exchange gifts. However, proving that they are not immune to the wider culture of Christmas, they do give children inexpensive and practical presents at Abib. In its April 16, 1916, issue, the *Megiddo Message* listed the gifts given to the children that year: handkerchiefs, neckties, stockings, gloves, Bibles, Testaments, pencil boxes, spelling books, sets of tools, dress goods, and "other articles of utility and usefulness which give more lasting pleasure and benefits than do the foolish worthless toys and nonsense usually distributed on such occasions." Beginning as early as 1914, the mission began to send Christmas gifts to children in the families of those who regularly corresponded with the mission. Letters from children and parents expressing appreciation for the gifts indicate that the gifts included Abib spoons, bookmarks, dress material and a collar, a comb and brush, and a coloring book with "a color set" (probably crayons or colored pencils). Pastor Ruth Sisson remembers that before she moved to Rochester in the 1960s, the mission sent her a manicure set for Abib that she still uses. Food items are included in the gifts given to the few children affiliated with the church today. The gifts are given "not in imitation of the meaningless orgy of commercialism which prevails in the world, but to encourage and reward the little ones for good behavior, even as our Heavenly Father has promised to reward us if we are good."[38]

In another capitulation to the popular American celebration of Christmas, the Megiddos produced Abib or True Christmas cards bearing spring themes on a regular basis for several years beginning in 1949 and have produced them occasionally since. They are viewed as an opportunity to share the message of True Christmas with family and friends who may not celebrate True Christmas.[39] Beginning in 1925, and continuing for many years thereafter, the mission offered free placards to be placed in windows to proclaim True Christmas. Cards placed in windows of Rochester members invited passersby to attend True Christmas services at the church.

Until 1966, a hardware business next to the church called the Six-in-One Ladder Company, which initially was owned by members of the church and later by the church itself, each year placed advertisements in local newspapers to introduce Rochesterians to True Christmas. One such advertisement read, in part, as follows:

TO OUR MANY FRIENDS, IN AND ABOUT ROCHESTER

Another year has passed and in accordance with our belief, we are about to celebrate the Christmas season.

May we invite you and your friends to join with us, regardless of your belief, race, creed, or color, in celebrating the birth of our Saviour through prayer and thanksgiving . . .

In our humble way, we have tried to depict portions from the life of the Teacher and have made them as floats, appearing in the Six-In-One Hardware store windows. . . . We cordially invite you and your loved ones to view these scenes. They are the fruits of many hours of loving labor by those of the Megiddo Mission.

We will be Closed April 7th in Observance of This Day.[40]

The store windows, which were often decorated as elaborately with religious themes as were the commercial Christmas windows in the downtown department stores, drew curious onlookers from throughout the Rochester area and were often featured in local newspapers.

People came from throughout the Rochester area to see the Abib displays in the windows of the Six-in-One Ladder Company, next door to the Megiddo Church. A family from the north side of Rochester posed for this photograph, which appeared in the *Rochester Democrat and Chronicle* in March of 1950. Reprinted with permission of the Gannett Rochester Newspapers, Rochester, N.Y.

Abib was also often celebrated by groups outside Rochester.[41] Beginning in 1916, the Megiddos often printed portions of the Christmas program in advance in the *Megiddo Message* so that distant groups would have them for their own worship services. For example, in the April 1918 issue, "for the interest of our brethren resident in Utica and Boonville, N.Y., Phoenix, Ariz., Portland, Ore., Meyers Falls, Wa. and our readers and friends scattered throughout the country," they published several poems, a sermon, and the program of the service to be held on Abib 1, or April 11. Beginning in 1946, and for several years thereafter, the *Message* published a special "home Christmas service" designed especially for distant celebrants.

In 1914, Everett Gillings of Meyers Falls, Washington, wrote to say that his family had celebrated True Christmas "very much as we do at Megiddo." In 1925, in response to a request published in the *Message,* the mission received letters indicating that more than six hundred people throughout the United States, and in Canada, Australia, and England, were planning to have True Christmas services either as individuals or in groups of up to forty people.

Letters from distant celebrants would become usual in issues of the *Message* in the weeks following Abib each year. For example, in 1963, "M. P." reported that a group gathered at Rock Island, Illinois, "sang Christmas songs and read a piece out of the *Message* on True Christmas, and then the drama. . . . We had our lunch at 11:30 so we would be eating at the same time that you would be." She went on to comment on the spring weather and to note that she "liked the drama very much." Over the years, celebrations were held by groups in Sparta, Kentucky, and Cypress, Tennessee (where in 1930 there were sixty-seven in attendance for dinner). A small group of worshipers in Clarence, Missouri, even presented the one-act Abib drama, "The Mystery of Wellsville," in 1934. An article titled "Abib Reflections" in the June 1976 *Message* reported on celebrations in Tennessee, Virginia, Kansas, Canada, Australia, England, and India.[42]

Under the ministry of Rev. Maud Hembree, who succeeded Nichols as pastor, the campaign against False Christmas intensified. True to the Restorationist tradition in which the Megiddos had their origins, Reverend Hembree emphasized the fact that the early Christians had not celebrated Christmas in December and praised "our late lamented leader, the Rev. L. T. Nichols, who . . . found evidence to prove the true date of Christmas."[43] In 1919, on December 25, "in order to counteract the possible allurements of witnessing any of the foolish customs and nonsense indulged in, in the mind of the youthful members of Megiddo's congregation," the Megiddos held a program that featured the children performing musical selections and reading essays on the true date for the celebration of Christ's birth and on other Bible subjects. Some of the essays were printed in the *Message.*[44]

Over the years, the Megiddos have promoted True Christmas and waged a campaign against False Christmas through tracts that explain True Christmas or condemn the celebration of False Christmas. One recent tract features a brightly colored Christmas scene with Santa Claus and a Christmas tree, with the title "Is This (Foolishness) for Christians?" Another tract, entitled "Christ the Savior Is Born," shows shepherds, sheep, and flowers in the field with a herald angel in the sky. The Megiddos encourage members and friends to send the tracts to others in December in lieu of Christmas cards. During the 1950s, they also ran newspaper advertisements at the time of False Christmas. In at least one year, 1927, carloads of Brethren distributed copies of the previous Christmas issue of the *Megiddo Message* door to door in Rochester and other communities on December 25.[45]

By the mid-1920s, the rejection of December 25 as Christmas and the celebration of True Christmas had become a litmus test for the true believer. The *Megiddo Message* reported at length on preparations for the Abib celebration and on the activities themselves. In addition, along with the descriptions of the celebrations held in distant cities, the *Message* printed testimonials from people expressing their gratitude for having been rescued from the error of celebrating False Christmas and given the knowledge of the true date of the Lord's birth. In 1937, a reader from Fort Lauderdale, Florida, wrote that she had read the notes that accompanied her copy of the Moffat translation of the Bible (a favorite translation among the Megiddos) and noted that they said Christmas was not December 25 but "did not say when it was." She said she was "glad to know the true date" and enclosed a donation to show her appreciation to the mission. A letter appeared in the January 9, 1916, issue of the *Message* in which the writer states that she "really didn't know I was a pagan before. I have just finished taking down the Christmas tree for I could not bear to look at it after what Rev. Nichols says in reference to keeping the old pagan day." The accounts of celebrations and testimonials continued to appear in the magazine on a regular basis into the 1960s.[46]

Today, the celebration of True Christmas remains much the same as it has for more than seventy years. Because there are fewer members, the celebration has been simplified. The floral decorations now consist mainly of potted plants and flowers lining the front of the stage, and the casts of the costumed dramas are small but enthusiastic. True to the spirit of their inventor-founder, the Megiddos are eager to embrace technological advances, as evidenced by electronic instruments, which compensate for the small size of the band, and computer-generated images projected on a screen, which now occupy a prominent place in some services. Attendance at the True Christmas dinner is limited to members and out-of-town guests.

Although Abib is also the start of the new year for Megiddos, there has been a limited emphasis on new beginnings, which pervades the secular New Year's celebration. However, in 1931, there was a short-lived attempt to institute something similar to the popular New Year's resolution. The mission distributed a daily record chart listing some of the "most familiar evils," with boxes in which to mark progress in eradicating them. Members were to "have these evils completely subjected to the law of Christ, and the virtues thriving in their place" two years hence. Each sheet was to last one month and supplies were offered on request. The form was somewhat complex, and this ministry appears to have met with little success. There is no indication that it lasted beyond the first year.[47]

The weeks following True Christmas include other holidays, the dates of which are computed in relation to Abib 1. New Passover is celebrated on Abib 13. The Megiddos believe that "the Jewish Passover fell on the fourteenth of Abib . . . [but] Jesus instituted the New Passover one day earlier so that He could partake of this last meal with His disciples before He suffered." Unlike their Restorationist forebears, the Disciples of Christ and the Christadelphians, who take Communion weekly, the Megiddos take Communion only once a year, at Passover, but they do so for the same reason the Disciples and Christadelphians do it weekly—they believe it replicates the practice of the first-century church. The Megiddos are also adamant that the Lord's Supper must be celebrated in the evening to truly duplicate the New Testament experience. Two days after New Passover, the Resurrection of Christ is celebrated with a special worship service. The Ascension of Christ into heaven is celebrated forty days after the Resurrection, and Pentecost is celebrated ten days after the Ascension.[48] In the early years of the mission, these additional holidays were celebrated with more ceremony than they are today. It was not unusual for out-of-town visitors to arrive for Abib 1 and stay until after True Easter, but this rarely, if ever, happens today.[49]

The description of True Christmas in the April 27, 1930, *Megiddo Message* described the celebration of the other Abib holidays that followed:

> The Lord's Supper was observed by the Megiddo congregation on Friday evening, April 11, which was the beginning of the 13th of Abib of Bible time, the true anniversary of the night Jesus met with his disciples and instituted the New Passover. . . .
>
> In partaking of these emblems we renew our covenant to eat every word of God and live it out daily, showing forth the Lord's death (death to sin) till he comes.
>
> The true Easter on Abib 15 . . . was observed with an early morning service in the Megiddo church. Four thirty found the whole congregation of the brethren, with several visitors who remained over from the Christmas celebration, congregated to commemorate with songs of praise, musical selections and words of exhortation, the anniversary of the glorious day of our Saviour's Resurrection. The service was opened by an overture by the band, "Hallelujah," followed by a soprano and alto duet, "He is Risen," by Brother A. Ploughwright and Sister Clara Thorne, the choir joining in the chorus. The Scripture lesson was Luke 24, followed by prayer. "Bright Beautiful Morning" was then sung by the congregation. Our pastor, Rev. M. Hembree, delivered a very impressive and earnest exhortation in which she admonished her hearers to greater efforts during the coming year to overcome evil and live worthy of the great Resurrection in the future, or to be ready to meet our Saviour at his coming, with joy and not with grief.

The men's chorus then sang "He has Triumphed," after which the service was closed with "The Holy City" by the band, and benediction.

In spite of positioning themselves outside mainstream American society, the members of the Megiddo Church have not ignored two traditional American holidays—Independence Day and Thanksgiving. Independence Day has been celebrated as a church holiday as far back as when the Christian Brethren were in Minnesota. At its June 1896 business meeting, the Minnesota ecclesia discussed having Independence Day activities but determined that the Brethren should decide for themselves how to celebrate the holiday; the following year, however, the members held a meeting and picnic on July 4th.

L. T. Nichols wrote the following regarding the importance of Independence Day: "We have a great deal to cause us to be thankful to our God, in that the Declaration of Independence was made on July 4th, 1776 . . . A Government sprang up for independence of religion and free thought, regardless of race or color. It declared we should have the right to worship God according to the dictates of our own conscience, without molestation, and the Government to protect and sustain us." This statement seems strange in light of the Megiddos' experiences in Oregon, Iowa, and Alton, Illinois, where they were victims rather than benefactors of free speech as practiced by the free press, and where the authorities at the very least had failed to protect their rights. Obviously, the intentions underlying the Constitution and the law were more important to Nichols than the practice.

Like many other Americans, L. T. Nichols had a special reverence for George Washington, who was viewed in the nineteenth and early twentieth centuries as a Moses-like figure divinely ordained to lead his people from the Egypt of tyranny to the promised land of liberty. According to Nichols,

> If it had not been for George Washington, where would we be today? still so bound that Truth could not fit its head. He was a great benefactor to America. . . . We are thankful for the freedom that has been given us through a Washington. . . . He was a man God made use of for the benefit of his people. Through his instrumentality we gained freedom and the right to worship God as we please. We should be thankful that there was such a man who, together with other brave men, had the courage to stand up and obtain a Declaration of Independence and a Fourth of July.

The Megiddos believe that the discovery of America and the establishment of the United States as a free country has religious significance and has "been Divinely ordained that God's plan for the earth might be fulfilled." Indeed, "it was all part of God's plan for ending of the long apostasy." The Megiddos also "love and respect the flag which protects us in the enjoyment of . . . inestimable privileges." Unlike some other religious groups, particularly Jehovah's Witnesses, they do not oppose saluting the flag, believing that the practice falls under the apostle Paul's command to "render therefore unto Caesar the things which are Caesar's." [50]

The members celebrate Independence Day with a variation of the traditional Fourth of July picnic and a program. The celebrations were initially held on the vast lawn at the church home, but later, after several members acquired automobiles, the festivities moved to the country. Typical of the elaborate early Independence Day celebrations was that held in 1920 and described in detail in the *Megiddo Message*. Beginning about 9:30 in the morning, fourteen automobiles began to make repeated trips to ferry the members to a site about three miles from the mission. A platform, decorated with flowers, was erected near a shady grove of trees with a carpeted square in front of it. Folding chairs that had been brought by truck from the mission were set up in front of the platform. Trees by the platform were decorated with flowers and flags. With some ceremony, the young men of the mission unveiled a large portrait of L. T. Nichols that had been hung in one of the trees. This was followed by a program of songs, patriotic and religious music played by the band, and recitations and essays "of an instructive, upbuilding nature." There was a picnic dinner, after which Rev. Maud Hembree gave a brief address on the significance of Independence Day. Finally, as the band played "Home, Sweet, Home," the mission members thanked their hosts and prepared to leave for home.[51]

Beginning in the 1930s, the celebration was often held in a tent purchased for the use of traveling missionaries. Smaller tents were also sometimes erected to provide dressing rooms for the band and for the actors when dramas were added to the celebration. The activities lasted into the evening. The celebration eventually was relocated to the large lawn of a member who lived near the church. This made it easier for disabled members to attend and for the celebration to be moved indoors to the church's ample basement in case of inclement weather. In the 1960s, the picnic moved to land owned by a member in the Bristol Hills south of Rochester. Apparently, "there was a problem of too close proximity to the gaze of the public, too much interference by noise and din; public or private retreats were often hard to secure, and there was always the problem of interference." In 1970, the mission erected a pavilion on that property that was used for the July 4 picnic until the land was sold in 1978. Today, the celebrations are held on a much smaller scale, but they are still held outdoors and still feature music and reflection on the advantages of living in the United States.[52]

Occasionally, the Independence Day celebration was combined with a work activity, as when the members of the mission refurbished the "somewhat rundown" farm that two members of the mission had purchased or when they painted the church and remodeled its front to add "utility space." However, this was the exception. Community work activities were often done on Memorial Day, when most of the men were off work but the mission did not have regularly scheduled activities.[53]

The Megiddo Church observes Thanksgiving to offer thanks to God for the many blessings the members have received in the previous year. In the past, members celebrated with a common meal and a program featuring appropriate

Scripture, poetry, readings, and songs. Sometime in the late 1930s or early 1940s, the women began serving a Thanksgiving dinner to the "unattached men" of the mission.

Children are a special focus of Thanksgiving Day. The *Megiddo Message* of November 28, 1915, reported that "Ideal weather prevailed on Thanksgiving Day, and the Mission just bristled with vim, and activity; for at the kind invitation of our pastor, Rev. Maud Hembree, the children of the Mission were invited to dinner at the residence of our late beloved Leader, a custom instituted by him. . . . This day might well be called 'Children's Day.'" Thirty-nine children attended, and after dinner the children presented a program under the direction of their teacher. The 2000 celebration of Thanksgiving featured a potluck meal in the church dining room and a treasure hunt for the children, "which was a great success. Outdoors in the snow, they had Bible questions to answer which translated into places to find the next question . . . and finally to a 'prize' [a big box of edibles]." [54]

The inclusion of Independence Day and Thanksgiving in the Megiddo calendar of holidays appears to have made the holidays less exclusively American and more religious if several items in the *Megiddo Message* relating to Canadian readers are representative. In a letter to the *Message,* two readers from Theodore, Saskatchewan, stated that it was "nice to read of Independence Day, when all the brothers and sisters met together on July 4th to glorify our Heavenly Father for His mercies bestowed upon us." On at least two occasions, Canadians attended the Independence Day celebration at the mission. In a news item, the editor of the *Message* noted that a letter had been received from one of five members of a family from Peterborough, Ontario, who had spent Thanksgiving at Megiddo. [55]

Music has been, and still is, an important part of not only holiday celebrations but also the entire life of the church. When the Brethren relocated to Rochester from the *Megiddo,* they brought their band instruments, and their bandwagon became a familiar sight near meetings. Shortly after L. T. Nichols's death, the band divided into two—the Progressive Band, which played at meetings held away from the mission, and the Home Band, which played at the mission and included, in addition to all the members of the Progressive Band, others who played instruments, including those who were just learning.

Shortly after the bands were formed, a professional musician, Frederick Melville, was hired to do hymn arrangements and train the band, giving private lessons to less accomplished players. Melville directed band rehearsals, but at the actual church programs the band was directed by mission member Harriet E. Payne. Eventually, the two directors clashed due to "differing tastes and directing techniques."

> Mr. Melville wanted to add saxophones to the ensemble, which [Mrs. Payne] opposed. [Payne] failed to take into consideration that saxophones could complete the tonal spectrum between the brass instruments and the

reeds in a concert band. (At the time, saxophones were becoming very popular as an instrument that easily produced a wailing tone which was desired in dance and jazz music, though in the hands of a capable player, they could add considerably to the tone of a concert band.) The band later added three saxophones.[56]

Beginning in October 1935, Harriet Payne's son, Newton H. Payne, became director of the band, a position he held for fifty-five years. In order to improve the quality of the band's performances, Newton Payne, with the assistance of mission member Ralph Barber, devised a plan to require all players to practice ten minutes a day.

The thought was that if they practiced at least ten minutes, they would practice longer . . . Each player was required to bring a chart to each rehearsal showing how much they practiced. It [the plan] worked from a musical standpoint, but Sister Hembree and Sister Skeels were concerned that it could cause rivalry among the members which would be adverse to their spiritual well-being, and that it placed too much emphasis on secondary matters when our main thrust should be on preparing ourselves and others for a place in God's kingdom. The plan was abandoned.[57]

To complement the band program, which was directed toward the men, Dorothy French formed the Ladies' Orchestra about 1930. When the members of the orchestra "felt that their efforts were being curtailed by the director, who was inclined to take most music at too slow a tempo," Estella Beck assumed responsibility for the orchestra. She was succeeded by band director

The Megiddo Mission Ladies' Orchestra, circa 1940s. Courtesy Megiddo Church, Rochester, N.Y.

Newton Payne, who, as a wind player, found the orchestra, with its stringed instruments, a challenge.

The vocal music program was developed by Estella Beck and her husband, David, graduates of LaFayette College, where David Beck performed with a male quartet. When the Becks joined the church in 1926, it had only a male quartet for vocal music, but David Beck soon organized a male ensemble and then a women's choir. He also formed a second male quartet, which became known as the "new" quartet, as opposed to the "old" quartet. David Beck directed the vocal organizations until the 1950s, when failing health forced him to turn responsibilities over to Dorothy French and Newton Payne.[58]

The mission initially began to experiment with sound recording in the early 1930s, when home recording was in its infancy and recording was done on a lacquered disk made of acetate, aluminum, or glass. L. L. French, a machinist, took initial responsibility for recording, which involved cutting a groove in the lacquered surface and was not an easy task. "If it was not cut deep enough, the pickup needle would not track properly and would skid across the disk. If it was cut too deep it would cut through the lacquer and dig up the aluminum or whatever the base was made of." [59] Eventually, French and his associates did manage to produce records, but they were fragile and sometimes of questionable quality or use because they could not be stopped and started like tape. Once one started to record on a disk, one had to keep recording regardless of the quality or continuity of the performance. "Sometimes the music would start softly and everything would seem to be working until suddenly the music would hit a loud spot and the cutter would make a too wide sweep and cut into the next groove." About 1950, tape recording became practical. The church has subsequently employed more and more sophisticated recording equipment, including a recently acquired compact disc writer/player.[60] The church also has video recording equipment, and holiday services are often recorded, edited, and made available to members who cannot attend services.[61]

An advertisement in the May 1975 issue of the *Megiddo Message* announced an audiotape ministry:

> The living Word of God is on the move these days—across the United States and Canada, to England and Australia. It is moving in the form of live recordings of church services, on magnetic tape reel and on cassette. It can come to your home, too.
>
> This is how it works:
>
> We record our Sunday morning church service each week. We mail one set of these (two recordings) every two weeks to the first subscriber on our list. He uses the recordings for approximately two weeks. Then he mails them on to the next subscriber on the list. The next subscriber does the same and so on.

Interested readers were directed to send a card to the mission in return for a packet containing a sample recording and a copy of the formal agreement each participant was required to sign. The service was free, except for the cost of postage. The plan had its drawbacks. "If someone forgot to mail [the tape], or damaged it, or decided to keep it, the rest on the [subscriber] list lost out." By 1977, the original program was replaced by a "cassette-loan plan." For one dollar a month, the subscriber would receive two cassettes to keep for a month and then return to the mission, which would then send two more tapes. If the subscriber wished to keep the tape, the cost was three dollars per tape.

The tape ministry developed a devoted following and the church received many letters of appreciation. One subscriber from England wrote, "What joyous hours I spend listening to the tapes. I sing within as I follow you and your choir. The admonitions from the pastor are a great help to me. . . . My cup runneth over with so much week after week." A subscriber from North Carolina wrote that she longed to "hear someone's voice from your church." When she received the tapes, she said they made her "feel closer" to the members of the mission, as if she were "right there" with them.[62]

The recorded audio ministry is still active and now includes compact discs. In recent years, a set of Bible studies has been added to the audio ministry, and the church is currently developing "a set on various books of the Bible," which are verse-by-verse studies of the books accompanied by printed lesson sheets.[63]

In contrast to the observances involving elaborate decorations and programs along with sumptuous meals is Self-Denial Week, a period of dietary restriction that occurs each February. It is viewed as "the chief means by which the body is brought into subjection, and . . . it is a benefit both to the physical and spiritual man."

The roots of Self-Denial Week are in the concern that L. T. Nichols expressed during the 1882 camp meeting that his followers eat only true nourishing food and avoid unnourishing items such as tea, coffee, and spices. The substances Nichols told his listeners to avoid were those commonly identified by the health reform movement as harmful, but Nichols put a biblical slant on the dietary rules by exhorting his listeners to be "not like our first parents [and] think that the subject of eating will not endanger our eternal life. As Adam and Eve were commanded not to eat of or touch a certain fruit. So we are commanded to be content with that which is food. And if we are not content, but partake of that which is not food, we will (like our first parents) be put to shame when Jesus comes."

Self-Denial Week also reflects Nichols's interest in fasting, which he encouraged at least as early as the time of his ministry in Oregon, when he said that "until we earnestly and willingly enter into fasting, we need not expect to get rid of all disobedience, of weights and besetting sins which so easily beset us . . . We must suffer with Christ in all the self-denial he requires." On the many benefits of fasting Nichols stated, "Not only does our fasting cause us to rule our own selves by the word of truth simply in obeying this command, but it also enables us to better grasp and comprehend the truth upon every point. It enables us to perceive quicker and better, and we can express our heart-felt desires with more clearness when we go to the throne of Grace. It is not only good for us in these respects, but it is also beneficial to our health." [64]

It is not known exactly when the Megiddos began to observe Self-Denial Week, but it was practiced in the early days of the ministry in Rochester, and there is a reference to it as an established event in a sermon preached by L. T. Nichols in 1910. The observance was originally two weeks long and occurred during the first two weeks in February. The entire diet consisted of all one wanted of cornbread and applesauce. The diet has now been expanded so that "only three things will be eaten at a meal, the selection to be made from vegetables, bread, cereals, butter, milk and common fruits. No meat, fish, poultry, game, eggs, or cheese, sugar, cake or pastry may be eaten." [65] Anyone who is ill or who has a special diet prescribed by a physician is exempt from observing Self-Denial Week.

In spite of its probable origins in the religious thought of L. T. Nichols, the reason for the practice of Self-Denial Week in Rochester was originally at least partly financial—to save money that would normally be spent on meals and use it to support the missionaries, many of whom were affected by hard economic times and did not have the resources to meet their expenses. By 1946, Self-Denial Week took on a more thoughtful character. The *Megiddo Message* indicated that as part of the observance, those participating in Self-Denial Week should be thankful that the Lord had been generous to them while others in the world were not adequately fed. In one of the *Message*'s few references to World War II, the same article mentioned that food rationing, although inconvenient, had been a blessing in disguise because it provided a more equal distribution of food.[66]

The holiday celebrations of the mission became focal points around which activities were planned and periodical issues designed. By focusing on doctrines and activities that did not necessarily relate directly to the holiday, the Megiddos were able to take advantage of the celebrations to draw public attention to their teachings and to present and clarify their beliefs for members and visitors.

6

Spreading the Megiddo Message

As the Megiddos became more established in Rochester, Captain Nichols gained a reputation as an outstanding public speaker and "one of the best versed men on Bible themes in the world." Among his most noteworthy messages were his attacks on Spiritualism, which had a significant presence in Rochester. Consequently, it is ironic that the mission was forced to vacate its rented facilities in Plymouth Church in August 1906, when the church was purchased by Spiritualists. Since Nichols was never one to avoid controversy, it is not surprising that his last sermon in the church was an attack on its future tenants in which he stated that he stood "ready to buy the Plymouth Church outright and make the Spiritualists a gift of it" if they could produce one phenomenon he could not explain "upon reasonable examination." [1]

The members of the mission continued to prosper as Captain Nichols purchased building lots on streets near the headquarters at Thurston Road and Sawyer Street. He sold these lots at cost to members of the mission, who, using lumber also purchased at cost from Nichols, helped one another build houses, much as they had done in Nashville. He also loaned money to members at 4.5 percent interest. When possible, each person built two houses, one in which to live and one to rent for income. Early issues of the mission magazine contain many items relating to the homes members were constructing on the streets near the mission. The houses were a most welcome addition not only to the mission members who wanted to be closer to the church but also to the city.

Rochester was experiencing a housing shortage due to an expanding economy and a large influx of immigrant workers.[2]

In his efforts to provide for the mission, Nichols also contributed to the development of the surrounding area. Although an early attempt failed when the Rochester Railway Company refused his $1,000 offer to help pay for the extension of its rail line to the mission area, Nichols's efforts eventually contributed substantially to the growth of the southwest side of Rochester and the nearby suburb of Gates when he arranged for the extension of water service to the mission and its neighborhood. Water was critical to development primarily because fire was a constant threat to life and property. Without water it was impossible to fight fires. As a result, housing costs were prohibitive in areas without dependable water supplies due to the high cost of fire insurance.

Captain Nichols petitioned the City of Rochester in 1908 for extension of water service to the mission. The city delayed action on Nichols's petition, and the impatient developer contracted for water service with the Lake Ontario Water Company, a private competitor to the city's waterworks. As a result of extending its mains to the mission, the water company was able to continue its lines to the adjacent suburb of Gates, thereby encouraging development in that area. Eventually, the City of Rochester acquired the Lake Ontario Water Company.[3] Nichols was also instrumental in convincing the New York State Railway to extend its trolley line so that it passed the mission property. The city soon paved the streets and sidewalks near the mission, and within a few years several stores and other businesses brought economic prosperity to Thurston Road.

After leaving Plymouth Church in 1906, the mission held services in the mission home until the following year, when Reverend Nichols decided that the mission needed its own worship facility and the Brethren began construction of a church building at the corner of Thurston Road and Sawyer Street, across from the home. Constructed partly from wood cut from the lot on which the church was built and processed in Nichols's own sawmill, the simple building measured eighty-one feet by thirty-six feet and had a seating capacity of four hundred people. The pews were constructed by the Brethren out of chestnut and the women made the cushions. The building cost about five thousand dollars, all of it raised within the Megiddo Mission community. It was dedicated on March 22, 1908, with about 250 people in attendance.

The rostrum and the front of the church were carpeted. Stained glass windows allowed natural light to come in, and electric lights were available when needed. According to a Rochester newspaper, the "the distinctive feature" of the church was a series of murals that decorated the walls. On "every available inch of space, excluding the ceilings, [were] Bible texts, which form the foundations of the Megiddo faith, in very artistic lettering." Over the rear door was a "ladder on each round of which are words indicating steps on the ladder of salvation." In apparent remembrance of their years on the rivers, next to the ladder was painted a riverboat. Above the door leading to the rostrum was a painting of the Holy City that will exist after the return of Christ.[4] The new building allowed the mission to hold both regular services and their elaborate public holiday celebrations.

Because the pastor received no salary, Nichols was still responsible for his own support. In 1906, in a move that seems incompatible with his aversion to military service, he applied to the government for a Civil War veteran's military pension, which became available to him when he turned sixty-two. The pension was granted and he received six dollars a month; the amount increased to twelve dollars a month in 1907. In 1909, in partnership with his brother-in-law Henry E. Skeels, Nichols patented the last of his inventions, an egg crate designed to permit the shipment of eggs with minimal breakage.[5]

Over the years, L. T. Nichols suffered occasional episodes of ill health. Early in 1912, one such episode led him to the famous Battle Creek (Michigan) Sanitarium, operated by the Kellogg family of cereal fame.[6] At the sanitarium, his health appeared to be improving, even to the point at which he was able to conduct religious services. Consequently, it came as a shock when on February 28, 1912, the years of dedicated mission work and studying until the wee hours of the morning finally took their toll and L. T. Nichols suddenly died.[7]

Word of Nichols's death reached the mission on the heels of positive news of his condition, and the mission members were thrown into deep mourning. His body was returned to Rochester, where it lay in state at the mission surrounded by members of his congregation. The church was decorated in black

Interior of the auditorium of the Megiddo Church showing Scripture passages on the walls and a mural depicting the gospel boat *Megiddo* at the back. Courtesy Megiddo Church, Rochester, N.Y.

and white for the funeral, with a banner reading "Beloved Leader" above the altar. Maud Hembree preached the funeral service.

Like many groups and institutions, the Megiddo Mission had purchased a section of Mount Hope Cemetery, a large Victorian cemetery on the south side of Rochester. A funeral cortege "that extended for blocks down Thurston Road" accompanied the flower-covered casket to the cemetery, where Reverend Hembree conducted a brief graveside service.[8]

According to an unidentified member of the mission who spoke to James Bristah and Margaret Frerichs, students at Colgate-Rochester Divinity School who did a study of the Megiddo Mission in the mid-1940s, some members of the mission identified L. T. Nichols with Elijah. After he died, they made visits to his grave to see if he had risen. Given that Nichols expected the actual prophet Elijah to return and that he rejected the idea of a new Elijah, it would seem contrary to his teachings for his followers to believe him to be Elijah. However, given the strong sense of expectation at the time, the high esteem in which Nichols was held by members of the mission, and the prosperity of the mission, which could easily have been mistaken for the beginning of the restoration of the earth in preparation for Christ's return, it is not unreasonable to believe that overzealous believers might mistake Nichols for Elijah.[9]

After Nichols's death, the members of the mission continued the annual dinner held in celebration of his October 1 birthday, in which he had taken "great joy and comfort" and at which he had "visited from table to table with words of kindly cheer and greeting exhorting all to so live that the pleasure might be his of meeting and eating with them in the Kingdom of God."[10] To the dinner was added a service at his grave, weather permitting, which included music, for which special permission was required from the cemetery commission,[11] and the placing of flowers on his grave. There has also usually been another observance either at the church or at the Church Home. Since Nichols is held in the highest esteem by the members of the Megiddo Church, as a holiday his birthday is second in importance only to Christmas. According to an article in the *Message,* "Christmas Day and October 1 are memorable days at Megiddo. It may be a mere coincidence that the birthday of our honored leader comes in the fall, while that of our coming King occurs in the early Spring, making about six months between the two events, both of which are celebrated by our congregation with great honor. As the programs require much preparation, this gives ample time for each." The holiday "is one of the cardinal points of the year and a time of pilgrimage for brethren residing in distant States and cities." Visitors have been known to visit from as far away as Louisiana and California for the occasion.[12]

In 1931, on the founder's birthday, a bronze plaque, which is now located in the vestibule of the church, was dedicated to his memory. In 1944, on the one hundredth anniversary of Nichols's birth, an elaborate celebration was held. The church building was painted on Independence Day in preparation for the event. A spectacular, though temporary, memorial arch was constructed over the entrance to the complex across from the church and remained in place from September 23 to October 7, bearing the inscription:

SO THE LORD ALONE DID LEAD HIM,

AND THERE WAS NO STRANGE

GOD WITH HIM

1844 OUR FOUNDER 1944

Although the arch appeared to be marble, it was actually made of plywood, and it was illuminated at night with blue and gold floodlights.[13]

The mission's twenty-four-by-forty-five-foot tent was set up on the lawn of the mission home. Inside, it was divided into two sections. In one section were nine paintings by mission member Charles M. Clarke that depicted scenes from the life of L. T. Nichols. There were also enlarged photographs of Nichols at various times in his life. In a glass case were some of Nichols's personal possessions—his lexicon, Bible, wallet, cane, and reading glasses. Two long glass-covered tables displayed newspaper clippings and photographs relating to the history of the mission. In a corner was a display showing the history of the mission magazine. There was also a life-size depiction of the biblical story of Mary and Martha, executed in wax. In the second section of the tent was an area for meditation with chairs and soft music. There were also two dioramas designed by members of the mission—one of the New Jerusalem of the future,

Temporary arch erected for celebration of the centennial of L. T. Nichols's birth, 1944. Courtesy Megiddo Church, Rochester, N.Y.

which was ten feet wide and five feet high, and a smaller one of Sodom and Gomorrah.

On Friday evening, September 29, in the flower-decorated church, Rev. Percy J. Thatcher gave a welcoming address and Brother E. C. Branham read one of Nichols's sermons. At 8:00 A.M. the following morning, there was a quiet hour and devotional service. A birthday dinner was served to 187 people at 12:30 P.M. and there was a graveside service at 3:00 P.M. There was a buffet supper at 6:00 P.M., followed by a program by the Maranatha sisters, the mission's women's organization, at 7:30 P.M.[14]

On Sunday morning, the church bell tolled one hundred times to commemorate the one hundred years since Nichols's birth, and there was another service followed by a dinner in the church basement. In two sessions, one at 2:00 P.M. and the other at 8:30 P.M., a two-part drama entitled "The Triumph of Truth Over Error" traced the development of religion from the time of Daniel to the appearance of Elijah, accompanied by Nichols, and the Resurrection. The service ended at midnight.[15]

In the years following the centennial celebration, Nichols increasingly ceased to be characterized simply as the exceptional human being that he had been portrayed to be by those who knew him, and he took on almost Christlike virtues in the minds of some members of the mission. Most of the October 1, 1949, issue of the *Message,* which featured Nichols on the cover, was devoted to "A Brief Biography of the Rev. L. T. Nichols," which concluded:

> In looking backward through his life among his people, his presence seems to fill the entire scene; his influence, predominating throughout, is reflected from everything that is holy and good. He moved into the position of a great leader because there was vacuum which none other could supply.
>
> His character and wisdom gave unity and dignity; his intelligence and knowledge of God's Word guided the whole. His perseverance, fortitude and inspiration were the support of all. He was before every man in his suggestions for the spread of the Gospel to a dying world, and was before everyone in the extent to which he contributed to its adoption. Brave, fearless, heroic, with prudence ever governing his impulses, the wisdom of God ever guiding his valor, he recognized a divine aid in all that he accomplished.
>
> He was a man with iron will and great intellectual force; a soldier of God with dauntless courage and stainless honor . . . stainless in character, kind and gracious of heart, modest, self-denying, self-sacrificing, declining all worldly honor, scorning gifts, charitable to the needy, forgiving injuries. His life, like Christ's, was for others.
>
> We love to record his heroic purposes, the power of his magnificent personality, his glorious achievements for mankind, his stalwart and unflinching devotion to the truth . . . The comforts of his home were always open to those who sought for the high, the elevating, the good

and pure. . . . The intensity of his tenderness was specially manifest with children.

Blessed are we above all people in the richness of our privileges to have been permitted to share in his inmost thoughts and to watch in all its sweetness and unaffectedness his daily life.—The flight of years seems only to enhance his hold upon us. He has become so centrally fixed in our hearts and minds that he is one of the greatest influences in our life and conduct . . . what is the meaning of his deathless hold upon our minds? It is because the impress of his life and character cannot be eradicated. He was a providential man, he was a man of destiny.[16]

Over the years, the reverence accorded Nichols, while still evident, has been tempered. Nichols is spoken of with great respect but without the extreme adulation evident in the period after the centennial. The editors of the *Megiddo Message,* influenced by Kenneth Flowerday, who knew Nichols and was probably aware of the potential for the general readership to misinterpret the Megiddos' devotion to Nichols, have given less space to writings of and about him, although *An Honest Man* has been serialized in the *Message* in recent years. In contrast to the *Message* of fifty years before, in the September/ October 1999 issue, in recognition of the anniversary of Nichols's birth, there was a three-page excerpt from his writings with a small box stating "In Memory of Our Founder, Born October 1, 1844."

The church still sells copies of *An Honest Man* as an anonymous work. While the language of other Megiddo publications, including those originally written by L. T. Nichols, has been updated, *An Honest Man* still appears in the late Victorian prose style of E. C. Branham, unlikely to hold the attention of the modern reader. Platitudes substitute where facts are unavailable. Where facts were almost certainly available from Ella Skeels, the author frequently resorts to tantalizing suggestions of an interesting story while leaving the reader unsatisfied. For example, in *An Honest Man* the persecution Nichols suffered in Oregon is described as the following:

the greater the man and the more public his mission, the more enemies he will make. Mr. Nichols . . . inevitably had his detractors and persecutors. The opposition . . . grew more bitter. Threats of violence were common, and in 1883 the persecution culminated in a vicious and cowardly assault on his person which endangered his life. So determined were his enemies to finish their foul work and eliminate this arch-heretic once and for all that it became necessary for him to obey the command of his Lord: "When they shall persecute you in this city, flee ye into another." Oregon, too, had proved unworthy and suffered, without knowing it, a most grievous loss.[17]

J. Gordon Melton, an expert on new religions, has pointed out that contrary to popular wisdom that the loss of a charismatic leader is life threatening to a group, "the average founder of a new religion is an important factor in the movement's growth and development. . . . However, once the founder articulates the group's teachings and practices, they exist independently of him/her and can and do develop a life of their own. . . . Once a single spokesperson for the founder arises, the possibility of transmitting the truth of the religion independently of the founder has been posited."[18] Rev. Maud Hembree was that "single spokesperson" who had, intentionally or unintentionally, been groomed by L. T. Nichols to be his successor. She was quickly elected as pastor of the mission. The transfer of authority was apparently smooth and set the tone for the future, in which the minister would serve for life and would be succeeded by one of her or his closest associates.[19]

The period of Nichols's leadership, particularly the period of the ministry that was spent on the water, is still looked upon as the golden age of the church. However, it was during the ministry of Maud Hembree that the Megiddo Mission enjoyed its greatest success.

By 1905, the mission had entered on an active program of evangelistic work outside Rochester, sending missionaries, often attention-getting groups of deaconesses dressed in their black dresses and deaconess bonnets, to such places as Buffalo and Watertown, New York, and Boston, as well as the Canadian cities of Toronto and St. Catharines. Everywhere they went, the press reported on their message of preparation for the Second Coming of Christ—and they rarely failed to mention the mission's past history on the gospel boat.[20]

The mission also engaged in outreach in the Rochester area. At any given time, four to twenty missionaries, supported by the tithes of mission members, were in the field, going from house to house and visiting businesses, talking to people, and distributing pamphlets and tracts.

When Reverend Hembree assumed leadership, years had passed, Elijah had not come, and the Megiddos found themselves in a similar position to that of the early Christians when Christ had not returned within a short period after his ascension. Given the assumption that failed prophecy threatens the viability of groups that experience it, the Megiddos should have been in danger of disbanding. However, as J. Gordon Melton has pointed out, although "media representatives, nonmillennial religious rivals and scholars" see "prophecy as the organizing principle for millennial groups," such is rarely the case. The groups actually tend to be organized around a comprehensive set of beliefs and "a group life within which ritual can be performed and individual interactions occur." Since they can focus on those things that truly bind them together, "times of testing tend to strengthen, not destroy, religious groups." In the case of the Megiddos, while many were undoubtedly disappointed with the continuing delay, their beliefs that the incorrect dates might be merely incomplete comprehension of Scripture and that the Bible can be continually mined for new insights positioned them to see the delay as a challenge to continue to search the Scriptures.[21]

No one was more aware of the opportunities presented by the delay in Elijah's return than Maud Hembree. Since the return of Elijah would occur at some indefinite future time, she realized that it might be possible to convert more people who would have enough time to perfect their lives before Christ's return. She gradually began to downplay the importance of the Bible chronology, which eventually disappeared from the Megiddo publications list, and other more sensational doctrines that had up to that point gained the mission much of the public attention it had received. In its place, she began to focus on the doctrine that was at the core of her faith and that had caused her to accept social ostracism and alienation from her family to follow L. T. Nichols: the belief that in order to be saved one must study Scripture diligently and scrupulously follow its mandates.

Guiding people to perfect lives required the ability to provide regular nurturing, and in the early 1910s the mission was not positioned to do this. The mission depended on distribution of the publications of L. T. Nichols and on visits by missionaries to interest people in the mission and to foster commitment and ongoing involvement. While some people repeatedly read Nichols's publications, they could not be expected to do so indefinitely, and time and the cost of travel limited who missionaries could reach and how often. The answer to this dilemma—a periodical that could provide ongoing support to both old and new believers—came about almost by accident, but once established it was used effectively by Maud Hembree and by subsequent ministers and editors to provide ongoing support to members in Rochester and elsewhere.

Periodicals were an important means by which religious ideas were disseminated and cohesion was established and maintained among geographically separated adherents in the nineteenth and early twentieth centuries. Almost all denominations had periodicals, and even a few, like the Church of God (Anderson, Indiana) were organized around them. Many smaller groups became known by the names of their publications, such as the Metropolitan Church Association, which is known by the more colorful name of its magazine, *The Burning Bush*.[22] Consequently, it is surprising that L. T. Nichols, with his printing press and active pamphlet ministry, had not published a periodical.

The beginnings of the Megiddo periodical were highly unofficial. Minnie Branham, the mother of two boys, aged twelve and fourteen, who had journalistic ambitions, suggested that they might fill a community need by publishing a newspaper to communicate news within the mission. Using an old typewriter, the boys prepared the first issue, laboriously typing each individual copy. This first "printing" of the *Megiddo News* occurred on March 31, 1914. It consisted of "two dingy little sheets, letter size typewriter paper, written on both sides. Contents,—'Extract of Sunday's Sermon,' 'Local News,' weather forecast and a space for advertising which lapsed into desuetude before many weeks had passed." It sold out quickly and more issues had to be typed.[23]

The young editors sold subscriptions to the publication, the few typed pages of which could hardly pass for either a newspaper or a magazine at the time. To speed production, carbon copies were used to produce two or three issues at a time. The papers were distributed at church on Sunday. The distribution system caused some problems, as a notice in the October 8, 1914, *Megiddo*

News indicates: "We are obliged to ask all our readers to pay up subscriptions for 6 months or a year so we will be able to keep correct account. When handing out the paper at church it is impossible to remember every one who hands us 5 or 10 cents and we have not the time to write it down."

After seven issues had been produced, the typewriter gave out. Recognizing the usefulness of the publication, the community quickly came to its support and purchased first a small hand-operated press and then a larger job press. By 1915, the success of the *Megiddo News* led the mission to replace it with its official periodical, the *Megiddo Message,* the first issue of which appeared April 18, 1915. The leadership of the mission quickly recognized the value of a periodical as part of the mission's outreach program. In addition to news of the mission, the *Megiddo Message* began to carry word of the imminent coming of Christ and the need to prepare for it. By the early 1920s, the *Message* had become a mainstay of the ministry, and the elements to be included in each issue were fairly well established. Most issues began with an L. T. Nichols sermon and then a message or sermon from Reverend Hembree. Other features were a column of news of activities at the mission and its outreach activities in the immediate Rochester area and a column of news of evangelistic outreach in more distant places. Letters from subscribers were a major feature. There was usually a list of Bible verses for study and, one of the most popular features, answers to questions from readers. Since the *Message* served as a teaching tool for new adherents, who were offered free six-month subscriptions, some sermons and many questions from readers were repeated periodically. As the mission acquired increasingly sophisticated printing equipment, illustrations, photographs, and eventually color covers were added. Under the current editor, Ruth Sisson, who operates a graphic arts business, the format features attractive color photographs and sophisticated graphics.[24]

Initially, subscriptions were sold by the traveling missionaries and offered to interested persons through the mail. In 1927, the mission urged each subscriber to sell one additional subscription, and many sold more than one. The following year saw a large increase in subscriptions when the mission divided its members into three teams—patriotically designated the Red, White, and Blue teams—and sponsored a contest to see which team could sell the most subscriptions between Independence Day and Thanksgiving. The campaign netted more than 3,000 subscriptions, bringing the total number of subscribers to 4,411.[25] For several years thereafter, similar contests were held and large numbers of subscriptions were entered. However, the majority of these appear to have been free six-month trial subscriptions that the church offered all new subscribers, and it is unknown how many of these actually turned into long-time paid subscriptions. Over the years, the church has provided the magazine free to libraries, which, at least in some cases, made it available to their users. Letters from readers occasionally indicated that they had first seen the magazine at public libraries in such cities as Los Angeles, Denver, Dayton, Ohio,

Auburn, New York, and the Pacific island of Fiji.[26] Union lists of serials show a few libraries holding runs of the magazine.

The *Megiddo Message* currently has a circulation of about fifteen thousand and is published ten times a year in the church's modern computerized printing plant; however, its content has changed little over the years.[27] The magazine still contains articles on Megiddo beliefs and answers to questions from readers, which have been its mainstays. The articles, until recently unsigned, have often been edited versions of previously published pieces. The magazine has recently begun to include a greater number of original articles. Besides being informative, the articles probably contribute to the maintenance of orthodoxy in the Megiddo Church and among its adherents outside Rochester. Letters from readers continue to be a feature of the *Message,* although there are fewer of them published than there were in the past. Many subscribers have been, and are, regular contributors to the letters column. Ironically, the periodical that was begun in order to inform members of mission activities now rarely carries news of the church. In fact, were it not for occasional obituaries and annual invitations to readers to attend holiday celebrations, a reader might think that the *Megiddo Message* was the product of a publishing company rather than of an active community of believers.

Publication distribution grew rapidly after 1915 when the Megiddo Mission began to place advertisements offering free literature through the mail. Advertisements were placed in periodicals aimed at a rural audience, and respondents received the pamphlets advertised along with sample issues of the *Megiddo Message.* The mission initially distributed a series of pamphlets written by L. T. Nichols, along with a hymnal that became available in 1910. In 1926, two items were added to the arsenal, the pamphlet titled "The Great Apostasy" and a prophecy chart that traced the history of the world from Bible times to the return of Christ but was not specific as to the date of Christ's return.[28] The various publications of the church have been edited and changed as new insights make old versions obsolete or when there is a need to clarify the subject under discussion. New publications are added as needed. The Victorian prose that characterized L. T. Nichols's writing has gradually been replaced with modern language and more concise writing. Recent editions of the booklets have featured colorful and attractive covers in contrast to the plain covers of the past.

Brief tracts have been added to the literature, most in the 1990s. The majority of these deal with the beliefs that distinguish the Megiddo Church from other religious groups. The Megiddos are aware of current religious interests and have recently produced publications on timely topics, as indicated by a tract on angels, produced in 1995–96, that capitalizes on the interest in angels that arose during the last decade of the twentieth century.[29]

The Megiddos usually deal with questions from readers about current social problems in the pages of the *Message.* The responses usually state the church's position briefly and identify the issue as a sign of the sorry state of the world that precedes the coming of Christ. For example, in response to the question as to whether or not the Megiddo Church opposes abortion, an article in the *Megiddo Message* stated the following:

> In a world under proper management and a proper moral code, abortion would never be an issue . . . We can be sure that after Christ sets up His Kingdom there will be no abortion necessary or allowed. . . . But in our world today, where lust and sensuality run wild and animal instincts are not restrained, the situation is very different. . . . God did not intend that children be born to parents that transmit disease to their offspring because of their own licentious and lustful living. Nor did God intend that children be born to those who are not able or willing to care for them. Add to all this the problems caused by drug and alcohol addiction, and we have a situation where abortion may actually save suffering. It is not desirable, it is not right, it is not part of what God intended, but it is part of the corrupt system under man's direction.[30]

The church has tended to avoid drawing attention to its positions on current issues via separate publications, probably in order to prevent its being identified or confused with other groups that take more public stands on controversial issues. Exceptions occurred in the mid-1990s with the publication of tracts condemning gambling and homosexuality, neither of which relates its subject to the state of the world.[31]

On the surface, many Megiddo positions on current social issues would appear to make them compatible with other conservative Protestant bodies. However, since the Megiddos emphasize individual salvation, mediated through the beliefs of the Megiddo Church, and conservative Christian groups tend to have, in the name of a popular book and audiovisual series, a "focus on the family," with the church occupying a somewhat secondary role, other similarities are rendered irrelevant.[32]

Megiddo publications were initially distributed in the Rochester area by missionaries who went door to door. The *Megiddo News* and the early issues of the *Megiddo Message* include reports of missionaries traveling into the countryside in cars, dubbed "Auto No. 1" and "Auto No. 2," to sell publications. One of the men would drive, and the missionaries, mostly women, would sell the tracts. Two more cars were eventually added. In addition to the auto ministry, young men from the mission would set up camping stations in rural areas several miles from Rochester. They would use bicycles, "from which more than one landed in mud, sand and ditches," to visit homes in the area to sell tracts and pamphlets.[33] Sales were brisk and, consequently, it is somewhat surprising that there appears to have been little interest on the part of the purchasers in joining the mission.[34] Perhaps the impression of a closed, structured society given by local newspapers discouraged readers from attempting to join the mission.

The membership grew largely from people who lived at a distance and were not exposed to the Rochester area media.

Missionaries traveled by train to spread the message of the Megiddo Mission throughout the country. For example, in 1915 and 1916, missionaries traveled to Akron (Ohio), Meadville (Pennsylvania), Duluth, Minneapolis, Chicago, Richmond, Little Rock, Dallas, and Long Beach (California). On their mission trips to distant cities, missionaries would often ship their tracts and pamphlets separately. Occasionally, a member would drive to the site of the mission, taking the materials for distribution while others traveled by train. On a 1938 trip, three of the men from the mission took a train to Oregon, where members of the Bryant family, who had been members of the True Christadelphians, provided a car and driver for them. In many cities, the missionaries would rent rooms and canvass the city, the surrounding countryside, and neighboring towns. One missionary, Sister Wittman from Tacoma, Washington, set out by bus to a place about fifteen miles from Tacoma but found that it was "only a hamlet." Obtaining only one subscriber but not wishing to waste the trip, she walked home on the state highway, "finally covering the entire distance in two days, obtaining a total of fifteen subscribers."[35]

Once settled in a location, the missionaries not only canvassed in residential areas but also visited offices, shops, restaurants, and barber shops. It is probably difficult for the reader of the early twenty-first century to imagine that businessmen would stop work to hold religious dialogue with the missionaries, but this often occurred. For example, in September 1919, William Pickering, one of the mission's most active canvassers,

> entered the office of a business man to find he had no time to spare, but who promised if our Brother would return, he would be glad to hear what he had to say. A few days later the second visit was paid, and they had not talked long before another caller entered who at once became a willing listener . . . The proprietor of the establishment called in another young man, and for three hours the business of one concern in Scranton was practically suspended to hear proof that the setting up of God's Kingdom was future. . . . each of the three men purchased a set of literature, expressing their heartfelt appreciation for the light which had been imparted to them.

In another instance, a Brother Engle entered a barber shop in Fayetteville, North Carolina, and initiated a discussion with the proprietor and his sons that lasted from 9:20 A.M. to 1:30 P.M.[36]

In spite of this success among businessmen, the more prosperous members of society were often not among those most interested in the Megiddos' message. Missionary Eunice Ingham complained in 1928 that she was having success among the servants of millionaires in Palm Beach, Florida, who were "much more receptive to Bible truth than are their proud and unapproachable employers."[37]

During the Spanish influenza epidemic of 1918, as part of an attempt to stop the spread of the disease in public meetings, the City of Rochester ordered all churches to suspend services. The mission church did not hold services from early October until November 7. The mission was fortunate not to lose any members to the epidemic. Neither did the flu have a serious impact on the mission outreach, although a mission trip to the Southwest was interrupted when one of the missionaries was stricken with the flu while in Albuquerque, New Mexico. He was cared for by the family with whom he and a fellow missionary were staying, and after a brief period of recovery he continued on his way. The *Message* noted that "despite certain restrictions imposed on account of the prevalence of influenza," William Pickering was having "good success" in Louisville, Kentucky.[38]

The flu was particularly virulent among army personnel in Europe and in the United States. One member of the mission, who was serving in a clerical capacity in the U.S. Army in France contracted the flu and was hospitalized for forty-six days. He recovered and returned to the United States in March 1919.[39]

The devastating effect the flu had on military personnel at home was observed by missionary Sister French, who was stopping in Maryland on the way to Florida with her husband and young son. She wrote,

> Yesterday we started out early in the morning, business taking us to the station where they were unloading the dead soldiers as they brought them from the camp to be shipped away, and oh! I never saw such a terrible, horrible sight in all my life. The bodies were piled one box on top of another all along the platform and army truck after truck waiting in line to unload. Two mule teams on other large wagons and all kinds of rigs, with as many as they could pile on, getting them to the station to be sent on the train. As the trains pulled in the soldiers would load them on and soon after they pulled out the waiting trucks would unload and in a short time, there were as many as before. There were so many you could scarcely realize the boxes all contained human bodies. A gentleman who lives here told us that was what they had seen every day for a whole month. . . . The cemeteries are just as thick as they can be with rough boxes and open graves; people cannot get either hearses or undertakers. One family near where we are all died. . . . Everywhere we go it's just the same, and since we came home tonight all we see are hearses going and coming. You cannot imagine what it is like. If ever the grave yards yawned opened mouthed for the dead it is right now.

The *Message* editor took the opportunity presented by Sister French's letter to admonish readers: "The age when 'the inhabitant shall not say "I am sick"' is drawing near, when 'God shall wipe away all tears from their eyes; and there shall be no more death, neither sorrow, nor crying, neither shall there be any more pain.' Why not get ready?"[40]

While Nichols and his followers were always adamantly opposed to involvement with the government, this did not stop the Megiddos from canvassing
civil servants and government officials. In 1915, a group of missionaries visited
the New York State capitol in Albany, where they were befriended by the custo-
dian of the Senate. Through his influence, the missionaries were able to spend
a day at the capitol, selling books to employees. The most notable sale was a set
of books to Governor Whitman.[41]

In another outreach to public employees, in June 1916, a party went from
Rochester by car to a state-run home for epileptics, which occupied the buildings of a former Shaker colony at Sonyea, New York, about fifty miles south of
Rochester. There, having obtained a permit to visit the homes of the employees,
they sold 150 books. This was part of a pattern of outreach activities directed
toward institutions. For example, two missionaries working in New Mexico in
1918 made "several visits to large institutions." At one of these, a tuberculosis
sanitarium, the missionaries visited the head physician, who purchased their literature and granted permission for them to visit the cottages in which the
patients resided. After leaving the sanitarium, the missionaries visited an Indian
school, where they interviewed the principal and teachers and left literature.[42]

The missionaries were always on the alert for interested listeners and often
approached fellow travelers on trains and streetcars. Even vacationers were not
safe from being proselytized by the missionaries. Vacationing members of the
mission took supplies of Megiddo publications to distribute to tourists in hopes
that they would take them to places the missionaries did not visit. When Estella
Dryden of Portland, Oregon, went to Trout Lake and Mount Rainier, Washington, on vacation, she "searched among the camping parties for those who had
honest hearts" and sold them literature. In 1916, missionaries attended a
reunion of Confederate army veterans in Birmingham, Alabama, and sold literature to some of the thirty-seven thousand attendees and visitors.[43]

One of the most effective vacation-related mission experiences occurred
when a member of the mission went on a fishing trip to Sunset Cove, a resort on
Lake Nippissing in Northern Ontario, operated by the Byers family. One evening
as the men sat around exchanging fishing stories with the owner of the resort,
the discussion got around to religion and to whether the thief on the cross joined
Jesus in paradise. Mr. Byers attempted to refute the claim of the mission member
that, indeed, the thief had not. He was unable to do so and, consequently,
became interested in the mission. The missionary went home to Megiddo,
returning two weeks later with another brother. The Byers family began to study
Megiddo literature and correspond with the mission on a regular basis, with several of their letters appearing in the *Message* over the years. They made frequent
trips to Rochester during the next seventeen years, and all eleven members of the
family moved to Rochester as soon as World War II ended.[44]

The Byerses are typical of the many people who, after years of contact with
the mission, moved to Rochester to worship at "the Fountainhead." In 1940, a

group of believers from Portland, Oregon, moved to Rochester, and another small group from southeastern Iowa arrived in Rochester in the mid-1950s. One of the members of the Iowa group provides an excellent example of the way in which the Megiddos look after each other's needs. Clifford and Donna Ruth Mathias moved to Rochester from Selma, Iowa, and Clifford, who had farmed and worked for a meat packing firm in Iowa, went to work for the Six-in-One Ladder Company, the hardware business owned by members of the mission. When the store was closed in the early 1960s, Clifford went to work for Payne Electric, also operated by a member of the mission. Clifford Mathias is now in charge of maintenance for the church, and Donna Ruth Mathias is subscriptions manager for the *Megiddo Message*. The couple live in a house reserved for the maintenance supervisor on the grounds of the church property.[45]

The church rejects faith healing, believing that because "the power of the Holy Spirit has been withdrawn, we are totally dependent upon the skill of the physician and the laws of healing which God has built into our bodies." In spite of this belief, the ministry of the Megiddo Church has had remarkable success among the chronically ill. For example, the Johnson family, who had lived in Rochester, was forced to locate first to Denver and then to Phoenix for Mr. Johnson's health. Throughout their ordeal, their faith in the mission's message never wavered. In Phoenix, they hosted missionaries and helped them develop an active group that held regular meetings, often at the Johnsonses' home. A Mrs. M. C. Mars of Philadelphia, who suffered from rheumatism and had been unable to walk for nearly a quarter of a century before she began to receive mission publications in the mail, became a faithful adherent, as did an equally frail woman in a town south of Rochester. To the ill and frail, the church offers the hope of the imminent return of Elijah, who, according to church doctrine, will restore the faithful to good health.[46]

The weather was often a factor in determining both the location and the effectiveness of mission work. For example, the visit to the home for epileptics noted above was undertaken during a break in a spell of bad weather that had forced the missionaries to abandon a mission trip to a lake about thirty-five miles south of Rochester. The rural roads that carried missionaries into the countryside and to places within driving distance of Rochester were often especially treacherous from late fall to spring due to ice and snow, so missionaries often went to more temperate locations in the south and southwest, such as the Carolinas, Florida, and California. But even these trips sometimes fell victim to the weather, such as when William Pickering went to Lexington, Kentucky, on a planned four-week trip late in 1917. When he arrived in Lexington, he found that the temperature had dropped to a highly unusual nine degrees below zero and a heavy snowstorm made travel difficult, so he sought a "warmer climate" by moving south to Chattanooga, Tennessee. Another encounter with inclement weather occurred on a trip by car to Oklahoma in 1923, when missionaries reported their safe arrival in Hoyt, Oklahoma, "after having navigated—yes, we say navigated because the roads were more liquid than solid, and seemed . . . to be unfathomable—12 miles of mud." A few weeks later, they reported that they had left McAlester, Oklahoma, "to brave more mud." They got past Kiowa, still in Oklahoma, when they found themselves "in another mud pit" and needed assistance. Taking every possible opportunity to spread the Gospel, the missionaries spent a pleasant evening discussing the Bible with the man who pulled them out of the mud.[47]

Wherever and whenever the missionaries traveled, if at all possible, they attempted to be home for Abib, Independence Day, the founder's birthday, and Thanksgiving. The importance of being home for holidays was demonstrated in 1922 when the missionaries were having such success at Watkins Glen, New York, that they almost felt compelled to delay their scheduled return home for the founder's birthday. Instead, they left the boat on which they were living at Watkins Glen, returned to the mission for the celebration, and then returned by car to the boat and resumed their mission work.[48]

Members of the mission took every opportunity to promote the mission's ideas, even when they were working at their jobs. For Brother Kingsley of the Utica ecclesia

> being employed by the government . . . in the delivery of the mails, abundant opportunity . . . presented itself to impress on the 600 families, of which our Brother's route is comprised, one truth as assuredly God-given as any other in the Bible. The majority of these families extended the familiar greeting "A Merry Christmas and a Happy New Year," but despite the rush and increase of work not a single instance was allowed to pass unchallenged, but in a few brief words each one was told that God's time for Christmas and New Year commenced with the 1st of Abib and not Dec. 25th and Jan. 1st of Pagan time.

Mission member Emmanuel Boyer visited people who had corresponded with the mission in the course of his travels to promote his inventions, which included a tractor-drawn cabbage harvester and a device for restaurants to use to slice onions for French fried onion rings.[49]

Periodically, the *Megiddo Message* would include summaries of the season's work. A summary for 1919, which appeared in the December 7, 1919, issue gives some indication of the geographic extent of the mission work and the amount of material distributed:

> Three missionaries who worked in Arizona and New Mex. placed 6,744 Megiddo publications in that section. They visited Phoenix and vicinity, Las Vegas, Albuquerque and Raton [New Mexico]. Brother Pickering, during seven trips, worked in Columbia, S.C., South Bend and Elkhart, Ind., Scranton and Bradford, Pa., Grand Rapids, Mich., and Minneapolis, Minn., leaving in those places 8,511 Megiddo publications . . . missionaries in three trips left 22,019 copies of Megiddo literature in the cities, villages

and surrounding country adjacent to the Barge Canal and Lakes Oneida and Cayuga; places to the number of 104 were visited, covering approximately 1,200 miles of roads. . . . Other workers have placed Megiddo literature in Florida, Massachusetts, and New York State to the extent of 4,533 of which our aged Brother Loomis of Utica disposed of more than 1,000. Work accomplished by autos in the country adjacent to Rochester, 3,394 publications. As a result of . . . advertising, 1,425 books have been mailed to 45 States in the Union and also to Canada. Other mail orders reached the total of 1,007. Total for the year 51,522. 12,905 copies of the bi-weekly *Megiddo Message* were distributed to all parts of the United States, Canada, England, New Zealand, and Australia.

The Rochester newspapers were also not unmindful of the Megiddos' outreach and often noted their work. For example, the *Union and Advertiser* of January 12, 1916, reported on the return of mission members from a trip to Texas and Oklahoma.

Many of the people who purchased literature shared it with family, friends, and neighbors. A few developed active ministries of their own, including Wade Helmar of Dayton, Ohio, who had received some of the Megiddo publications on a visit to California in 1915. Helmar began a street preaching ministry and spoke to as many as six hundred people at a time. An adherent in Fort Saskatchewan, Alberta, started a small Sunday school with an attendance of about twenty children in a community without a church. A "Mrs. R. M." in Cape Girardeau, Missouri, mailed copies of the *Megiddo Message* to people whose names she selected at random from the local telephone directory.

Some adherents were very creative in the means they developed to spread the word from Megiddo. A woman reader of the *Message* from Prince Albert, Saskatchewan, having a number of issues of the *Megiddo Message* she no longer needed, wrapped them in paper on which she wrote "The Gospel as Jesus and the Apostles preached it. Help yourself," and she left them, with permission, in the lobby of the local post office. Canadian adherent John Gizen went one step further. He placed advertisements in local publications in Alberta and mailed out literature at his own expense to those who responded.[50] In 1915, Everett Gillings of Meyers Fall, Washington, acquired a typewriter and began typing copies of L. T. Nichols's sermons for distribution.

Several readers of the *Message* reported having first encountered the publication at hospitals, and one reader read the copy that was received at the office where he or she worked. Sometimes people discovered Megiddo literature by accident. A North Carolina resident subscribed to the *Message* after having a copy left in his post office box by mistake. Barbara C. Hornum found Megiddo literature in a wastebasket in 1950. She eventually moved to Rochester to join the community.[51]

One of the most successful ministries outside of Rochester was that of Estella S. Dryden. Dryden first encountered the True Christadelphians when her family attended the Oregon camp meeting, but she did not become committed to the church until 1906, when she was living in Portland. Over the next six decades, she maintained a small congregation in Portland, which drew as many as sixty people to its Abib services. In 1915, Brother and Sister Gillings from Meyers Falls, Washington, even relocated to Portland, "enabling them to have the companionship of the brethren already assembled there." Dryden was assisted by Adalaide Buckingham, a convert of the Oregon ministry who had relocated to Minneapolis, where she became reacquainted with the Brethren. Upon returning to Oregon, she joined Estella Dryden in her ministry. As early as 1915, the *Megiddo Message* reported that Dryden and Buckingham were canvassing for the mission. The *Message* also reported that a newspaper, the *Portland Evening Telegram,* printed one of Reverend Hembree's sermons, probably at the behest of Dryden. Over the years, Dryden and Buckingham traveled throughout the Northwest distributing tracts. Dryden also conducted funerals, taught Bible classes, and ran a religious counseling service. Reports of her work and news of her small ecclesia were often featured in the *Message.* Late in her life, she relocated to Rochester, where she lived with a niece until her death in 1966 at the age of ninety-two.[52]

In "A Letter to You," published by the Megiddo Mission in 1919, Maud Hembree reported on the success of the mission work: "For the first two years of our work in Rochester (1904–1905) no account was kept of our traveling expenses, but since then we have paid out for railroad fare for our workers and to send books to interested ones $22,889.00." She noted that this wes in spite of never having asked for a contribution and the fact that "we are a working class of people, and have not a rich man or woman in our band, only one of our members has an income of two thousand dollars a year."[53]

Members of the Megiddo Mission have generally been oriented toward middle-class lifestyles, and there are indications that this is the class from which members have continued to be drawn. James Bristah and Margaret Frerichs, in their study of the Megiddos in the mid-1940s, state, without noting a source, that "apparently the members have always been drawn from the lower middle class of people." They do not define "lower middle class." It is possible that the economic prosperity of the mission for which Nichols bore major responsibility may have held particular significance for members with middle-class values and goals. This would seem to be born out in an article in the October 2, 1948, issue of the *Message,* in which the unidentified author, possibly pastor and editor Percy Thatcher, wrote that Nichols's "first thought was for the welfare of his brethren, taking full responsibility of supplying them all with work, teaching them economy and helping them to get a start in life so they could better serve the Lord and enjoy their later years in comfort and not have to mingle with the world."[54]

The economic prosperity of its members formed a financial basis that supported the Mission's outreach program. In future years, it would allow the mission to take advantage of opportunities to use advances in transportation and technology to get its message to more people in more distant places.

Outreach was a major focus of the ministry of Maud Hembree. Under her direction, the mission continued to produce pamphlets and established the magazine that gave the mission a systematic means of keeping in contact with distant followers. Megiddo missionaries traveled widely, taking their message door to door, engaging in religious discussions, and selling publications. The contacts they made would form the basis for the growth of the mission in the years to come.

7

Back on the Water and Out on the Road

In addition to the work of individual missionaries, the mission supported the work of groups who not only distributed literature but also conducted religious services. In 1913, a group of young men organized themselves as the Megiddo Progressive Workers, or, as they were usually called, "The Progressives," in order to revive the group's boat ministry, albeit on a much smaller scale. In 1914, a yacht was purchased and named *Megiddo II*. It cruised western and central New York via the Erie Canal and adjacent waterways during the summer of 1915, stopping at various places where the evangelists tied the boat and pitched a tent in which they lived while they canvassed villages and the countryside on foot and by bicycle.

The missionaries were well received in their travels. Wherever they went, they "made a deep impression on the people of the neighborhood who treated them with every kindness and consideration." People brought them "dishes of baked beans, stewed apples, potatoes" and even cots and blankets. The boat made three trips and the missionaries distributed 11,090 "books." [1]

Megiddo II proved to be inadequate for the needs of the missionaries and a larger gasoline-powered boat, *Megiddo III,* was purchased in 1916. This boat provided comfortable living accommodations for six young men and made it unnecessary for them to carry a tent. The lower deck included sleeping berths, lockers, cupboards, a dining table, stove, and pump-operated sink. It even had curtains on the windows. The boat measured forty feet long by twelve feet wide, and its twenty-five-horsepower engine propelled it at a speed of nine miles per hour. It was launched with much ceremony, with members of the mission sitting in folding chairs on the shore while the Progressives presented a program of speeches and music from the upper deck. Reverend Hembree spoke some words of encouragement and the Progressives headed off, traveling the newly opened Barge Canal to Syracuse and then the Seneca River. They camped in Oswego and then went out onto Lake Ontario. *Megiddo III* spent one summer on the water before pressures caused by World War I and the young men's occupations caused the ministry to be abandoned for two years. During that time, the boat was placed in dry dock and "remodeled and enlarged to such an extent that it might almost be called a new boat."[2]

On July 11, 1919, the boat was launched a second time, again with great fanfare, from a park near mission headquarters. It traveled on the Barge Canal, making brief stops at several towns until it reached Utica, where the missionaries were hosted by the small community of followers who lived there. Over the next several years, the yacht visited ports on the canals, on the upper Hudson River and Lake Champlain, and on the Finger Lakes in central and western New York. The boat usually operated from June to September, returning to Rochester when the men needed fresh supplies of literature to distribute. Other workers used automobiles to travel to places where the boat was tied for long periods of time to support the ministry. In addition to feet and bicycles, the evangelists added motorcycles to the means used to cover areas away from the ports. As with the original boat ministry, occasionally the missionaries were offered the opportunity to speak in churches, which they enthusiastically accepted. They also received attention from the press.[3]

The yacht mission was very successful in converting many who would remain lifelong adherents to the doctrines of the Megiddo Mission, some of whom would eventually move to Rochester. However, by 1923, most of the areas that could be reached by the yacht had been covered, and at the end of the navigation season the decision was made to abandon the boat in favor of a gospel car.

In 1924, the mission purchased a two-and-one-half-ton truck chassis from the Brockway Motor Truck Corporation on which members of the Progressives, particularly Kenneth Flowerday and Percy J. Thatcher, built a new vehicle for the mission's ministry. Beginning with a ceremonial dedication at the 1924 Independence Day celebration, the "Megiddo Mission Gospel Car," as the lettering on its side proclaimed, traveled throughout New York, Ohio, and Pennsylvania, stopping at small towns, in rural areas, and even at an Indian reservation. Hardly a car—it resembled a motor home—the vehicle was twenty-four feet long, seven and a half feet wide, and ten and a half feet high (seven and a half feet high inside). It had a thirty-six horsepower motor. The interior was furnished in oak with ivory trim. It had electric lights, a stove, a sink, and a table, and it could sleep six.

When the gospel car arrived at a likely location, the missionaries circulated a four-page flyer that announced, among other things, that "The Megiddo Missionaries of Rochester, N.Y., are now in your vicinity to visit every home. . . . They are paid no salary nor solicit money or take collections at their meetings. . . . While in your vicinity we will be pleased to accept invitations to hold services Sunday morning, afternoon, or evening, at Mid-week meetings, Christian Endeavor, . . . Cottage meetings, Sunday School, or Bible Classes." The flyer then listed seven topics on which addresses were delivered, including "The Great Battle of Armageddon" and "The Modernists' and the Fundamentalists' Battle. Are Both Wrong?" It concluded with this admonition: "Do not confuse us with Mormonism, Adventism, or Russellism; we are in no way connected with them."[4]

Initially, the missionaries canvassed door to door and held services in churches of various denominations, including Baptist, Methodist, and Presbyterian, but since churches were not always available, the missionaries acquired a twenty-four-by-forty-five-foot tent with a seating capacity of 150; chairs were carried in a separate trailer.[5] The gospel car was often accompanied by other cars with additional missionaries and with band members and instruments so

The Megiddo Mission band in front of the Megiddo Mission gospel car, 1926. Courtesy Gannett Rochester Newspapers, Rochester, N.Y.

that the music characteristic of Megiddo Mission services could be provided. Sometimes the car would park at one location for several days or weeks and other workers would drive to the location to assist with services. The gospel car's staff changed throughout the summer as employed men in the community used their vacations to do mission work and then returned to Rochester to be replaced by other vacationers. The car was a great curiosity and the men gave tours of the vehicle. On a visit to Watertown, in northern New York State, more than two hundred of the curious, including many tourists, were shown through it.[6]

The gospel car mission to Warsaw, New York, southwest of Rochester, was typical.

[The missionaries] decided to move on to Warsaw, where they are now pleasantly located on the Masonic Temple grounds and where their welfare has been carefully looked after by a well known and influential resident . . . who has manifested great interest in their work.

Friday evening a telephone message was received . . . stating that two meetings had been arranged for Sunday, and the reserve musicians would be needed . . . ; so Sunday morning three auto loads of helpers, 15 in all, with the necessary instruments . . . , were on their way bright and early, arriving in Warsaw about 10 o'clock.

Our mission workers now divided up, attending three different churches where they explained the object of our work, and at the end of the services hand bills were distributed announcing the afternoon meetings.

After dinner, . . . the autos were brought into service to convey the workers to Oatka, about 5 miles from Warsaw, where a church had been secured for the service. . . . Upon arriving they found a number of autos parked outside and soon the church was filled to the number of about 130 persons . . . In the evening another service was held at S. Warsaw . . . where about 60 were present.

A service has been arranged for Wednesday evening in the Congregational Church. . . . The "reserves" all returned home Sunday night, expecting to return to Warsaw for the mid-week service. About 1000 books have been disposed of so far and 14 subscriptions to the *Message* have been secured by these willing workers.[7]

Among those attending services were often people who had become interested as a result of other trips by the gospel car and who traveled some distance to hear the message again.[8]

Occasionally, the missionaries would be invited to conduct services in private homes. This often led to fairly cramped quarters. Alice Cummings remembers a service held in a home in Corfu, New York. During the service, the person conducting it asked a question and called on Kenneth Flowerday to answer it. There was some delay while Flowerday made his way in from the sun porch, where the band had been forced to locate, to the living room, where the attendees were seated.[9]

After operating for seven years, the gospel car ministry was abandoned. Car trips by individual missionaries, often using their vacations from work, continued. In 1933, Kenneth Flowerday, who had been among the most enthusiastic of the gospel car evangelists, constructed a trailer that he pulled behind his car. The trailer provided living accommodations for himself and one other brother while they carried the message and distributed literature to other parts of New York State and to Pennsylvania, Virginia, West Virginia, and even Brownsville, Texas. Usually they arranged to visit *Message* subscribers, who often provided accommodations, or others who had ties to the mission. Beginning in 1946, the missionaries on these trips took copies of the *Message* and placed them in or on parked cars as they traveled.[10]

Some mission brothers worked for the U.S. Post Office and for Eastman Kodak Company, Rochester's largest employer, and for several companies that had plants on the west side of Rochester within an hour's walk of the mission complex, including Taylor Instrument Company, a manufacturer of thermometers, and General Railway Signal Company.

Mirroring the entrepreneurial spirit of L. T. Nichols, several members had their own businesses, many of which allowed them the flexibility necessary to spend considerable amounts of time in the mission field. Kenneth Flowerday worked as an interior decorator. Newton Payne operated an electrical contracting business from 1925 until his retirement in 1975. The business employed several men and women from the mission. Percy Thatcher and Byron Simmons had a fireplace business, and David and Estella Beck operated an insurance agency. Ralph and Clarence Barber operated a heating business and employed their sister Ethel.

The business most clearly identified with the mission in the minds of the public was the Six-in-One Ladder Company, which was located next to the church building. Because Abib decorations appeared in the company's windows each spring for many years and because a number of the conservatively dressed Megiddo women worked in the store, many people outside the mission thought the mission owned the business, contributing to the impression that the mission was a communal society. Actually, the company was founded in 1926 by William R. and Ruth E. Hughes. The Hugheses wanted to go into business but were at a loss as to what to do, until an older member of the mission suggested that they manufacture an extension ladder he had invented that could be positioned in six different ways. It is likely the older member was Henry E. Skeels, L. T. Nichols's brother-in-law, and that the ladder was an extension ladder that he had patented in 1892, or some variation thereof.

The Six-in-One Ladder Company was formed and quickly experienced considerable success. In 1949, when William R. Hughes died suddenly in an automobile accident, Ruth Hughes assumed direction of the company. By that time, the company had shifted its focus from extension ladders to storm windows, eventually becoming one of New York State's largest manufacturers of wooden storm windows and doors. By 1949, the Six-in-One Ladder Company employed about forty people, slightly less than one-half of whom were members of the mission. Ruth Hughes died tragically in 1963 when she either leaned or fell onto a second-floor railing that gave way, sending her plummeting to the concrete below. At that time, ownership of the company fell to the mission, which was named the major beneficiary in Ruth Hughes's will.[11]

When the Six-in-One Ladder Company ceased operation after Ruth Hughes's death, mission member Dorothy French continued a mailing service business that had been part of the company. Commercial Mailers operated until French sold it about 1968. Several members of the mission worked for her, including Ruth Sisson. Other employees of the ladder company worked for the person to whom the mission leased the company's building until they went to work for Digitech Publishing, a company formed by Ruth Sisson and Margaret Tremblay.

Some women worked outside the mission community. Because of their reputation for honesty, Megiddo women were in demand as domestic workers, but many found more lucrative employment. Several of the women worked as caregivers. After Edith Heywood moved to Rochester, she worked as a nurse at the Iola Sanitarium, a hospital for tuberculosis patients, until she became concerned that she would catch the disease. She then worked as a domestic for a well-to-do family who lived a few blocks from the mission. She also worked for the Six-in-One Ladder Company. Joyce Manktelow worked as personal secretary to the president of the Harris Seed Company, one of the many firms that contributed to Rochester being known as the "Flower City." [12]

Women also traveled away from Rochester as missionaries. Although the mission stopped sending out groups of deaconesses early in the Rochester ministry, on a few occasions, women left their jobs or household duties to go on mission trips. For example, on July 10, 1950, five of the sisters, equipped with "an abundant supply of literature," a tape recorder, and an accordion, left by car for Winnipeg, Manitoba. On their trip, they, stopped to visit interested *Message* readers in Michigan, Wisconsin, Minnesota, Ohio, and Manitoba and distributed about two thousand pieces of literature.[13]

Occasionally, Reverend Hembree and Ella Skeels also made missionary trips. For example, in 1921, they traveled to Philadelphia and to Reading, Pennsylvania. The stated purpose of the trip was to rescue some followers who had come under the influence of Jehovah's Witnesses, but they also visited the invalid Mrs. Mars, who was a frequent correspondent to the *Message*.[14]

Considering the number of miles covered by the missionaries, as many as 7,700 miles on a single trip, it is amazing that they had so few problems. There were the usual car problems, but several of the missionaries had mechanical skills and could make their own repairs. The trips also appear to have been free of serious accidents, except for a 1949 trip to the Midwest, Pacific Northwest, and California. Near Ukiah, California, the missionaries' car left the highway and plunged down a steep embankment. William R. Hughes, a veteran of the yacht and gospel car missions, was fatally injured, and the other two missionaries suffered minor injuries.[15]

In 1930, seeds were sown for a new missionary outreach involving the women of the church, who were often left at home while the Progressives and other men from the mission went out to sell literature. The ladies' orchestra formed a group called the Maranatha Society.[16] Initially, the group met between the early afternoon Sunday school period and the Sunday evening service because it was too far for some people to go home and return for the later service. The women presented short talks on Bible topics to each other, and soon they were joined by other women from the church. For the following two decades, articles based on the talks became a mainstay of the *Megiddo Message,* sometimes with several Maranatha papers appearing in a single issue.

In 1933, the Maranatha Society devised an outreach to women who were too far away to attend church. They began to send out a monthly letter that invited the recipients to respond. When readers replied, the sisters sent personal letters. The Maranatha letter became an important point of contact for many distant and often isolated women, such as "M." of Sundance, Wyoming, who had visited the mission. She later wrote the following:

> Maranatha! I will not only try to answer your Maranatha letter, but also your good letter received this noon. I just can't wait for the mail man these days, and usually begin to watch for him about 11:30. As his truck comes into view to the top of our Sunny Divide, the next quarter mile to our mail box is an anxious one. For I begin to wonder then, which of the Sisters of mine are paying me a visit this morning. And when I finally get the letter I always look at the signature. It is easy now to picture you as I read your words of comfort and help, and I feel very close to you. Do please keep up writing and I know that answering is helping me to keep my 'eyes on the prize.'[17]

Shortly after the formation of the Maranatha Society, the Progressives began similar activities, and Progressive papers appeared alongside the Maranatha papers in the *Message.* The Progressives also wrote a monthly letter; occasionally, responses to that letter appeared in the *Message,* but given the difference between the numbers of published responses to Maranatha and Progressive letters, it is apparent that women were much more likely to respond to the monthly mailings than men.

The respondents to the Maranatha and Progressive letters developed a sense of having a personal relationship with the people who wrote the letters. They often wrote missives that included questions that were printed in "Items from Our Mail Bag" without answers, suggesting that the questions were answered in personal letters. In 1986, the Maranatha and Progressive letters were combined into *Maranatha Musings,* which is printed on church bulletin forms and which continues to be an important point of contact between the church and its distant members and friends.[18]

Adhering to Megiddo doctrines in locations far from Rochester was often difficult and lonely. As one follower from Canastota, New York, wrote: "We are surely growing, spiritually speaking. Our friends and neighbors shun us and call us 'funny.' We are working hard now, very seriously, on our conduct, manner and speech. . . . Our son, is adjusting very nicely to this kind of life and we all are very proud of him. He said he would rather study Bible verses than play and by his conduct can say that he surely does." A reader from Wallkill, New York, wrote the following to the *Message:*

> Since your visit with our family many changes are taking place. . . P——— and I are not going to the club sponsored by the F——— B——— Church in our school.
>
> I have learned twelve verses and they are getting easier and easier to learn. Every morning we recite the verses we learned the day before.
>
> I like school even if it is hard to do what is right when everyone else is doing something else. One thing that is assuring is that after we have learned to do right, we will be worthy to live in the Kingdom of God on earth.

A former member of the Megiddo Mission whose family eventually moved to Rochester remembers that she was "sneered at" by her schoolmates because of her conservative dress. Her mother had to accompany the children in her family home from school to keep them from being pelted with stones. A *Message* reader from Baton Rouge, Louisiana, complained in the April 1980 issue of the *Message* that when he discussed religion and Christianity with people on the Louisiana State University campus "they thought I was really 'cracked' in the brain."

Richard Kucharski, who later moved to Rochester with his family, wrote from Poland that "we depend upon what we receive from you, as we feel quite alone here in Poland. Your correspondence brings us nearer to the Megiddo Church." A *Message* reader from Erie, Tennessee, wrote that he considered it a "one in a million" chance that a man from Chicago who had come to work in the factory where he worked had read Megiddo literature and subscribed to the *Message.* The reader thought the man "seemed deeply religious and seemed to believe most if not all of the truth." [19]

Many of the people who have been visited by missionaries or who have become acquainted with the mission through its advertising ministry have visited for Sunday services, holidays, or for extended periods of time. The *Message* has often carried stories of visitors coming from distant places to spend time at the "fountainhead" or staying after a holiday for an extended visit. For example, in 1921, Brother Kingsley, a frequent visitor to the mission from the Utica ecclesia, spent his two-week vacation from his job with the U.S. Post Office at the mission for what might be called a retreat. In 1936, when missionaries visited the Goertzen family in northern Saskatchewan, they offered to take any of the family members who wanted to go back to Rochester with them. Eva Goertzen, a young woman in her early twenties, accepted the invitation, went to Rochester, and never returned to Saskatchewan.[20]

Some interested followers visited frequently, often prior to moving to Rochester to become regular participants in the mission. Alice Cummings recalls her family's biweekly drives to Rochester during the 1930s from their home just outside of Akron, New York, about fifty-four miles southwest of the city. The drive in their Model A Ford took about one and a half hours. When the weather was cold, there were piles of quilts and blankets in the backseat, which kept Alice and her sister Agnes warm. When the bedding failed to provide enough warmth, a kerosene heater, about three feet tall and eighteen inches in diameter, was placed in the middle of the floor in the backseat. The Cummingses moved to Rochester in 1944.[21]

The *Message* printed many letters from visitors reflecting on their time at Megiddo and expressing a desire to return. Typical of these is a letter from a mother and daughter from Iowa who visited for the Independence Day celebration in 1946: "We were both sorry we had to leave 'Dear Megiddo,' but our visit with you shall be a dear memory. We know it is the only place in all the world where we can obtain the water of life, clear as crystal, that will prepare us for the Kingdom, where God shall wipe away all tears from their eyes, and there shall be no more death, neither sorrow, nor crying, neither shall there be any more pain."[22]

The Megiddo Mission has not engaged in systematic overseas mission work. When questioned on this point in light of the so-called Great Commission, the biblical mandate from Jesus to his apostles to evangelize the world, the Megiddos have often replied that that mandate applied only to the Apostles and that they fulfilled the commission according to Acts 8:4, when "they that were scattered abroad went everywhere preaching the word." L. T. Nichols believed missions were a waste of effort because, prior to the return of Jesus, the world was destined to "grow worse and worse." As he wrote, "It is but a wild fancy of the human brain that all the churches have got into their minds, sending out missionaries off to India, and all other heathen countries, with the expectation of converting the world." Nichols also thought the residents of some foreign places might lack the ability to understand and receive his message. In a sermon in which he was addressing the need to evangelize "every city in the North and South" in the United States, he noted that "we are not missionaries to the wilds of Africa or India or to the Fiji Islands, but to a more intelligent people."[23] Currently, when asked why they do not engage in foreign missions, the Megiddos say that they can only do so much and there is so much crime, vice, immorality, and wickedness in America, they feel there is sufficient work to be done to prepare their own nation for the coming return of Christ without entering a foreign field.

The best established overseas ministry was a small group of believers in Swansea, Wales. The origins of the Swansea community rest in the visit Nichols and his wife made in 1891 to England, where he lectured and found several willing listeners. Since Swansea is a seaside city, it is possible, even likely, that the initial Swansea followers were the people who, according to *An Honest Man,* had been swayed by Nichols's success in a debate with Robert Roberts and had been baptized by Nichols in the sea. The Haywards, a couple with one child, had become so interested that they traveled to the United States in 1900 to visit the Brethren, staying for two years before returning to Swansea. After Mr. Hayward's death in 1909, his wife and daughter took up permanent residence at the mission home in Rochester. Others continued the ministry in Swansea, holding outdoor meetings, distributing Megiddo literature, and maintaining an active correspondence with the mission.[24]

The emphasis on domestic missions did not prevent individuals from proselytizing abroad. In 1920, Sister Bertha B. Johnson traveled to England with 300 Megiddo publications and two hymnals, a supply that proved inadequate, as she had to send for 258 more publications.[25] In 1958, a *Megiddo Message* reader from Morrisville in central New York traveled to his native Holland with a supply of Megiddo literature. He reported that he had given the captain of the ship he was on a Megiddo leaflet and "always had some pamphlets in [his] coat pocket and left one here and there." He translated the tract "Christ the Hope of the World" into Dutch "so some of the Hollanders could read it." In Holland, he went from village to village and used a series of Bible lessons that the mission published to point out edifying Bible verses that people could read and study for themselves.[26]

In 1955, two men from the mission made a missionary trip to the British Isles. "They left many samples of literature, visited many homes . . . and encouraged as many of our readers as they were able to contact." Apparently, they also proselytized en route, as a few months after their journey, the *Megiddo Message* published a letter from a "Capt. W. R. D.," who asked for four issues of the *Message* because "I was greatly impressed with your [leaflet] 'Divine Radar' which was given to me on the *SS. Queen Elizabeth* by one of your missionaries. . . . While at sea, I have time on my hands, and reading the words of Truth in your booklet gave me inspiration."[27]

About 1920, Alexander Ploughwright, a British convert of L. T. Nichols who had moved to Rochester in 1913, devised an advertising campaign, known as the "Elijah campaign," that would make the name of the Megiddo Mission familiar to people throughout the United States and Canada. The mission placed advertisements in publications, primarily in the Midwest, offering a free book on the coming of the prophet Elijah as a forerunner to the return of Christ. According to the *Megiddo Message,* the magazines were selected to target "the salt of the earth, the rural communities" because "when Jesus called his disciples he chose them from among the humblest toilers of his day, the fisherman." The *Message* article went on to bemoan the futility of trying to reach businessmen: "We have tried to reach the well-to-do business men, but the proverb, 'There is no friendship in business,' should have been 'There is no religion in business,'—no insinuations, there are exceptions to every rule,—but two wrongs do not make a right; first the modern business man thinks he has no time for religion on week days, and secondly he can make up the deficit on Sunday."[28]

The Elijah campaign advertisements quickly piqued the interest of the public. The campaign was an immediate success, and it became one of the mission's most effective and enduring means of missionary outreach. By 1925, an average of between five and six hundred requests for free literature were being answered weekly.[29]

The Elijah campaign was gradually expanded to reach other than rural people. Advertisements appeared in magazines aimed at many segments of the American population, particularly publications with readerships that would probably respond to a rational approach to religion. Among these publications were *Saturday Review,* a popular literary magazine, and the more counterculture *Prevention,* a magazine focused on natural healing.

Advertising was another way in which the church reached a foreign audience. Advertisements were placed not only in American magazines but also in magazines in other English-speaking countries, including England, Australia, and New Zealand. As a result of these advertisements, the message reached people throughout the English-speaking world, especially those in the former British colonies.

8

The Known Bible and Its Defense

Like their Restorationist forebears, the Megiddos reflect a trend in nineteenth-century Protestantism to reject creeds and depend on the Bible as the sole authority for tenets of faith. However, Restorationists did not have one single view of the Bible. For example, the Disciples of Christ placed their trust most firmly in the New Testament, downplaying but not totally rejecting the Old Testament. The Christadelphians treated the Old and New Testaments as having equal authority, probably due to John Thomas's reliance on Old Testament Scripture for his eschatology.[1] The Megiddos reject the ceremonial law of the Old Testament, but they accept the Old Testament as a historical record and as a critical element in defining their eschatology while focusing primarily on the New Testament for direction for their lives.

The Megiddos look to the writings of their founder for guidance on biblical interpretation, and in this they are not alone. For example, Charles Lippy notes that for the Christadelphians, the writings of John Thomas stand as a second "primary source," and Bryan Wilson confirms that at least some Christadelphians "believe that they have achieved a final and absolute understanding [of Scripture] through the exegesis offered by Dr. Thomas." But while the Megiddos often cite L. T. Nichols's interpretations of Scripture, they are not totally dependent on them for their beliefs. As they have published new editions of the booklets Nichols wrote, many changes in interpretation and emphasis have occurred.[2]

Beginning with Nichols, the reliability of the Bible has been critical for members of the Megiddo Church, who believe that "since God spoke to John on the Isle of Patmos, no one has ever heard a single item from heaven, whether by wireless telegraphy or other means." The Megiddos also reject conscience as a guide, and they believe that the Holy Spirit, which operated in the Apostolic Age and will be renewed when Elijah and Christ return, does not operate now. Consequently, to the Megiddos, the Bible is the sole basis on which they can determine the will of God and the requirements for salvation.[3]

To the Megiddos, the Bible is inerrant, but only in its original autographs, or "the original originals." "God did not promise to keep copyists from copying inaccurately, or to prevent printing presses from duplicating errors, or to keep translators from choosing the wrong word when translating."[4] Many apparent inconsistencies and errors in Scripture are attributed to faulty translation, ministers with inadequate knowledge of the Bible, or

> private translation [when] instead of letting the Bible interpret itself, men begin to read into it false teachings and doctrines that are extant in the world. [Or] . . . they approach the Bible, not with an open mind, but with "an axe to grind"—a theory to confirm or a system of theology to uphold. By isolating texts from their connection and telling what they think the meaning to be, they sometimes succeed in wrestling the Scriptures to an apparent confirmation of a creed which can be traced back to a pagan source.[5]

Many errors are thought to result from attempts to interpret symbolic passages literally.

L. T. Nichols, who taught himself to read Hebrew and Greek, believed that "with the help of the original Hebrew and Greek, every vital error can be fairly taken away." As he stated, "while translators have made many mistakes, the blessed volume [the Bible], as delivered in the language in which God caused it to be written, is free from every error." He dealt with the problems of translation error in his tract "What Must We Do to Be Saved?" in which he told the story of a discussion he had regarding how many windows there were in Noah's ark. His opponent stated that in light of the fact that it takes 420 cubic inches of air per minute for a human being to breathe, and the ark, containing eight people and a large number of animals, had, according to Scripture, only one window, there must be an inaccuracy in the story. To resolve the controversy, Nichols consulted his Hebrew Bible and his lexicon and determined that the passage in Gen. 6:16 had been mistranslated. The word translated as "window" should have been translated as "windows."[6] In his continuing criticism of the professional clergy, Nichols blamed them for "not hav[ing] given you this light which causes the Bible to come forth victorious and infidelity fairly put to flight." He further accused ministers of "hav[ing] studied to please their hearers, instead of studying to know the word of God."[7]

In order to determine which passages may be interpreted literally and which symbolically, in true Restorationist fashion, reason is applied to Scripture. If something appears reasonable, it probably may be interpreted literally; if it is unreasonable, it should be interpreted symbolically. For example, the story of Noah's ark is interpreted literally because the description of the ark and its specific dimensions as given in Genesis 6 seems to favor a literal ark. Noah as a "preacher of righteousness" was an individual man. The ark was to be constructed of gopher wood, a literal substance. The flood water was literal; it resulted in the drowning of people in the portion of the world that it engulfed. On the other hand, the creation story in the first three chapters of Genesis is interpreted symbolically because several elements of the story defy reasonable explanation: a tree of knowledge; a talking serpent; Cain going into another land and finding a wife when his parents were the first people created on earth.[8]

In line with the Restorationist tradition, the Megiddos essentially agree with Thomas Campbell, father of Alexander Campbell, who coined the phrase "Where the Bible speaks, we speak; where the Bible is silent, we are silent." They do not believe that the Bible specifically addresses every issue that may arise in one's life. However, they do believe that there are biblical principles that govern all aspects of life even if they are not directly addressed in Scripture.

In 1932, Maud Hembree began a book designed to explain the Bible and answer all objections to it. *The Known Bible and Its Defense,* largely derived from Reverend Hembree's sermons, many of which had already appeared in the *Megiddo Message,* was completed in 1934. It was 816 pages in length and was published in two volumes. Among the subjects covered in a random order were the nature of God, the doctrine of original sin, miracles, the Jewish national homeland, women's roles in the church, the kingdom of God, death, the Atonement, the humanity of Jesus, and the true date of Christ's birth.

After the publication of *The Known Bible and Its Defense,* one goal of mission trips became placing sets of the book, free of charge, in libraries throughout the country. In subsequent years, mission reports in the *Megiddo Message* often indicated how many copies of the set the missionaries had placed. As of 1979, an estimated three thousand copies of the work had been placed in public, high school, and college libraries. Although few copies of it appear to be available in libraries today, the book was well received by at least one reader from Pinckneyville, Illinois, who wrote that coming into possession of it "is the only thing that has ever happened in my life worthy of mention."[9]

For several years the church has planned a new edition of *The Known Bible and Its Defense,* with its contents being printed as articles in the *Megiddo Message* before publication of the book. However, because the original book addresses many issues not currently of interest and thought in the church has changed on some issues that are addressed, the undertaking has proven to be beyond currently available resources and publication has been postponed indefinitely.

Although L. T. Nichols used several translations of the Bible, the Megiddos have shown a preference for the King James Version (KJV). However, as Rev. Kenneth Flowerday noted, they are "conscious of the fact that errors have occurred due to dependence on the King James Version, which contains some errors in translation." They also recognize that the KJV contains archaic language and obsolete words. Consequently, they also use other translations and paraphrases in which passages are more clearly translated for the contemporary reader. Among the translations and paraphrases they use, or have used in the past, are the Revised Standard Version, Moffatt, American Standard, Weymouth, Phillips, the Living Bible, New English Bible, the New Century Version, and the New International Version.[10] Surprisingly, in spite of his strong anti-Catholic stance, Nichols numbered the Catholic Douay Bible among those he used, at one point noting that Luke 13:22 "as it reads in the Douay Bible [is] in harmony with the Greek" and that the Douay has the correct division of verses for the following verse. The Megiddos also use the Jerusalem Bible, a modern Catholic translation.[11] When asked how the Megiddos determine which Bible translations are acceptable, Ruth Sisson replied, "it seems like we have to differentiate between two types of use: descriptive and authoritative. Some are paraphrases, and we use these only selectively. Among the translations, some are definitely superior to others in accuracy, but at some points we still consult the original definitions as every translator must use his/her judgment at times." [12]

L. T. Nichols was well aware that the original text of the Bible was not divided into verses, but this did not trouble him. He frequently cited combinations of individual verses and even portions of verses to prove his points. Memorization of individual verses or passages of Scripture was a characteristic of Megiddo education. Maud Hembree knew "literally hundreds" of passages of Scripture by heart. She often quoted Scripture from memory. She was also known for "fingering the pages of her Bible to find the passage she had almost, by then, finished quoting." [13] Even today, as part of the services held in the Megiddo church home, members take turns reciting, or occasionally reading, Bible verses.

The Megiddos' unusual interpretations of Scripture and the body of literature that has resulted have attracted a small but devoted body of believers. Over the years, the *Megiddo Message* has contained letters, news items, and obituaries that recount the stories of people converted by the mission's various outreach programs who maintained lifelong relationships with the Megiddo Mission. Membership grew slowly, but there was a spurt of growth immediately after World War II and until the mid-1950s, the membership of the mission was at least stable.[14]

The addition of new members occasionally made it necessary to remodel and enlarge the church. In preparation for the Abib services in 1922, the church building underwent a major remodeling partially to remove two small rooms next to the platform to make more space for the choir and band. Two windows were added, new art glass was put in existing windows for better lighting, and ventilation was improved. In September 1924, the exterior of the church was remodeled, a new roof was installed, and the church was painted. The steep, unsafe entrance steps were replaced with concrete steps enclosed in a "terraced wall of tapestry brick, surmounted by a granite cap and six electric lights on cast-stone columns."[15]

A two-story wing, twenty-four feet by sixteen feet, was added to the church in 1938 to provide classrooms and storage for musical instruments. In 1951, a new ceiling, wall panels, wood trim, and new carpeting were installed, and the sanctuary was completely refurnished.

About 1930, the mission purchased a church sound system marketed by Western Electric Company. It was designed to provide assistance to members who were hard of hearing, but over the years it evolved to meet the particular needs of the church. According to Newton Payne, who was active in the development of the sound system, "when Sister Hembree came to church on Sunday morning she never knew what to expect on the pulpit. I am afraid I was responsible for her developing a dislike of microphones."

A distributed sound system developed whereby "any member could have a loud speaker in their own room and could hear any service from either the assembly room or the church." Two men connected with the Stromberg-Carlson

The Megiddo Church building at the corner of Thurston Road and Sawyer Street, Rochester, New York. Courtesy Megiddo Church, Rochester, N.Y.

Company, a local manufacturer of high-quality sound equipment, and a local merchant arranged for an engineer from Stromberg-Carlson to work with the mission on Saturdays and evenings to help with the sound system. Newton Payne's company, Payne Electric, was able to do the wiring, and members did not have to pay for labor to have their homes wired.

The location of the church across the street from the mission home created a challenge for those who were doing the wiring. Initially an overhead cable containing circuits for a private telephone system and loudspeakers was run above the street. Several years later, a conduit was run underground. Unfortunately, the mission failed to register the conduit with the city, and around 1945 it was cut by contractors making improvements to Thurston Road who were unaware of its existence. The conduit was replaced, and this time the mission obtained a permit to do the work and registered its location with the City of Rochester. By 1953, there was "an exceptionally complete and elaborate system of sound and light controls, and the services [were] broadcast" by wire to Megiddo homes in the vicinity for the benefit of those unable to attend. For many years, programs of music and readings were broadcast to homes each year on Thanksgiving. The sound system is currently used to provide material for evening services in the church home assembly room. In the home and the church there are also headsets available for the hard of hearing. Electric chimes from the steeple announce services on Sunday.[16]

Sunday morning worship services were almost always held in the church building. An exception occurred in the summer of 1922, when services were briefly held in the mission home, due to the absence of Reverend Hembree, who had taken two weeks' vacation. The moving of the services suggests that there was some significance attached to the presence of the pastor and that either there were fewer in attendance when the pastor was not there or that services were viewed differently when she was absent.[17]

In 1924, death took two significant links to the mission's past. On May 20, Maggie Millican, the blind Oregon convert who had been Maud Hembree's companion for forty-two years, died at the age of seventy-six. Nine days later, Hattie Nichols, widow of the founder, died, barely a month after her eightieth birthday. After the death of her husband, Hattie Nichols had assumed responsibility for answering requests for Nichols's publications and was held in high esteem by the congregation.[18]

In 1925, in one of the few instances of the Megiddos' publicly addressing an issue of popular interest, Reverend Hembree—who was always looking for ways to promote the mission's stand on biblical interpretation—with her "assistant friend" Ella Skeels, attended the Scopes Trial in Dayton, Tennessee, for ten days. The two women decided to take the trip on short notice. They took a train to get to Dayton as quickly as possible and were met in Dayton by Percy Thatcher and Kenneth Flowerday, who had arrived by motorcycle. In order that Hembree and Skeels, "who are no longer young," might have access to a car while in Dayton, Ruth and W. R. Hughes left Rochester in their car the same night the women left. They arrived in Dayton two days later.

Reverend Hembree had faint praise for the judge of the trial, "an intelligent, impartial judge" who, "if he had only understood the true teachings of the Bible . . . and had been able to grasp the folly of worldly evolution . . . would have made a fine judge." She commented "forcibly on the pitiful lack of evidence and woefully imperfect knowledge of the Bible displayed by counsel on both sides," and she was particularly critical of Clarence Darrow, who, she claimed, was "positively childish in his ignorance of the word of God." She had an opportunity to meet with a Mr. Hayes, one of the defense attorneys who was a former resident of Rochester. The meeting lasted for two hours, and Sister Skeels reported that "later Mr. Hayes delivered an address in the courtroom, in which he embodied the principal points covered in their . . . talk, giving Scripture evidence for the same." [19]

The subject of evolution and the Scopes Trial occupied the pages of the *Megiddo Message* for the issue preceding the trip to Dayton and for several issues after the ladies' return. Reverend Hembree castigated both attorneys Darrow and William Jennings Bryan as "two of a kind in their supreme ignorance of the Bible and their unwillingness to listen to reason and evidence." She then carefully presented the church's position on each issue raised at the trial. The issue of the *Message* that contained Reverend Hembree's article on evolution was subsequently sold by missionaries as a separate document, much like a tract.[20]

From the beginning of their existence, the Megiddos have diligently looked for the signs of the end times, the period when events occur that many believe are designated in the Bible as indications that the Second Coming of Christ, or in the case of the Megiddos, the coming of Elijah, is imminent. About 1905, L. T. Nichols identified signs of the times when he wrote, "It cannot be denied but what the inhabitants of our fair land are groaning under the heavy burden of poverty, weakness, sickness, disease and death, besides the misappropriation of billions of wealth brought about by misguided judgment, in others rascality, and right down meanness in many. Pride, brought about by lust, [is] running rampant in every direction in search of evil in which to satiate its unlawful desires." [21]

Reverend Hembree saw signs of the end times in terms of lawlessness, vice, and immorality. In 1922, she wrote an article for the *Megiddo Message* in which she identified several signs of the end times, including a rapid increase in crime in Rochester; the involvement of people in worldly amusements, especially a YWCA circus that featured, among other things, a "fortune-telling wizard"; and, echoing L. T. Nichols, the reading of "pernicious novels." She also noted that while President Harding was involved in peace negotiations, the nations were preparing for war. She returned to the theme of preparations for war in future writings, as in 1930, when she saw Bible prophecy being fulfilled in the peace negotiations and arms race leading to war in Europe.[22] In 1929, a column entitled "World Events in the Light of Bible Prophecy" began to appear on an irregular basis in the *Megiddo Message*. The author of the column, probably either Percy Thatcher or Clyde Branham, examined world events in order to divine signs of the fulfillment of biblical prophecies that predicted the near arrival of Elijah and the return of Christ. As the "World Events" column reported, "For a generation the nations have been crying peace, yet in fulfillment of Joel 3:9 they have been preparing mightily for war . . . Here we find two prophecies apparently opposed to each other being fulfilled at the same time before our very eyes, a sure proof of the inspiration and infallibility of the Bible." [23]

In 1938, on the eve of World War II, the *Message* reported, "Today we see the vast, seething world on the very brink of a dreadful cataclysm, which perils civilization itself . . . Beyond question the nations are mad. Destruction looms directly ahead, yet they rush blindly toward the precipice. And as these things come to pass, as we see prophecy after prophecy of the Scriptures fulfilled in swift succession, let us look up, and lift up our heads; for our redemption draweth nigh." [24]

In a 1943 article in the *Megiddo Message,* titled "Is the World Growing Better?" the author, Clyde Branham, noted, in words not unfamiliar in the first decade of the twenty-first century, that although there had been progress in areas such as provision for needs of the handicapped, the humane treatment of animals, medicine, surgery, public health and sanitation,

> the periodic and increasingly violent outbreaks of war, with its studied and deliberate cruelty, more than offset these gains in civilian life. . . . On the political front, there has been a steady disintegration of public virtue and public conscience. . . . Conveniences and luxuries are more widely distributed, but if we measure the results in terms of human happiness, contentment and security, we fear that this column shows a definite loss. . . . Personal morality has sunk to a new low under the pressure of several decades of godlessness and materialism, plus the demoralizing impact of war. The home—the foundation and supposed guardian of our social order—is not doing so well in molding the character of the rising generation. Disrespect for parental and school authority leads directly to disrespect for all law, as the constantly rising tide of crime and delinquency testifies. Racial prejudice and class friction are on the increase, even in the "land of the free." [25]

Branham went on to identify biblical passages that indicated that these characteristics of modern society were signs of the end times.

One result of the Megiddos' sense of the inevitability of the world's growing worse before the coming of Christ is that it makes them appear complacent in the face of the world's numerous problems. However, while they do not provide direct services to people outside the mission, they have a history of making contributions to social service organizations such as the Red Cross. Some members have even gone door-to-door collecting for charitable causes.

In the post–World War II era, although many premillennial groups focused on the potential nuclear holocaust as the defining event in the end times scenario, the Megiddos, while aware of the possibility of nuclear war, continued to see the signs of the end times as numerous, with the threat of nuclear war as only one of many. An article in the *Megiddo Message* in 1961 identified as signs of the end times that "men are proud, blasphemers, lovers of pleasure more than God, children are disobedient to parents, unthankful, unholy despisers of those that are good . . . [there] is worldwide preparation for war with atomics and missiles at the same time the peace cry increases." "These Things Shall Be," a 1983 publication of the Megiddo Church, identified impending overpopulation, famine, depletion of natural resources, and "a moral and spiritual dilemma [that] has overtaken the world" as signs of the imminent return of Elijah.[26]

Typical of the Megiddo view of world events is the church's response to the air attacks on the World Trade Center and the Pentagon in September of 2001. The editor of the *Megiddo Message,* stated that the events were not "a judgment from God," "a signal of the arrival of doomsday," or "an early step toward worldwide domination by terrorists or worldwide devastation." Instead, they were "a confirmation that the last days (the time before Jesus' return) will be a 'time of peril,'" "a warning that life is uncertain," and a "wake-up call: Get Ready!" even though "we do not know how near the end of the age is."[27]

To the Megiddos, signs of the end times are limited to events and problems for which humankind is responsible. Natural disasters are not seen as signs of the times, nor are accidents such as plane crashes. As Reverend Flowerday wrote, "as far as trying to relate physical phenomena, such as earthquakes, storms, pestilences, etc., with Bible prophecy, we do not believe Jesus applied these signs to our day. . . . Such phenomena have always occurred."[28]

Somewhat surprisingly, the Great Depression of the 1930s received minimal attention as a possible sign of the imminent return of Christ. This may have been because the depression had a limited effect on the mission and its members. Mission members entered the depression debt-free, and most members owned their own homes and continued to receive income from their rental properties. A number of the men held jobs with the U.S. Post Office or worked in businesses or trades that were less sensitive to the depression than were jobs in manufacturing. It is also possible that mission members who owned businesses were more willing to forgo some of their profits in order to keep other members employed. In addition, a community garden and the high degree of cooperation among members of the mission always serve to mitigate the effects of economic hard times.[29]

There are two other issues on which the Megiddos differ from many other apocalyptic groups—the Antichrist and the number 666. In post–World War II popular eschatology, there have been many attempts to identify a specific person as the Antichrist, an evil power, usually identified as a person—mentioned in the New Testament books of 1 and 2 John but interpreted through passages in Daniel and Revelation—who will enjoy a brief reign over the world before being defeated by the army of Christ at Armageddon. Readers of Megiddo literature have often asked the Megiddos about their view of the Antichrist. Their response, which interprets the passages in 1 and 2 John in a way that is more compatible with mainline Protestantism, has been that they "do not see any reason to attempt to identify a specific person as the Antichrist mentioned by the Apostle John." Instead, they see as the Antichrist "an idea or person that denies or opposes Christ," and they take John's warning as a "call to remain steadfast against any opposition" to Christ.[30]

Many of the same people who seek to identify an Antichrist also attach eschatological significance to the number 666, which is mentioned in the book of Revelation. These people often devise elaborate formulas to make the number add up to the name of the Antichrist. The number 666 has also been associated with "the Mark of the Beast," mentioned in Revelation, which will be required by Satan before anyone will be allowed to transact business. Consequently, in some popular prophecy systems the number has been identified with credit cards, computers, and dates. The Megiddos no longer attach significance to the number 666, as L. T. Nichols did, but, as with the Antichrist, the number does elicit questions from readers of the *Message*. In response to one question, editor Ruth Sisson noted that the number only appears in one verse of Scripture (Rev. 13:18) and that "it would seem possible that it refers to the same system of darkness that controlled religious doctrine at the time. Very likely it has much more meaning than can easily be discovered." She further stated that "some . . . religious teachers and evangelists have applied an almost superstitious meaning to the number, and related it to the use of credit cards, UDC codes, bar codes, etc., as though these were indications of the power of darkness. All such conclusions are only human and have no Biblical basis."[31]

One sign of the end times that has frequently been addressed by the Megiddos is the appearance of false prophets in the form of many religious groups whose beliefs the Megiddos consider particularly contrary to the truth as it appears in Scripture. Over the years, the *Megiddo Message* has carried numerous references to the Christadelphians and to the doctrines on which they and the Megiddos are in disagreement. This was especially true in the early period, when the content of the *Message* was largely composed of the writings of L. T. Nichols and Maud Hembree, veterans of the True Christadelphian period of the mission, but it has persisted into the 1990s. The references have probably been mystifying to the *Message*'s largely rural and small-town readership who were unaware of the mission's prior affiliation and who may well have been unfamiliar with the Christadelphians, who have never been very numerous.[32]

It is difficult to determine the number of Christadelphians in the United States. Reference books do not have up-to-date statistics. Estimates from Internet sites range from 30,000 worldwide, with the majority in Great Britain, to 20,000 in the United States. An article in the April 2, 1958, *Rochester (N.Y.) Times-Union* indicated that there were thirty-five members of the Rochester ecclesia at that time. There was another small Christadelphian group in Rochester that relocated to Marion, New York, in the mid-1940s.

The dialogue between the two groups continues, with Christadelphians viewing the Megiddo Church as a heretical daughter denomination and the Megiddos viewing themselves as the bearers of the truth that Christadelphians refuse to acknowledge. Since the final split in 1891, the two groups have moved further and further apart. At present, while the groups share a common interest in the end times and expectation of the imminent return of Christ, they have little else in common, the dispensationalist Megiddos denying the efficacy of the sacraments, particularly water baptism, which are critical to the Restorationist Christadelphians' replication of the experience of the early church. If Bryan Wilson is correct in stating that the Christadelphians thrive on controversy, perhaps this is one of the last vestiges of their Christadelphian heritage that is evident in the Megiddos.

Among the other groups singled out for special attention have been Spiritualists, who were the subject of not only condemnatory sermons by L. T. Nichols but also of many articles in the *Megiddo Message;* Mormons, who L. T. Nichols called "a dark blot upon our civilization"; Christian Scientists; and Jehovah's Witnesses.[33]

Like many smaller sects, the Megiddos have been plagued by the tendency of the public to confuse them with other more familiar religious groups. As early as 1883, the True Christadelphians were apparently confused with Mormons, if not in the public imagination at least in the mind of the editor of the *Yamhill County Reporter,* who wrote that "so much of their history as you can get here" indicated that Nichols arrived from Salt Lake and that Nichols's tenets were "new in some respects but smacking strongly of Mormonism in their general features." The confusion is somewhat ironic given that the True Christadelphians were characterized by sexual abstinence and an avoidance of armed conflict, while the Mormons were most notorious at the time for their practice of polygamy and the internal violence that resulted in intervention by the U.S. Army in 1857. The editor obviously was either unwilling or unable to distinguish between the two groups whose views he found offensive. The main similarity between the True Christadelphians and the Mormons in 1883, which would have distinguished them to some degree from other Protestant groups, was an emphasis on salvation through individual merit and good works, but given the importance of good works to a broad spectrum of Christianity, from Roman Catholicism to the holiness movement, this would probably not have excited much attention in Oregon at the time.[34]

The public confusion of the Megiddos with Mormons may have been strengthened around the turn of the century, when L. T. Nichols began to preach and write on the existence of life on other planets. It would be easy for the public to confuse the Mormon belief in the plurality of worlds with that of the Megiddos, even though the Mormons believed that other planets and their inhabitants were very different from the earth and its inhabitants, while the

Megiddos believed that other planets were inhabited by humans who were at one or another of the stages of the process through which their worlds would become the site of an eternal kingdom of God.[35]

The Megiddos had particular problems with being confused with the Jehovah's Witnesses, probably largely due to similarities in beliefs and emphases that would be likely to lead a public that was not familiar with the fine points of the two groups' beliefs to find it difficult to distinguish between them.[36] Both groups have strong beliefs in the imminent return of Christ, special roles for 144,000 faithful believers, and an eternal kingdom on earth. Furthermore, the Megiddos and the much more numerous Jehovah's Witnesses also employed door-to-door canvassing as a primary means of introducing their beliefs to the public. Articles critical of Jehovah's Witnesses and pointing out differences between the two groups appear often in the *Megiddo Message*. Of particular note is a series that appeared in the issues of August 15, August 29, and September 12, 1953, in which Rev. Percy Thatcher gave a short history of Jehovah's Witnesses, briefly described some points on which the Megiddos and Jehovah's Witnesses agreed (such as the consistency and truth of Scripture and the existence of only one true faith), and outlined at length the errors of the Witnesses.

An article in the *Megiddo Message* in 1973 about "some of the unusual religions of our day" included both the Mormons and Jehovah's Witness as well as the African American cult figure Father Divine. It also featured two groups that became popular in the 1960s and 1970s—the Baha'i Faith and the Divine Light Mission of the boy prophet Maharaj Ji.[37]

Roman Catholicism continued to have particular significance for the Megiddos. Among the world events that were identified as being particularly portentous was the creation of the Vatican state in 1929. A "World Events" article in the *Message* identified the papacy as the beast "dreadful and terrible and strong exceedingly" of Daniel 7 and noted that L. T. Nichols had announced that "Babylon, the Great" of Revelation 17, which was the papacy, would increase in strength. The author states that "from now on we shall look for other signs of increasing strength," which will eventually result in Rome's leading an assault on the returned Christ as predicted in Rev. 17:13–14.

While the Megiddos identify signs of the end times, unlike many premillennial groups, they do not claim to know exactly what events must occur in order for Christ or Elijah to return. As Kenneth Flowerday stated in answer to a question from a reader of the *Megiddo Message,* "Many of [the signs shown by Jesus' foretelling the end of this system of things] have been fulfilled, but of course we do not know just to what extent they must be fulfilled." This contributes to the sense that Elijah's return could come at any moment.[38]

To bolster her historical arguments regarding the progress of the world, Maud Hembree continued to use Mosheim's *Ecclesiastical History.* She also used many other reference works that L. T. Nichols cited, including *Hastings' Encyclopedia of Religion and Ethics.* To these she added *A New Standard Bible Dictionary* and the *Abingdon Bible Commentary;* magazines such as *Christian*

Century, Pulpit, and *American Magazine;* and the *New York Times.* She also cited popular religious and social science books of the day, often to refute their authors. One of her most devoted followers, Fanella Porter, wrote, "When you came to Church on Sunday morning, it was not unusual to see the pulpit piled high with historical reference works, catechisms, and various books she was going to cite—a line here, a paragraph there—in her effort to express the truthfulness of the Word of God."[39]

Rev. Maud Hembree with her extensive library, circa 1933. Courtesy Megiddo Church, Rochester, N.Y.

In keeping with the view of public education that the Christian Brethren held, the members felt it was important to operate their own school as they had on the *Megiddo*. The school was never very large, seldom having more than a dozen students, and it was taught by a member of the mission.[40] Edith Thatcher, a Massachusetts native who moved to Rochester with her husband, Percy, was the school's teacher for more than thirty-five years, and she was principal for twenty years. According to one of her students, she was very nice but did not allow her students to get away with anything. The curriculum focused on the basic skills needed for life, generally reading, writing, and mathematics, good behavior, and, most important, knowledge of the Bible. When asked what was taught at the high school level, a former student recently said "not much." Most students looked forward to careers in practical jobs learned through apprenticeship or experience. A former member who had completed several years of public school before moving to Rochester said that she realized immediately that in attending the Megiddo school she was "just putting in time" without getting much of an education. She did, however, take the opportunity to learn household skills and business skills from some of the accomplished members of the mission.[41]

Reverend Hembree devoted considerable effort to recognizing the efforts of the students in the Megiddo school, and there were frequent children's programs. Each year at the end of the school year, around the first of June, exercises were held to give students the opportunity to demonstrate their learning and talents through dialogues, essays, songs, recitations, and musical selections. Special opportunities were provided for graduating students to exhibit what they had learned. Essays written by the students were often printed in the *Megiddo Message*. An essay titled "The School of Schools," which appeared in the June 12, 1920, *Message* gives an idea of the emphases of the school and the way the students were taught to feel about their education. In the essay, the unidentified student author criticized public and private schools for teaching "dancing, dress, tennis, golf playing and all other manner of sport and pleasure" and praised "this humble school of perhaps twelve or thirteen pupils" because there they did not have to "learn a lot of things that will be of no use to us" but instead were taught to "be of a humble and contrite spirit." Each school day began with a Bible verse and a song. Good behavior was considered important, and apparently Reverend Hembree was not above using bribery to achieve it. One student author reported that Sister Hembree went to the school every three months and gave prizes to the children who had been good.

In what was probably an attempt to speed children along the way to perfection and enhance their chances to perform enough good works to achieve salvation at as early an age as possible, the mission by the 1920s had implemented a system under which children reported each morning on their behavior of the day before. These reports were initially registered in a ledger and later recorded as gold stars or black marks on cards that were known as "deportment cards" or "conduct cards." Rev. Newton H. Payne remembers that the prospect of these daily reports made children approach morning exercises with some trepidation; a former member remembers that some children were punished as result of the marks on the cards. The practice was abandoned long ago. Few people who went through this variation on the practice of mutual correction have remained with the church. One can only speculate on its possible long-term negative impact on the retention of the mission's young people.[42]

The Megiddo school was closed in 1968 largely because its small student body made it impractical to make changes, such as the addition of a gymnasium, that would have been required to meet state standards. The mission has since negotiated with various private Christian schools that have been willing to educate their children while excusing them from participation in activities that would be contrary to the doctrines of the church. Until recently, a few children associated with the church have attended a Christian school in East Bloomfield, New York, about fifteen miles from Rochester, at the church's expense. Recently, the children's parents have decided to attempt home schooling.

L. T. Nichols was also opposed to higher education. He felt college did not prepare anyone to receive the truth and, in fact, left students "entirely spoiled for the reception of it."[43] Consequently, for most of their existence, the Megiddos have discouraged young people from seeking higher education, believing that the study of Scripture provides sufficient knowledge to meet their needs. However, because higher education is now necessary for many members to achieve levels of employment that members have traditionally occupied, young people are permitted to attend local colleges if they wish. In 1998, there were three members of the Megiddo Church enrolled in college—two at Roberts Wesleyan College, a Free Methodist institution located in the Rochester suburb of North Chili, and one at the Rochester Institute of Technology.

9

An Eroding Public Image

On November 22, 1935, Rev. Maud Hembree died at the age of eighty-two, having led her flock for more than twenty-three years. Her passing was commemorated with much ceremony. Her body lay in state at her home on the mission grounds from Friday until Monday, the open casket surrounded by flowers, an honor guard of young men and women taking turns standing at the head and foot of the coffin in one- and two-hour shifts. A procession of women dressed in white satin dresses with black sashes and men in their choir uniforms accompanied the casket, carried by six pall bearers, across the street to the church. Clyde Branham read one of Reverend Hembree's sermons as part of the farewell service, and Percy J. Thatcher gave the eulogy. At the conclusion of the service, the mourners, who had come from throughout western and central New York, as well as Pennsylvania, Vermont, and Ontario, Canada, filed solemnly by for one last look at their leader. Following a brief graveside service, Reverend Hembree was buried in the mission section of Mount Hope Cemetery, next to the grave of L. T. Nichols.[1]

In April 1935, a temporary fountain was erected on the lawn of the mission home and was illuminated with red, green, and yellow lights. A positive public response to the fountain led Reverend Hembree, "always alert for ways to advertise the wonderful truths of the Bible," to decide to erect a permanent fountain. Set in the middle of a rock garden, the fountain was flanked by large signs containing Bible verses. On the Independence Day following her death, the fountain was dedicated in memory of Reverend Hembree.[2]

An article in the *Megiddo Message* following Reverend Hembree's death praised her as "a woman of strong personality and profound spirituality, with a keen and judicial mind, and a great amount of practical business ability." Her accomplishments were listed as guiding the church debt-free through difficult financial times, the development of the printing plant and the *Megiddo Message,* the gospel boat and gospel car ministries, and the completion of *The Known Bible and Its Defense.*[3]

In the decades following her death, Maud Hembree was occasionally featured in the *Megiddo Message,* but her contributions to the mission were overshadowed by those of L. T. Nichols. In 1981, Ruth Sisson, fearing that the legacy of Reverend Hembree was becoming lost, edited a special issue of the *Message* devoted to Maud Hembree. This effort has led to a renewed interest in her life and work within the church. In the mid-1980s, a series of excerpts from her writings ran for several months in the *Message* under the title "And Still She Speaks." She is the most highly regarded person in the history of the

Fountain in front of the Megiddo Church Home, dedicated to the memory of Rev. Maud Hembree in 1936. Courtesy Megiddo Church, Rochester, N.Y.

church, next to L. T. Nichols, but in spite of the crucial roll she played in the growth of the mission, the adulation accorded her has never approached that of the founder.

Rev. Ella Skeels succeeded Maud Hembree as pastor of the mission. The younger sister of L. T. Nichols, she had been with the movement from its beginning. She was a charismatic person, but her frailty made her a less dynamic leader than Reverend Hembree. Reverend Skeels did not preach, delegating that responsibility to Percy J. Thatcher, but she did write poetry and gave "morning talks" at the morning prayer services. The talks "were 'homey' and [contained] lots of good advice." Ella Skeels had a keen mind and is remembered for her sensitivity in counseling. She focused her ministry on keeping the mission true to the teachings of her late brother.[4] Under her direction, the mission program continued much as it had under Reverend Hembree, with the publication of the magazine and tracts and with missionaries traveling the country to visit people interested in the mission's teachings. Reverend Skeels went on a few trips when her health permitted.

The two decades following World War I witnessed a series of scandals and legal actions involving religious groups in the United States that helped to fuel a general suspicion of sects outside the religious mainstream. This suspicion affected the public perception of new religious groups in general and particularly of groups perceived to be communal, such as the Megiddo Mission. This was to have an effect on the mission during the last years of Maud Hembree's ministry and the succeeding decade.

Among the most prominent figures to become a focus of negative public attention was George Baker, who called himself "Father Divine" and claimed to be God. Father Divine developed a biracial but mainly African American communitarian organization with centers throughout the country. He was arrested many times and charged with crimes against the public order and with being insane. He established his first community in Sayville, Long Island, New York, in 1919. In 1931, after years of controversy with his neighbors—who were concerned about the biracial nature of the community and the increasing amounts of property controlled by its members—Father Divine was arrested for maintaining a public nuisance. When he was finally convicted the following year, in words reminiscent of the accusations leveled against L. T. Nichols in Oregon and Iowa, he was declared by the sentencing judge to be a "menace to society" who "broke up families, tricked his congregation out of thousands of dollars, and destroyed the mental health of his followers."[5]

In 1937, in the most highly publicized scandal of Father Divine's ministry, one of his white lieutenants was arrested for violation of the Mann Act, which prohibited the transportation of a female across state lines for immoral purposes. William Randolph Hearst's *New York Evening Journal* purchased the story from the family of the young girl involved in the case and "exploited [it] to its fullest," bringing discredit to Father Divine's ministry. In the years following, the ministry was the subject of legal actions and intense government scrutiny.[6]

Unfortunately for the Megiddos, one of the groups that attracted the most public censure was one with which they were often confused in the public mind—the Jehovah's Witnesses. Ridiculed for their failed prophetic pronouncements, the Witnesses were also castigated by many who were offended by their aggressive door-to-door evangelism and eventually by their noisome public proselytizing. However, the issue that had the greatest effect on the public image of the Witnesses and on their treatment by the legal establishment was their refusal to salute the flag on the grounds that the practice was tantamount to according the flag an honor that should be reserved only for God. The issue came to public attention when the Minersville, Pennsylvania, public school system, with the blessing of the Pennsylvania state attorney general, expelled Witnesses Billy and Lillian Gobitis from school for refusing to salute the flag. The Gobitis family sued the school board. The case wound its way through the courts, eventually reaching the U.S. Supreme Court, which ruled in the school board's favor in 1940. The result was a "wave of persecution" of Jehovah's Witnesses, as some members of the public and even law enforcement officers interpreted the court's opinion as declaring the Witnesses to be virtually traitors in an era when the threat to European democracies posed by Nazi Germany was fueling a patriotic fervor in the American people. Witnesses were beaten, arrested, and expelled by vigilantes from communities where they were attempting to evangelize. Their meeting places were ransacked and burned.[7]

In this volatile religious atmosphere, several court cases involving the always law-abiding Megiddos brought the mission, which had always enjoyed a positive image in the Rochester area, much unwanted publicity. This publicity affected the way the mission was portrayed in the Rochester press and consequently how it was viewed by the people of Rochester.[8]

Three cases involving property left to the mission came to the attention of the Rochester press in the 1930s. According to notes in the mission's constitution and bylaws, "Before the Church was incorporated if anyone desired to leave money in their will for the work of the Church, it could only be done by willing it to an individual member."[9] This practice caused the mission to become involved in several court cases concerning property willed to members. In one case, the children Maud Hembree left behind in Oregon, with whom she had maintained some contact, attempted to claim her estate, valued at $85,178, a considerable sum for the time. The estate included "the Mission home, two dormitories, and two garages on Thurston Road; six houses with five garages in Flanders Street occupied by Mission members; a three-car garage in West Sawyer Place; and two summer cottages in Forestport, Oneida County." The children contended that Reverend Hembree had not been of sound mind and that the mission had unduly influenced her when she made out her will. The mission, which claimed that she owned all of the property in her capacity as pastor of the mission, prevailed and the case was dropped.[10]

In a second case, Isadora N. Bryant, widow of Z. A. Bryant, died leaving a will that named her nephew George H. Bryant, who was a member of the mission, as beneficiary. Her son, who lived in West Concord, Minnesota, sued for the estate, claiming that the conveyance of the property to the nephew was "in furtherance of an agreement between his cousin and Mrs. Ella Skeels, as head of the Megiddo Mission, to deprive the Minnesotan of his right to inherit property." The case was settled when the nephew agreed to pay Mrs. Bryant's son $4,500 in exchange for his relinquishing his claim to the several pieces of property mentioned in the will.[11]

It was a third property case that probably generated the most negative publicity for the mission. On December 24, 1938, longtime member Mary Olaevia Greene died, leaving $30,000 in real estate and $10,000 in personal property to "persons connected with the Megiddo Mission." The following month, under the headlines "Blind Cult Founder Seeks Estate Share" and "Megiddo Member Claims Wife's Holdings Illegally Deeded," the *Rochester (N.Y.) Evening News* printed a photograph of the obviously blind Ellis D. Greene, who had sued to recover the property his wife had deeded to the mission. In addition to presenting Greene's claim that the property was fraudulently conveyed to Percy Thatcher, Ella M. Skeels, Emma McDaniel, the Megiddo Mission, and others who, according to the suit, "entered into a conspiracy to defraud her and to convert her property unlawfully to their own use," the paper reported that the mission was attempting to evict Greene from an apartment on the mission grounds, part of which he claimed he "built with his own hands, and at his own expense." The court granted Greene limited administration of the estate, and there are no further actions on the case recorded in the files of the Monroe County, New York, surrogate's court. Greene left the mission; no one at the mission knows what became of him, although they believe that he continued to operate his janitorial supply business in Rochester. When he died in 1949, his obituary in the newspaper listed him as "formerly of 481 Thurston Road," the address of the mission home. He is buried next to his wife in the Megiddo section of Mt. Hope Cemetery, but there is no marker on his grave.[12]

To correct the problems concerning control of property deeded to the mission, the constitution and bylaws adopted in 1958 set up an investment board as a "temporary arrangement to allow those individuals who had received funds to manage those funds." By 1996, all the members of the investment board had died and the board of trustees became responsible for all of the property of the church, including all funds donated to it. Today the church has a finance committee, appointed by the board, that oversees assets and investments.[13]

In 1941, in another legal case, the mission sought tax exemption for the property in the entire mission complex, most of which was residential. Rochester corporate counsel Samuel D. DiPasquale contended that in order for the property to be tax exempt, the forty-two mission members who lived in the two houses and seven cottages on the property had to be employed exclusively in religious work. The attorney for the mission, Charles Bechtold, argued that the workers gave donations to the mission rather than paying rent, and, therefore, the property deserved to be tax exempt. Reverend Skeels and Percy

Thatcher testified on behalf of the mission, Thatcher claiming that two-thirds of the residents of the property devoted full time to mission work. After reviewing the occupations of the mission members, the court ruled against the mission. The original mission buildings were left untaxed.[14]

The most widely covered case in which the mission was involved concerned the custody of a child. When the gospel car stopped near Sherburne, Chenango County, New York, about 1930, Howard Sisson, a local produce broker, became interested in the teachings of the mission. He took his daughter Beverly to Rochester biweekly to attend services at the mission church. His wife, Blanche Bingham Sisson, who was an invalid, eventually objected to her daughter's attending mission activities, preferring the Presbyterian Sunday school Beverly attended when she was not at the mission. In 1934, Mrs. Sisson sued her husband for custody of Beverly, claiming that the father had alienated the child from her and that the child had become "too religious." The case caused an immediate sensation and became a focus of public attention. This was at least partly because it was unusual, if not unique, for one parent to bring a custody suit against the other parent when the two were still married to each other and living in the same household.[15]

On July 26, 1934, the *Norwich (N.Y.) Sun,* published in the county seat of Chenango County, reported that a children's court hearing had been held at the "spacious" Sisson home south of Sherburne. The plaintiff, Blanche Sisson, was a "helpless invalid" who had been bedridden for six years due to arthritis and was unable to travel to Norwich, New York, for a hearing. In her petition, Mrs. Sisson stated that she objected both to her daughter's continued absence from home to attend the Megiddo Mission and to Megiddo teachings. Blanche Sisson presented a record she had kept from January to July 1934 indicating that Beverly had been in Rochester for fifty of the two hundred days and that for nine days in July, Beverly had been staying in Rochester at the home of a Megiddo family, without her father being present. Mrs. Sisson stated the following:

> These trips are taken very much against my wishes. Once Mr. Sisson took Beverly to Rochester when she had a broken arm and couldn't even dress herself and other times she has been taken to the mission when she was suffering from the itch, when she had colds, and when she was in an over-nervous condition.
>
> I have pleaded with my husband to leave Beverly home where she can have the supervision of her mother . . . She is growing indifferent and acts with increasing nervousness.

Blanche Sisson presented Beverly as an unhappy child. She further stated that Beverly was forced to deceive her father in order to enjoy her childish pursuits. Mrs. Sisson reported seeing her daughter playing with two puzzles, "one a regular jig-saw puzzle and another which makes the saying, 'The Lord is my Shepherd.' If her father comes in . . . the regular puzzle goes under the rug."

She also reported that Beverly hid her dolls from her father. Beverly was also afraid to let her father see her listening to the radio.

Mrs. Sisson reported being awakened every morning between 4:45 and 6:00 A.M. by the sound of her husband giving her daughter instruction in the Megiddo faith. This was repeated for an hour after dinner, the result of which was, according to Blanche Sisson, that her daughter "hardly ever gets more than nine hours sleep when she should be getting 10 or 11." Mrs. Sisson claimed that she had asked to be present when Beverly received religious instruction, but her request had been denied.

The unusual clothing styles worn by the women of the mission were also an issue in the case. According to Blanche Sisson,

> When she is in Rochester, Beverly wears the particular clothes insisted upon by the Megiddos. They are long stockings, long sleeves, and long skirts. At home, she is not allowed to wear pajamas any more. Once, when Beverly reached for something . . . my husband measured her skirt to see how far above the knee it reached. He has said that the present day clothes have been the "cause of the crime wave."
>
> In order to satisfy my husband I ordered six dresses . . . with sleeves and to be at least 30 inches long, so as to cover the knees. When they arrived, we selected two, but her father would not let Beverly wear them. He said her elbow should be covered.
>
> I have had hems let down on dresses that already were long enough to be conspicuous. I have seen children laughing at Beverly and pointing fingers when she got out of the school bus in front of the house.

The dresses were presented as evidence, and images of Beverly in the two competing clothing styles appeared in the press.

Mrs. Sisson stated that her daughter told her she did not want to do good work in school because "not many wise will be chosen," and her standing in class had dropped from first to fifth. Mrs. Sisson then offered her daughter a swimsuit as a reward for getting good marks. As might have been expected, the swimsuit Mrs. Sisson purchased did not meet with her husband's approval, and she found it replaced with two other suits that were offered as evidence. One of the suits "was bright red and looked more like a suit of long underwear than anything else. It had long sleeves, long legs, and a high, button-up neck. Elastic was in the cuffs of both sleeves and legs." The other suit was similar but of a different color.

Following Mrs. Sisson's testimony, court was adjourned until afternoon, when it reconvened in Norwich to hear the testimony of "pretty" eight-year-old Beverly Sisson. When it was time for the session to begin, in a move that seems counterproductive for a group attempting to avoid being perceived as communitarian, "about 20 members of the Megiddo Mission . . . trouped soberly into the courtroom." "The Megiddo men were attired in dark suits and wore small black bow ties. The women wore long, high-neck dresses with long sleeves and, in the case of two elderly women, said to be eighty-four years old, wore little bonnets on their heads. The two older women, thought to be 'spiritual advisors' of the sect, wore long black skirts, one with a white satin blouse and the other entirely in black. The other women's gowns were of light blue, plain material." The Megiddos "were promptly banished . . . by Judge Brown . . . in order to give the attorneys an opportunity to question the child alone."

According to the *Norwich (N.Y.) Sun* reporter, during more than an hour of testimony, Beverly "proved to be an astounding witness for one of her years." She testified that the main reason that she liked to go to Rochester was because "her father liked to have her keep him company," but she also liked the parks and the animals in them and she liked to go to church because it was "fun." She also stated that she liked her clothes and did not like dresses that did not have sleeves. Contradicting her mother's testimony, she stated that although she had dolls, she found it "kind of babyish to play with dolls." She further stated that she would rather repeat Bible verses than play. In response to prompting from the judge, Beverly then recited the Twenty-third Psalm. A statement from a physician was introduced indicating that Beverly was "in normal physical and mental health and above average both physically and mentally."

Judge Brown stated that he wished the attorneys and parents could work out a plan agreed upon by all parties but that he did not suppose that was possible. He ordered that Beverly not be taken out of Chenango County and reserved decision in the case. Court was adjourned.[16]

Having been denied the opportunity to testify at the hearing in Norwich, the mission quickly prepared a statement of its position in the Sisson case and asked that it be published in the *Rochester (N.Y.) Democrat and Chronicle.* In the July 30, 1934, edition, the paper included the statement in an article on page 13 headlined "Megiddo Mission Denies Influence Bad for Child." The article's author elected to begin it with two of the more extreme statements from the Megiddos' defense: "Better dig up a bathing suit of the early nineties than send your daughter to a nudist's camp" and "war is terrible but immodesty saps the vitals of any nation." There followed the text of the lengthy statement "issued by Percy J. Thatcher, Megiddo secretary":

> The statement to the effect that our religion is in any wise detrimental to the health or happiness of any child or adult is absolutely false. The life and happiness of our people is a testimony to prove this. Neither has any member young or old ever been denied any lawful pleasure of which it becomes a Christian to partake.
>
> To be a Christian is to be like Christ our Master and Great Example. Then to be a Christian would be to be found doing what Christ would have done, to be saying what He would have us say, and be found going to places that He would have us go. To follow such a course brings joy, peace and happiness both now and in the age to come.

. . . The children of the Megiddo Mission enjoy useful presents: the boys have their little wheelbarrows, carts, shovels, rakes and hoes, drawing sets, building blocks, construction toys, also their pet rabbits and chickens. They are taken on fishing trips and hikes and have their lunch around camp fires and have many other good wholesome pleasures that the child may be able to face the stern realities of life.

The little girls enjoy music, sewing, boating and bathing and picnics. The animals at the zoo are studied to help the child in natural history. The claim made by Blanche Sisson that her girl has been denied playing with dolls is too ridiculous when thousands of girls at the age of eight years have passed beyond the "doll" age.

The statement went on to describe the Megiddo school, in which "no one who has attended is forced to learn beyond his capacity." Thatcher further claimed that "the Megiddo Mission has never taught that the wise would not stand among the best in God's kingdom but rather that a man must read, understand and keep the sayings of the Book of all books, if worthy to stand as the survival of the fittest."

Addressing a complaint by Blanche Sisson that Beverly had removed bacon from her mother's tray, stating that the Megiddos did not eat pork, Thatcher contended that "a false charge" had been made to the effect that members of the mission did not eat pork. "Many of our members," he wrote, "have eaten bacon recommended by many of the best doctors as wholesome food . . . The Megiddo Mission has no rule governing the diet or food of its members." Thatcher went on to state that Mr. and Mrs. Sisson had shared in the religious instruction of Beverly and that the child had attended church with both parents. Addressing the issue of clothing were the statements with which the article had begun and a phrase that echoed the statement that Mrs. Sisson had attributed to her husband regarding immodesty as the cause of "much of the crime wave sweeping the land."

In Chenango County, the case was reduced to acrimonious exchanges between the disputing parties, which appeared in the *Norwich (N.Y.) Sun.* In a lengthy letter to the *Sun,* printed under the sympathetic title "The Revelation of a Father's Heart," Howard Sisson, responding to his wife's contention that she had never found any good in the Megiddos' teachings, stated that he had written proof to the contrary. He further stated that "the coming of the Megiddo Mission and its teachings into my home were not the beginning of my family troubles. Peace and happiness never attended my footsteps for years before I came into contact with the people that my wife and others now bitterly assail." Sisson's statements that there had been problems in the marriage before he had become affiliated with the Megiddos suggest that the Megiddos may have been the unwitting focus of the wrath of Mrs. Sisson. Rather than being embroiled in a religious controversy, they had inadvertently become involved in a long-running family squabble.[17]

It probably did not escape the notice of readers of the Rochester *Democrat and Chronicle* that the way in which several of the statements were phrased, such as those on childhood amusements and the consumption of pork, confirmed Mrs. Sisson's charges. Furthermore, the thinly veiled attack on Mrs. Sisson, who had been portrayed in the press as a helpless invalid acting in the best interests of her child, probably did not endear the mission to the newspaper's readers. The mere fact that the mission was intervening in what would have appeared to many to be a family matter may also have offended some readers. Finally, the attempt to defend the mission emphasized the ways in which the mission' beliefs and practices were different from those of most people in the Rochester community and may well have increased the sense among many Rochesterians, including the press, that the members of the mission were most peculiar people.

In an attempt to defend Sisson and the Megiddo position, Ward Truesdell, who is mentioned in the *Norwich (N.Y.) Sun* of July 26, 1934, as one of the legal counsels to Howard Sisson, wrote a letter to the editor of the *Sun* which appeared in the "People's Forum" on July 31. In the letter, Truesdell stated, "The Megiddos are Christians and its [*sic*] teachings are wholly Christian." He then presented two letters to show that the Megiddos were respected in the Rochester community. The first letter was from the Federation of Churches of Rochester and Monroe County, and it stated that the federation held the Megiddos "in the highest respect." The second letter was from the Rochester Chamber of Commerce and claimed that "we have always regarded the Megiddo Mission as a splendid organization. We admire their thrift, independence, honesty and religious principles to the greatest degree." The writer of the letter noted that two members of the mission were members of the Chamber of Commerce. There is no information about the way in which the letters were solicited, when they were written, and whether or not the writers of the letters were aware of the purpose for which the letters were to be used, but since they appeared within days of the first hearing in the case, one can probably assume that they were solicited well in advance of the hearing.

Mr. Truesdell concluded by contending that freedom of religion was at the heart of the Sisson case. He proposed that the appearance of the Megiddos at the hearing indicated that "the case will be fought to its ultimate conclusion."

The day after Truesdell's letter appeared, the "People's Forum" featured a response to it by one Louis R. Starr, who apparently sent some Megiddo publications with his letter, asking that the newspaper print them so that readers could judge for themselves. He went on to describe some Megiddo beliefs in a way that was not designed to win them acceptance from the newspaper's readers. He wrote, "Megeddo [*sic*] . . . teaches that all Protestant churches and people are the daughters of the 'Harlot' and are damned. That the Megeddo are the only true church; the only spiritually minded people, the 144,000 of Revelation; that all will have to believe their doctrine and be educated as they are or be lost. That salvation is by faith in their interpretation of the word and by works." Starr concluded by suggesting that "Mr. Truesdell stick to his law books until such time as he becomes satisfied to take the 'Book of Books' and study it for edification." [18]

It was evident that the Sisson case had excited considerable interest in Chenango County when the *Sun* published a letter from Howard Sisson that occupied more than a full page in the August 18, 1934, edition of the newspaper. Starting on page 3, under the title "Reply to Mr. Starr's Criticism of Megiddo Teachings," Sisson noted that those who knew him would agree that he was not among those "who followed every sect that came in our midst proclaiming their doctrines." Sisson claimed that he had at first been skeptical of Megiddo teachings and had come to accept them only after careful study. He contended that with regard to his daughter, he had "endeavoured to teach her what I believe to be the truth."

Following the initial disclaimer, the letter went on to address various Megiddo doctrines that Mr. Starr had mentioned in his letter, including hell, the Atonement, the Trinity, original sin, and works righteousness. While this discussion appeared above Howard Sisson's name, much of the text of the article was quoted directly, or was at least paraphrased, from material that appeared in Maud Hembree's book *The Known Bible and Its Defense,* raising the likelihood that much of the letter was prepared by Maud Hembree or other members of the mission and was another attempt by the mission to defend itself to the public. [19]

In September 1934, Judge Brown dismissed the case on the grounds that the court had no jurisdiction in the matter. In rendering his decision, however, the judge did not let Howard Sisson or the Megiddos off the hook, stating, "It is apparent from the evidence that the father is subordinating the natural development of a normal life in this child in a blind and almost idolatrous devotion to the doctrines and teachings of the Megiddo cult." He further asserted that "because of the mother's condition . . . the father is in position to take unfair advantage and impose his will on the child's mind and she is growing up under restrictions, for he is obsessed with the false idea that the Megiddo religion and creed is the only religion that should be followed." [20]

Blanche Sisson appealed her case to the New York State Supreme Court, which Judge Eli W. Personius of Elmira decided had jurisdiction. The case was heard in December 1934, at which time Mrs. Sisson's testimony was again taken at her home. Members of the mission were allowed to testify at this stage of the case, and Maud Hembree and Percy Thatcher spoke for the mission. Reverend Hembree testified on the history of the mission and Thatcher described the school, presenting photographs.

When the supreme court ruled in favor of Blanche Sisson, the press response made it clear that, at least to the media, the case was not "Sisson versus Sisson," as it read on the court docket, but "Sisson versus the Megiddos." A

Binghamton paper headlined "Megiddo Loses Control of Girl by Court Order," while a Rochester paper countered with "Megiddo Leader Sure She Will Win Child Back." The case was appealed.

When the final decision was rendered by the court of appeals in May 1936, the Megiddos' beliefs and practices proved not to be an issue. The parents were awarded joint custody purely on the basis of the welfare of the child, the court finding that because the moral, mental, and physical conditions were not "so bad as seriously to affect the health or morals" of the child, the court could not "regulate by its processes the internal affairs of the home." The ruling further stated that "in the proceedings for custody of children, the courts have reiterated that their sole point of view is the welfare of the child. The parents of this child are obviously interested only in her welfare. When they realize that for the good of the child it is necessary for them to repress to some extent the natural desire of each to have the child educated solely according to his or her point of view, the remaining sources of difficulty will doubtless disappear."[21] Thus, after nearly two years of litigation, debate, and public posturing, the case was resolved in a manner generally favorable to Howard Sisson and the mission but based on issues that had nothing to do with Howard Sisson's religious views or those of the Megiddo Mission. Beverly Sisson moved to Rochester to join the Megiddo community in 1945. She left in 1959.

Mrs. Sisson died shortly after the case was resolved, and Howard Sisson and his daughter became active participants in the mission. Beginning in 1936, Sisson occasionally accompanied other members of the mission on trips to such distant places as Florida and the West Coast. He continued to be a successful and respected businessman. He remarried and in the 1960s relocated to Rochester with his second wife and his daughter from his second marriage, Ruth Sisson, now pastor of the Megiddo Church and executive editor of the *Megiddo Message*. Ruth Sisson writes fondly of her father. Education was particularly important to him, and he served on the local school board in the district in which Ruth was a pupil. In terms of religious education, Ruth states that her father was a "homeschooler" who "would not have trusted [schooling] to anyone else." He "gave it regular time every evening, every Sunday afternoon and evening, and whenever we went anywhere in the car."[22]

Another legal case in which the mission became involved focused on the conscientious objector status of the men of the mission. When conscription was instituted at the beginning of World War II, responsibility for processing applications for status as a conscientious objector was given to local draft boards. Most draft boards accepted the applications of members of religious groups that had previously established the right of their men to conscientious objector status and assigned them appropriate classifications: 1-A-O, noncombatant status, under which the draftee would serve with the military but would not be required to bear arms, or 4E status, under which the draftee would serve in a Civilian Public Service camp performing service in the national interest that did not involve the military. The camps were operated by three of the historic peace churches—Mennonites, Society of Friends (Quakers), and Church of the Brethren. Many religious groups accepted 1-A-O status, most notably the Seventh-Day Adventists; others, including the Megiddos, refused to accept 1-A-O status, officially because it put them under military authority but also because, as the war progressed, it was clear that the military put pressure on noncombatants to take up arms and fight.[23]

Ella Skeels and Maud Hembree went to Washington, D.C. in 1918 and induced the War Department to grant conscientious objector status to the mission's members. The mission's position is as follows:

> During the period when God was actively involved in the affairs of His people, the children of Israel were required to wage war with some of their heathen neighbors. In these and such cases, war was just and the taking of life was not only allowed but commanded. . . . Again, when Christ returns . . . the only way He will be able to subdue the wicked nations will be to wage the Battle of Armageddon.
>
> War under divine guidance would be justified, and the taking of life would be honorable, not sinful. War under human authority is something else. Man without Holy Spirit power cannot read the mind of an individual; he cannot know whether another man is worthy to live or worthy to die. . . . We believe it is wrong to serve in an army under man's direction.[24]

Members of the church will "serve in work of national importance, but will not serve with the armed forces."

During World War I, most of the mission's young men worked on farms; during World War II, most remained on farms or in factories to work, while some performed alternate service. One member, Charles Wesley Daigh, who was classified I-A-O, noncombatant, refused to report for induction. When he was subsequently arrested in the spring of 1942, Percy Thatcher posted a $2,000 property bond on his behalf. The case dragged on for a year before the government eventually reclassified Daigh 4E and the matter was dropped. Percy Thatcher made several trips to Washington in connection with the case.[25]

The patriotism of conscientious objectors to military service tends to be questioned in wartime, particularly when the war is popular. Draft resisters in World War II did not experience the persecution that those with similar views often suffered during World War I. However, many people questioned the patriotism of conscientious objectors and many more did not understand the difference between those who would accept noncombatant service and those who would not. In the most notable case, acclaimed motion picture actor Lew Ayres applied for and was granted conscientious objector status, and, as a result, theaters canceled showings of his films and the press declared his film career over. The press coverage of the Daigh case was generally neutral, and while the case probably did not do severe damage to the public image of the Megiddos, it did call their much vaunted patriotism into question and contributed to their increasingly becoming objects of curiosity.[26]

The one factor beyond the control of the mission that has had the most profound effect on its public image was, and still is, the distinctive appearance of its female members. Women's clothing styles, which had been basically static for nearly a century, underwent a transformation during the period of Reverend Hembree's ministry. This transformation had a powerful impact on the way the women of Megiddo were viewed by the public.

Newspaper photograph of Megiddo Mission member Margaret Tremblay with mannequin at a Rochester Museum exhibit on "Rochester and Religion, 1817-1900," April 1966. Titled "Unchanging Attire," the caption noted that "the years have made little change in attire worn by members of the Megiddo Mission." Courtesy Gannett Rochester Newspapers, Rochester, N.Y.

Women's clothing styles had always been a particular concern to the mission, and there are suggestions in the church's literature that women have a special tendency to follow the dictates of fashion and to dress in an immodest and unchristian manner. In the minutes of the 1882 Oregon camp meeting, L. T. Nichols singled out women's fashionable attire for special condemnation, and this concern has surfaced in items in the *Megiddo Message* over the years. In 1956, for example, in answer to a question concerning how a family could overcome "financial worries and mounting debts," the author states, "Women's idea of style is an unnecessary drain on many a husband's purse. Follow the Bible commands to dress in 'modest apparel' which is 'not conformed to the world' (I Tim. 2:9; Rom. 12:2), and you will save expense, time, and headaches." Even Maud Hembree wrote, "Paul knew that women's besetting sins were and are pride and vanity. I do not mean every woman is thus beset, but the majority are. The Apostle had given the command: *'Be not conformed to this world'* (Rom. 12:1,2), but he knew that many would pay no heed to this command, that only a few would obey. Their desire to conform to the fashions of the worldly throng would cause many to forget the lesson of modesty." Hembree went on to tell of looking out the window on a "cold, bleak, wintry day" and "seeing men and women who were passing continually—the men warmly clad, their limbs protected from the cold, while most of the women, with dresses to their knees and limbs almost bare, were a living example of the vanity of their sex."[27]

With the rapid changes in clothing styles in the 1960s and, particularly with the advent of the miniskirt, women's fashions became a frequent subject of articles in the *Megiddo Message.* Pastor and *Message* editor Kenneth Flowerday wrote, "In these days when women undress boldly and clothing manufacturers promote mini-minis (or as termed in the Fiji Islands, micro-minis) in full-fashion advertisement and fabric so sheer as to expose the human form, the Biblical commands regarding modest apparel become ever more meaningful." Using the fall of the society of ancient Crete as an example of a civilization that was destroyed suddenly due to its low moral standards, characterized by the "elaborate hair-dos, fancy jewelry, and sheer fabric and tightly clinging garments" of its women, he admonished readers not to be lulled into complacency by God's apparent silence at the present time, but to heed the words of the prophet and adhere to the prescriptions of Scripture to "be not partakers of her [Babylon's] sins."[28]

The issue of women's dress resulted in two of the few instances in which the *Message* reprinted articles from other sources. An article produced by Faith Publishing House, the publishing arm of the Church of God (Guthrie, Oklahoma) was reprinted in the April 1968 issue under the heading "Woman's 'Undress,'" and an article from the conservative Christian evangelical magazine *Eternity* appeared in the August 1970 issue under the heading "The Eleventh Commandment—Thou Shalt Clothe Thyself." In response to the former article, a reader wrote that she planned to show the article to her granddaughter, who "intends to marry a future minister, but wears her skirts far to short," hoping that the article would "alert her to the danger."[29]

In spite of the numerous changes in women's fashion, the women of the mission continued to dress much as they had when the first Megiddos arrived in Rochester in 1904, and while the image of the grandmotherly Maud Hembree in her old-fashioned clothing was quite endearing to Rochesterians, the same clothing styles on younger Megiddo women served to separate them from the general public. To the women of Megiddo, modest dress was viewed as an expression of their obedience to the mandates of Scripture and their duty to the mission, which also contributed to the mission's witness to the world. However, to those outside the mission, their dress styles made the women of the mission seem not only odd but also unapproachable. As styles continued to change, the mission women's attire became increasingly strange to Rochesterians, especially to people born after World War I, and this contributed to the perception that the mission was a communal society and to the mission's becoming increasingly isolated from the rest of Rochester society. Consequently, they were isolated from many of the very people the Megiddos claimed to be attempting to evangelize.[30]

The conservative dress of the Megiddo women also surprised at least one reader of the *History of the Megiddo Mission.* He or she wrote to the mission, "I have never met any of you people and never heard of your religion before. I was so interested in the history of the Mission and the happy faces, but due to the dress, I thought the pictures were of earlier years." The reader then asked for clarification of the mission's views on dress.[31]

The unusual dress style of the mission women also contributed to the increasing tendency of Rochester newspapers to focus on mission peculiarities and not to take the mission seriously. While in the early 1930s Maud Hembree's sermons were occasionally featured in a newspaper column called "From Rochester Pulpits," after 1935, newspaper coverage was largely confined to stories about various legal matters in which the mission was involved, the Abib celebration, and, beginning in the 1940s, the boat ministry. These stories rarely failed to mention the women's attire.

Dress remains an important consideration to the Megiddos, and the most recent edition of the "Synopsis of the Principal Beliefs and Practices of the Megiddo Church" contains guidelines from Scripture on proper attire and lists ways in which the scriptural passages may be applied to dress. The applications include prohibitions against "abbreviated clothing," "tight form-fitting clothing" for both men and women; shorts; make-up; ornamental jewelry; "spiked-heel, open-toe, or open-heel shoes"; and any change in dress style "to conform with fashion." In addition, men should not wear shirts with more than one button unbuttoned and "one- or two-piece bathing suits are not to be worn in mixed company at any time." Women are admonished not to wear "slacks, pants, jeans, or overalls at any time," an exception being made when employed "in an industry where a skirt might pose a hazard and would be against company rules." Women are advised to "AVOID" such employment if possible.[32]

The court cases of the 1930s and 1940s, coupled with the rapid changes in American society, had a devastating effect on the public image of the Megiddo

Mission and permanently changed the way the press viewed the mission. From being a small but vital force in the Rochester religious community, the mission came to be seen as a curiosity—a group of people who dressed strangely, celebrated Christmas at an odd time, and were constantly experiencing legal difficulties caused by forces from both within and without.

Members of the mission were not unaware of the way they were viewed locally and were, perhaps, somewhat defensive about it. An article in the May 1, 1948, issue of the *Message* noted the following:

> A recent article in a Rochester newspaper, reviewing the history of the various "peculiar" sects which have arisen in Western New York, described the Megiddo Mission as a group of honest, quiet, hard-working people who attract little attention except at this season of the year when they celebrate Christmas and New Year. In the past forty years this celebration has come to be something of an institution in our city, respected by many, regarded by others, no doubt, as a harmless aberration.

The author of the *Message* article concluded that while some people took a "perverse delight in being different, out of step, eccentric," this was not the case with the Megiddos. On the contrary, their goal was to encourage others to keep "God's time" with them because God's people were "a peculiar people, not from choice but from the force of circumstances and surroundings in which they find themselves. The 'peculiarity' depends upon the angle from which we look at it."[33]

During the 1940s, articles about the mission's activities, particularly missionary trips, and some obituaries began to appear in the *Community News,* a small newspaper that on the journalistic continuum would probably fall somewhere between a weekly newspaper and the modern so-called shopper. Information for the stories that appeared in the *Community News,* or even the stories themselves, were usually provided by the subjects, and it is probable that the mission supplied information or articles to the paper in order to improve its public image in the wake of the negative publicity. The articles concerned such mission activities as missionary trips and donations to the Red Cross.[34]

By 1942, Rev. Ella Skeels was becoming increasingly frail and required assistance to attend mission activities. By 1944, she had begun to delegate her responsibilities to others. She relinquished her Bible school teaching duties and Percy J. Thatcher assumed her pastoral responsibilities. Ella Skeels died November 12, 1945, and on November 21, Percy Thatcher was elected to succeed her as president of the mission and editor and publisher of the *Message.*[35]

Thatcher was born in Williamsburg, Massachusetts, in 1880. A toolmaker by trade, he relocated to Rochester in response to an advertisement for workers at General Railway Signal Company, a manufacturing firm located a few blocks from the mission. At work, he became acquainted with a member of the mission and joined the mission in time to be present for the first public celebration of True Christmas in 1906. In 1908, he was appointed teacher of the Young

Men's Bible class by Reverend Nichols, a position he held until he was named assistant pastor in 1935 and assumed responsibility for the Adult Bible class. He continued to teach the Bible class after he became pastor.[36]

Under Thatcher's leadership, a ministry to children was established. Headed by mission pioneer Ruth E. Hughes, the program produced three Bible story books, *Daniel, The Story of Joseph,* and *Samuel,* each more colorful than the one before; Bible coloring books; a periodical, *Children's Doings;* and "interest-catching, attractive, colorful" Sunday school leaflets "for all, from tots to teen-agers."[37]

The Thatcher years also saw many improvements to the physical plant of the mission. Responding to the increasing numbers of followers in the Rochester area, the auditorium that was located in a large building on the grounds in which the members of the mission had met nightly since the acquisition of the property was enlarged. Seating was increased by forty or more, fluorescent lighting and air-conditioning were installed, the latter quite unusual for the time. This expansion was made possible by the acquisition of new printing equipment that occupied less space.[38]

A combination school and printing plant building were eventually completed, construction having been delayed due to scarcity of materials during World War II. Attached to the education building was a central boiler room that provided heat for most of the buildings on the mission property, including the large mission home. The building improvements were made possible by income from investments that prospered due to a rising stock market.[39]

Although there is no indication of increased outreach to areas outside the United States, during the Thatcher years increasing numbers of letters to the *Megiddo Message* came from other countries, especially England and Canada. In 1958, the church was contacted by a Nigerian who said he knew of a group of people who wanted to form a Megiddo congregation. The mission provided financial support and received letters requesting additional copies of the *Message* for distribution, stating that the Nigerian was "in the field calling women, children, and men of good will to the Mountain of the Lord's House." The church also received pictures of supposed members of the church and a church building under construction. So firm was the mission's commitment to the program in Nigeria that in response to a reader's question regarding whether there were churches other than the one in Rochester, the September 20, 1958, issue of the *Megiddo Message* reported that there was a "newly organized branch" in Abraka, Nigeria. In January 1964, the *Message* printed a letter from Nigeria that reported on a "Commemoration Feast" held in honor of Reverend Thatcher. According to the letter, "There were many visitors who came to watch the feast and how it was staged. It was amazing. We served everybody who came with fresh Palm wine, rice, orange fruits, biscuits and baked breads. After this distribution of literal food, then they were generally served with spiritual food from the Holy Book—The Bible." The account went on to list several songs from the Megiddo Church hymnal that were sung. Unfortunately, the church planting proved to be a fraud and the people in the photographs unknown to its supposed leader. In the 1970s and 1980s, the church also supported missions in Liberia and Haiti, but neither led to the establishment of a congregation.[40]

The minutes for a meeting held on February 10, 1958, to announce a new system of church government appear ominous in light of subsequent events. In May 1958, E. C. Branham, an assistant minister, was married to a member of the mission in a civil ceremony. Later the same day, Branham performed a marriage ceremony for another mission couple with other members of the mission in attendance. According to the front pages of the Rochester newspapers, the couples faced censure by the mission because mission doctrine prohibited marriage on the grounds that it was likely to interfere with members' abilities to serve Christ fully.

While the mission discouraged marriage, it had never actually forbidden it. Married couples who joined the mission remained married and lived as families in their own private quarters. However, according to a former member of the mission who was interviewed by Bristah and Frerichs, L. T. Nichols specifically discouraged the remarriage of a widowed father with two sons who wanted to marry a Megiddo woman after he joined the mission. The former member also told the story of another young widower who wanted to marry but was repeatedly talked out of it, after which he would lock himself in his room for from one to three weeks. In spite of his disappointment, he apparently did not leave the mission.[41]

According to Bristah and Frerichs, who in addition to talking to former members of the church had extensive interviews with Percy J. Thatcher, married couples "are not to have any children because of Paul's injunctions and because it is wrong to 'give way to our low desires.'" A couple on the mission boat had a child, and "at the time a big fuss was raised." Later, however, they repented and were accepted back into the church. Another couple who had a child were chastised by Captain Nichols, but apparently their excuse that the child was conceived while the husband was comforting his wife during a thunderstorm was accepted and they were also reconciled with the mission.[42]

In spite of the fact that marriage was discouraged, members of the mission did marry over the years. The major difference in the case in 1958 was that a marriage had been performed in the context of the church community, while in the past couples had married outside the mission, in most cases in civil ceremonies.

The reasons behind the public marriage and the resulting controversy within the mission became centered around seemingly trivial issues, such as allowing men and women to swim together, but the roots of the problem were actually much more complex and involved such things as the reorganization and centralization of the structure of the church. Positioning to determine the direction of the church and the selection of its leadership with the inevitable imminent passing of the aging Percy Thatcher may also have contributed to the dissension.

The mission reacted to the rebellion of the members by meeting to consider whether or not the couples were out of fellowship with the mission. It was decided that they should serve a period of probation, at the end of which it would be determined whether or not they were to be restored to fellowship with the other members of the mission. The dissidents refused the offer of probation and left the mission, as did several other mission families. Current members of the church attribute some of the departures to a mistaken sense that the noble experiment that was the Megiddo Mission was over and that the mission had no future.[43]

People from a wide spectrum of the mission's membership were included among those who departed at the time of the split or shortly thereafter, although most were recent converts. E. C. Branham was one of the mainstays of the mission as a writer, missionary, and representative of the mission at funerals in distant cities. Orla Thayer's name appeared frequently in the *Megiddo Message* in conjunction with a variety of activities. Barbara Wiejak was involved in many of the mission's worship services, often doing readings, and was a major contributor to the L. T. Nichols centennial celebration in 1944. Another family, whose daughter was a favorite of local press photographers at Abib time, were members of the mission for many years. The P—— family was associated with the mission for several years and moved to Rochester from New Jersey in the early 1950s. The H—— family, a mother and two adolescent daughters, moved to Rochester from Canada in 1957.[44]

Ironically, many of the changes that the departing families advocated were made in 1958, when the mission adopted its constitution and centralized its structure. However, only one of the families returned, and they did not stay. Those who left intended to form their own church but were unsuccessful in doing so, and they went their separate ways. Children of some of the families enrolled in public school but continued to dress as they would have had they stayed at the mission. The girls wore loose tops and skirts that were much longer than fashion dictated, and all but one of the girls kept her hair in the drawn-up style of the mission. The boys wore conservative clothes, but they were not obviously out of fashion. As students, the former mission members were above average to excellent, and several went on to attend college. It should be noted, however, that because their families had not been affiliated with the mission in Rochester for very many years before the split, some of the young people received considerable portions of their education in public schools rather than at the Megiddo school.

Bristah and Frerichs noted in the 1940s that there did not appear to be a formal method by which people were dismissed from the mission. Percy Thatcher stated that they were just "disfellowshipped." A woman who had been a member for many years and wished to leave told Bristah that if a person decided not to live according to accepted Megiddo standards they just "evaporated."[45] The informality of the procedure for disciplining dissident members exacerbated the difficulties in 1958, and the new constitution and bylaws, which set the previously noted membership requirements, also anticipated possible future internal conflicts. It provided for a means for resolution "should unhappy differences arise between members." The procedure is based on Matt. 18:15–17 and encourages settling the differences between individual members with resort to public or private hearings with the pastor and board of trustees only in "case of gross disobedience" or when the "offense cannot be removed privately." All proceedings "shall be pervaded by a spirit of Christian kindness and forbearance." This provision has proved effective in resolving conflicts within the church.[46]

In reflecting on E. C. Branham and the events of 1958, Rev. Newton Payne expresses more regret and disappointment than animosity:

> [E. C. Branham] possessed a good mind. As an assistant leader he read the sermons on Sunday nights and Thursday nights. . . . He could ad lib a very meaningful prayer any time any place. He never lacked for words. . . . He had a good knowledge of the scriptures. He could explain the doctrine in an interesting manner, in a word, he was an interesting person.
>
> Brother Branham felt that the church was drifting more to traditionalism and away from godliness. . . . Unfortunately, as Clyde tried to correct some flaws, his efforts took two directions. One was gradually widening out the narrow way, the other was making beneficial changes. Clyde was the architect of the constitution and the incorporation of the church. These have proved a great blessing over the years. And we believe that God was silently working to make this possible. On the other hand, he was doing much harm by bringing in worldly ideas and practices. . . . Being the attractive leader that he was, he thought he could lead his own group away from the "little flock." He actually thought that this would be the end of the followers of L. T. Nichols, but the exact opposite occurred, I can't say that the church has been blessed with members but God has surely made it possible for us to keep spreading the truth.
>
> . . . With Brother Branham's talent and potential for good, it is sad to see that he wasted so much of it. Of course, God is the final judge.[47]

Rev. Percy Thatcher died on November 13, 1958, in the midst of the mission's difficulties. He was succeeded by Kenneth Flowerday, who had assumed the title of assistant pastor in 1955.[48]

10

Thy Kingdom Come

The press quickly lost interest in the dissension within the mission and it ceased to be a focus of public scrutiny, although it would remain in the memories of many Rochesterians. During the years of Reverend Flowerday's administration (1958–85), the mission became a stable organization focused on maintenance of its outreach ministries, particularly the Elijah campaign.

Reverend Flowerday had a special concern for clarification of Megiddo doctrine, which has had a lasting effect on the church, especially on pastor Ruth Sisson, who wrote the following:

> Bro. Flowerday was my youthful mentor and paragon (I was in my early teens when he became pastor), who always had time for my hard or easy questions, and always left me with a desire to go after more. I admired his very logical, systematic approach to the Bible, and his tremendous personal insights. It just seemed like his knowledge of the Bible was like a deep well—there was always something more to draw up!
>
> By nature a student/teacher, he reasoned that God has given us minds and he intends us to use them, so he never objected to questions. (He used to tell of his own youthful days, when he was one of several boys who delighted in spending Sunday afternoons sitting cross-legged on the floor in Sister Hembree's study, asking questions and listening as she explained the Bible to them.)

Our beliefs, he said, are not something we should take on blind faith but which we should really understand, and when he became pastor he made a major effort to research and explain Bible passages and concepts which earlier generations had more or less accepted. I liked especially his honest, systematic approach, and his genuine appreciation of the evidence underlying our beliefs. And not infrequently he would mention the principle of our founder, that "if I can't give you Bible for it, don't believe it."

Some of my earliest memories of him were of his Bible studies, which were never long enough or frequent enough to satisfy me. It just seemed like he had a special talent for making difficult concepts understandable. I remember one time asking him if we couldn't have Bible Study more often, maybe twice a week instead of once? I don't remember his answer, but I know it didn't happen . . . I lacked appreciation for the time and effort that he put into preparing them![1]

Flowerday's interest in doctrine is reflected in *Megiddo Message* articles and in responses to readers' questions. According to Ruth Sisson, "When he was answering a question, whether it came from a member, a subscriber, or only a curious inquirer, Brother Flowerday didn't give simplistic answers. He assumed that the person asking wanted to know, and he explained it, A-to-Z style. . . . His answers to current questions were a source of ready copy for the *Message,* which was his responsibility at that time. It was also a way to share (and preserve) the results of his study/research." [2]

Under Flowerday's editorship, the *Megiddo Message* dealt much more directly with current events than it had at any time in the past. A regular feature of the *Message* was "Timely Topics," a series of articles on issues of the day. They were written by Liot L. Snyder, a longtime member of the Rochester congregation, and Newton H. Payne, who would succeed Flowerday as pastor of the church.[3] The issues addressed in "Timely Topics" were presented in a variety of ways—sometimes as examples of worldly activities to avoid, sometimes as signs of the declining state of the world presaging the return of Christ, and occasionally as the bases of object lessons. Among the issues addressed in the "Timely Topics" column and in articles were divorce, the occult, the so-called new morality, "skyrocketing" crime, alcoholism, drugs, advertising, pollution, and obscenity. The column even briefly noted the controversy over President Gerald Ford's pardoning of former President Nixon for any crime he may have committed while in office. While the author noted that "only God can judge" the rightness of Ford's action, the public outcry did serve as evidence of "a deep-seated weakness of human nature: the reluctance of one man to forgive another." [4]

In the tradition of L. T. Nichols's complaints about novel reading and other leisure pursuits, the *Message* contained attacks on activities believed to be a waste of time and potentially negative influences on people trying to work out their salvation. There was particular concern about the influence of the entertainment industry.

In two articles the *Message* expressed sentiments echoed by contemporary critics of commercial television:

Saturday morning coming around—its magic hours of freedom seduce many good-intentioned parents into abandoning their offspring. It is all too easy to forget the day's obligations and stay in bed longer, while the little ones toddle into the living room for a rendezvous with that reliable pacifier, the television. So loyal an audience are they that they will park themselves obediently before the tube whatever the fare. Even the tiniest will stare enchanted at the continually changing patterns . . .

. . . Most parents have never thought of taking their children to night clubs, theaters, or other places of filthy and questionable amusement. But what about the TV set, on which all forms of immorality—drinking, smoking, lust, unclad people, dancing, drugs—and crimes . . . are flaunted before young and old alike, and right in the home!

Television, according to the author, was not inherently evil, and he noted that it had "proven beneficial to mankind in various ways" in such areas as education, hospitals, industry, and space exploration. Even commercial television was not all bad. The news, musical programs, religious dramas, and historical programs could be beneficial. However, in order to be a commercial success, programs "must appeal to the lower or animal nature" and this is where the problem arose. He concluded that "for those who wish to be morally and spiritually strong, TV is a curse and not a blessing. It is too great a temptation, and the results are too tragic for the serious Christian to risk."[5]

The PTL scandal in which evangelist Jim Bakker was accused of cheating contributors to his ministry elicited a direct statement about televangelism in the *Megiddo Message*. According to the author, Ruth Sisson, "TV religion . . . has suddenly shown itself to be what it really is: only another form of public entertainment, show business, operated for the enrichment of the producers." She further compared televangelists with greedy religious teachers of the Old Testament who were accused of teaching in exchange for money.[6]

In another attack on the entertainment industry, Newton H. Payne turned his considerable rhetorical skills to a criticism of the rock musical *Jesus Christ, Superstar,* which he accused of "drag[ging] down to the level of the gutter the noble life of the greatest Man who ever lived." Payne was particularly critical of the portrayal of Jesus as "inconsistent and unsure," which was "the exact opposite of the Jesus of the Scriptures." He found the music to be "banal and repetitious with a persistent beat more suited to the wilds of Africa than to the Christian Church" and in a style that "stimulates basic animal instincts." He thought the singing came "closer to the wailing of a banshee than the utterance of a civilized vocalist," and the lyrics, some of which were quoted in the article, were described as "vulgar, slangy and irreligious." He compared the musical unfavorably to Handel's *Messiah* and Bach's *Christmas Oratorio* and decried the commercialism at the root of the production. He concluded that to present such an image of Jesus to the youth of the day was not only evil but also "a crime." He was certain that "when Jesus returns to earth, He will condemn this sort of blasphemy in the strongest terms and action."[7]

The attack on *Jesus Christ, Superstar* resonated with some readers of the *Message*. Two responses appeared in the "Letters" column in the following months. In one, a reader said she was going to show the article to her Catholic altar boy nephew with whom she had been arguing about the merits of the musical. Another reader commended the editor for the article and agreed that "our Saviour should not be used as a tool for making money [or] held up to ridicule."[8]

Genealogy was another activity that was considered a waste of time and detrimental to Christian progress, according to Flowerday. In response to a query from a reader regarding the sinfulness of doing family genealogy, Flowerday cited two passages of Scripture that he contended placed genealogies "in a class of needless wranglings that gender [*sic*] strife and do not edify. Searching one's genealogy is time-consuming, and is of questionable profit—what practical benefit can there be? If our first interest is to prepare to live in God's future Kingdom, we will find far more profitable occupation for our time than tracing our ancestors."[9]

An issue on which Reverend Flowerday took a particularly strong stand was race relations. A reader wrote the following: "What is your position on the integrating of Negroes and the white race? I believe the race of man extends back over 50 million or more years, a slow heritage of mental, spiritual and physical unfoldment. The Negro race have not this heritage, but are descendants of apes, and gorillas—only a few hundred years ago they were cannibals, savages, natives. And now they demand equality with the white race. What is your position?" Flowerday responded forcefully:

> Where is there any proof for your statement that the white race has been developing for the past fifty million years, while the black race has not? Where is your proof that the black races are descendants of apes and gorillas? Isaiah the prophet says that God "made the earth, and created man upon it"—God created man, *every* man, whatever the color of his skin.
>
> In regard to the Negro, it is unfair to condemn all Negroes for the actions or misbehavior of some. There are undoubtedly many Negroes who fit your description of near-savages, and you would be justified in wanting to segregate yourself from such. However, that same feeling of repulsion should apply to the white, red, yellow or brown person of low character; the gangster, gambler, drunkard, dope addict, thief, or murderer, whatever the color of his skin. . . . It is the character and conduct of the person that should determine his or her acceptability, not the color of the skin.

Flowerday concluded that "God does not allow us to respect race. *God respects character only* . . . . in the sight of God, one race is as acceptable as another . . . . Observe that those worthy to sing the new song (Rev. 5:9, 10) were redeemed to God 'out of every kindred, and tongue, and people, and nation'—no segregation here."[10]

In another instance, when a reader asked if the church was "composed of white, or colored people or both," Flowerday replied, "Our church is integrated. . . . We are largely white, but this is accidental, not intentional." In fact, the mission had one black family as active members for many years. In the early 1920s, a Megiddo missionary visited Jeannette Hill Porter, an African American woman who lived in Scranton, Pennsylvania, and sold her a set of books. Porter began a correspondence with the mission that resulted in her moving to Rochester in 1924 with her two daughters, Edith and Fanella. Initially, Fanella did not like life at the mission and longed to return to Scranton, but she responded to the teachings of Maud Hembree and decided to stay. Fanella Porter was "a colorful and gifted actress, dramatist and playwright." She and her sister wrote and directed religious dramas and performed in church. She also occasionally wrote for the *Megiddo Message* and was actively involved in ministry to children. Her love of travel took her from the Atlantic Coast to the Indian Ocean. Sister Fanella was well known for her "exceptionally keen" memory, and even into her eighties she continued to memorize large portions of Scripture, a skill much admired among the Megiddos. She also memorized religious poetry. Sister Fanella died on January 6, 2000, at the age of ninety-one. Two other African American families were involved with the mission for short periods of time.[11]

Many of the issues addressed in the *Message* during Kenneth Flowerday's editorship related to youth culture. These included the aforementioned "new morality" and drugs. Campus unrest was another aspect of youth culture that was addressed. The *Message* came unusually close to taking a political stand on this issue:

> Recent events underscore the fact that man without divine guidance is totally unable to govern himself. Young people going to college in America today have infinitely more freedom and advantages than any people on this planet have ever enjoyed. If students behind the Iron Curtain should revolt, we might be able to sympathize with them. But American students rioting, throwing stones, hurling molotof [*sic*] cocktails, burning buildings, desecrating the American flag (the symbol of their liberty) is not only unjustified, it is criminal. Perhaps a sinister conspiracy, such as Communism, has brainwashed these immature minds. They have become willing tools in fomenting revolt and anarchy in this country, all under the pretense of a just and high-sounding cause.

The author went on to identify the causes of campus unrest as "a lack of respect for authority . . . ; parental permissiveness; the absence of religious instruction and the discrediting of belief in a Supreme Being to whom mankind is answerable for his conduct; the extremes to which the principle of free speech has been carried . . . ; [and] the replacement of the wisdom of Solomon with the muddled thinking of Dr. Spock." He concluded that it is not "necessary, wise, or prudent to demonstrate against authority" and that Christians should not participate in such activities. He averred, however, that the "trouble and perplexity" that characterized the world had been prophesied "centuries ago" and that "demonstrations against divine authority will not be permitted" during the millennial reign of Christ.[12]

In a departure from past practice, in the 1960s and 1970s the *Message* reprinted several articles from a wide range of sources other than Megiddo Mission publications. These included an article by FBI director J. Edgar Hoover that appeared in *Christianity Today,* the previously mentioned article on women's dress, an article from *Pulpit Digest,* and the text of a radio broadcast from *The Lutheran Hour.*[13]

Under Flowerday's editorship, the *Message* also devoted much more space to materials directed at teaching the Bible and Megiddo doctrines to children. Various series aimed at children appeared in the magazine's pages, including Bible stories, lives of biblical figures, and puzzles and quizzes. In the 1960s and 1970s, the *Megiddo Message* emphasized self-control, which was reflected not only in the articles but also in the publication of testimonial letters from readers who reported on their striving to achieve a state of perfection.

By the 1970s, the church had long ago abandoned setting a date for the coming of Elijah. In February 1933, Maud Hembree completed a section of *The Known Bible and Its Defense,* which pointed out the inaccuracies of the dates set by Jehovah's Witnesses for Christ's return by simply noting that Elijah had not yet come.[14] However, Megiddos still believe strongly in the need to study prophecy and that the return of Elijah is imminent. For example, in 1955, a *Megiddo Message* reader asked if there was "any definite indication that Elijah will come within the next 50 years?" The author responded with a definite "yes." [15] The response reflects the degree to which the sense of the imminence of Elijah's return pervades the life and thought of the Megiddo Church.

In the 1970s, the Megiddos' sense that the millennium would begin soon positioned them to capitalize on the sudden explosion of interest in the end times and the future of the world that was evident in the popularity of Hal Lindsey's book *The Late Great Planet Earth.* Purportedly based on notes Lindsey took while a student at Dallas Theological Seminary, an institution with a strong focus on dispensationalism and premillennialism, *The Late Great Planet Earth* used references to Scripture, particularly the book of Revelation, to depict the destruction of the earth through nuclear holocaust, the horrific effects of which Lindsey described in graphic detail. The book, published in 1970, was the best-selling nonfiction book of the 1970s with nine million copies in print by 1978 and twenty-eight million by 1990. It was followed by other best-selling premillennial works by Lindsey and by numerous imitations by other authors.[16]

In 1980, the Megiddos produced their own addition to what Paul Boyer has called "the hundreds of prophecy paperbacks [that] fed an apparently insatiable market" in the form of the anonymous book *Millennium Superworld*. The book was based on a series of Bible studies by Eva Goertzen, many of which had previously appeared as articles in the *Message*. The studies were expanded with additional materials by Ruth Sisson, who edited the final manuscript. The book was sold through advertisements in the *Megiddo Message* for two dollars. It was very well received by readers, who within months of its release sent testimonial letters to the *Message*. Responses ranged from "very useful to a better understanding of this great Bible theme" to "it fired me with enthusiasm, to win at all costs." A reader from England read the book twice and began reading it a third time because she "might have missed a vital point." [17]

The 1980 edition of *Millennium Superworld* was superceded in 1997 with a new edition attributed to the pseudonymous author R. Chris Connolly. The new edition was issued to coincide with the millennial fervor excited by the approach of 2000—this in spite of the fact that the Megiddos fully recognize that the numbering of the years is purely a human convention with no theological significance and that the true date of the event on which it is based, the birth of Christ, is uncertain and probably deviates from year 1 by three or four years.

Millennium Superworld does not claim to be a factual representation of future events. Rather, "using Bible evidence as our foundation . . . we feel justified in letting our imagination picture to a limited extent the wonders of the Superworld that is coming." The author further feels that no one can condemn using one's "God-given imagination to picture what may be—within the scope of what is revealed so long as Scripture is not contradicted . . . Time will prove—or disprove—the accuracy of the details." [18]

Contrary to *The Late Great Planet Earth* or the more recently popular Left Behind Series, *Millennium Superworld* is a very upbeat account of Christ's establishment of his kingdom on earth. The account begins with, but does not dwell upon, the return of Elijah. His return is followed by the battle of Armageddon between Christ and those who refuse to submit to him. "The battle will be costly, but only to the evil"—but the evil, even though they comprise two-thirds of the world's population, are not the focus here. [19]

The Superworld is a material place and as such owes much to currents that were active in America in the intellectual and religious climate of the nineteenth and early twentieth centuries, a period when, according to James H. Moorhead, "the image of heaven . . . changed. Protestant portrayals of the celestial [that] had emphasized pictures of release from earthly struggle, total abolition of sin, and unceasing adoration of God" were replaced with a heaven that was "becoming continuous with the present life; it was a place where the best of this world would be writ large and where the realization of earthly dreams would be at least as important as the glory of God." [20]

Among the forces driving this change in the view of the afterlife were the ideas of Emanuel Swedenborg (1688–1772). According to historian Sydney Ahlstrom:

> Of all the unconventional currents streaming through the many levels of American religion during the antebellum half-century, none proved more attractive to more diverse types of dissenters from established denominations than those which stemmed from Emanuel Swedenborg. His influence was seen everywhere: in Transcendentalism . . . , in spiritualism and the free love movement, in the craze for communitarian experiments, in faith healing, and a half dozen medical cults; [and] among great intellectuals.[21]

Similar to L. T. Nichols's claim to have been given insight into the true essence of Scripture in 1880, Swedenborg claimed to have been given the key to the meaning of the Word of God in what he believed to be the true Second Coming of Christ. Swedenborg's claims might easily have been dismissed as the ravings of a madman had he not had a long career as a renowned scientist, mathematician, and engineer, a career for which he is virtually unknown today but that gave him a certain aura of credibility.

Swedenborg's most influential writing was *Heaven and Hell* (1758), in which he described heaven as it was revealed to him on a visit he made, while fully awake, in the company of angels. Unlike the heaven of the previous generations, which was very unlike earth, the heaven of Swedenborg was a continuation of the earthly life. It was, according to Colleen McDannell and Bernhard Lang, "the distilled essence of the true and beautiful found in earthly existence."[22] Characteristics of Swedenborg's heaven were adopted by both secular and religious writers to describe life after death and contributed substantially to the development of the idea of a material heaven that most Americans envision today. Many of these characteristics appear in the writings of L. T. Nichols and in *Millennium Superworld*.

The new view of the afterlife was popularized in the writings of Elizabeth Stuart Phelps (1844–1911), the author of two accounts of the afterlife that were widely read in the nineteenth century: *The Gates Ajar* (1867) and *Beyond the Gates* (1885). *The Gates Ajar*, "appealing nakedly to the wishful thinking of its readers," was eagerly read by thousands seeking comfort in their grief over the loss of loved ones in the Civil War. Phelps's two books sold more than 100,000 copies in the United States alone and spawned an industry that produced *Gates Ajar* capes, collars, musical compositions, and even cigars.[23]

The idea of continuity between the present life and the afterlife, which began to prevail in the second half of the nineteenth century and is reflected in *Beyond the Gates*, tended to blur the passage between the two. Mary, the protagonist of *Beyond the Gates*, fails to realize that she has died and evinces only mild surprise when her long-dead father appears in her bedroom to guide her into the afterlife. The transition to the other world is easy and natural.[24] The basis of the other world for Phelps is in the familiar. On entering a dwelling, Mary finds the "familiar furniture of a modest home" but also "much that was unfamiliar mingled therewith," and such is the case with the Superworld of the Megiddos.[25]

According to *Millennium Superworld,* Christ will establish his kingdom in Jerusalem, but not the Jerusalem that exists prior to his coming. It will be "a rebuilt city of modern times," like the cities Swedenborg claimed to have seen in heaven. The New Jerusalem will be set in a valley "created by a physical earthquake and the removing of the mountains currently on the site of Jerusalem," as the Megiddos believe is predicted in Zech. 14:4–5.[26]

The new government will be the "the first ideal government in the earth's history," and it will be a dictatorship because Christ is supremely qualified to be an absolute ruler. He will be assisted by 144,000 administrators, chosen from among the righteous. The Megiddos expect to be among those chosen, but it is not clear who the others will be. L. T. Nichols left open the possibility that even members of other churches might qualify for selection: "It does not matter whether you are called a Methodist, a Baptist, a Christian, or a Presbyterian, &c., if you will believe all truths revealed in the blessed word, conforming your lives to the divine standard, and become a peculiar people zealous of good works, looking for his glorious appearing, you will be accepted at his coming."[27]

Those chosen for administrative positions shall be the "new Royalty" and will receive the gift of immortality. Their bodies will be changed into "a substance superior to flesh and blood," but "you will still be you, but you will be a much better 'you.'" They shall have "the glory that shall never tarnish, beauty that shall never fade, and life that shall never end." They will be distinguished by their shining white clothing, and they will sit on thrones and have access to Christ. Like the angels of Swedenborg's heaven who had greatly increased senses, the immortals of the Superworld will "have eyes that see a much broader spectrum of color than can be seen by mortals." They shall rule as "kings" and "lords" over mortal multitudes, some of whom will be alive at the beginning of the millennium and others of whom will be born during the millennium. These mortals will have the opportunity to prove themselves to Christ during the millennium, and those who are found acceptable will be rewarded with eternal life.[28]

An important activity of the government of the Superworld will be formal education, which will focus on three areas: first, "the building of upright and moral character; second, . . . the development of a new society; third, . . . the means of livelihood."[29] According to the Megiddos, Isaiah suggests that the teachers will be angels who, Megiddos believe, are immortal humans from planets that have already experienced resurrection of the dead.[30] In addition to the angels, some of the "new immortals," the 144,000 administrators, may also be teachers.

The education program envisioned by the author of *Millennium Super-world* will be highly structured, with a level of "basics" that will include understanding God and creation, character development, self-discipline, and personal responsibility. On a secondary level, students will be trained in the "newest and best methods" of such disciplines as horticulture, food science, economics, and administration.[31]

In the Superworld, the arts and sciences will be developed to a point now only imagined by writers of science fiction and fantasy. For example, advanced study in "communication systems, interplanetary communications, and inter-galaxy communications" will address the "effective use of words, sound, color and light, both as they may be employed on earth and between earth and other worlds."[32]

Information in the Superworld will be "closely monitored and controlled, so that nothing is released or circulated that is untrue or in any way detrimental to the health and spiritual well-being of the people." Echoing Kenneth Flowerday's concern about campus unrest, student dissension will not be tolerated. Leaders, from Christ to even the "humblest teacher . . . will brook no opposition. All will have Divine authority at their command and students who refuse to cooperate will be reprimanded and dismissed immediately. . . . If one obeys the laws, he will live in happiness and blessing; if he refuses to obey, he will die . . . . There will be no tolerance for deviant behaviors or willful disobedience."[33]

The world will become increasingly more beautiful. "Smoke, smog, and gas fumes" will be swept away and replaced with air that is "crystal clear" and the "fragrance of blossoms, pine, and sweet spice." The description of the loveliness of the Superworld was anticipated by L. T. Nichols when he wrote that "the earth will be a garden of flowers and sweet perfume. . . . We have never seen a lovely day nor smelled a sweet perfume when compared to that we will see and smell when the gladsome kingdom of God rolls in." A similar image appeared in the sermon preached at the first public Abib celebration in 1906, when Nichols stated that the flowers that decorated the church for the celebration were there to remind those attending the service of "how grand, lofty, beautiful and altogether lovely the old earth will be when the desert shall blossom abundantly as the rose, wafting sweet perfume in its remotest bounds."[34]

In the Superworld, all that is immoral or decadent, such as "slums, . . . casinos, taverns, . . . dance halls, and porn shops, and all dens of lust and iniquity, will be reduced to rubble and carried away. Then will begin the construction of the new and beautiful." The "raucous, distressing, grating" sounds that characterize the world today will be replaced by "pleasing harmony and melody that will transcend the finest melody you have ever heard."[35]

In the Superworld, all who suffer from disease or a physical disability will be healed, and there will be no pain or illness. All mortals will live for several centuries and will die of old age. Family life will be directed toward the production of multitudes of children who will have the potential to achieve immortality. "The sexual aspect of human relationship, so abused for centuries, the most perverted of all God's marvelous designs for humankind, will be wholesome under the control of Divine law and will be respected by all." Toward the end of the millennium, however, God will cause the bearing of children to cease, because "if He did not, there would be children brought forth for trouble—there would be a multitude of little children and infants at the close of the Millennium who would have no time in which to develop the character God requires in all."[36]

At the end of the millennium, Satan, or evil, which has been suppressed for the thousand years will be unleashed for a brief period in order that those who are secretly evil can be revealed. Satan will then be cast into a lake of fire and evil will disappear from the world. The dead will be raised, a second judgment will occur, and those who did not take advantage of the opportunities provided for them to achieve salvation will be cast into a lake of fire and annihilated. Then death will also be cast into the lake of fire. With no more death in the world, all those remaining will become immortal. Then, "another planet [will have] gloriously concluded its long period of development and [be] welcomed into the heavenly family of perfect worlds, among whom it will shine forever and ever." The perfect world created at the end of the thousand-year reign will be on earth and it will be eternal. There will be "eternal growth, eternal expansion, eternal improvement, eternal productivity."[37]

The Megiddos are not unaware of scientific predictions that the earth has a finite existence and will eventually be destroyed. This was addressed by assistant minister Gerald R. Payne in an article in the August 2000 issue of the *Megiddo Message*. He described various theories about the possible destruction of the earth from natural or man-made forces and then dismissed them all: "Those who make these claims have been challenged by One of higher authority, the Lord Himself." He then proceeded to cite the passages on which the Megiddos base their belief in an eternal earth.[38]

The Megiddos' belief that other worlds have already gone through the same process the earth will experience and have achieved eternal existence is unusual. The belief in other worlds and the ability to contact them or travel to them is not unique in Christianity, but individuals or groups who believe in other worlds usually see them as inferior and not the chosen planets of God. For example, the Swiss theologian Johann Kaspar Lavater (1741–1801), who was a contemporary of Swedenborg and familiar with his works, believed that after death one would be able to travel to other worlds, but the earth "as the place where Christ lived, [provided] 'the natural climate of the blessed.'"[39] The Megiddos believe that the light emitted by distant unknown planets may be a result of their being occupied by luminous immortal beings. Consequently, they evince an interest in astronomy, especially in discoveries of other solar systems with planets that might prove to be inhabited by immortals.

With such a positive view of the world of the millennium, it is hardly surprising that the Megiddos eagerly anticipate the return of Elijah. Meanwhile, the church continues much as it has for decades. In a 1969 article in the *Rochester Democrat and Chronicle,* Emily Ribble, treasurer of the mission, indicated that the mission had substantial resources. With the growing economy and increased property values, it is likely that the church has prospered in recent years and remains financially stable. It still owns the complex of buildings across the street from the church building, and about thirty-five people live there. In 1984, Newton Payne was responsible for the conversion of one of the buildings into a health care facility that offers round-the-clock skilled temporary or long-term care for members who are ill or frail. The facility is called COTE, which stands for "Care of the Elderly," although members of any age in need of care may stay there. Reverend Payne has become one of the residents of COTE, where he has spacious, attractively furnished quarters with a computer, slide projector, and other items he needs to pursue his various interests. His pet dog is even welcome to stay with him.[40]

Megiddo members requiring health care visit physicians, dentists, chiropractors, and other practitioners. They have hospital care when necessary and take prescribed medications, although many prefer to use natural remedies from health food stores instead of drugs whenever possible.

The Megiddo Church property in 2001. *Left,* the health care facility; *right,* the church home. Courtesy Megiddo Church, Rochester, N.Y.

There continues to be a community garden occupying a large tract of land in back of the church home. The church maintenance person plows and disks the land and marks the rows. Members claim as many rows as they want, marking them with stakes. Each gardener plants what he or she wishes and then maintains the rows and harvests the crops. In the fall, the maintenance person prepares the garden for winter, occasionally planting a cover crop to enrich the soil.[41]

Most of the houses on neighborhood streets that once belonged to mission members have been sold to people who have no connection with the church, although the church still owns a number of houses that provide income from rent. The building that housed the Six-in-One Ladder Company belongs to the church and will probably continue to do so as the infrastructure of that building and the church are interconnected. The Six-in-One building was converted into offices in 1964 and is occupied by Ruth Sisson's business.

Shortly after the Megiddos settled in Rochester, L. T. Nichols "had 'board meetings' at which business issues were discussed. No doubt he realized the need for shared responsibility for decision making, especially as he became older."[42] However, no one knows how the board was selected, and the church did not have an official organization until it adopted a constitution and bylaws in 1958, under which it has been governed by a board of trustees composed of six members elected for terms of two years each. The church's buildings are well maintained, and the interior of the church and the entrance to the complex have been remodeled and redesigned in recent years.

The membership of the Megiddo Church, as the mission is now called, has declined gradually, and fewer visitors than in the past come from distant places for church holidays. There are occasional additions to the community. Several years ago, a Polish family joined after a member of the family discovered a mission advertisement in a periodical. The family members visited the mission and then decided to join. They represent a very limited number of converts from outside the English-speaking world.

The small membership has never been of particular concern to the church. In fact, in commenting on the large numbers of converts of the Jehovah's Witnesses (4,640 baptized in one day) in a series of articles in the *Megiddo Message* in 1953, Reverend Thatcher quoted Isa. 1:8, 9: "Except the Lord of hosts had left unto us a very small remnant, we should have been as Sodom and . . . like unto Gomorrah" and stated that, "You will note that it is not only a remnant, but a *very small* remnant. No wonder our Lord and Master brought consolation to the few when He proclaimed in Luke 12:32, 'Fear not, little flock; for it is your Father's good pleasure to give you the kingdom.' Remember, when the flock grows large, the promise is made void. While the great masses walk the broad road to destruction, but a few will enter the narrow way that leads to life."[43] Furthermore, as Rev. Newton Payne notes, numbers do not necessarily affect the ability to spread the Megiddos' message. "With the *Message* and books and pamphlets being distributed throughout the U.S.A. and the Web Site available world wide, our message is reaching more people than ever."[44]

Although the church has evinced a healthy suspicion of the Worldwide Web, recognizing that "much on the internet is worse than worthless—polluted, corrupt, rotten," it also views it as "another means to make our material available to those who seek." In fact, "it seems that God is opening another means of communication; another means of making His voice heard on earth." To this end, the church has developed an attractive page to promote itself through a link from the online church directory of the *Rochester Democrat and Chronicle.*[45]

Most Megiddo Church outreach is still done largely through the mails, with free trial subscriptions to the *Megiddo Message* still available. However, there is still occasional missionary travel. In the tradition of the dedicated Megiddo missionaries of the past, church member Daniel Wiselka uses his vacations to visit readers of the *Megiddo Message* and other interested people in various parts of the United States, often taking other members of the church with him. The vacations are somewhat of a busman's holiday for Wiselka, as he is employed as a courier for Ruth Sisson's Digitech business. According to Alice Cummings, who has accompanied Wiselka, destinations for the trips have included Virginia, Georgia, several states in the Midwest, and Canada. An average trip involves about three or four visits in a week, each visit lasting three to four hours and usually including music by Wiselka, who has an outstanding singing voice, short readings, and the opportunity for questions. A meal is a usual part of the visit, with the missionaries taking an individual or family out to dinner. In one case, a member of the family had had a stroke and could not go out to dinner. Brother Wiselka brought in food from a fried chicken restaurant chain. Many of the people Wiselka visits correspond regularly with him, and some have even visited the church.[46]

The church, as always, provides someone to perform funeral services for believers outside the Rochester area. Over the years, funeral services have been performed by representatives of the church in many communities throughout western and central New York and in such places as Vermont, West Virginia, California, Nebraska, and Ontario. Rev. Newton Payne remembers with great fondness his experiences with distant funerals, although they were not always easy trips. He drove whenever possible, flying only when the funerals were in distant locations, such as Wausau, Wisconsin. In Hamilton, Ontario, Reverend Payne followed a large truck into Hamilton, using the grooves made by the truck to navigate his way through deep snow. On the day of the funeral, it was so cold at the cemetery that he could hardly speak. Needless to say, it was a short graveside service.

The church still holds weekly worship services and Sunday school in the church building at the corner of Thurston Road and Sawyer Street. Outsiders attending the Megiddo Church find much that is familiar. The services contain the elements of most Protestant worship services: Scripture, prayer, music, and sermons. Hymns are sung from editions of the *Megiddo Hymnal.* Most of the hymn tunes are from the late Victorian period and are seldom used by churches today. Several hymns in the hymnals appear at first to be well-known popular hymns, but almost all have verses altered to be compatible with Megiddo theology.

Music for the Sunday services is provided by the band and choir, which is composed largely of the members of the band. The sermon, which is usually written by Ruth Sisson, is read rather than preached. Brother Ronald Hicks, who has read the sermon since 1976, has a clear voice and distinct diction, and his reading is much admired and appreciated by members of the congregation. The worship service is followed by Sunday school. Members in Rochester also meet at the church home each morning, except on Sunday, and most evenings with some evenings free for letter writing and other personal activities.

The women of the church are still recognized for their distinctive dress. Many of the women wear dresses with long sleeves and hems about two inches above the ankle. Long-sleeved blouses with long skirts are also considered appropriate. The tops of dresses are often loose and gathered at the waist, concealing the bust line. Jackets or sweaters may be worn over blouses. Specific patterns and colors of clothing are a matter of personal choice, and several of the women wear bright colors. White collars are popular. It is now even possible for women to buy ready-made clothing that is considered sufficiently modest. The women wear no makeup, and their hair is long and gathered into buns; unlike members of some conservative groups, they do cut their hair when it becomes "inconveniently long." Some of the women also wear simple jewelry. Given the wide variety of styles adopted by American women today, only a very few of the women would draw immediate attention outside the mission.

Men, who are more likely to work in environments in which certain dress styles are expected, tend to wear conservative suits and functional work clothes. Neckties are considered appropriate. Because they believe that clothes should be worn as long as they give good service, men may be seen in styles considered out of fashion.[47]

In spite of their strict dress code, the Megiddos are tolerant of the dress of those outside the church and welcome visitors who may be dressed in what they consider more worldly styles. Among women who attend Megiddo services are a few who have short hair, skirts with hems at midcalf, and tops with short sleeves and even scoop necks. There is every indication that these women are as welcome as the more conservatively dressed members. A young woman employee of the health care facility even wears pants and has a dark magenta streak dyed in her otherwise black hair. When asked about her, the Megiddos simply say that she is a good worker and make no mention of her appearance.

When possible, the Megiddos avoid involvement with the government and politics. They neither vote nor serve on juries. They do meticulously pay their taxes, however, and they obey all laws that do not conflict with their religious beliefs. They cooperate fully with the government. For example, in 1981, a man in the neighborhood near the church killed three people, including his mother and a teller at the bank across the street from the church building, where he held police at bay. Members occupying the church-owned office building next to the church allowed the police to set up a negotiations center in the office building. Later, the church allowed the police to occupy a room on the second floor of the church building from which a police officer shot and killed the assailant.[48]

While members of the church believe that the arrival of Elijah and the Second Coming of Jesus are imminent, their experience makes it clear that they do not know when these events will occur. Consequently, they participate in Social Security and pension plans and purchase insurance to cover losses.[49]

Megiddos do not watch television, although they may view edifying videotapes. They avoid motion pictures; dancing; cardplaying; coffee, tea, and alcoholic beverages; smoking; spectator sports (they are especially critical of boxing and wrestling); and other activities they consider detrimental to their goal of dedication to religious work. However, they do participate in other forms of relaxation and entertainment, such as reading wholesome and edifying literature and listening to news and some classical music on the radio. They also engage in outdoor activities, such as swimming, fishing, and picnicking, and they travel. For many years, David and Marie Sutton used their vacations to travel to remote locations, lugging heavy professional quality camera equipment to photograph scenery, particularly waterfalls. Their beautiful photographs now grace the covers of the *Megiddo Message.*

Since about 1918, the church has owned residential property at McKeever on the Moose River in the western Adirondack Mountains. The property, variously known as "Megiddo Rest" and "Camp Megiddo," can accommodate up to twenty people at one time. Over the years, the camp has been used for pastors' and members' vacations and for group social activities.

There is little or no sense of frustration or deprivation associated with being unable to participate in what the members of the church consider worldly activities. Dedication to the church supplants all other concerns, and the members who remain are vitally interested and active in the church and are committed to its mission.[50]

The lifestyle of a member of the Megiddo Church is very demanding and many try it and find it too difficult. Consequently, the membership has been fluid over the years, with many people coming and going, some leaving after many years of attempting to live the life that strict adherence to Scripture demands. The members view those who leave with pity rather than anger or resentment. Many members continue to have friendly personal relationships with friends and relatives who have left the church. Members Elva and Shirley Byers are still close to two sisters who are former members of the church and who are employed by the church's health care facility.[51]

The general policy of the church is not always reflected in its individual members, and some family relationships are strained when family members leave. One former member wrote that when she left the church as a young woman, her mother told her that her prayers would reach no higher than the back of her chair. After several decades, the ex-member remains hurt by the statement.[52]

The church has always had committed members willing to serve in whatever capacity they can to promote and advance the ministry. George W. Sawyer, who died in 1980, gave

> long and useful service to the organization. . . . As an electrician, he donated literally thousands of hours to installing and operating of lights in the church and on the church grounds. As a writer, he contributed numerous thought-provoking articles and letters which were published or circulated and widely appreciated for the spiritual uplift and encouragement they provided. As a missionary, he made three major trips, distributing literature and attempting to interest others in living the Christian life. When in declining years he was unable to do any strenuous work, he took very seriously the various hand tasks associated with mailing our literature and was always an eager helper.

The church is able to compensate for its declining membership by reassigning responsibilities and modifying programs to make effective use of the personnel resources available. Many women have been flexible in terms of their service to the church. Eva Goertzen was active in the Maranatha Society, performed in church dramas, served as hostess for guests, sang in the choir, wrote for the *Message,* served on the church board and as superintendent of the Bible school, and went on several missionary trips in the United States, England, and Australia.[53]

Recently, the church made an important move to avoid discontinuity when clergy become unable to perform to full capacity due to age or infirmity. When physical ill health made it impossible for Rev. Newton H. Payne to continue to perform the duties of pastor, assistant pastor Ruth Sisson assumed the pastoral duties of the church. Reverend Payne is still a vital part of the community, attending church activities when he is able and serving as the memory of the church and mentor to younger members. His knowledge, opinions, and sense of humor are highly valued. Recently, he has undertaken to organize a large collection of slides that document the church's recent history, and he has initiated some improvements in the church's electrical system.

Gerald R. Payne has been selected to be assistant pastor to help Sisson. In order to meet his obligations to the church, he has resigned his position as a quality control technician with the Electronic Systems Group of Lithonia Lighting. He lives in Georgia, but he and his wife, Barbara, have committed themselves to visiting the church four times a year for two weeks each time. Payne is a regular contributor to the *Message.* Many of his articles employ scientific themes, particularly from astronomy and the biological sciences.

The ministers of the Megiddo Mission and the Megiddo Church. *Counterclockwise from the right:* L. T. Nichols, Maud Hembree, Ella M. Skeels, Percy J. Thatcher, Kenneth E. Flowerday, Newton H. Payne, and current pastor Ruth E. Sisson. Courtesy Megiddo Church, Rochester, N.Y.

Ruth Sisson is a bright, energetic, effective, and practical leader of the church. In the tradition of L. T. Nichols and Maud Hembree, she is a student of the Bible, making use of resources available at the nearby Colgate Rochester-Bexley Hall-Crozier Theological Seminary. She has been willing to delegate management responsibilities for her graphic arts business to a person from outside the mission in order to meet her obligations to the church. Sisson has made several moves to streamline the church's operations, to adjust the church's program to the needs and abilities of the members, and to enhance the church's ministry. She has reduced the number of meetings held during the week and the number of issues of the *Message* so that she and members have time to address other requirements of the church. She has also begun to use carefully selected, commercially produced Sunday school materials to reduce the burden of Sunday school preparation. She has focused on updating some of the church's tracts and pamphlets to reflect the new insights of recent years. One example of her practicality is the new, revised edition of *Millennium Superworld,* which she has encouraged members to try to place in bookstores in addition to selling it through the *Message.* She has been responsible for the publication of the *Megiddo Message* for several years and, using what she has learned from her graphic arts business, has produced a more colorful, modern, and visually pleasing publication, although it still retains its sectarian title. In order to put a face on the church that it has not had since news of mission activities ceased to be an integral part of the *Message,* Sisson has begun to include signed articles, and the new edition of *Millennium Superworld* was issued with its pseudonymous author, R. Chris Connolly. Currently, Ruth Sisson and Margaret Tremblay are devoting considerable effort to the development of a Web-based Bible study. They are also planning an interactive question-and-answer section on the church's Web site (www.megiddo.com).

The members of the church have had some difficulty adjusting to the changes in their neighborhood. Through the first half of the twentieth century, much of the adjacent neighborhood was occupied by members of the church. As the membership became smaller, the houses were sold to other middle-class people. In the last two decades, the neighborhood, while still primarily middle class and appearing much as it has since World War II, has become increasingly African American. In spite of the attractiveness of the neighborhood and the high property values, some members of the mission perceive some of their neighbors as being economically disadvantaged. This appears to be largely because there are significant numbers of people and automobiles on the street well after midnight.[54] Furthermore, there are no African Americans involved with the church. Consequently, mission members have little contact with their neighbors.

New local businesses are another problem. Unlike the merchants of the past, new business owners do not know the Megiddos and are not accustomed

Assistant Pastor Gerald Payne. Courtesy
Megiddo Church, Rochester, N.Y

to their unique characteristics.[55] As in any community undergoing rapid change, there is less stability, neighbors do not know neighbors, and, although the neighborhood is generally safe, crime has increased. Particularly troubling to the Megiddos is the presence of a bar very near the church. The church building and members' homes are protected by security systems, but many feel unsafe in a neighborhood no longer familiar to them.

Only time will tell whether the recent changes the church has made will result in more effective outreach and increased public interest in the church's doctrines. The rational nature of the Megiddos' message may find few adherents in a religious atmosphere in which the influence of popular Christian and New Age spirituality is becoming pervasive. Further, it may be impossible to promote True Christmas in a society that has long ago given up the pretense that Christmas has anything to do with the birth of Christ; to call people to a more godly life in a society in which most churches have abandoned the call to repentance in favor of making their highly individualistic members feel good about themselves; to instill a desire for an active afterlife in people who may see death as a welcome relief from the rigors of modern life; or to bring people to faith and commitment in a society where the emphasis is on respectability and acquisitiveness. However, regardless of the success or failure of their outreach, the Megiddos will remain for many years to come a faithful remnant eagerly anticipating the prophet Elijah coming before Christ.

Appendix

Excerpts from a Diary Kept on the Gospel Boat Megiddo

The following are excerpts from a diary kept by Mary Eastman Lee from November 16, 1901 to November 4, 1903.[1] According to an obituary that appeared in the *Megiddo Message* on October 11, 1931, Mary Lee was born in Royalton, Ohio, in 1841. She became a schoolteacher in Wisconsin, where she met L. T. Nichols and followed him to Oregon. She was married to Martin G. Lee in Chicago in 1888 and became a member of the Christian Brethren's Davenport, Iowa, and Barry, Illinois, congregations. In 1901, she joined other members of the Barry church on the mission boat, where she served as a teacher. After the mission was established in Rochester, she taught Sunday school, composed songs for the Megiddo hymnal, and wrote poetry that appeared in the *Megiddo Message*.

On the Mississippi on Board the Mission Ship *Megiddo*

November 16, 1901

Left Lyons, Iowa with 97 on board. The first trip of our new boat. She floats the water like a duck, but we scarcely have time to think of it for all our stuff is dumped aboard in a confused mass. We have beds to set up, furniture to arrange, goods to unpack and put in place; in fact, everything to do to bring order out of chaos. We finished moving on to the boat the evening of the 15th and got our beds up to sleep in but all else is in confusion. However time, work and patience accomplished the work and we went along merrily. The machinery worked [illegible] no mishap, nothing to worry about or [page torn] . . .

But go back a little to the tim[e of] our coming to Lyons from M[inneapolis]. We arrived in Lyons, 46 of us, on the 11 of Oct. Bro N. came the night before and was there to receive us and pilot us to the old Randall house where he had 5 bales of straw & we soon improvised beds and slept.[2] Next morning (Sat.), we swept & scrubbed & settled ourselves for the month to come. The brethren worked on the boat day & also nights some of the time. Launched it, the band played & Bro N delivered an address and finally, after some delay in getting the engines, they came and were put in place, machinery got in order and we were ready to sail although the boat was far from being finished, but what did that matter, we were anxious to get through the locks before freez[in]g of the river as they usually close [abou]t the 18 of Nov. This, the maiden trip [of the] *Megiddo,* was a success, she glided [down] the river with perfect ease and gr[ace.][3]

November 18–19, 1901

Stayed at Quincy that night . . . and part of the next day. Sisters Sweet and Ogram joined us here. Mr and Mrs Klein and Mr Penner came on board. Sold my Barry home. Reached Hannibal at 5 that evening.[4]

November 20, 1901

[The boat reached St. Louis on November 21 and stayed there until November 28.]

December 17, 1901

Were obliged to tie up at Fletcher's before noon on account of high wind.

December 18, 1901

Left there and moved down to Island Fort[y?]. During the evening, ice began to float down the river and continued for three days and three nights, growing worse & worse, so much so that the ship was in great danger of being cut to pieces. The brethren watched constantly, working for three nights to protect the ship by undergirding with trees cut from the island. Finally the ice floe grew so much worse that we felt there could be no safety in remaining there but less danger in trying to flee from the ice. Consequently early on

December 22–23, 1901

Sunday morning we steamed up, watched for an opening, and escaped for our lives. We crossed the river and tied up at Oscar[?] Lights. From thence we went to Memphis and moored along side of Hopefield on the Arkansas side where we remained until Jan 3, 1902 when we crossed over and up the Hatchie[5] a little ways but as the water was getting very low we moved up (the Wolf) and tied at Williams Landing, Tenn. Here we procured lumber and built the barge, pitched our tent and held some meeting[s]. A few seemed to be interested. The Lesters left us here.

Started school for the children while at Memphis.

March 27, 1902

Left Memphis Tenn. and the Wolf River and tied up overnight by the river on the Tennessee side.

April 3, 1902

Were hindered in the morning by the breaking of a bolt, but that was soon remedied and we went up to Kimmswick. Laid over to paint the boat.

April 7, 1902

Steamed up and started for St Louis, painting the deck on the way. Reached St Louis about noon. Some of the brethren got work here. Bro & Sis Lind left us here returning to Minneapolis. They went out from us because they were not of us.

Mr Ogram came on and stayed several days.

April 23–May 8, 1902

Left St Louis and reached Alton [Illinois] in the evening. Pitched the tent here and [held] meetings. A good audience and quite a number [of] interested ones. Bro. Shepard, a Methodist minister, came to hear and then advertised in the paper to puncture Bro N's bicycle, but got all the wind knocked out of his own. Remained in Alton 16 days and left a little band of believers who now number 18. Some of them came to the boat in the evening of May 8 and five of them gave in their names for membership that evening.

May 9–11, 1902

Left Alton and reached Louisiana [Missouri], 113 miles from St Louis. Stayed over Sunday and in [the] afternoon preached from the ship to a crowd on the shore. Sister Ogram got off here and ran up to Barry.

May 13–15, 1902 [dates combined]

From Quincy [Illinois] to Keokuk [Iowa] From Keokuk thro the "locks" to Fort Madison [Iowa], arriving at 2 P.M. We secured ground and pitched our tent; holding meeting every evening except Saturday. The audience is not nearly as large as at Alton and very few attend regularly; however, they are well behaved, pay good attention, no opposition and no outside annoyance. Fort Madison is a clean city, clean streets, good walks and a clean wharf. A good place except that there is not God there. God is not in all their thoughts, the people are not religious. However, we hope some seed has been sown that will not perish, but when the times of refreshing shall come, will spring up into everlasting life.

May 30, 1902

This national holiday the band has been to play for the G.A.R. exercises.[6] Cloudy and cool, has been all week.

June 1, 1902

Sunday noon. This is probably our last day here, as we expect to leave for Lyons tomorrow morning. Has been raining since early morning, quite a downpour some of the time. A gentleman attempted to get a picture of the boat at 7:30 this morning, but the sky became so overcast I fear it will be a failure. We have an appointment to hold meeting in the park at 3 o'clock but the rains may prevent. We have not organized a band here as at Alton. Quite a number say it is the truth but do not seem to care to come out and take a stand on the Lord's side.

A Miss Dunn has been to talk with Sr Hembree several times and evinces considerable interest. All the ministers keep away from us.

The band came home Friday, tired but feeling that they had made a good impression. Took in $20. that day.

What a work this is, noble, grand. Would that I could more fully realize its greatness, have a deeper sense of the high calling to which we have been called. A stronger faith in the word of God. I long to have these glorious promises seem more real, to be able to picture before my mind the glories of the world to come just as vividly as I can the lovely things of nature by which we are surrounded. The landscape from my window is very lovely, the banks sloping backward and upward to the bluffs, some little islands near the opposite bank, and all in its fresh robe of green, trees and grassy hills. What will this earth be when it is made new?

June 2, 1902

Monday. 8 A.M. We left Fort Madison about 5:30 [A.M.] and are gliding smoothly up the river. It is a lovely morning, and warmer than it has been the past week. The rain ceased Sunday P.M. so we were able to have our meeting in the park. Sr H spoke, followed by Bro N—Theme, the second coming of Christ. There was a good attentive audience and several hands went up to testify that they believed these things were true. The Christian minister was present and talked quite insultingly to Bro N. after meeting but left very suddenly when he saw the crowd gathering around them.

The people shook hands very cordially and expressed regrets that we [were] leaving so soon and hoping we would come again.[7]

This morning as we steamed away, Mr & Mrs Currier waved goodby's from their home. While I was at breakfast we passed through the bridge and Fort Madison was left behind.

Very warm today. Grandpa Bryant seems to sink because of the heat.

We reached Burlington [Iowa] about 9 o'clock, stopped a half hour and then on up the river, stopping at Muscatine Island for the night. Got pieplant in abundance and milk and fine water from a farmers well.

June 3, 1902

Started early Tuesday morning. Passed Davenport at 10:10 and reached Clinton [Iowa] about 4:15. Decided to remain here a little time and hold meetings. The band played in the evening and a crowd gathered at the wharf which is a fine one. A good place to land. Bro N made a few remarks to the people assembled, telling them we were to pitch a tent and hold meetings.

June 4, 1902

Have a place for the tent close by, right here on the river front. The evening paper is just in with a nice little notice of our arrival here.

June 7, 1902

Sat. morning. Our tent was erected and ready for meeting last evening but the heavy rain and wind storm of yesterday made the attendance very small. During the afternoon we had a good deal of rain, and when the storm first came up the wind blew the tent down and broke the stern line of our boat.

June 10, 1902

The worst storm known for years in some sections of the country, did a good deal of damage in Minnesota and also in Illinois in Peoria and adjoining country.

June 12, 1902

Went to Davenport on business. Saw Mr. Pierce and rec'd $135 on the Bridge Ave. lot, and note for $100. More when the estate is settled.

June 17, 1902

Left Clinton early this morning on our trip north. Had a lovely day, just perfect it seemed, and we made good headway, going 91 m and stopping over an hour at Dubuque. Above Dubuque we passed portions of a wreck and finally the hull of the *Ravena*. Fifteen persons went down on her in the storm.[8]

June 18, 1902

Early this morning it rained, but now the sun is shining. Tied up last night by an island where was an old deserted cabin. The scenery along the river is beautiful, especially on the Wisconsin side. The high bluffs covered with green and the hinge rocks projecting out here and there are very picturesque. We have just passed the beautiful little town of Glen Haven [Wisconsin].

June 26, 1902

At Winona [Minnesota]. A full week since I have looked into my book. We have been anchored in front of Riverside park since last Thursday noon, just one week. We have [a] beautiful location, the surroundings as agreeable as we can expect under this arrangement of things, but there is no interest in religion here. It proves the bible true that there is no fear of God before their eyes, and few there will be that will go in the straight and narrow way. We are holding our meetings in an old rink, six blocks from our landing. It is a long rough building not nearly so pleasant as our tent but we could not readily find a place for the tent and this was offered us with lights free of charge. The weather is fine with cool air. There are occasional destructive storms along the river and over the country but none have crossed our path.

June 30, 1902

This last day of June finds us at Wabasha [Minnesota]. Held meetings Saturday eve. and Sunday afternoon and eve in the opera house which was given us free and the Electric Light Co. gave us light free also. It is very evident that people of the world have little interest in religion. We have small congregations but probably large compared to most of the churches. It seems very strange to us for people to get up and go out in the midst of a sermon, and such sermons as these, but sometimes half the congregation will leave in that way. Leave for St Paul tomorrow.

August 1902

Have kept the school up all through July as the weather was cool and we did not have meetings. The sisters and children are doing a good business in shawls and all who have means are investing in real estate and the brothers are busy fixing up the houses.

October 1–3, 1902

Bro N. returned from a visit to his sister, Iron Mountain, Mich.[9] Tuesday morning and on Wednesday the 1st eve., we had a few exercises on the occasion of his [Bro N's] birthday. 58 years old. Had a long table in the dining room where 4 of us ate supper and others ate in the small dining room. On the following Friday evening, Bro & Sr N & Bro & Sr. Skeels went to Virginia, Minn. to visit nephews and nieces, returning Monday Evening.

October 4, 1902

Sr Hembree went to Valton to visit her daughter, returning on Tuesday Eve.[10]

October 9, 1902

On Thursday about 3 o'clock we steamed away from St Paul. leaving Mrs Hatch and Mrs Wright watching us from the bank and waving good by. Our Dear Sister, whom we were obliged to leave behind, had left [the] boat before and was on her way to Minneapolis. Could not bear to see us go & leave her behind. We sailed through Lake Pipin and tied up across from Prescott [Wisconsin] at night. Bro Dean stayed at Minneapolis to finish up his work on the house he and Sr Dibble own.

October 10, 1902

The wind was strong and the river low which made sailing dangerous, but we got through the day safely although there was collision with some piles that did a little damage to the boat, and the barge rode on top of a raft for a little way in passing it. Tied up at night opposite Fountain City [Wisconsin].

October 11, 1902

Left Fountain City this morning and tied up at night opposite DeSoto [Wisconsin] having run about 77 miles. The day exceptionally fine and the scenery beautiful as it has been all along the river (especially on the Wisconsin side).

October 12, 1902

We are lying along side of an island covered with timber, a lovely spot (as also our landing place at Fountain City was). The picturesque bluffs with the varied hues of the autumn foliage, the river, the island, everything in nature is beautiful, but how soon these lovely colors will fade and the bleak winds of winter will lock the river in its icy slumber, while we will travel away from the winter to a more congenial clime.

There is a way that leads to a land of perpetual summer. There is a land a summer land, whose skies are ever bright, and I would travel the way that leads to it.[11]

Evening. Our morning meeting over. Had a good sermon as we always do, good for us, if we will profit by it. Prov 6 for a lesson, urging us to awake, to be no longer slothful. Awake to righteousness and sin not. I feel that it is indeed good to be here, and I feel that it is of the Lord's mercy that I am thus privileged. One thing impressed upon our minds was the tendency of the human mind to become wearied, dissatisfied with present blessings and fail to realize how great they are. When situated as we are, our pleasures and enjoyment should continually increase and the blessing of being associated together here where we can have such help should take away all thought of weariness or burden, and yet with some at least its effect is quite the contrary. This life becomes monotonous and irksome. No wonder the Lord said, "Thou sluggard." Paul said awake, arouse. The time is far spent, the day is at hand. Yes, it is nigh at hand and what we do must be done quickly. Instead of our lives becoming monotonous to us, our pleasures should be continually increasing, and we growing in favor with the Lord and in knowledge every day.

Contrast our situation now with what it was one year ago. Here we are settled on our boat with the work done and we have every needed comfort and more, "Having food and raiment let us therewith be content." That heavenly food and that raiment pure and white, let us not rest, not be content, until we have/get it.

October 13, 1902

Did not move from our moorings as there was a leak in the boiler and were in need of an engineer. Rev N went to Lansing [Iowa] in one of the small boats, telephoned to the boiler inspector at Dubuque and got permission to repair it so we could move on, and engaged an engineer.

October 14–15, 1902

Remained at Dubuque one day on account of repairs need[ed] to [the] boiler.

October 16–17, 1902

Boiler being mended. Baptist minister came aboard this morning to talk with Bro N. Am sending a chinchilla shawl to Mrs Haskin. Several are over town trying to sell crocheted work.

October 18, 1902

We reached Rock Island [Illinois] at about a quarter to eleven, had to get a new engineer so were delayed a little. While waiting, Mr Gartland came aboard. He must have been watching for the boat and came hurrying over the river to see me. His mission was to tell me that Mrs. C. R. Lee had decided to accept proposition and settle on that basis. I will be only too happy to have the trouble end and hope it will be so easily done without more recourse to law. Evening. We are moored on the Iowa side near New Boston, a small town of about 1,000 people.

October 19, 1902

Last evening, some of the brethren went with the rowboat to New Boston, saw the Christian minister and got an invitation for Bro N to fill his pulpit on Sunday A.M. and P.M. Bro N decided to go this (P.M.), so we are at home this morning.

Evening. We held meeting in the hall where the Christian church hold forth. Had a good attentive and, judging from appearances, a very much interested audience, and have an invitation to go this evening.

October 20, 1902

Had quite a meeting at the hall last evening, a large congregation, five hundred at the least, very attentive and expressed many regrets that we were going so soon. Took in over eight dollars in contributions at the hall and on the boat. Today, Monday, the men are getting wood, have several cords.

October 21, 1902

I must not skip over our stop at Fort Madison. After we got the mail, Bro N decided to move on instead of staying all night as he at first intended to do. Got my bedstead fixture in the mail here. Mrs. Currier waved to us from the house and we got milk from them.

Some time past midnight, a large steamer passed, and a little later the watchman found one of our small boats had broken loose and was gone. Bros Rowland & Prose went in search of it in the little boat. We found it down the river a little way, drifted against the bank, and a little later overtook the two brothers. Bro Brown stopped at Fort Madison to work awhile.

October 22–31, 1902

The last day of October. More than a week has passed since last I wrote in my book. We have gone down through the canal, spending a night in it, near the lower lock, and from thence on to Louisiana [Missouri] where we had meetings in the Christian church twice on Sunday through the persistent efforts of Dr. Keith. Thursday, Friday and Saturday night held meeting in Court Hall. Had fair audiences except that Sunday P.M. the ladies went home, or rather went to Bro Wharton's meeting, and left us with empty benches.

Rec'd reply from C R Lee accepting my proposition and I went to Barry with Mr Ogram Monday Eve to see Mr Klein. Have filled out papers which if properly signed will settle his worrisome will business.

Came to Clarksville [Missouri] Wednesday A.M., arriving about noon. The boat came here Tuesday A.M. Have had three meetings, first in the Opera house and two in the Baptist church. The audience quite large and attentive. The city authorities will not allow us to sell shawls or anything else; not even take orders.

This evening the band and preachers will cross the river, where they will be met with teams to take them to Pleasant Hill [Illinois] where they are to hold meeting tonight. Home of Sr Hembree's relations, and where she preached her first sermon.

From Louisiana we went out for pecans twice, but did not get many.

November 1, 1902

The brethren returned from Pleasant Hill a little before midnight, well pleased with their meeting there, the house full and many outside, and the people were anxious to hear more.

November 2, 1902

At Alton, having arrived about 4 o'clock yesterday. Not very long after, our Bro Gillings came on board, also Bro Patton called. In the evening quite a goodly number came to meeting. Bro Howell among them, full of the fair chance theory. Bro N gave him enough testimony to convince any one with a shadow of ears to hear, but he seemed obdurate. Time will tell the result. The others seemed to drink it in. Bro Weble said, "That is just what I wanted to hear," and Bro Leonard drank the sermon in with open mouth and sparkling eyes.

Just at dark the wharf master came blustering up, sent, no doubt, by the churches, but he cannot harm us, we can move on if we cannot stay here peacably. This seems like a May morning, warm soft air.

Captain Wild and Mr Wilson left for Rock Island last evening.

Later. This morning some of the Alton brethren came on board and at 11:30 Mr Howell and Mr. Rodgers, the Millennial Dawn man from St Louis.[12] They invited Bro N to join them at the hall at 2 o'clock. Said they would occupy about three fourths of an hour and Bro N could have the remainder of the time. This settled, Mr. R asked us to have services, so Bro N gave a stirring sermon showing no resurrection for those out of Christ.

November 6, 1902

At St. Louis. Came down from Alton yesterday morning. (Foot of Biddle St) Had some strange experiences there. On Sunday afternoon we all repaired to the hall, got there ahead of the others. When Mr Rodgers came in with his party, they asked Bro N to play and sing a hymn as they were not quite ready to begin their meeting. Then he asked for another and still another; then they practiced five pieces in their book and then opened their meeting which they kept up for an hour and a half, putting in all the time they could, hoping to leave us without an audience at the last, but not so. Rodgers, Howell and their party got offended and left after a little. They could not stand the sword of the spirit, it cut them [illegible] but most of the Alton people stayed. Among them a street preacher and his wife, who kept Bro. N there until quite late, asking him questions. Had meeting on the boat in the evening, our little chapel full. Among them Howell and the street preacher. They came for fight. The preacher kept interrupting until Bro N told him he must keep still. Well, it is hard to describe the meeting, suffice to say that he tried to preach after Bro N got through and kept it up until all were so tired that Bro N stopped him and then he & his party went home in a passion. Bro Gillings came on board the next morning, 5 hr and stayed until we started away.

Expect to stay and have the boiler repaired.

November 9, 1902

Sunday morning and the sun is shining. The first sun we saw since arriving in St Louis was yesterday. Are having some trouble to get the boiler repaired. All the boiler makers are union men and none of them will touch it because our own brethren have taken out the old ring.

Have looked some for a place to hold meetings but not settled one yet. Last evening two ladies called and Sr. Hembree had a little talk with them. They are quite a wonder as they believe that we must stand on our own merits and not on the righteousness of Christ. Expect to see them at meetings today. Their stay was short last evening as it was growing dark and they would not be out here after dark. Bro Leonard's wife & child of Alton came last evening.

November 10, 1902

Yesterday was another wonderful day. In the morning we had a grand sermon, such a one as no one but Bro N can give, bringing out the seven wonderful things of eternity from Rev. 2 & 3 viz.:

1—To eat of the tree of life; 2—To not be hurt of the second death; 3—To eat of the hidden manna & the white stone with the new name; 4—Power over the nations; 5—To be clothed in white raiment and his name not blotted out of the book of life but confessed before the Father and the holy angels; 6—To be made a pillar in the temple of God and go no more out forever. And I will write upon him my new name; 7—To sit with Christ upon his throne

A few curiosity seekers were on the boat. After dinner, Bro Gillings came, and toward evening, strangers. Mr. Sturgeon, another new light, who said that Jesus Christ is not only the eternal God but the everlasting mother. He didn't do like the street preacher, get mad, but he kept very calm, but was bound to have his say. His pants were darned beyond anything I ever saw before.

Bro Len from Alton went home before the evening meeting, but Bro Gillings, stayed until 9 o'clock. Three of his friends were here, a gentleman and two ladies.

November 13, 1902

Evening. Time flies, this week over half gone. Have been over town yesterday and today, did a little shopping for myself and some for [the] others. No public meetings yet. Have not settled on any place to hold meetings. The brethren got plenty of work, several are working nights.

An old man, I think a Christadelphian, called one day this week and talked awhile.

The weather is fine and warm, warm enough for tent meetings, but it is liable to change any time now.

November 19, 1902

Wednesday Eve and the last night of our stay in St Louis. Have quite a chapter to chronicle since one week ago. We succeeded in getting the privilege of holding meeting in the Full Bible Church on Sunday P.M. and at the People's Church in the evening. The day was unpleasant, raining much of the time, and the audiences small. At the First Full Bible Church, the minister was present and a few others who seemed to accept much of what Bro N said in his sermon but in the after talk it showed what manner of men they were of. The blood of Jesus did the work and set them free. I could hear but very little of the conversation as they were gathered in a group and talked low. One of the most remarkable features of the company was a lady who introduced herself to Sister Hembree as Elijah, said she is the true, the genuine and Dowie a counterfeit. A Salvation Army man told his experience in proof that the holy ghost is still given to the children of men, and work in them. The man in the darned pants was there but said nothing. Bro Leonard from Alton came on Sunday A.M. and was at the afternoon meeting. Went from there to see some friends and did not come in the evening, perhaps he could not find the church.

In the evening we repaired to the Peoples Church where we had empty benches mostly. 25 or such a matter of the strangers. The darned trousers among them. One man came in and took his seat in front who we judged to be a minister. Bro N spoke on perfection, no salvation aside from keeping the commandments. At his close the minister got up to speak, said he agreed with the bother but from fear of getting mistaken ideas, he wished to make some explanation. What the worthy brother had said was all right, it was to the church members but he had something to say to the sinners. "To you, poor sinners, come just as you are, give yourself to Jesus, such a strain.["] Well, when he got through, Bro N started in on him, very mild at first, but grew strong[er] & stronger until he, as an Adventist who was present said, he walloped him good. Then the meeting closed and we came home. Thus passed our second Sunday in St Louis.

Monday Eve. two people came on board, members of the Christian church, and Bro N gave us a grand sermon on the Kingdom. Tuesday evening an old German came in, another strange character, a great bible student and intelligent but there is something peculiar about him. However, he seems to have many ideas near to the truth and might learn it if he could keep his head straight and have an opportunity. Made some striking remarks. One was that we do not know how we are blessed here on this boat. The [word missing] called today for a short time

There were several in last evening to meeting. Some old acquaintances of our Barry brethren and 4 gentlemen, from the First Full Bible Church I believe.

This morning I received a letter from Mr Crawford regarding the sale of the Mostland place. Have written Sister Maxwell and Mr Klein today and this is the first trial on a new fountain pen bought today.

The evening is cool and my steam pipes are warming the room, a little.

November 20, 1902

Moored at a bank near the little old town of Kaskaskia [Illinois] having traveled a little less than 80 miles. Struck a sand bar once that shook us up some.

Capt. Little is too blind to trust. Didn't succeed in getting any one to identify me so could not have the deed executed. Will sign my name and send on to Mr Crawford as the notary at the bank advised.

November 22, 1902

At Cape Girardeau [Missouri], arrived 3 P.M. The town and wharf reminds us of Fort Madison. Had the first meeting last eve in the Baptist church which was offered us free. A fairly good attendance for such short notice.

The band went out soon after landing and played on the street, so helping to spread the news of the meeting. Are to have the Court H[ouse], tonight through the courtesy of the Presbyterians. Have had quite a number of visitors on board today as also we had yesterday after landing.

The people seem quite taken with the introductory sermon which was grand, on the all important theme.

Some of our party have been out with their crochet work with good success, the mayor giving permission to sell.

November 23, 1902

Sunday. Meeting in the court house, 2 P.M. & 7:30. A good audience in the afternoon and a crowded house in the evening. Bro N speaking, followed by Sr Hembree. Several expressed regrets that we could not stay.

November 24, 1902

Left this P.M. and sailed down until about 4 o'clock. Were obliged to tie up at the bank. A heavy fog made it unsafe to go farther.

Today was the commencement of our school. The new schoolroom is completed, cleaned and carpeted. But I was not allowed to look into it until today. Then I was led to the door, requested to close my eyes, led in to a chair and seated. When I opened my eyes, the children were in two lines, one each side of the room. Bro & Sr N, Sr Hembree and several others were there; then the girls began reciting verses in concert, 15 verses I believe. Then each girl recited some singly, except Esther & Ruth, they recited together. Then followed a song, then recitations by the boys and nearly the whole program was gotten up by the children. They seem delighted with the new school room.

November 26, 1902

Have had my school as usual. This morning some of the brothers procured some tame geese and several have been prepared for Thanksgiving dinner, beside two wild geese and two wild ducks which were obtained yesterday. Bro Dean went out peddling today & got lost. Came in about 5:45.

Brethren getting wood today. The bank here is high, about even with the cabin deck at this stage of water.

November 28, 1902

At Cairo [Illinois], arrived about noon. Had Thanksgiving dinner together, two wild geese, 5 tame ones and two wild ducks with plenty of dressing, gravy, potatoes, good bread and butter, apple, cherry & squash pie and canned peaches & piles of apples were the main articles of food. All passed off very pleasantly and all had enough to eat. Were we all thankful to the giver of all good things? Do we esteem the words of truth of more value than our necessary food? or did we care more for that dinner than we did to hear the words of counsel and warning that are so constantly being sounded in our ears? These are things that all need to consider well. Bro N is not at all well, could not eat of the dinner, but sat at table with us.

Found letters from Mr. Klein and Mr. Crawford awaiting one here. Business no nearer a settlement than before.

November 29, 1902

Paducah, Kentucky. Arrived about 4 o'clock. Had a smooth run up the Ohio, no incident. Bro Leonard went by train to Mound City last evening, a distance of 8 miles and had to walk back in the evening to Cairo. Captain Little leaves us here.

December 9, 1902

Still in Paducah. Have had a few meetings, beginning Thursday eve. . . . Small attendance except on Sunday. The people seem quite friendly and we were given the use of the 2 [Second] Presbyterian church free. Paid $1.50 for gas light.

December 14, 1902

Sunday eve, at Nashville, Tenn. Left Paducah Thursday. Started in the morning but were not far from our landing place when the packing blew out of the boiler, filling the boat with steam. We tied up at the bank for repairs, got fixed up and started on our way about 11:30. Reached our present landing about 3 P.M. Saturday. Weather much warmer.

Captain Ryman did not meet us here as he promised but his son came on board to explain that his father was obliged to leave before our arrival. His two daughters called in the evening to see the boat in the evening. But about Capt. Ryman. A Capt. Warner whom we ran across when hunting for a pilot, is in his employ and was so pleased with our boat that he brought him to see us and our boat, he is so delighted with it that he has promised us $100.— and the use of their tabernacle and band wagon.

Today it rains and Bro. N is not well. We may hold meetings Tuesday evening perhaps.

December 17, 1902

Last evening Capt. Ryman, Mr. Buchanan and little Walton Reeves called. Master Walton sang three songs for us, one Diamonds in the Rough. The boy left first as he was to sing at an entertainment. The Capt. and Mr. Buchanan stopped a little while and the Capt. said he would give us his band wagon ($750.), if we could carry it. It seems we have struck the right place. River still rising.

December 25, 1902

Nashville Tenn. Christmas Day on Megiddo. The children have been trying for a month to do right and are to have a supper and presents according as their conduct has been to lay their conduct before Bro N, he to be the judge and grade them accordingly. Sr. Hembree has written an excellent dialogue for the children, Sr. H, Sr. Skeels and myself to take part in it.

December 26, 1902

The supper came off last eve, but first came the examination before Bro N and it was truly a solemn occasion. Their misdeeds were brought up and talked over and the sinfulness of each transgression and disobedience pressed home and the children seemed to feel it keenly. It certainly should be a lesson to us who are on probation for a far greater prize and will we be wiser than our children.

At the supper table they were seated near to Bro N according to their merits. Muriel at the head & the only one who wore the [page torn, word missing]. After supper the dialogue was rendered and the evening spent in profitable conversation.

December 28, 1902

Sunday and my 61 birthday . . . The bell rung just before 11 o'clock this morning and soon all were assembled in the chapel, and the first thing Bro N did was to call all the children up before him and told them to form in line. Then they commenced to recite some verses in concert to their teacher and then presented a beautiful little clock, a birthday present from my pupils, just what I wanted and just the kind of thank you [page torn, line missing].

January 1903

New Years has come and gone. Had a pleasant day. Capt. Ryman, wife, two daughters and two lady friends took dinner with us. A long table was set in each dining room, and a second table in the large room. The band played some instrumen[tal] pieces, and at table had a song of thanks. After dinner repaired to the parlor. The choir gave a New Years greeting and welcome to the guests in a little song. The children presented a shawl to Mrs Ryman, the choir gave us a song to the tune Swanee River. Bro N gave an address and the children sang a New Years greeting. The exercises ended, our guests soon departed, and we had the rest of the day to ourselves.

January 4, 1903

Sunday. Meeting at 11 A.M. at the tabernacle. Rather unpleasant weather although not raining, but few out, perhaps 100. Evening, meeting again at 7:30. Perhaps 300 out.

The lesson read in the morning. Heb 2. In his discourse Bro N pressed home the importance of heeding what God has said, quoting Heb 1:1–2. He referred to Paul's conversion and to the fact that Paul verily thought he was doing the will of God when he was persecuting the followers of Christ. He had a conscience void of offense then, thus showing that conscience is no criterion to go by. Our conscience is just what it has been educated to be. When our conscience is guided by the Bible, it is all right. We must learn what the Lord has said is right and wrong. He urged upon us the necessity of keeping these things in mind so as to not let them slip.

[There are no entries between January 4 and September 22, 1903, or the pages are missing.]

September 22–24, 1903

Arrived at Madison [Indiana]. P.M. Pitched our tent on the Siersdorf lot and began meetings . . . Have had the tent well filled and more than filled, some of the time people going home because they could not get in. People listen attentively. Sunday meeting at 2:30 & 7:30 o'clock. Many went home at night because they could not get where they could hear.

September 28, 1903

Monday a gentleman educated a Catholic called to talk with Bro N. Has read the bible much and got a better understanding of it than most people. (Spiritualist lady called)

September 29, 1903

Tuesday a Methodist minister living at Jennings, Trimble Co., Ky. named Walsh called and had a long interesting talk with Bro N. Quick to grasp and ready to receive the truth.

October 6, 1903

Carrollton, Ky. Left Madison this A.M. Closed our meetings there Sunday Eve. Had a full and overflowing tent, many more than could get in, and much interest manifested. At least 300 arose at the close of the meeting to show their appreciation of what they had heard and their determination to lead better lives.

Held meeting at Milton [Kentucky] at 10:30 A.M. Sun—a full to overflowing church.

Came from Madison in about two hours. Are anchored in the mouth of the Kentucky River. A good harbor but no view of the town.

October 14, 1903

Bro N has been sick ever since we came here. Was up yesterday and went downstairs to dinner and supper, up again this A.M. but is not feeling as well. Has been in his room ever since morning.

A gentleman called this Sunday week to talk with Bro N. Sis H talked with him for some [word missing] and the band played & sang at his request. Is an intelligent well read man, a retired farmer living about 40 miles from Indianapolis.

October 16, 1903

Cleaned my room yesterday. Had my dresser and commode stained to match the bed and secretary today. Bro N up but not well by a long ways. Eunice, Madie & Ruth have chicken pox. Ohio River is rising and backing up into the Kentucky so it is much higher where we are than it was when we came.

October 21, 1903

Began our meetings in Court House first night, moved to [the] opera house. Closed Sunday Eve, full house

November 4, 1903

Leave Aurora [Indiana] this A.M. Held meetings in the First Baptist Church Friday & Saturday Eve. Went to the Odd Fellow's hall Sunday P.M. & Eve. At the Church, Rev. Davies got offended and interrupted. Showed himself. Monday afternoon several called and Sis Hembree talked to them on the thief. In the evening some came aboard. One couple, Mr. & Mrs. Oneil, seemed intelligent and earnest. Bro Davies came Tuesday forenoon to talk with Bro N. Is greatly exercised over our teaching. Dismissed school to hear the talk. [The diary ends here.]

Notes

Introduction

1. As of July 2001, the Evangelical Christian Church (Disciples of Christ) maintained a website, which gave a Rockville, Indiana, address for its "national pastor."
2. One of the first things Ruth Sisson of the Megiddo Church did when I met her in 1996 was assure me that the church was not a communal society.
3. Philip Jenkins notes that during the late nineteenth century the news media became increasingly sensational in its coverage of new religious groups, many communal societies among them. In fact, "some papers developed a minor specialization in cult debunking." Philip Jenkins, *Mystics and Messiahs: Cults and New Religions in American History* (New York: Oxford Univ. Press, 2000), 33–34, 42–43.
4. Donald E. Pitzer, *America's Communal Utopias* (Chapel Hill: Univ. of North Carolina Press, 1997), xvii. Katherine Tingley's theosophical community, founded in Pont Loma, California, in 1899, is a notable example of a communal society in which giving up one's private property was optional (405).
5. *St. Paul Pioneer Press,* July 9, 1902. Dolores Hayden, *Seven American Utopias* (Cambridge, Mass.: MIT Press, 1976), 6. The practice of celibacy and the reconstituting of membership through converts was also characteristic of the Shakers, who were among the most enduring of communal societies. The failure to produce subsequent generations, however, does have the drawback of forcing the community to focus heavily on evangelism to maintain a viable membership.
6. R. Laurence Moore, *Religious Outsiders and the Making of Americans* (New York: Oxford Univ. Press, 1986), 208.
7. Critics have pointed out that under this definition, most religions would qualify as cults.
8. There are many discussions of the use of the terms *cult, sect,* and *denomination* to describe religious groups. Among the more useful or accessible are in Jenkins, *Mystics and Messiahs,* 13–18, 48–50, and Ruth A. Tucker, *Another Gospel: Alternative Religions and the New Age Movement* (Grand Rapids, Mich.: Zondervan, 1989), 15–30.

1. A New Faith on a New Frontier

1. The fact that Nichols was given only his father's initials as a name often warranted explanation. As he stated in a military pension application in 1906, "My Father's name was Lemuel Truesdale and my parents took the initials of my Father's name and named me simply as I have always signed . . . L. T. Nichols."

2. *An Honest Man: The Life and Work of L. T. Nichols* (Rochester, N.Y.: Megiddo Press, n.d.), 10. Two additional children were born after the move to Wisconsin, including Ella M. (born in Lomira, Wisconsin, in 1858). Only Ella would stay with L. T. Nichols throughout his ministry. Information on the Nichols family was provided by the Nichols family genealogist, Owen J. Nichols. It is interesting to note that in an autobiographical article composed of material from Nichols's sermons, Nichols was quoted as saying that at the age of fourteen he had "an invalid father, a devoted mother, a loving sister," his other siblings seeming to have been forgotten. (L. T. Nichols, "Told by Himself," *Megiddo Message*, Oct. 4, 1936, 1).

3. Mark Wyman, *The Wisconsin Frontier* (Bloomington: Indiana Univ. Press, 1998), 179.

4. Information about the state of Wisconsin is from Richard N. Current, *The History of Wisconsin,* vol. 2, *The Civil War Era, 1848–1873* (Madison: State Historical Society of Wisconsin, 1976), 3–41.

5. *An Honest Man,* 10–11.

6. It is probable that E. C. Branham was the author, but the degree to which he was responsible for the content is impossible to determine. *An Honest Man* is, of course, adulatory. It is heavily weighted toward impression rather than fact, but what facts can be verified from other sources have essentially been shown to be generally accurate. Information about the origins of the book *An Honest Man* was provided by Ruth Sisson, pastor of the Megiddo Church and executive editor of the *Megiddo Message* (E-mail, Ruth Sisson to author, July 12, 1999).

7. L. T. Nichols, "True Christmas and New Year: They Changed Times and Laws," sermon preached Mar. 28, 1909, printed in the *Megiddo Message,* Mar. 31, 1919. L. T. Nichols, "Fear Not, Little Flock," sermon preached Jan. 6, 1907, printed in *Megiddo Message,* July 25, 1920, 3. An article published in the *Utica (N.Y.) Globe* at the time of Nichols's death in 1912 states that his parents were "deeply religious under the old Methodist style." The source of the information for that article is unknown. According to Mary Schroeder, archivist of the Wisconsin Annual Conference of the United Methodist Church, there was no Methodist work in Lomira during Nichols's youth, but there was in Fond du Lac, which is about nineteen miles from the town of Lomira (E-mail, Mary Schroeder to author, Sept. 23, 1999). There may also have been preaching points in the Lomira area at which Methodist circuit riders held services. In an excellent chapter on religion in frontier Wisconsin, Mark Wyman describes a Methodist circuit that would have come very close to Lomira (Wyman, *Wisconsin Frontier,* 205–6).

8. Maud Hembree, "The Faithful and Wise Servant of God Who Gave Meat in Due Season," *Megiddo Message,* Oct. 7, 1944, 1. Membership List (Goshen, Ind.: Washingtonian Temperance Society, n.d.) (courtesy of Owen J. Nichols). The Washingtonian

Temperance Society originated among reformed drinkers in Baltimore in 1840 and from there spread throughout the East and to the Midwest. The organization grew to include not only those who had been drinkers but also those who pledged to refrain from drinking. It was the only major temperance organization that involved mainly members of the lower middle and working classes. Women's groups, known as Martha Washington Societies, developed, often as auxiliaries to the men's organizations. Ruth M. Alexander, "'We Are Engaged as a Band of Sisters': Class and Domesticity in the Washingtonian Temperance Movement, 1840–1850," *Journal of American History* 75 (Dec. 1988): 763–85. For an excellent brief history of the Washingtonian movement, see Alice Felt Tyler, *Freedom's Ferment: Phases of American Social History from the Colonial Period to the Outbreak of the Civil War* (Minneapolis: Univ. of Minnesota Press, 1944; reprint, New York: Harper & Row, 1962), 338–46 (page citations are to reprint edition).

9. Frank L. Klement, *Wisconsin in the Civil War: The Home Front and the Battle Front, 1861–1865* (Madison: State Historical Society of Wisconsin, 1997), 28–29. Current, *History of Wisconsin,* 324–25. The quotation is from Carolyn J. Mattern, *Soldiers When They Go: The Story of Camp Randall, 1861–1865* (Madison: State Historical Society of Wisconsin for the Dept. of History, Univ. of Wisconsin, 1981), 98–99. Prior to German unification in 1871, the term *German* referred to people from various German principalities, including Prussia, as well as to Austrians, Belgians, and Swiss.

10. L. T. Nichols, *Bible Chronology* (West Concord, Minn.: author, 1899), 17.

11. Mattern, *Soldiers When They Go,* 11–14, 99. Throughout the war there was considerable tension between the camp and the city of Madison. Rowdy and drunken soldiers created disturbances and assaulted citizens. The city blamed the camp; officers at the camp blamed tavern keepers who sold alcohol to the soldiers.

12. B. J. Humble, "The Influence of the Civil War," *Restoration Quarterly* 8 (1965): 233–35. Humble notes that pacifism was not the only reason leaders counseled against military service. Some saw nonparticipation in the war as the only chance the church had for preserving unity between its northern and southern congregations. Unfortunately, "the Civil War . . . so shattered the sense of brotherhood between northern and southern [churches] that they could never again be called 'one people' in any meaningful sense" (246). John Howard Yoder, *The Priestly Kingdom* (Notre Dame, Ind.: Univ. of Notre Dame Press, 1984), 131.

13. Edward Needles Wright, *Conscientious Objectors in the Civil War* (Philadelphia: Univ. of Pennsylvania Press, 1931), 83. This volume contains accounts of soldiers petitioning President Lincoln to establish conscientious objector status, and it is possible that Nichols did so, as stated in *An Honest Man,* 39.

14. Nichols notes in his account that he was allowed to go home for twenty days during his brief term of service, perhaps for the planting season. Nichols's description of his Civil War duties is found in a compilation of biographical material contained in his sermons "Told by Himself," 5. Muster and Descriptive Roll of a Detachment of Drafted Men and Substitutes, May 1, 1865; Hospital Muster Roll, Mar. and Apr. 1865; George Worthington Adams, *Doctors in Blue: The Medical History of the Union Army in the Civil War* (New York: Henry Schuman, 1952), 184–86. The sources of

information concerning Camp Randall and the soldiers stationed there in the last months of the war are scanty. Carolyn J. Mattern notes that between September 1864 and the end of the war seven regiments "passed through the gates of Camp Randall. . . . None was in camp more than several weeks. . . . None had enough of a service record to warrant a regimental history." Furthermore, the newspapers had lost interest in the camp; "instead they carried news from Virginia where Wisconsin soldiers were preparing to come home" (Mattern, *Soldiers When They Go,* 105–6).

15. *An Honest Man,* 39, 40.

16. Whitney R. Cross, *The Burned-Over District: The Social and Intellectual History of Enthusiastic Religion in Western New York, 1800–1850* (Ithaca, N.Y.: Cornell Univ. Press, 1950; reprint, 1982), 354–55 (page references are to reprint edition). Place-names such as Rochester and Genesee, which were transferred from New York to Wisconsin with the westward migration, are evidence of the roots of many early Wisconsinites in the burned-over district. For an excellent map that shows the migration from New England to the Midwest that carried the ideas of the burned-over district to Wisconsin, see William Warren Sweet, *Religion on the American Frontier, 1783–1850,* vol. 3, *The Congregationalists* (Chicago: Univ. of Chicago Press, 1939), frontispiece.

17. For information about John Thomas and the early years of the Christadelphians, see Robert Roberts, *Dr. Thomas: His Life and Work: A Biography Illustrative of the Process by Which the System of Truth Revealed in the Bible Has Been Extricated in Modern Times from the Obscuration of Romish and Protestant Tradition* (Birmingham, U.K., 1911); and Charles H. Lippy, *The Christadelphians in North America* (Lewiston, N.Y.: Edwin Mellen Press, 1989). Roberts was Thomas's successor as leader of the Christadelphians; consequently, his life of Thomas cannot be considered objective.

18. In 1899, there were active communities of Christadelphians in the central Wisconsin towns of Camp Douglas, New Lisbon, and Hustler. It is not known whether the roots of these communities predated Nichols's contact with the Christadelphians. *The Life and Works of Thomas Williams* (n.p.: Christadelphian Advocate Committee, 1974), 18. *An Honest Man,* 12; [L. T. Nichols], *Second Pamphlet of the Condensed Report of the Annual Meeting of the True Christadelphians of Oregon Which Commenced May the Twenty-seventh Eighteen Hundred and Eighty Two and Continued Over Three Sundays. Holding in all Nineteen Days and a Half: And an Entire Night. During Which Time, the Authority, Publisher and Printer of This Report: Delivered Fifty-seven Discourses, Which Will Be Sent Out as Fast as Printed* (McMinnville, Ore.: author, 1882), 113. Since Nichols reported having traveled to the Thomas lecture with a group of people, he may have been involved with others of like persuasion, or he may already have gathered around him a small group of followers. (Subsequent references to volumes in the six-pamphlet series of camp meeting minutes will be designated *First Pamphlet, Second Pamphlet,* etc.). Thomas is known to have traveled to Milwaukee in 1866 and 1868.

19. Wisconsin was for many an intermediate stop on the way west, and native Wisconsinites accounted for a significant number of those who relocated farther west. As

the Nicholses arrived in Wisconsin, thousands left the state for the California gold fields. According to the 1860 census, 31,185 Wisconsin natives were living outside the state, as were countless others who had lived in Wisconsin but whose origins were elsewhere. Current, *History of Wisconsin,* 71–74.

20. "Articles of Association and Agreement of Citizens of Wisconsin and the North West to form a settlement in the State of Kansas or southern part of Nebraska." All of the Nicholses sold their property between January and April 1872. Property transfer records, pp. 279, 283, and 273. Records of the Northwest Colony are included in "Northwest Colony and Russell Townsite Company Ledger, 1871–1874" (Manuscript Dept., Kansas State Historical Society, Topeka). An L. T. Nichols is mentioned in the records as having served on a committee to pursue some advantages for the colonists, but since all men are designated in the records by their initials, it is impossible to determine whether the person mentioned was L. T. or Lemuel Truesdale.

21. *Understanding the Bible: Apostasy and Restoration* (Rochester, N.Y.: Megiddo Church, n.d.), 29. The Megiddos make much of L. T. Nichols's origins as a "frontier youth." Dean May, *Three Frontiers: Family, Land and Society in the American West, 1850–1900* (New York: Cambridge Univ. Press, 1994), 209–12.

Oregon is often considered historically to be a hotbed of new, unusual, and often controversial religious activity. In his book *Mystics and Messiahs,* Philip Jenkins identifies several groups on the religious fringe in Oregon (see, for example, 44, 96–97, 169, 205). According to historian Susie C. Stanley, who has done considerable research on holiness and Pentecostal groups in Oregon, "All I've ever seen is brief references to these groups gradually moving west until they couldn't go any farther. It just seems to be a general presupposition that everyone accepts at face value. I've never seen any 'scientific' data to back up the claim but it's one of those that just seems to make sense. It's easy to live off the land in Oregon so that would be a factor in keeping people there rather than returning back East" (E-mail, Susie C. Stanley to author, Mar. 21, 2001).

22. "United States," *Christadelphian,* Sept. 1, 1877; [Letter], *The Christadelphian,* Mar. 1, 1879.

23. Bryan R. Wilson, *Sects and Society: A Sociological Study of the Elim Tabernacle, Christian Science, and Christadelphians* (Berkeley, Calif.: Univ. of California Press, 1961), 298. Women are not permitted to speak at services unless there are no men available, although they are permitted to teach Sunday school to children and youth. For a description of women's roles in the Christadelphian church, see Lippy, *Christadelphians,* 198–202.

24. U.S. Census, Yamhill County Oregon, 1880; Wilson, *Sects and Society,* 300.

25. Charles H. Lippy, "Waiting for the End: The Social Context of American Apocalyptic Religion," in *The Apocalyptic Vision in America: Interdisciplinary Essays on Myth and Culture,* ed. Lois Parkinson Zamora (Bowling Green, Ohio: Bowling Green Univ. Popular Press, 1982), 38, 43.

26. The word *ecclesia,* the Greek word for "church," is used by Christadelphians to designate a congregation.

27. Barton W. Stone directed the 1801 camp meeting at Cane Ridge, Kentucky, which is considered one of the most important of the early camp meetings. On camp meetings, see John B. Boles, *The Great Revival: Beginnings of the Bible Belt* (Lexington: Univ. Press of Kentucky, 1996). On the holiness movement, see Melvin E. Dieter, *The Holiness Revival of the Nineteenth Century* (Lanham, Md.: Scarecrow Press, 1996). Nichols was well aware of the association between camp meetings and the holiness movement. In the second session of the first day of his 1882 camp meeting, he told his audience that he realized many had come "expecting to hear me talk upon perfection, holiness, and entire sanctification" (Nichols, *First Pamphlet,* 53). He then proceeded to tell them his version of the meanings of perfection and sanctification. He continued his criticism of the holiness movement on the following day of the camp meeting in a public "Interview with a Holiness Preacher" (88–106).

28. Lester G. McAllister and William E. Tucker, *Journey in Faith: A History of the Christian Church (Disciples of Christ)* (St. Louis: CBP Press, 1975), 123–27. McAllister and Tucker note that "while the debates did much to promote knowledge of Alexander Campbell as a brilliant forensic master, they did little to further the aims of the united church."

29. Hembree, "The Faithful and Wise Servant," 3. "Debate at Carlton," *Pacific Christian Messenger,* July 12, 1877; "United States," *Christadelphian,* Sept. 1, 1877. Thomas Campbell (d. 1893) is an important figure in the history of the Christian Church (Disciples of Christ) in the Pacific Northwest. He was called to Oregon, where he changed the fortunes of the struggling Christian College in Monmouth and made it an important educational institution that produced many prominent leaders of early Oregon. He also founded the *Pacific Christian Messenger,* which "became the leading family magazine among Christians of Oregon for many years." K. E. Burke, "Influence of Thomas Campbell and Alexander Campbell in the Oregon Country," *Christian Standard* 69 (May 5, 1934): 309. Christian College is now Western Oregon University. Interestingly, the advertisements for the debate that appeared in the *Pacific Christian Messenger* did not identify Nichols as a Christadelphian. The issue that should have been appeared immediately following the debate is missing from the microfilm edition of the *Pacific Christian Messenger* and may not have been published.

30. According to *An Honest Man,* Maud Galloway "received her education at the Convent of the Sacred Heart in Salem." Sister Rosemary Kasper, SNJM, archivist for the Oregon Province of the Sisters of the Holy Names of Jesus and Mary, the congregation that operated Sacred Heart Academy in Salem from 1863 until 1984, could find no record of a Maud Galloway attending the school (Letter, Sr. Rosemary Kasper to author, Feb. 13, 1996). It is possible that the records are incomplete or that someone at some time made an error in recording Mrs. Hembree's educational history. It is uncertain what Maud Hembree's religious affiliation was at the time she first heard Nichols preach, but according to information located by Joan Marie Meyering, Hembree's first child was baptized by a Roman Catholic priest in 1875, and she was likely still to have been Roman Catholic. In a reminiscence reprinted in the *Megiddo Message* in 1989, Hembree made no mention of being a Roman Catholic and stated

only that she "had believed the old creeds . . . and never heard anything else." As an adult, Hembree did not use the first name "Sarah."

31. Lippy, *Christadelphians,* 61–62, 66.

32. L. T. Nichols, *Adam before He Sinned* (Portland, Ore.: Schwar & Anderson, 1881), 3, 23–27, 35. The number 144,000 refers to a passage in the Bible (Rev. 14:1–3) that reads, "And I looked, and lo, a Lamb stood on the mount Sion, and with him an hundred forty and four thousand, having his Father's name written in their foreheads. . . . And I heard a voice from heaven . . . and I heard the voice of harpers harping . . . And they sung as it were a new song . . . and no man could learn that song but the hundred and forty and four thousand, which were redeemed from the earth." Unless necessary for the sake of clarity, all Bible quotations are from the King James Version, the preferred translation but not the only one used by the Megiddo Church. The 144,000 have been identified by various premillennial groups, most notably Jehovah's Witnesses, as comprising either all or part of those who will be saved when Christ returns.

   According to Nichols's pamphlet, he planned to send it out free, asking those who received it to send him the cost of printing—fifteen cents. The frequent references to Thomas and Roberts indicate the intended audience was other Christadelphians.

33. Since in claiming victory in his debate with L. T. Nichols, Thomas Campbell reported in the August 5, 1877, issue of the *Pacific Christian Messenger* that H. C. Plummer, "the Christadelphian soul sleeper," was pleased with the result of the debate, the difficulties between Plummer and Nichols appear to have started at least by that time. *Yamhill County (McMinnville, Ore.) Reporter,* Aug. 29, 1878. See *The Christadelphian,* July 1, 1879, 336; May 1, 1880; Aug. 1, 1880; Sept. 1, 1880; Feb. 1, 1882, 96. Sister Wade, "Attending Funerals," *Christadelphian,* June 1, 1881, 267; Brother Gunn, in "Pseudo-Christadelphianism," *Christadelphian,* Dec. 1, 1881, 557. There are no known extant copies of this early edition of the "Synopsis." The church that was planted at Scholls Ferry, which was known as the "Soul Sleepers or Church of God," constructed a small building in 1893. Pastor Skeels baptized twenty-eight converts in a nearby creek. The fate of the congregation is unknown, but the church building was used by other denominations after 1900 (Margaret Putnam Hess, *Scholls Ferry Tales* [Medford, Ore.: Groner Womens Club, 1994], 35). I am indebted to Joan Marie Meyering for drawing my attention to this information.

34. For a classic brief description of Campbell's thought on the Mosaic law and the New Testament law, see Winfred Ernest Garrison, *Alexander Campbell's Theology: Its Sources and Historical Setting* (St. Louis: Christian Publishing Co., 1900), 161–82. In Campbell's writings, see *The Christian System in Reference to the Union of Christians, and a Restoration of Primitive Christianity, as Plead in the Current Reformation* (Cincinnati: H. S. Bosworth, 1866; reprint, Salem, N.H.: Ayer Co. Publishers, 1988), 138–158.

   According to the Megiddos, "the Law of Moses was only a secular or civil law for Israel, and never would give eternal life" ("Questions and Answers," *Megiddo Message,* Feb. 18, 1961, 11). It should be noted here that while the Megiddos believe "the Mosaic law remains today only as part of historical Scripture," they are quick to point out similarities between the Mosaic law and what they call the "Law of Faith" or "Royal Law." See *Understanding the Bible, Section 20: The Mosaic Law—Its Significance* (Rochester, N.Y.: Megiddo Mission, n.d.), which includes a table of parallels between the two legal systems and descriptions of where in the New Testament specific issues raised by the Ten Commandments can be found.

35. Nichols, *Fifth Pamphlet,* 383. Nichols's claims to have discovered the true meanings of Bible texts are not unlike claims made by the Christadelphians for John Thomas.

36. Campbell used the term *Great Apostasy* in his work *The Christian System,* 3. Since Christian unity was the focus of Campbell's ministry, the Great Apostasy referred to the period during which the church became divided. The term *Great Apostasy* has been used by many other religious leaders and groups, notably by Daniel S. Warner (1842–1925), founder of the Church of God movement. Richard T. Hughes, "The Meaning of the Restoration Vision," in *The Primitive Church in the Modern World,* ed. Richard T. Hughes (Urbana: Univ. of Illinois Press, 1995), x. John Thomas used the term *apostasy.*

37. *The Great Apostasy* (Rochester, N.Y.: Megiddo Mission), 10.

38. On perfectionism, see Dieter, *Holiness Revival,* and John L. Peters, *Christian Perfection in American Methodism* (Nashville: Abingdon Press, 1956).

39. Richard T. Hughes, "Christian Primitivism as Perfectionism: From Anabaptists to Pentecostals," in *Reaching Beyond: Chapters in the History of Perfectionism,* ed. Stanley M. Burgess (Peabody, Mass.: Hendrickson Publishers, 1986), 213.

40. Nichols, *Fifth Pamphlet,* 337–86. In the camp meeting report, Nichols noted that a Sister Sweet had had a chronology he had written in her scrapbook printed without his consent. He states he was glad she had it printed even though he "had not the matter arranged as yet so that I felt free to have it go out to the world." As far as members of the Megiddo Church know, there are no extant copies of the earlier chronology. Nichols reported in his *Bible Chronology* that he had been disappointed when the date appointed by Thomas for the return of Christ had come and nothing happened.

41. Nichols, *Fifth Pamphlet,* 382; Maud Hembree, *The Known Bible and Its Defense* (Rochester, N.Y.: author, 1933–34), 1:263, 266. See also L. T. Nichols, *Natural Israel, or Spiritual Israel, Which One Will Be Restored: By Whom, When and How?* (Rochester, N.Y.: Megiddo Mission, n.d.). For excellent brief descriptions of the roles of Russia and Israel in American prophecy, see Paul Boyer, *When Time Shall Be No More: Prophecy Belief in Modern American Culture* (Cambridge, Mass.: Belknap Press of Harvard Univ. Press, 1992), 154–66, 181–224.

42. Nathan Hatch, *The Democratization of American Christianity* (New Haven, Conn.: Yale Univ. Press, 1989), 206.

43. Nichols, *Adam before He Sinned,* 60. Hembree, "The Faithful and Wise Servant," 3. In the *Third Pamphlet,* Nichols reported that the first part of one session of the camp meeting was "taken up by reading a letter from the beloved brethren of Barry Illinois . . . [and] tears of love and joy flowed from heart to heart as all longed to see

the brethren of Barry and converse with them . . . And no doubt the letters from Oregon to them cause their hearts to beat with the same love" (244–45).

44. Maud Hembree, "Who Brought Forth Truth after the Apostasy?" *Megiddo Message,* Oct. 26, 1940, 3.

45. Nichols, *Second Pamphlet,* 107, 133.

46. *Who Are the Christadelphians?* (Birmingham, U.K.: Christadelphian Publishing Office, n.d.), 7; *Understanding the Bible, Section 3: Of Life, Death, and Immortality* (Rochester, N.Y.: Megiddo Church, n.d.), 4, 13.

47. Nichols, *Fifth Pamphlet,* 392–409.

48. John Thomas, *Elpis Israel* (London: author, 1849), 108–10.

49. Robert Roberts, *Seasons of Conflict at the Table of the Lord, Being Fifty-two Addresses at the Breaking of Bread, or Sunday Mornings at Birmingham (Principally)* (Birmingham, England, 1880), 83. It is possible that Nichols adopted a position favoring increased roles for women in the church before 1880, and this may account for the number of single women among his converts. He also may have encountered women in leadership roles in the church at a very early age. Mark Wyman notes that due to a shortage of clergy, women were allowed to preach in Methodist churches and were permitted to pray aloud in public in Congregational and Presbyterian settings in frontier Wisconsin. Wyman, *Frontier Wisconsin,* 205.

50. Nichols, *Second Pamphlet,* 91.

51. The first woman to be ordained by a denomination in the United States was Antoinette Brown, who was ordained as a Congregational minister in 1853. At the ordination service, Luther Lee, a Wesleyan Methodist minister, gave a spirited defense of women's ministry. The text of Lee's message is included in Luther Lee, *Five Sermons and a Tract* (Chicago: Holrad House, 1975), 77–100. Later defenses of women's ministry were written by such people as Benjamin Titus Roberts (*The Right of Women to Preach the Gospel* [1872]), one of the founders of the Free Methodist Church, and by Salvation Army cofounder Catherine Booth (*Female Ministry* [1859]). See also a chapter on the evangelical roots of feminism in Donald W. Dayton, *Discovering an Evangelical Heritage* (New York: Harper & Row, 1976), 85–98.

52. Constitution and Bylaws of the Megiddo Church, Inc., 4, 10. In fairness, it should be noted that there is a tendency among churches of many denominations to favor the placing of men on boards of trustees probably because of the perception that they will be better able to deal with problems concerning the church's physical plant, for which the board is usually responsible.

53. Gerald R. Payne, "Dialogue: Should Women Teach in Church?" *Megiddo Message,* Nov. 1998, 14. The article goes on to defend the right of women to occupy positions of responsibility in the church and to describe the roles of many important women mentioned in the Bible.

2. Despised and Rejected

1. Frederick Jackson Turner, *The Significance of the Frontier in American History* (Washington: Government Printing Office, 1894; reprint, Redex Microprint Corporation, 1966), 226.

2. Among the biblical passages that mention the holy kiss are Rom. 16:16; 1 Cor. 16:20, and 2 Cor. 13:12. L. Herman Shuman, "Kiss, Holy," in *Brethren Encyclopedia* (Philadelphia: Brethren Encyclopedia, 1983).

3. The German Baptist Brethren, who later experienced several splits, was primarily an Anabaptist and Pietist group, which was strongly influenced by the Restorationist movement in the nineteenth century, as evidenced by the fact that most of its congregations in Kentucky and southern Indiana eventually joined the Disciples of Christ. Conservative groups with ties to the German Baptist Brethren still practice the holy kiss but only between members of the same sex.

   Admittedly, the references to Thurman in Nichols's writings are scant and vague. They appear in the *Fifth Pamphlet* and in later editions of *Bible Chronology* (1899 and 1911), which are heavily dependent on the *Fifth Pamphlet*. According to Church of the Brethren historian Donald F. Durnbaugh, who has done considerable work on Thurman, Thurman predicted three dates for the coming of Christ (1868, 1875, and 1876) and led a group of his followers out of the German Baptist Brethren. He died in poverty in 1906, claiming that Christ would come in 1917. Thurman's most noted eschatological work was *The Sealed Book of Daniel Opened,* first published in 1864. Donald F. Durnbaugh, "'How Long the Vision?' William C. Thurman and His Adventist Following," unpublished paper, 1999.

4. Nichols, *Fourth Pamphlet,* 319, 325–27.

5. *Yamhill County Reporter,* Aug. 8, 1878.

6. Ibid.

7. Ibid., Sept. 5, 1878, Aug. 8, 1878.

8. Ibid., June 14, 1883. Nichols was not the only minister to have been the object of controversy over the holy kiss. In one of the most complex cases, the holy kiss was implicated in a romantic relationship that resulted in the suicide deaths of a married clergyman and a young woman when a newspaper clipping headlined "Holy Kiss Causes Stir in Church" was found in the young woman's effects. The clipping, which was datelined St. Paul, reported an incident in Woodstock (Minnesota?) in which a clergyman excused his kissing of a married female parishioner on the "ground that the kiss was holy, and could be of no harm" (*St. Louis Post-Dispatch,* Nov. 9, 1902).

9. On sexual practices of the Oneida Community, the Shakers, and Mormons, see Lawrence Foster, *Religion and Sexuality: Three American Communal Experiments of the Nineteenth Century* (New York: Oxford Univ. Press, 1981).

10. For information on the teachings of Sylvester Graham relating to sex, see Stephen Nissenbaum, *Sex, Diet, and Debility in Jacksonian America: Sylvester Graham and Health Reform* (Westport, Conn.: Greenwood Press, 1980), 30–33. Information about the marital purity movement in general appears in Nancy A. Hardesty, "Marital Purity, Holiness, and Early Pentecostal Teachings on Sexuality," unpublished paper. It is also possible that Nichols felt that he had support for his views on marital purity from John Thomas, who suggested in his description of the fall of Adam in the Garden of Eden that sexual relations were sinful (Thomas, *Elpis Israel,* 14th ed. [Birmingham, U.K.: Christadelphians, 1949], 74–85). However, if he was influenced by Thomas on this matter, he appears to have been alone, as Charles Lippy, author of *The Christadelphians in North America,* does not know of any other

Christadelphian group that has ever practiced marital purity (E-mail, Charles Lippy to the author, Aug. 19, 1999). Nichols, *Second Pamphlet,* 110. At this point in his sermon, Nichols mentioned a series of ten lectures he had delivered the previous fall on "marriage relation, and its duties." The contents of the lectures are unknown.

11. References to these lifestyle elements are scattered throughout the camp meeting minutes and many are repeated. Examples are included in Nichols, *First Pamphlet,* 11, 15, 19, and Nichols, *Fourth Pamphlet,* 321, 335.

12. Nichols, *Third Pamphlet,* 247, 249; Nichols, *Sixth Pamphlet,* 483; Nichols, *First Pamphlet,* 15–17; Nichols, *Fourth Pamphlet,* 335.

13. Nichols, *Bible Chronology* (1899); L. T. Nichols, *What Must We Do to Be Saved?* (Rochester, N.Y.: author, 1905), 39–40.

14. Nichols, *Fourth Pamphlet,* 316; Nichols, *Sixth Pamphlet,* 444.

15. Lawrence Foster, "Free Love and Community: John Humphrey Noyes and the Oneida Perfectionists," in Donald E. Pitzer, ed. *America's Communal Utopias* (Chapel Hill: Univ. of North Carolina Press, 1997), 259.

16. Nichols, *Third Pamphlet,* 174; Jenkins, *Mystics and Messiahs,* 42–45.

17. As noted above, indications are that the membership of the Oregon church was about equally male and female, but more women than men remained with Nichols after he left Oregon. This may have been because the women who left tended to be single and the men who remained did so for economic reasons. There were still men in Oregon who retained ties with the True Christadelphians after they left.

18. *Buckingham* vs. *Buckingham,* undated transcript of court case, Yamhill County Historical Society, McMinnville, Ore.

19. *Hembree* vs. *Hembree,* undated transcript of court case, Yamhill County Courthouse, McMinnville, Ore. I am indebted to Jennifer Blacke for locating a complete copy of this document. The date for the filing of the case comes from testimony contained in *Buckingham* vs. *Buckingham.*

20. "A Sermon Delivered by the Reverend Maud Hembree, Megiddo Church, Rochester, N.Y., Sunday A.M., Nov. 12, 1933. According to Ruth Sisson, telling the story without identifying her husband "was her way of stating it formally 'in the pulpit.'" That it was her husband "was relayed to people who knew her personally and heard her preach." Fanella Porter, a particular disciple of Reverend Hembree, "told the story in greater detail" and remarked that Reverend Hembree was of an "extremely compassionate nature, very easily hurt, and it was a really hard trial to her to see anything made to suffer" (E-mail, Ruth Sisson to the author, Aug. 2, 2001).

21. Glenda Riley, *Building and Breaking Families in the American West* (Albuquerque: Univ. of New Mexico Press, 1996), 141. Contrary to popular assumptions, divorce was not uncommon in the American West in the nineteenth century, but religious differences were seldom identified as the cause.

22. Thomas, *Elpis Israel,* 122–23. Thomas's view on a woman's relationship to her non-believing husband is drawn from the teachings of Paul in 1 Cor. 7:13–14.

23. *Yamhill County Reporter,* June 14, 1883. Other than accusations from sources outside the church, there is no evidence that Nichols ever promoted community of goods among his followers.

24. *An Honest Man,* 49. The deed for the purchase of Nichols's property is dated July 22, 1875. Deeds for sale of property are dated August 20, 1875, and October 30, 1877.

25. The only evidence that Nichols carried his ministry outside the United States, other than to England, is a reference in the *Fourth Pamphlet* (277) to a lecture given at New Westminster, British Columbia.

26. Nichols, *Sixth Pamphlet,* 493–99.

27. According to a notice in the *Yamhill County Reporter* of June 13, 1878, a "grove meeting" was to be held by the Christadelphians from Friday, June 21, to the following Sunday "three quarters of a mile south-east of McMinnville (across the covered bridge) on Mrs. E. Martin's place." The notice is signed "L. T. Nichols, Christadelphian Minister." Later the same year a notice appeared stating that L. T. Nichols would lecture "on the camp ground near the Martin farm" (*Yamhill County Reporter,* Sept. 19 1878). Since Nichols did not seem to have qualms about putting a notice of the camp meeting in the newspaper, it appears that his aversion to newspapers may have developed after his later harsh treatment by the *Yamhill County Reporter.*

28. *Yamhill County Reporter,* June 14, 1883. Another article in the same edition of the *Reporter* states that Nichols taught his followers that he could not be hurt and that the shooting proved this was not true. There is no evidence in Nichols's writings that he claimed any such special attributes.

3. A Church of Their Own

1. "Mary J. Morehouse" (obituary), *Megiddo Message,* June 9, 1918. Both Dodge counties are named after Henry Dodge (1782–1867), first territorial governor of Wisconsin and later U.S. senator from Wisconsin. Dodge County, Minnesota, newspapers for the period during which Nichols lived there contain frequent references to trips made by residents to visit family and friends in Dodge County, Wisconsin, and the surrounding area.

2. Hatch, *Democratization,* 188.

3. Nichols, "Told by Himself," 2. Edward Everett (1794–1865) was one of the most famous orators of nineteenth-century America and was the principal speaker at Gettysburg when Lincoln gave his famous address.

4. Nichols, *Bible Chronology* (1899), 54.

5. J. Gordon Melton, "Introduction: When Prophets Die: The Succession Crisis in New Religions," in *When Prophets Die: The Postcharismatic Fate of New Religious Movements,* ed. Timothy Miller (Albany: State Univ. of New York Press, 1991), 2. The Megiddos do not believe in revelation, and Nichols's discovery of biblical truth is attributed to his own efforts.

6. According to a published history of Barry, Illinois, the Barry congregation was composed largely of people who had moved from Oregon and who were also apparently prosperous. "They built a church and good homes . . . and seemed a happy flock. Only a few Barry citizens embraced the religion." W. W. Watson, *History of Barry* (Barry, Ill.: Barry Advocate, 1903), 16.

7. Nichols, *Bible Chronology* (1899), 49.

8. *An Honest Man,* 113–16; *Owatonna (Minn.) People's Press,* Sept. 5, 1890.

9. *Dodge County Republican,* Oct. 9, 1890. The debate was transcribed by "two of the best court stenographers in the state of Minnesota." It was printed in the *Megiddo Message* October–December 1979 and February, March, May, July, and September 1980.

10. There is no record of the Nichols-Hull debate that, according to *Life and Work of the Rev. L. T. Nichols* (59), occurred in October 1891. In October and November of 1891, the Hulls spent a month in Minnesota helping the fledgling Spiritual and Liberal Research Society of Duluth (*Banner of Light,* Nov. 14, 1891), and Mattie Hull spent two Sundays with the Spiritualists in St. Paul (*Banner of Light,* Nov. 7, 1891). The Hulls' activities were reported regularly in the *Banner of Light,* a Spiritualist newspaper published in Boston. Hull also edited a free love newspaper, *Hull's Crucible,* in the early 1870s. There is a biased account of Hull's departure from the Seventh-Day Adventists in Arthur L. White, *Ellen G. White,* vol. 2, *The Progressive Years, 1862–1876* (Washington, D.C.: Review and Herald, 1986), 53–58.

    It is likely that Nichols's acquaintance with Spiritualism dates to his youth. The area in which his family settled was home to the Wisconsin Phalanx, a communal society led by Spiritualist Warren Chase. The colony closed about the time the Nicholses arrived in Wisconsin, but Chase lectured in the Fond du Lac area at least into the 1860s. Warren Chase, *Forty Years on the Spiritual Rostrum* (Boston: Colby and Rich, 1888), 90.

11. Lippy, *Christadelphians,* 65.

12. This debate is not included in the list of Nichols's debates in *An Honest Man.* Williams claims in his article in the *Advocate* (1892) that he offered to have the debate transcribed and published if Nichols would help to defray the cost, but Nichols refused. Consequently, no transcript of the debate exists and the information provided by Williams is all that is available.

13. *Christadelphian Advocate* (1892), 13–14.

14. Ibid., 156.

15. Nichols, *An Honest Man,* 64–65. Peter McNaughton Reekie, a British Christadelphian publisher, disputes this account of Nichols's meeting with Roberts: "The reference to 'Roberts fleeing' from the debate with Nichols is hardly credible. . . . The only circumstances under which I could visualise Robert Roberts 'fleeing' would be if his opponent was grossly blasphemous" (Letter, Peter McNaughton Reekie to the author, Mar. 28, 1996). Mr. Reekie could find no references to Nichols's meeting with Roberts in the British Christadelphian literature of the period. Roberts traveled to the United States three times between 1886 and 1888, but there is no evidence that Nichols met with him on any of those visits.

16. Apparently at some point after the 1882 camp meeting, Nichols stopped qualifying the name of his ecclesia with the word *true.* Newspaper announcements of services in Minneapolis appeared as "Christadelphian meeting." See, for example, *Minneapolis Times,* Oct. 4, 1891. Members of the Dodge County (Minnesota) Historical Society still refer to the group as Christadelphians.

17. It is unclear whether Nichols left the Christadelphians, they "disfellowshipped" him, or perhaps both. It is uncertain exactly when Nichols's followers changed their name to Christian Brethren; however, Williams indicates that the change occurred in 1891, and it certainly had occurred by mid-1893, when a notice appeared in the *Owatonna (Minn.) People's Press* announcing a new meeting place for the Christian Brethren church. In 1899, a Davenport, Iowa, newspaper noted that the Brethren seemed "to go a step or two farther than Christadelphianism," and the Brethren denied that they were Christadelphians (*Davenport [Iowa] Daily Leader,* Mar. 2, 3, 1899). It is interesting to note that both the names Christadelphian and Christian Brethren were used in the original document John Thomas prepared to establish a denominational identity. The document was necessary for the church to be recognized by the U.S. government, allowing church members to qualify for conscientious objector status during the Civil War.

18. Garrison is quoted in a chapter that focuses on the split in the Disciples of Christ that created the Church of Christ in McAllister and Tucker, *Journey in Faith,* 234. According to Bryan Wilson, during the first quarter century of their existence, twelve heresies arose among the Christadelphians, several of which resulted in schism. The most significant of the many splits experienced by the Christadelphians occurred in 1893 when the two main existing bodies of Christadelphians, now known as the Amended and the Unamended, separated. Wilson, *Sects and Society,* 244, 351, 341. Dr. Wilson notes that "one might almost say that Christadelphians appeared to thrive on disputation!" (Letter, Bryan R. Wilson to the author, Mar. 10, 1996). In *Sects and Society,* Wilson notes, "Among the Christadelphians with local assemblies enjoying wide autonomy, it is still only leading brethren who can promote widespread divisions, and they must be men of wide influence if their dispute is to spread further than to a few local ecclesias" (339).

19. On the importance of baptism to present-day Christadelphians, see *Who Are the Christadelphians?* (Birmingham, U.K.: Christadelphian Publishing Office, n.d.), 10, and *The Christadelphians: Who Are They? What Do They Believe?* (Unattributed tract), 12. Both publications were being distributed by Christadelphian Action Society of Elgin, Illinois, in 1996.

20. *Understanding the Bible, Section 9: Baptism and Baptism* (Rochester, N.Y.: Megiddo Church, n.d.), 10.

21. Constitution and Bylaws of the Megiddo Church, 3, 10–12. *The Synopsis of the Principles* has undergone several revisions, including, of course, the title as Megiddo Church, which is of recent vintage.

22. There is some evidence that the holy kiss was practiced after the Brethren moved to Minnesota. A report in a Davenport, Iowa, newspaper states that it was "the custom of members of the church to greet each other with a kiss," but since the otherwise highly critical article does not mention that the kiss was practiced between men and women, it may have been exchanged only between members of the same sex. *Davenport (Iowa) Daily Republican,* Mar. 5, 1899.

23. Nichols, *First Pamphlet,* 7. *Owatonna (Minn.) People's Press,* Sept. 10, 1886; Sept. 24, 1886; Oct. 15, 1886; Dec. 2, 1887. The obituary for Fanny Amelia Darby appears

in *Owatonna (Minn.) People's Press,* Nov. 25, 1887. *Owatonna (Minn.) Journal and Herald,* Dec. 2, 9, 1887. Information about Darby's other child is from *History of Steele and Waseca Counties, Minnesota* (Chicago: Union Publishing Co., 1887), 111.

24. *Megiddo Message,* Dec. 3, 1955, 9; May 3, 1958, 11; July 7, 1969, 23; Ruth Sisson, interview, Apr. 16, 1999.

25. According to Flowerday, "Mrs. Borden corresponded for some years afterward with the Mission . . . but nothing further than that was known of her" ([Kenneth Flowerday], "Experiences of Mission Life on Three Rivers, Mississippi—Ohio—Cumberland, Oct. 24, 1901—January, 1904," 22–23; this unattributed memoir was certainly written by Kenneth Flowerday.)

In commenting on the contention that the threat of eternal torment was necessary to foster good behavior, Nichols noted the law-abiding behavior of the Brethren and further commented, "Look at the Universalists; they do not believe in eternal torment and where could you find a more law-abiding people? . . . If it were true, that to not believe the terrible doctrine makes men and women lawless, then an extra force of police would be necessary to guard the Universalists, and all who have discarded the fearful doctrine." L. T. Nichols, *Treatise on Hell* (Rochester, N.Y.: Megiddo Mission Band, 1905), 5.

26. *Owatonna (Minn.) People's Press,* Jan. 30, 1891.

27. Ibid., Oct. 19, 1888; *West Concord People,* July 19, 1893.

28. William Lass, *Minnesota: A History* (New York: W. W. Norton, 1977; reprint, Nashville: American Association for State and Local History, 1983), 132. U.S. patent numbers 327,894; 339,007; 339,071; 452,280; 458,478; 491,064; and 580,705. In 1902, a reporter for the *St. Paul Pioneer Press* suggested that Nichols's inventions were not limited to the practical items he patented. The report identified Nichols as "an up-to-date evangelist with a fine capacity for merging this world with the next. He had invented a theology and a windmill, an infallible chronology and an acetlene [*sic*] gas machine" (July 9, 1902, 2).

29. The information about the Steele County Fair was quoted in the *Mantorville (Minn.) Express,* Nov. 4, 1889. Z. A. Bryant was born in Oregon in 1856 and joined the True Christadelphians there. He followed Nichols to Minnesota and settled on a nearby farm. He was a follower of Nichols for the remainder of his life. "Zephaniah Albert Bryant" (obituary), *Megiddo Message,* June 3, 1944, 7.

30. In his book *When Time Shall Be No More,* Paul Boyer notes that "a striking number of post-1945 prophecy writers had backgrounds in science or engineering" (305). Boyer also comments on the fact that a significant number of recent popular writers of prophecy books had no formal theological training.

31. *Davenport (Iowa) Daily Leader,* Mar. 6, 1899; *Davenport (Iowa) Daily Republican,* Feb. 25, 1899.

32. An obituary for J. P. Byrd that appeared in the December 17, 1933, issue of the *Megiddo Message* noted that "he was led into the light of Truth over forty years ago when the Rev. M. Hembree was engaged in missionary work in Texas." Hembree stayed at the Morrison home on her visit to Texas. ("Ethel Morrison" [obituary],

Megiddo Message, Jan. 1980, 27.) Hembree's and Nichols's trips to Texas, combined with the fact that Nichols considered relocating to Texas when he left Oregon, indicate that there may have been people interested in the Brethren there at any early date.

33. The *West Concord Enterprise* reported on two occasions that Nichols traveled to Minneapolis, probably on trips to visit the ecclesia there. *West Concord (Minn.) Enterprise,* March 30, 1899; Nov. 27, 1900. In Minneapolis, Maud Hembree preached on the topic "Does the Bible Forbid Women to Preach?" *Minneapolis Times,* Oct. 23, 1891.

34. On the Owatonna ecclesia, see *Owatonna (Minn.) People's Press,* June 9, 30, 1893; Nov. 2, 1894.

35. *Barry Breeze,* May 2, 1901; *Davenport (Iowa) Daily Leader,* Apr. 29, 1901.

36. The reporter combines and confuses the Brethren belief that children do not have time to earn salvation, their rejection of the concept of the immortal soul, and their belief that those who do not achieve eternal salvation are annihilated. The reporter states that "according to the teachings of the prophet Nichol's [*sic*] children have no souls and if one dies before reaching the adult age he simply perishes, is annihilated." *Davenport (Iowa) Daily Republican,* Mar. 2, 1899; Mar. 5, 1899; Feb. 26, 1899.

37. *Davenport (Iowa) Daily Republican,* Feb. 25, 1899; Feb. 26, 1899.

38. *Davenport (Iowa) Daily Leader,* Feb. 26, 1899. The Davenport ecclesia is called "Brethren in Christ" by both newspapers, suggesting the Davenport ecclesia was known by that name in the community.

39. *Davenport (Iowa) Daily Leader,* Mar. 2, 1899. C. R. Lee was probably M. G. Lee's son, Clinton R., although an article in the April 29, 1901, edition of the *Davenport (Iowa) Democrat* indicated that Clinton R. Lee had moved to Lincoln, Nebraska, "a number of years" before.

40. *Davenport (Iowa) Daily Leader,* Mar. 2, 1899; *Davenport (Iowa) Daily Republican,* Feb. 26, 1899; Mar. 2, 1899. Tirzah and Margaret Smith remained followers of Nichols for the remainder of their lives. Margaret died in 1947 and Tirzah in 1955; "Margaret P. Smith" (obituary), *Megiddo Message,* Nov. 15, 1947; "Tirzah Smith" (obituary), *Megiddo Message,* Sept. 10, 1955, 9. The Davenport ecclesia had at least one other British member. An obituary in the December 11, 1927, issue of the *Megiddo Message* states that Thomas Phillips of the Rochester congregation had heard L. T. Nichols preach in Swansea, Wales, in 1891. In 1893 he moved to Davenport. Later he moved to Minnesota "for the purpose of worshiping with those of like precious faith."

41. *Davenport (Iowa) Daily Leader,* Mar. 3, 1899; *Davenport (Iowa) Daily Republican,* Mar. 3, 1899. For a discussion on the Megiddos as a communal society, see the introduction. The Megiddos believe that community of goods in the first-century Christian church was "adopted as a temporary measure to unite the new movement and all its resources in an all-out missionary effort, which was eminently successful." They also believe that it was practiced only in Jerusalem and that it was abandoned very early since it is not mentioned after the sixth chapter of the book of Acts (*Megiddo Message,* Feb. 11, 1956, 11; June 13, 1959, 11).

42. *Davenport (Iowa) Daily Republican,* Feb. 26, 1899, and Feb. 10, 1899. The identity of the disfellowshipped member and the nature and duration of his association with the Brethren are unknown.

43. *Davenport (Iowa) Democrat,* Apr. 29, 1901.

44. *Davenport (Iowa) Daily Leader,* Feb. 26, 1899. According to the Davenport Public Library, the name of L. T. Nichols does not appear in available court and police docket indexes (E-mail, Special Collections, Davenport Public Library, to author, June 12, 2001). John C. Snyder remained a member of the Megiddo Mission for the rest of his life, although he was somewhat estranged from the mission in his later years. "John C. Snyder," (obituary), *Megiddo Message,* Nov. 26, 1938, 8. Newton H. Payne, interview, July 20, 2001.

45. *Davenport (Iowa) Democrat,* May 3, 1901; *Barry (Ill.) Adage,* Aug. 30, 1900.

46. *Davenport (Iowa) Democrat,* May 3, 1901; *Davenport (Iowa) Daily Leader,* May 27, 1901. There is no evidence that the people to whom Lee sold the Davenport property were in any way associated with the Brethren.

47. There is also evidence that the ecclesias attempted to help each other's members. In a letter from Emeline Nichols to her son, written in March 1892, she reported that some of the Minnesota members were attempting to find work for a Barry member.

48. At least two of the hymnals listed in the minutes were standard Protestant hymnals of the time: *The Finest of the Wheat, No. 2* (Chicago: R. R. McCabe, 1894) and *Gospel Hymns* (New York: Biglow & Main Co., 1894). The source of the third hymnal, *Joyful Greetings,* is unknown. The Pealing Chord, a library that maintains one of the largest collections of hymnals in the United States (nearly 15,000 in 1999) has no information on this title. There is no indication in the minutes as to whether hymns were merely selected to be compatible with Brethren doctrine or altered to suit the congregation's needs.

49. For several weeks in the fall of 1891, the services were announced in Minneapolis newspapers. *Minneapolis Times,* Oct. 4, 1891; *Minneapolis Tribune,* Oct. 17, 1891; *Minneapolis Times,* Oct. 23, Nov. 8, 15, 22, 29, 1891. There were no announcements after November 29.

50. The evidence that the ecclesia was meeting on an upper floor comes from references to the need for a sign "on the first floor" to direct people to the meetings. (Minutes, Sept. 27, 1896.)

51. It is possible that allowing children to contribute financially to the church was viewed as a means of providing them with the opportunity to accumulate the good works required for salvation.

52. "Ada Boddy" (obituary), *Megiddo Message,* Sept. 15, 1962, 5.

53. *West Concord (Minn.) People,* Oct. 26, 1900; "Edward A. Flowerday" (obituary), *Megiddo Message,* Dec. 6, 1931. Interview with Kenneth Flowerday, son of E. A. Flowerday, undated typescript, Megiddo Church Home, Rochester, N.Y. The *West Concord (Minn.) People* contains occasional references to work E. A. Flowerday was doing for property owners in the Ellington area. "May Adeline Flowerday" (obituary), *Megiddo Message,* Oct. 14, 1939, 4.

54. Kenneth Flowerday, untitled and undated manuscript. The manuscript is partially written by Flowerday and partly in the form of questions by someone else, followed by Flowerday's answers. It may have been prepared in the late 1930s or early 1940s under the auspices of E. C. Branham in preparation for the centennial of Nichols's birth.

55. The cost of the trip to Florida may have been covered by the sale of some of Nichols's property in Ellington. The *Mantorville (Minn.) Express* (Nov. 17, 1893) reported the sale of property for $1,600. However, at the same time, Harriet Nichols purchased a small lot for $400. *The New Map of Dodge County, Minnesota* (St. Paul: Brown, Treacy and Co., 1894), plate 18, shows the Nicholses' property almost completely surrounded by property belonging to their relatives. *Megiddo Message,* Mar. 2, 1963, 2. For example, the letter appeared in the *Message* in October 1975. The October 14, 1961, issue of the *Message* reported that the service commemorating the founder's birthday had included the reading of the general letter, which was identified as one of Nichols's "most masterful works" (7).

56. L. T. Nichols, *A General Letter to All the Churches,* memorial ed. (Rochester, N.Y.: Megiddo Mission, 1941), 4–5.

57. Ibid., 3, 7–8.

58. The August 6, 1899, minutes state money was appropriated to purchase a dozen each of two publications to sell, one of which was Nichols's *Fifth Pamphlet.*

59. *Minneapolis Times,* Oct. 4, 1891; Nov. 8, 1891; Nov. 22, 1891.

60. The *Bible Chronology* and the *Fifth Pamphlet* are very similar, but there are changes in the structure of the links or periods into which it is divided (e.g., link twelve becomes part of link eleven), and there are additional text and changes made necessary by events occurring after 1882.

61. Nichols, *Bible Chronology* (1899), 49, 52. Nichols states that "there is a possibility that the truth was not all out until 1887."

62. Ibid., 106. The new dates for the period in which the Second Coming would occur are clearly stated on the cover of the pamphlet: "Bible Chronology, Fifteen Links Reaching from Adam to the Millennial Day of the Lord. Exposition of the Seven Times of Daniel, also of the 1260, 1290, and 1335 Years of Daniel 12 and the 42 Months, 1260 Days and 3 1/2 Years of Revelations 11. Profane and Ecclesiastical History Both Testify to the 1260 Years in Which No One Had the Truth of the Bible. All Demonstrating That the Lord Will Come in 1901 to 1909 and Renovate the Earth, Spread Peace and Plenty, Broadcast until All Nations Shall Own and Bless His Name. This Good Time Is Coming Soon. Though Men Scoff, the Day of the Lord Will Come—2nd Peter 3. Therefore Get Ready." References to Thomas and/or Roberts appear, for example, on pages 3–6, 50, 80.

4. Sailing into the Millennium

1. L. T. Nichols, "In Quarantine," delivered at Ellington, Minn., Feb. 2, 1900, 17.

2. L. T. Nichols, "The Megiddo Mission Boat, Where Built, When and by Whom, Its Object and Mission" (Evansville, Ind.: n.p., n.d.), 12–13. This pamphlet, which has a

photograph of L. T. Nichols on its cover, was probably printed in 1903, when the Brethren stopped to conduct meetings at Evansville.

3. Kenneth Flowerday, "Recollections," *Megiddo Message,* Oct. 21, 1944, 3.

4. Nichols, *Bible Chronology* (1899), 69.

5. H. M. Riggle, *Pioneer Evangelism, or Experiences and Observations at Home and Abroad* (Anderson, Ind.: Gospel Trumpet Co., 1924), 89–90. Lucy S. Furman, "The Floating Bethel," *Century Magazine,* Dec. 1894, 297–301. On I. R. B. Arnold, see Helen Arnold, *Under Southern Skies* (Atlanta: Repairer Publishing Co., 1924).

6. Nichols and H. E. Skeels sold their farm property in Ellington for $12,000, and Nichols sold his farm equipment and other goods at an auction at which "bidding was brisk and everything was sold at good prices." William Pickering, who was married to Harriet Nichols's sister and who had been a member of the Oregon ecclesia, sold his property and possessions shortly after Nichols. *West Concord Enterprise,* Apr. 11, 1901; May 2, 1901; Sept. 26, 1901. Although they left Ellington, the Brethren were not forgotten. In 1963, when Megiddo missionaries from the mission visited Ellington and Owatonna, they were shown the Ellington church and met an "old timer" who very well remembered the group as the "Nicholites" and expressed great admiration for L. T. Nichols. *Megiddo Message,* Aug. 1963, 16. The church is no longer standing, but the interest remains according to Idella Conwell of the Dodge County Historical Society (Telephone interview, Idella Conwell with the author, Jan. 15, 1999).

7. Flowerday, "Experiences of Mission Life," 2–3.

8. The *Quincy Whig* is quoted in the *Barry (Ill.) Adage,* Nov. 21, 1901. *St. Paul Dispatch,* July 5, 1902.

9. *History of the Megiddo Mission* (Rochester, N.Y.: Megiddo Mission, 1979), 17. This history was first published in 1905 and has been revised and republished several times since, often with substantial changes. Estelle Le Prevost Youle, *History of Clinton County, Iowa* (Iowa: n.p., 1946), 103. The steamboats on the Mississippi and Ohio Rivers at the same time as the gospel boat carried such colorful shows as the "Great American Water Circus," the "Eisenbarth-Henderson Floating Theatre— The New Great Temple of Amusement," and the "New Grand Floating Palace." For more information on showboats, see Philip Graham, *Showboats: The History of an American Institution* (Austin: Univ. of Texas Press, 1951). *St. Paul Dispatch,* July 6, 1902. Some information on the appearance of the boat was taken from the *(Cloverport, Ky.) Breckinridge News,* Dec. 9, 1903, and describes how the boat appeared in 1903. It was repainted as needed and the signs and banners were added and perhaps changed over time. In an early photograph, the boat does not have the banner between the smokestacks or the open Bible on the bow. Precisely when these were added is unknown.

10. *Clinton (Iowa) Advertiser,* Oct. 25, 1901, reprinted in the *Barry (Ill.) Adage,* Oct. 31, 1901. The *Barry (Ill.) Adage* followed the fortunes of the *Megiddo* throughout its travels, reprinting items from other newspapers and reporting news received from Barry residents aboard the boat. Even visits to the boat by residents of Barry in Louisiana, Missouri, when the *Megiddo* stopped there or the sighting of the boat

by Barry residents while on an outing warranted a brief article (*Barry [Ill.] Adage,* Oct. 30, Nov. 6, 1902).

11. The numbers of individuals and families aboard the *Megiddo* changed over time and vary from account to account. A list of the members of the Barry congregation who joined the boat ministry was printed in the *Barry (Ill.) Adage,* Nov. 21, 1901.

12. *St. Paul Dispatch,* July 6, 1902; *Clarksville (Tenn.) Daily Leaf Chronicle,* June 5, 1903.

13. Flowerday, "Recollections," 3.

14. (*Cloverport, Ky.*) *Breckinridge News,* December 9, 1903; *St. Paul Pioneer Press,* July 9, 1902.

15. *St. Paul Dispatch,* July 6, 1902.

16. One reporter noted that the *Megiddo* would probably return to Nashville for the winter of 1903–4 because the men from the ship had found work there the previous winter. *Clarksville (Tenn.) Daily Leaf Chronicle,* June 8, 1903. (*Owensboro, Ky.*) *Messenger,* Aug. 22, 1903. L. T. Nichols, quoted in "Glad Tidings," in an unidentified Madison, Ind., newspaper, Sept. 1903, quoted in *Megiddo Message,* Oct. 1980, 21. [Flowerday], "Experiences of Mission Life," 4. The occupations of the men may give an indication of the economic status of the members of the Minneapolis ecclesia who were unlikely to have been farmers.

17. George Dzurica, "Megiddos" *(Rochester, N.Y.) Upstate Magazine, Democrat and Chronicle,* July 15, 1984; Del Ray, "The Last Gospel Mariner," *Rochester (N.Y.) Times-Union,* Apr. 16, 1976.

18. Handbill in a scrapbook at the Megiddo Church Home, Rochester, N.Y. The *St. Paul Pioneer Press* (July 9, 1902) reported that the men on the boat were "laboring to develop a patent windmill and improved gas machine." Neither item was patented, unless the patents were in names other than those of Nichols or Skeels.

19. Flowerday, "Experiences of Mission Life," 3–4. The *St. Paul Dispatch* quoted Maud Hembree as stating that while the boat was at St. Paul, the Brethren ordered $104 worth of wool that was made into "fancy shawls and other articles . . . to be sold at a good price."

20. *St. Paul Pioneer Press,* July 9, 1902. *Cincinnati Enquirer,* Nov. 6, 1906. *St. Paul Dispatch,* July 6, 1902. *Evansville (Ind.) Courier,* July 18, 1903. Flowerday, "Experiences of Mission Life," 3–4.

21. (*Owensboro, Ky.*) *Messenger,* Aug. 22, 1903; *St. Paul Pioneer Press,* July 9, 1902.

22. *St. Paul Pioneer Press,* July 9, 1902.

23. *Nashville Banner,* Mar. 9, Apr. 13, 1903.

24. *Cincinnati Enquirer,* Nov. 6, 1903. While Nashville was not the first place the Brethren acquired real estate for profit, it is probably the first place where real estate was systematically developed as a means of supporting them in their ministry. It is likely that rather than underwriting the cost of the houses in Nashville and then deeding them over to his followers, Nichols, as he would in the future, purchased building materials in bulk and then sold them to the Brethren at cost. He may also have made low-interest loans to the Brethren, as he was later known to do.

25. Mary A. Lee, "On the Mississippi on Board the Mission Ship *Megiddo*" (unpublished diary, Megiddo Church Home, Rochester, N.Y.), Aug., Oct. 9, 22–31, Nov. 28, 1902. For the edited text of the diary, see the appendix in this volume.

26. *St. Paul Dispatch,* July 6, 1902. *Cincinnati Enquirer,* Nov. 6, 1903; *Clarksville (Tenn.) Daily Leaf Chronicle,* June 5, 1903.

27. Lee, "On the Mississippi," June 7, 1902. *Cincinnati Post,* Nov. 5, 1903. Flowerday, undated and untitled manuscript. *Evansville (Ind.) Courier,* July 18, 1903. *St. Paul Dispatch,* July 6, 1902.

28. *Winona (Minn.) Republican and Herald,* June 20, 25, 1902.

29. Flowerday, "Experiences of Mission Life," 8.

30. *Nashville Banner,* Dec. 20, 1902.

31. Flowerday, "Experiences of Mission Life," 8–9. Flowerday noted that "for a person of wealth and position and generosity to become interested in the humble, little sect, was indeed rare—a fact which led Bro. Nichols to remark . . . 'We have caught a fish with money in its mouth.'"

32. *Nashville Banner,* Feb. 2, Feb. 23, 1903; Mar. 2, 9, 16, 23, 1903; Apr. 6, 1903; May 11, 18, 1903. When Ryman died in 1904, Sam Jones preached at his funeral service before a crowd of about four thousand people. At that time, Jones suggested that the tabernacle be renamed Ryman Auditorium. Under this name, in 1941, the hall became the home of the *Grand Ole Opry,* the premier country and western music radio program. The *Opry* left the Ryman Auditorium in 1975, but the auditorium, which has recently been restored, is still used for musical events and is a tourist attraction for fans of country music.

33. Flowerday, "Experiences of Mission Life," 10 ; *(Clinton, Iowa) Tri-Weekly Herald,* Sept. 12, 1901. According to the *Clinton (Iowa) Herald* (November 1901), Nichols planned to leave an order for the barge, the lower portion of which was to house a machine shop for the manufacturing of articles to be sold and the upper portion to be a meeting hall to be used instead of the tent.

34. Lee, "On the Mississippi," Dec. 17, 1902; *Evansville (Ind.) Courier,* July 18, 1903; *St. Paul Pioneer Press,* July 2, 1902. The uniforms apparently reminded the *Pioneer Press* reporter of the Salvation Army, and he noted that unlike the Salvation Army the Brethren were not interested in "institutional or reformatory work." The reporter referred to them somewhat derisively as the "Salvation Navy."

35. *Evansville (Ind.) Courier,* Aug. 1, 1903; *St. Paul Pioneer Press,* July 9, 1902. An unidentified Henderson, Ky., newspaper, probably the *Daily Gleaner,* June 1903, in scrapbook at Megiddo Church Home. No Henderson newspapers for 1903 have been located by the Kentucky Newspaper Project. Kenneth Flowerday, "The Man I Knew," *Megiddo Message,* Oct. 1969, 15.

36. *St. Paul Dispatch,* July 6, 1902. For a brief discussion of women in preaching ministries, see Nancy A. Hardesty, *Women Called to Witness: Evangelical Feminism in the Nineteenth Century* (Nashville: Abingdon Press, 1984), 86–103.

37. Maud Hembree, "Women's Role in the Church," *Megiddo Message,* Feb. 1993, 20–23; "Questions: I Am Wondering about the Biblical Position on the Status of Women," *Megiddo Message,* Feb. 1977, 23–25. "Your Question Answered: Do You Consider It Proper for a Woman to Speak in a Church, or to Be a Minister?" *Megiddo Message,* Aug. 10, 1957, 11.

38. *St. Paul Dispatch,* July 5, 1902. "Elder Nichols and the Megiddoites Are Here," Henderson, Kentucky, newspaper, June 1903. "Searching the Scriptures," Henderson, Kentucky, newspaper, June 1903. These articles are reprinted in the *Megiddo Message,* Oct. 1980, 15, 20. *Evansville (Ind.) Courier,* Aug. 1, 1903; July 18, 1903; *Clarksville Daily Leaf Chronicle,* June 5, 1903; *Nashville Banner,* Dec. 20, 1902; *(Owensboro, Ky.) Messenger,* Aug. 22, 1903.

39. Nichols, "The Megiddo Mission Boat," 15. For accounts of attendance at the tent services, see Henderson, Kentucky, newspaper, June 1903 and Madison, Indiana, newspaper, September 1903, reprinted in *Megiddo Message,* Oct. 1980, 16, 20; *Evansville (Ind.) Courier,* July 23, 1903; also, *Clarksville Daily Leaf Chronicle,* May 25, June 1, 1903. There are no known existing issues of Madison, Indiana, newspapers for the period between 1901 and 1908. The Henderson and Madison articles are located in scrapbooks at the Megiddo Church home.

40. Flowerday, undated and untitled manuscript.

41. Lee, "On the Mississippi," Apr. 23, 1902. *Clarksville Daily Leaf Chronicle,* May 26, 1903.

42. Nichols, "The Megiddo Mission Boat," 9.

43. *Paducah (Ky.) News-Democrat,* Dec. 26, 1903; Lee, "On the Mississippi," Oct. 17, 1902; Sept. 29, 1903.

44. *Alton Weekly Telegraph,* April 24, 1902; May 8, 1902; May 15, 1902. Lee, "On the Mississippi," April 23, 1902. *St. Louis Post-Dispatch,* May 3, May 8, 1902. The controversy was also reported in the *St. Louis Globe-Democrat* and that coverage was copied by the *Barry Adage.*

45. *Alton (Ill.) Telegraph,* Nov. 3, 4, 6, 1902. Further evidence of the possibility that Nichols's Alton followers were influenced by Jehovah's Witnesses is found in Mary Lee's diary, in which she indicates that some people the Brethren knew had visited the *Megiddo* at Alton in the company of some representatives of another group that would later be part of Jehovah's Witnesses. Nichols held services or a debate with them a few days later in St. Louis. (Lee, "On the Mississippi," Nov. 2, 6, 1902).

46. *Alton (Ill.) Telegraph,* May 15, 1902, Nov. 6, 1902; *St. Paul Pioneer Press,* July 9, 1902.

47. Accounts of events in Evansville appear in the *Evansville (Ind.) Courier,* July 26, 27, 29, 1903.

48. Flowerday, "Experiences of Mission Life," 22. The act of shaking the dust off their feet was in imitation of Jesus' instructions to his disciples in Luke 9:5 to shake the dust off of their feet when leaving towns where they were not welcomed. Jews at the time shook the dust from their feet when leaving a gentile city to remove what was ceremonially unclean before returning to their own homes. (I. Howard Marshall, *Commentary on Luke* [Grand Rapids, Mich.: William B. Eerdmans, 1978], 354).

49. *Evansville (Ind.) Courier,* July 29, 1903. Flowerday, "Experiences of Mission Life," 22.

50. *Minneapolis Times,* Oct. 6, 1902. The article also noted that "a man from Ohio left a wife and several small children on account of this new religious venture." The reference is to John C. Snyder from the Davenport, Iowa, congregation, who lived in Springfield, Ohio, prior to moving to Davenport.

51. The Maxwells were members of the Minneapolis ecclesia. Mrs. Maxwell served on committees for the church. (Minutes of the Christian Brethren, May 1899, for example.)

52. *Barry (Ill.) Adage,* July 17, 1902.

53. Ibid., Sept. 11, 1902. According to the obituary for Laura M. Suiter in the *Megiddo Message* (May 18, 1957, 9), she was born September 11, 1870, making her thirty-one years old at the time the letter appeared. The obituary lists the child who wrote the letter and another child as survivors. There were no further articles on this matter in the newspaper. Laura Martin Suiter was probably no stranger to controversy, being a member of the family that the *Yamhill County (McMinnville, Ore.) Reporter* suggested might be responsible for the shooting of L. T. Nichols.

54. *Davenport (Iowa) Democrat,* June 5, 1902.

55. A change in plans would also account for the canceling of plans for an additional barge to be towed by the *Megiddo.*

56. *Paducah (Ky.) News-Democrat,* Dec. 23, 1903.

57. Ibid. *(Owensboro, Ky.) Messenger,* Aug. 19, 22, 24, 1903. *St. Louis Post-Dispatch,* Nov. 1, 1903.

    In her diary, Mary Lee noted that Nichols was ill at least from October 6 through 16, 1903. He also may have had health problems while the Brethren were located in Minnesota. The *Owatonna (Minn.) People's Press* reported in its January 24, 1890, edition that a short funeral service was held for Louisa Rosencrans on January 21, with N. Griffis conducting the service because L. T. Nichols was ill. It further stated that the full funeral sermon would be preached by Nichols at a later date. It was not until July 18 that the newspaper announced the time and place for Nichols's sermon in honor of Rosencrans.

    One problem the community on the boat experienced in the latter stages of the ministry were the deaths of two members. One woman died while the boat was at Henderson, Kentucky, in June 1903, and she was buried there. A few weeks later, Harriet Nichols's father died. He was taken back to Henderson and buried in the same cemetery (Flowerday, undated and untitled manuscript).

58. Paducah, Kentucky, newspaper, Dec. 23, 1903, clipping in scrapbook at Megiddo Church Home. The boat did not long occupy its new role. It ran aground and sank in the Tennessee River on May 24, 1904. *Paducah Daily Register,* May 25, 1904. Kenneth Flowerday, undated and untitled manuscript.

59. *Megiddo Message,* Aug. 4, 1918, 7. The December 5, 1915, issue of the *Message* reported that some Megiddo missionaries had met a man on a train who recalled the visit of the *Megiddo* to Owensboro, Kentucky, and the March 16, 1919, issue of the *Message* included a letter from a man who had met Brother Nichols on the *Megiddo* at Clarksville, Tennessee, in 1903.

60. Evidence of the enduring sense of curiosity aroused by the *Megiddo* is its appearance in *Ripley's Believe It or Not,* undated clipping from the 1960s, in a scrapbook at the Megiddo Church Home.

5. "Peculiar Religious Views"

1. *Rochester Herald,* Jan. 27, 1904.

2. Thomas Williams, whom Nichols had debated in Iowa in 1891, visited the Christadelphians in Rochester at least twice after Nichols relocated there. There is no evidence that Nichols even knew of Williams's visits, much less attempted to renew their dialogue. *Life and Works of Thomas Williams,* 30, 33, 39.

3. Unidentified Rochester, N.Y., newspaper, March 1906, clipping in scrapbook at Megiddo Church Home, Rochester, N.Y.

4. Nichols continued to use the title "Captain," although he was also referred to as "Reverend Nichols." The Christian Brethren did not practice ordination, and "Reverend" was, as it still is in the Megiddo Church, an honorary title bestowed on gifted leaders of the church. "Christian Brethren," unidentified Rochester, N.Y., newspaper for Jan. 25, 1904, quoted in *Megiddo Message,* Nov. 1980, 13. *Rochester (N.Y.) Herald,* Jan. 28, 1904. All but two of the families that had been on the *Megiddo* relocated to Rochester.

5. *Rochester (N.Y.) Democrat and Chronicle,* Jan. 30, 1904. *Rochester (N.Y.) Herald,* Mar. 27, 1904; "Rochester's New Citizens," unidentified Rochester, N.Y., newspaper for Feb. 20, 1904, quoted in *Megiddo Message,* Nov. 1980, 14.

6. *Rochester (N.Y.) Saturday Globe,* Aug. 20, 1904; *Rochester (N.Y.) Herald,* Mar. 27, 1904; "How Members of the Megiddo Mission Band Live," unidentified Rochester, N.Y., newspaper for Mar. 27, 1904, quoted in *Megiddo Message,* Nov. 1980, 14. "Owe No Man Anything," *Megiddo Message,* Sept. 1984, 12–13. It should be noted here that the names Christian Brethren, Megiddo Mission, Megiddo Mission Band, and Megiddoites were used by Nichols's followers during this period. Later they adopted the name Megiddo Mission. Recently, the name has been changed to Megiddo Church because the term *mission* has come to be associated with rescue missions. Members of the community are popularly known in Rochester as Megiddos (or Megiddoes), and, according to Ruth Sisson, the members are not offended by this designation. For the sake of simplicity, *Megiddos* will be used for the remainder of the book.

7. Incorporated into the buildings were cupboards that had been removed from the *Megiddo* when it was refitted. Megiddo buildings are characterized by large numbers of cabinets and cupboards.

8. *Rochester (N.Y.) Herald,* Aug. 23, 1904; *Rochester (N.Y.) Democrat and Chronicle,* Aug. 28, 1904; Sept. 18, 1904. Services for members of the mission were also held in the assembly room in the largest building on the mission property. On at least one occasion, Nichols lectured in an established Rochester church, giving a temperance address on behalf of the Prohibition Alliance at the Genesee Baptist Church. (*Rochester [N.Y.] Evening Times,* Sept. 24, 1904).

9. Ruth Sisson (E-mail, Ruth Sisson to author, Oct. 7, 1999). The *Alton (Ill.) Telegraph* of April 24, 1902, noted that the Brethren had "only once" taken up a collection. According to Charles Lippy, some local Christadelphian ecclesias do not accept

offerings from visitors because they believe that only gifts from baptized believers are acceptable. Lippy, *Christadelphians,* 189.

10. "Reminiscences of the Life of the Rev. L. T. Nichols," *Megiddo Message,* Sept. 29, 1951, 3; "What We Believe," *Megiddo Message,* Mar. 29, 1952, 7. "Sending the Light," *Megiddo Message,* Dec. 13, 1936, 7. *Megiddo Message,* Apr. 20, 1957, 11. Ruth Sisson (interview with author, Oct. 2, 1999). *Megiddo Message,* Aug. 26, 1944, 9.

11. Kenneth Flowerday, "On Paying Tithes," *Megiddo Message,* May 1973, 19.

12. L. T. Nichols, *Treatise on the Coming of Jesus and Elijah,* 8th ed. (Rochester, N.Y.: Megiddo Mission, n.d.), 39. Nichols, *What Must We Do,* 39–40.

13. "New and Novel: Leader of Megiddo Band Advances Some Novel Beliefs at First Tent Meeting—His Conceptions Are Sometimes Stupendous," *Rochester (N.Y.) Democrat and Chronicle,* 1904, reprinted in the *Megiddo Message,* Oct. 1970, 15.

14. Aharon Wiener, *The Prophet Elijah in the Development of Judaism: A Depth Psychological Study* (Boston: Routledge and Kegan Paul, 1978), 35.

15. Ralph L. Smith, *Word Biblical Commentary: Micah-Malachi* (Waco, Tex.: Word Book, Publisher, 1984), 342.

16. Nichols, *Treatise on the Coming of Jesus and Elijah,* 33.

17. Thomas, *Elpis Israel,* 404–5. This reference to Elijah is brief and is clearly not a major emphasis of Thomas's apocalyptic scenario.

18. *Nashville Banner,* Mar. 2, 1903. As evidence of Dowie's newsworthiness, during the time that the mission boat *Megiddo* was docked at St. Paul, Minnesota, the *St. Paul Daily Pioneer Press* ran three front-page articles about Dowie (Sept. 8, Sept. 26, Oct. 6, 1902). Nichols, *Bible Chronology* (1911), 27. In a sermon titled "Is the World Growing Better?" Nichols mentions having attended "one of Mr. Dowie's meetings" (reprinted in the *Megiddo Message,* Sept. 9, 1944, 1–6). Church historian William Kostlevy has suggested that Nichols may have heard Dowie when he attended the Columbian Exposition, where Dowie had erected a small tabernacle near the entrance to the exposition. According to *Life and Work of the Rev. L. T. Nichols,* Nichols applied for inclusion in the World Parliament of Religions at the Columbian Exposition in Chicago, but his request was denied because he did not believe in the "common Fatherhood of God and brotherhood of man" (35). *An Honest Man,* 91; *Rochester (N.Y.) Evening Times,* May 15, 1905. On John Alexander Dowie, see Philip L. Cook, *Zion City, Illinois: Twentieth-Century Utopia* (Syracuse, N.Y.: Syracuse Univ. Press, 1996). Dowie, aware of the belief that John the Baptist was the Elijah mentioned in Scripture, declared himself to be a third Elijah.

19. *Rochester (N.Y.) Democrat and Chronicle,* Aug. 6, 1906. For a critical assessment of Sandford, see Shirley Nelson, *Fair, Clear, and Terrible: The Story of Shiloh, Maine* (Latham, N.Y.: British American Publishing Co., 1989); for the authorized biography of Sandford, see Frank S. Murray, *The Sublimity of Faith: The Life and Work of Frank W. Sandford* (Amherst, N.H.: Kingdom Press, 1981).

20. Nichols, *Treatise on the Coming of Jesus,* 32–33. "Megiddo Band to Have Wings," unidentified Rochester, N.Y., newspaper, May 22, 1905, in scrapbook at the Megiddo Church Home; *Rochester (N.Y.) Herald,* May 22, 1905; *Rochester (N.Y.) Evening Times,* June 12, 1905. Nichols, *Treatise on the Coming of Jesus,* 27–29; *Elijah Then*

Christ (Rochester, N.Y.: Megiddo Press, 1982), 10. See also, *The Coming of Elijah and Jesus and the Kingdom of God* (Rochester, N.Y.: Megiddo Mission Church, 1972).

21. "Advance Guard in Our Midst," *Rochester (N.Y.) Post Express,* undated clipping, probably from 1905, in scrapbook at the Megiddo Church Home. The new chronology also confidently stated that "1914 will pass and there will be no millennium here, and it will prove Russell all wrong," referring to one of the several predictions of the date of the millennium by leaders of the Jehovah's Witnesses.

22. Charles H. Lippy, *Being Religious, American Style* (Westport, Conn.: Praeger, 1994), 6, 156–57.

23. L. T. Nichols, *Treatise on Christmas and New Year's* (Rochester, N.Y., 1906), 3.

24. Adam Clarke, *The New Testament of Our Lord and Saviour Jesus Christ. The Text Carefully Printed from the Most Correct Copies of the Present Authorised Version. Including the Marginal Readings and Parallel Texts with a Commentary and Critical Notes Designed as a Help to a Better Understanding of the Sacred Writings* (New York: Methodist Episcopal Church, 1833), 347–48. Neither the Megiddo Church nor I know of any other religious group that celebrates Christmas in the spring. However, with hundreds of small Christian sects in the United States and elsewhere, some as small as one congregation, it is possible, even likely, that there are others.

25. Minutes of the Christian Brethren, Nov. 1895, Nov. 1896, Nov. 1897. For a more complete description of the 1902 Christmas celebration, see the appendix. *Paducah (Ky.) News-Democrat,* Dec. 31, 1903.

26. L. T. Nichols, "True Christmas and New Year."

27. Nichols, *Treatise on Christmas,* 12. For a later criticism of Santa Claus, see "Celebrating Santa-Mas?" *Megiddo Message,* Dec. 1975, 25.

28. The Worldwide Church of God (WCG), an American Adventist sect founded in the 1930s, has recognized Abib 1 as the beginning of the sacred year but not as Christmas. Believing that it is a holiday of pagan origin that is celebrated today largely for commercial reasons, Christmas is not celebrated by the WCG.

29. *Rochester (N.Y.) Union Advertiser,* Mar. 26, 1906; "The Unique Celebration," unidentified Rochester, N.Y., newspaper, Mar. 24, 1906, quoted in *Megiddo Message,* Nov. 1980, 24–25. The newspaper stories indicated that the mission planned to leave the decorations up for about two weeks, after which some would be sold and others kept for future use.

30. *Rochester (N.Y.) Union Advertiser,* Mar. 26, 1906; *Rochester (N.Y.) Herald,* Mar. 26, 1906; *Rochester (N.Y.) Democrat and Chronicle,* Mar. 26, 1906.

31. *Rochester (N.Y.) Union Advertiser,* Mar. 26, 1906.

32. *Rochester (N.Y.) Herald,* Mar. 15, 1915. *Megiddo Message,* Feb. 18, May 6, 1917. James Bristah and Margaret Frerichs, "A Study of the Megiddo Mission," student paper, Colgate-Rochester Divinity School, 1946, 23. *Megiddo Message,* Apr. 24, 1943, 7. "Tomorrow Is the New Moon," *Megiddo Message,* Apr. 24, 1954, 4.

33. *Rochester (N.Y.) Herald,* Mar. 20, 1909.

34. *Megiddo Message,* Mar. 4, 1928, 8; "Christmas Program Broadcast," *Megiddo Message,* Mar. 4, 1929, 9.

35. "Christmas Activities," *Megiddo Message,* Apr. 8, 1934, 8. Newton H. Payne, interview with author, Apr. 25, 1998. *Megiddo Message,* Jan. 31, 1932, 1.

36. "Christmas Jottings," *Megiddo Message,* Apr. 28, 1929, 5. The celebration of Abib 1 has occasionally centered around the life of Christ. In 1970, the "main feature of the program" was a drama titled "The Choice," which depicted "scenes from the ministry of Christ." "Abib Echoes," *Megiddo Message,* May 1970, 8.

37. At this point in the article there is a lengthy list of out-of-town visitors to the Abib celebration.

38. *Megiddo Message,* May 12, 1950, 9; Apr. 26, 1952, 9; May 9, 1953, 9; Apr. 16, 1938, 7. Ruth Sisson, interview with author, Oct. 2, 1999. *Megiddo News,* Apr. 11, 1914.

39. A notice in the *Megiddo Message,* Mar. 5, 1949, 7, offered small Christmas cards at no charge to anyone who wrote for them. Similar notices appeared in subsequent years.

40. *Rochester (N.Y.) Democrat and Chronicle,* Apr. 1, 1951.

41. Some of these groups were considered to be ecclesias. It is unclear what constituted an ecclesia to the mission. As of 1918, the Megiddos recognized three ecclesias outside of Rochester, at Utica and Boonville, New York, and at Portland, Oregon. An item in the *Megiddo Message* for November 6, 1943 (p. 7), makes reference to a "little Santa Monica ecclesia" and an article in the September 6, 1955 (p. 6), issue identifies a group meeting in southeastern Iowa as an ecclesia. It is possible that the definition of what constituted an ecclesia changed over the years, or, since the mission was not incorporated until 1958, the designation had little or no significance. The Megiddo Church currently refers to the congregation in Rochester as a church and to bodies of believers elsewhere as ecclesias. Ruth Sisson, interview with author, Apr. 16, 1999.

42. *Megiddo News,* Apr. 11, 1914. *Megiddo Message,* Oct. 10, 1918; Apr. 18, 1920; Apr. 2, 1916; "A Home Christmas Service," *Megiddo Message,* Mar. 23, 1946, 31. *Megiddo Message,* Apr. 5, 1925, 6; Apr. 13, 1963, 2; "Abib—Far and Near," *Megiddo Message,* May 6, 1934, 7.

43. Hembree, *Known Bible,* 2: 338.

44. *Megiddo Message,* Jan. 4, 1920.

45. *Megiddo Message,* Mar. 18, 1928, 22. In addition to Rochester, communities visited include Batavia, LeRoy, Canandaigua, and Caledonia.

46. See especially *Megiddo Message* issues for Mar. 18 to May 13, 1928. *Megiddo Message,* May 30, 1937, 9.

47. *Megiddo Message,* Apr. 12, 1931, 7–8.

48. "This Abib Season," *Megiddo Message,* Mar. 1982, 17; "The Sacred Season," *Megiddo Message,* Mar. 1974, 10. On the Lord's Supper, see "The Lord's Supper or New Passover, Easter, and Pentecost," *Megiddo Message,* Apr. 2, 1949, 15.

49. In 1957, a reader wrote to question the use of the word *Easter* because of its pagan origin. The response was that, although it is true the word is of pagan origin, "our present system of life demands that we use words common in our language if we desire to convey our thoughts to the reading or listening public" (*Megiddo Message,* Apr. 6, 1957, 11). The same practical reasoning applies to the use of the standard calendar instead of a calendar based on the month of Abib.

50. *Understanding the Bible: Apostasy and Restoration,* 28; Minutes of the Christian Brethren, June 1896; June 1897; L. T. Nichols, "Excerpts from 'Our Day of Freedom,'" *Megiddo Message,* July 3, 1954, 9."Independence Day at Megiddo," *Megiddo Message,* July 19, 1941, 8. On the American view of George Washington as a Moses figure, see Robert P. Hay, "George Washington: American Moses," *American Quarterly* 21 (1969): 780–91. "Questions and Answers: Would You Please Explain Your Views About Saluting the Flag?" *Megiddo Message,* Nov. 1963, 23.

51. *Megiddo Message,* July 11, 1920, 7–8.

52. Like True Christmas, Independence Day was also celebrated by some distant members. The *Megiddo Message* of July 21, 1918, reported the celebration at Portland, Oregon, consisted of recitations, songs, and readings. "Independence Day Services," *Megiddo Message,* July 15, 1934, 7; "Independence Day Celebration," *Megiddo Message,* July 18, 1926, 8; "The Independence Day Service," *Megiddo Message,* July 16, 1933. The quotation is from [Fanella Porter], "Our New Pavilion," *Megiddo Message,* Sept. 1970, 16–17, 20. Ruth Sisson, E-mail to author, Nov. 27, 2000; interview with author, Apr. 24, 1998.

53. "Independence Day Memories," *Megiddo Message,* July 18, 1942, 7; "Independence Day," July 21, 1951, 7. "Decoration Day," *Megiddo Message,* June 9, 1929, 8.

54. Ruth Sisson, E-mail to author, Nov. 27, 2000.

55. *Megiddo Message,* Aug. 28, 1943, 9; Dec. 30, 1944, 9; July 27, 1946, 9; and July 24, 1948, 9.

56. Newton H. Payne, "The Band," attached to E-mail, Ruth Sisson to the author, Nov. 1999.

57. Ibid.

58. Newton H. Payne, "The Orchestra" and "Vocal Music," attached to E-mail, Ruth Sisson to the author, Nov. 1999.

59. Newton H. Payne, "Sound System and Recording," attached to E-mail, Ruth Sisson to the author, Nov. 1999.

60. "Thanksgiving Memories," *Megiddo Message,* Dec. 18, 1943, 7. "The Thanksgiving Celebration," *Megiddo Message,* Dec. 15, 1945, 7. Payne, "Sound System and Recording," Nov. 1999.

61. *Megiddo Message,* May 24, 1941, 9; Newton H. Payne, interview with author, Oct. 2, 1999. According to Reverend Payne, several unsuccessful attempts were made to record Maud Hembree. Ella Skeels, who succeeded Hembree as pastor, was successfully recorded.

62. "We're on the Move!" *Megiddo Mission,* May 1975, 27. *Megiddo Message,* Apr. 1977, 25. *Megiddo Message,* Nov. 1979, 27; Apr. 1981, 27; Dec. 1986, 19.

63. In the early 1990s, Rev. Newton Payne, who had been doing the analog recording and editing, became concerned about the preservation of the recorded messages. After exploring various methods of preservation, he decided that compact disc was the most practical. Clifford Mathias undertook the task of "recovering the unplayable tape archives by a tedious 'baking' process and immediately copying them to CD." Ruth Sisson, E-mail to author, Nov. 27, 2000.

64. Nichols, *Sixth Pamphlet*, 442; Nichols, *First Pamphlet*, 15–17. For information on the natural foods movement, see Gerald Carson, *Cornflake Crusade* (New York: Rinehart & Co., 1957), and Nissenbaum, *Sex, Diet, and Debility*.

65. "Self-Denial Week," *Megiddo Message*, Jan. 19, 1930, 8; Jan. 18, 1931, 8. Pastor Ruth Sisson believes that she has heard that Self-Denial Week was practiced on the mission boat *Megiddo*, but there is no confirmation of this in existing records. Information on the early celebration of Self-Denial Week was provided by Ruth Sisson and other members of the Megiddo Church based on their recollections and stories they heard as young people. Ruth Sisson, E-mail to author, Aug. 15, 1999. For an unknown reason, even though cheese is not permitted during Self-Denial Week, cottage cheese is.

66. *Megiddo Message*, Jan. 26, 1946, 7.

6. Spreading the Megiddo Message

1. *The Saturday Globe*, Aug. 20, 1904. *An Honest Man*, 88. Nichols used the device of offering to wager money as a means of assuring his listeners of his confidence in his ideas. During one of the public meetings that occurred when the *Megiddo* was docked at Evansville, Indiana, Nichols got into a discussion regarding how many windows there were in Noah's ark. He offered one hundred dollars to his opponent if the opponent could find the singular form of the Hebrew word for window in the Genesis account of the Flood. (*Evansville [Ind.] Courier*, July 20, 1903.) According to *An Honest Man*, "standing offers were made by him of large sums of money to any minister of Rochester who would meet him on the platform in an old-fashioned religious discussion" (116). Apparently, there were no takers.

2. *Rochester (N.Y.) Herald*, Mar. 11, 1911. For example, in May 1914, the *Megiddo News* reported that "Mr. Payne has a new house started and Bro. Plowright has a foundation in." Flowerday, "Recollections," 3. *Rochester (N.Y.) Democrat and Chronicle*, Aug. 5, 1906. Blake McKelvey, "A History of City Planning in Rochester," *Rochester History* 6 (Oct. 1944): 8. For information about the economic development of Rochester during the early twentieth century, see Blake McKelvey, *Rochester, the Quest for Quality, 1890–1925* (Cambridge, Mass.: Harvard Univ. Press, 1956).

3. Blake McKelvey, "Water for Rochester," *Rochester History* 34 (July 1972): 16.

4. *An Honest Man*, 92; *Rochester (N.Y.) Herald*, Mar. 20, 1908, and "Worshiped in New Building," unidentified Rochester, N.Y., newspaper, Mar. 22, 1908, quoted in the *Megiddo Message*, Nov. 1980, 25–26.

5. Pension application, Department of the Interior, Bureau of Pensions, Oct. 26, 1906. The Roosevelt administration issued Order No. 78, which declared that all honorably discharged Civil War veterans with ninety days of service who had reached the age of sixty-two were to be considered at least partially disabled and eligible for pensions. U.S. patent 968,592, filed Aug. 31, 1909.

6. The Kellogg family were Seventh-Day Adventists and, consequently, the Sabbath was observed on Saturday. There were also religious services twice a day every day at the sanitarium. In his book *Cornflake Crusade*, Gerald Carson notes that among the

rules for the support staff at the sanitarium were requirements that they attend religious services and not argue theology with the clients, who came from many religious persuasions (103–4). This latter admonition probably stood them in good stead when caring for Brother Nichols. Among the Battle Creek Sanitarium's most noted clients was Seventh-Day Adventist founder Ellen G. White.

7. Hembree, "The Faithful and Wise Servant," 4. Nichols's death certificate lists the cause of death as "angina pectoris." Certified copy of death certificate, Calhoun County, Mich. Date of record: Aug. 6, 1912.

8. F. O. Downer, a Nichols follower who lived in Battle Creek, accompanied Harriet Nichols and Ella Skeels along with Nichols's body back to Rochester. Downer later moved to Indianapolis and carried on a ministry there (*Megiddo Message*, Nov. 7, 1921, 10). Mount Hope Cemetery is on the National Register of Historic Places and is the burial place of many other prominent Rochesterians, most notably Frederick Douglass and Susan B. Anthony. See Frank A. Gillespie and Richard O. Reisem, *Mount Hope: Rochester, New York; America's First Municipal Victorian Cemetery* (Rochester, N.Y.: authors, 1994); the account of the funeral appeared in the *Rochester (N.Y.) Herald*, Mar. 3, 1912. A lengthy article about Nichols and an account of the funeral also appeared in the *Utica (N.Y.) Globe*, Mar. 9, 1912. Harriet Nichols applied for a widow's pension two months after L. T. Nichols died, and it provided her with at least a small amount of support for the remainder of her life. (Initially she received the twelve dollars per month that her husband had received, but this was increased to twenty dollars a month in 1916 and to thirty dollars at some later date).

9. Bristah and Frerichs, "A Study of the Megiddo Mission," 33.

10. *Megiddo Message*, Sept. 29, 1918.

11. In its October 4, 1914, issue, the *Megiddo News* printed the letter from the Mount Hope Cemetery Commission granting permission for the band to play in the cemetery. The one stipulation was that the band members arrive separately and assemble at the grave.

12. "Birthday Mention," *Megiddo Message*, Oct. 11, 1931, 8. "The Anniversary," *Megiddo Message*, Oct. 13, 1951, 7. The founder's birthday was also celebrated by the Portland ecclesia with a program and dinner. *Megiddo Message*, Oct. 29, 1916.

13. Information about the composition of the arch was provided by Newton H. Payne, interview with author, Oct. 2, 1999.

14. *Rochester (N.Y.) Democrat and Chronicle*, Oct. 2, 1944. "Centennial Memories," *Megiddo Message*, Oct. 7, 1944, 5–8.

15. The play presented in 1944 bears a strong resemblance to a silent drama presented at the time of the founder's birthday in 1930, in which Christian history was traced from the time of Jesus, climaxing in the dispelling of the darkness of error by "our loving, faithful Captain and father, the Rev. L. T. Nichols," *Megiddo Message*, Oct. 12, 1930, 7.

16. This article contains material excerpted from *Life and Work of the Rev. L. T. Nichols*. The entire article was probably written by E. C. Branham.

17. *An Honest Man*, 56.

18. J. Gordon Melton, "Introduction: When Prophets Die: The Succession Crisis in New Religions," in *When Prophets Die: The Postcharismatic Fate of New Religious Movements,* ed. Timothy Miller (Albany: State Univ. of New York Press, 1991), 1, 8.

19. The meeting held May 6, 1912, to elect Maud Hembree as successor to L. T. Nichols as minister is the first entry in a book of minutes that contains minutes to only nine other meetings, mainly held to fill vacant positions in the mission leadership. There are also two early membership lists in the book.

20. "Advance Guard in Our Midst," *Rochester (N.Y.) Post Express;* undated clipping; *Watertown Daily Standard,* Aug. 8, 1905; *Toronto Mail and Empire,* Sept. 27, 1905; "Deaconesses Here," undated clipping, probably from 1905, from St. Catharines, Ontario. All clippings in a scrapbook at the Megiddo Church Home.

21. J. Gordon Melton, "Spiritualization and Reaffirmation: What Really Happens When Prophecy Fails," *American Studies* 26 (fall 1985): 17–20.

22. Several of the groups known by the names of their periodicals are discussed in Charles Edwin Jones, *Perfectionist Persuasion: The Holiness Movement and American Methodism, 1867–1936* (Metuchen, N.J.: Scarecrow Press, 1974). Ironically, the Church of God (Anderson), one of the larger denominations to grow out of the holiness movement, started as a group of subscribers to the antidenominational magazine *The Gospel Trumpet,* published by Daniel Sidney Warner. On the Burning Bush, see William Kostlevy, "The Burning Bush Movement: A Wisconsin Utopian Religious Community," *Wisconsin Magazine of History* 83 (summer 2000): 226–57.

23. "After Ten Years," *Megiddo Message,* Apr. 5, 1924, 10. "After 60 Years the Work Goes On," *Megiddo Message,* Apr. 1975, 8–9. Copies of the earliest issues of the *Megiddo News* are located at the Megiddo Church Home. They are not included in the microfiche edition of the *Megiddo Message,* which begins with 1915.

24. The church has made a conscious effort to employ the most modern printing methods for its publications, and the acquisition of new equipment or the adoption of new methods has been reported with obvious pride to the readership of the *Megiddo Message.* For example, in the October 1980 issue, the *Message* devoted almost an entire page to a description of its change from letterpress to off-set printing.

25. *Megiddo Message,* June 12, 1927, 8; Dec. 9, 1928, 8.

26. *Megiddo Message,* Aug. 23, 1947, 9; Aug. 21, 1948, 9; May 19, 1956, 2; September 1985, 26; Feb. 1987, 26. At least one person became interested in the *Message* after finding it in a college library at Milton College in Wisconsin (*Megiddo Message,* Dec. 13, 1958, 2).

27. The frequency with which the *Message* is published has changed over the years. Initially it was biweekly. In 1963, it became monthly, and since 1998 has been published ten times a year.

28. In "A Letter to You," a publication that was apparently distributed by the missionaries, Maud Hembree included a medicine show–style endorsement of Nichols's publications: "Send for his works and you will find that he was truly the greatest Bible student and discoverer of truth in these latter days, and the greatest benefactor to

mankind." Descriptions of the Nichols publications available from the mission followed (n.p., 1919, 8). A prophecy chart is still distributed as part of the book *Millennium Superworld* (1997).

29. *Who Are the Angels?* (Rochester, N.Y.: Megiddo Press, [1995–96]).

30. "Serving One's Country," *Megiddo Message,* Feb. 1992, 25.

31. "The Gambling Trap" (Rochester, N.Y.: Megiddo Press); "Sin as in Sodom" (Rochester, N.Y.: Megiddo Press).

32. "Focus on the Family" is a book, audiovisual, and radio ministry of psychologist Dr. James Dobson, which has a large following throughout conservative Protestantism and even among many mainline Protestants. The Megiddo emphasis on individual salvation should not be taken to mean that the family is not important to them. They do not recognize divorce, and they expect members who have families to be responsible spouses and parents. (See, for example, "Can a Divorced Person Remarry?" *Megiddo Message,* May 1995, 13.)

33. A scrapbook at the Megiddo Church Home contains clippings from unidentified Rochester, N.Y., newspapers reporting on the mission work outside of the Rochester area. *Megiddo Message,* Oct. 31, 1915.

34. Not all forays into the areas around Rochester were successful. The August 2, 1914, issue of the *Megiddo News* noted that two sisters had returned from Summerville, a community on Lake Ontario, reporting that "the people were pleasure mad and were not interested in the books."

35. *Megiddo Message,* Jan. 24, 1937, 6; Jan. 1, 1922, 10.

36. *Megiddo Message,* Nov. 23, 1919, 8; Sept. 28, 1919, 7. Other accounts of visits to business offices appear in the *Message* for August 17, 1919, and June 13, 1920. When Pickering and his wife went on mission trips together, he would often visit businesses while she called on private homes, where she was more likely to encounter women. *Megiddo Message,* Feb. 4, 1923, 7–8.

37. *Megiddo Message,* Mar. 18, 1928, 24.

38. Ibid., Oct. 27, 1918; Nov. 10, 1918; Jan. 5, 1919; Jan. 19, 1919; Oct. 13, 1918.

39. Ibid., Mar. 16, 1919.

40. Ibid., Oct. 27, 1918.

41. Ibid., Sept. 26, 1915.

42. Ibid., June 25, 1916; Jan. 19, 1918.

43. Ibid., Nov. 12, 1922, 8; May 28, 1916.

44. Elva Byers, interview with author, May 1998. The Byerses' move to Rochester was celebrated with a sixteen-stanza poem, composed by one of the daughters, with parts for each member of the family. The poem was published in the *Megiddo Message,* May 4, 1946, 7. As of 2001, two of the daughters, Elva and Shirley, are active in the church, maintain the church home, and host visitors.

45. "Rosa M. Elliott," (obituary), *Megiddo Message,* Feb. 16, 1952, 7. Clifford and Donna Ruth Mathias, interview with author, Oct. 2, 1999.

46. "Donation of Vital Organs," *Megiddo Message,* June 1988, 25. "Question: Why Does Not God Prevent Sickness and Disease?" *Megiddo Message,* Jan. 31, 1915; Jan. 20, 1924, 4; Jan. 15, 1922, 7; Mar. 29, 1922, 20; Dec. 7, 1924, 8; Oct. 25, 1925, 8.

47. *Megiddo Message,* Dec. 12, 1917; Sept. 3, 1922, 8; Dec. 23, 1923, 8; Feb. 3, 1924, 8. On one trip to Florida, missionaries reported having arranged an interview with William Jennings Bryan, who "expressed his desire to read any religious writings of so reasonable a nature" (*Megiddo Message,* Mar. 2, 1924, 8).
48. *Megiddo Message,* Oct. 15, 1922, 8.
49. Ibid., Jan. 16, 1916. It is not known whether it was Mr. Kingsley or another letter carrier who converted Caroline B. Schubert, who, "after learning of [the Megiddos'] work through her postman at Oneida Castle, N.Y., subsequently moved to Rochester in 1926." "Caroline B. Schubert" (obituary), *Megiddo Message,* Nov. 24, 1962, 9. "Emmanuel F. Boyer" (obituary), *Megiddo Message,* Apr. 1990, 26. Alice Cummings, interview with author, July 20, 2001.
50. *Megiddo Message,* Mar. 19, 1916; Apr. 30, 1916; Oct. 29, 1916; Nov. 26, 1916; Mar. 2, 1919; July 6, 1919; May 4, 1924, 8; Apr. 21, 1956, 2; Oct. 5, 1946, 9. "John Gizen" (obituary), *Megiddo Message,* July/Aug. 1983, 27.
51. *Megiddo Message,* July/Aug. 1986, 27; May 1992, 25; Sept. 1995, 21. "Barbara C. Hornum" (obituary), *Megiddo Message,* June 1988, 26.
52. *Megiddo Message,* June 13, 1915; July 18, 1915; Sept. 27, 1914. "Adalaide Buckingham" (obituary), *Megiddo Message,* Nov. 26, 1922, 8. In spite of a slight difference in the spelling of the first name, it can probably be assumed that Buckingham is the "Adeline" Buckingham of the *Buckingham* vs. *Buckingham* divorce. Mrs. Buckingham is mentioned as a financial contributor to and is presumably a member of the Minneapolis ecclesia. Minutes of the Christian Brethren. She was buried at Yamhill, Oregon, where one of her daughters resided. "Estella Dryden" (obituary), *Megiddo Message,* Feb. 1966, 7. "Gladys Sanders" (obituary), *Megiddo Message,* July/Aug. 1988, 26; "Gleanings from the Mission Field," *Megiddo Message,* Oct. 25, 1925, 8.
53. Maud Hembree, "A Letter to You," Feb. 28, 1919, 13.
54. Bristah and Frerichs, "A Study of the Megiddo Mission," 34; *Megiddo Message,* Oct. 1948, 7. Bristah and Frerichs may have gotten their idea of the Megiddos' social location from Percy Thatcher, whom they interviewed at length.

7. Back on the Water and Out on the Road

1. *Megiddo News,* Sept. 6, 1914; "Mission Work: Boat II," typescript in scrapbook, Megiddo Church Home. The word *book* is used to describe any publication other than the magazine regardless of its size.
2. *Megiddo Message,* May 28, 1916; Aug. 6, 1916.
3. "Echoes of Home Work," *Megiddo Message,* June 13, 1920, 7; "Megiddo III Dedicated," *Megiddo Message,* July 20, 1919, 7–8; "Missionary Activities during the Pastorate of Rev. Maud Hembree: In the Service of the King," *Megiddo Message,* Sept. 1981, 20–21; *Megiddo Message,* Aug. 8, 1920, 8; Aug. 3, 1919, 8; Sept. 28, 1919, 7. *Utica Daily Press,* Aug. 9, 1919; *Ovid Gazette,* quoted in *Megiddo Message,* Sept. 28, 1919, 7. On at least one occasion, the gospel car missionaries were asked to substitute for a vacationing clergyman (*Megiddo Message,* Mar. 18, 1928).

4. *Megiddo Message,* Apr. 20, 1924, 8; July 13, 1924. Flyer in scrapbook at the Megiddo Church Home. The car was briefly dubbed *Megiddo IV,* but apparently the name did not stick (*Megiddo Message,* Aug. 24, 1924, 6).

5. *Megiddo Message,* July 18, 1926, 7.

6. Ibid., July 18, 1926, 7; Apr. 2, 1927, 13; Mar. 18, 1928, 22; Aug. 24, 1924, 6.

7. Ibid., June 28, 1925, 8.

8. Ibid., June 19, 1921, 8.

9. Alice Cummings, interview with author, July 20, 2001.

10. The gospel car was such a distinctive vehicle that it was easily recognized by missionaries Newton Payne and Earl Zimmer, who encountered it in Portland, Maine, a few years after it had been sold (Newton H. Payne, interview, Oct. 2, 1999). "Missionary Efforts," *Megiddo Message,* Nov. 5, 1933, 8; "Gleanings from the Mission Field," *Megiddo Message,* Nov. 4, 1934, 7; "In the Mission Field," *Megiddo Message,* Dec. 28, 1946, 7; "The Mid-Winter Missionary Trip," *Megiddo Message,* Mar. 22, 1947, 7.

11. U.S. Patent 470,615. H. E. Skeels, Extension Ladder, Mar. 8 1892. According to a letter written in 1892 by Emeline Dunbar Nichols to her son L. T., who was in England at the time, Skeels had quite a bit of success selling his ladder (E. Nichols to L. T. Nichols, Mar. 16, 1892). Ruth Sisson, interview with author, Mar. 12, 1996; E-mail, Ruth Sisson to author, July 4, 2001; *Rochester (N.Y.) Times-Union,* Dec. 19, 1949, Mar. 26, 1964. When Ruth Hughes died, her estate was valued at $283,170. She willed a $10,000 cottage on a lake near Rochester and her personal effects to her housekeeper, who was also a member of the mission. The remainder of the estate went to the mission.

12. Ruth Sisson, E-mail to author, July 4, 2001.

13. "The Megiddo Missionaries," *Megiddo Message,* Aug. 5, 1950, 6.

14. *Megiddo Message,* Nov. 20, 1921, 8.

15. Ibid., Sept. 1, 1951, 7; "William Rue Hughes" (obituary), *Megiddo Message,* Nov. 26, 1949, 6.

16. The word *maranatha* is from the Greek and translates to "Christ is coming."

17. *Megiddo Message,* Apr. 19, 1936, 5–6; Mar. 27, 1943, 9.

18. Information about *Maranatha Musings* was provided by Margaret Tremblay, interview with author, Oct. 2, 1999.

19. *Megiddo Message,* Mar. 4, 1961, 2; December 1969, 19; December 1980, 25; May 26, 1962, 2. Former member, E-mail to author, July 7, 2001. The former member says that it was a relief when her family moved to Rochester and she no longer had to suffer the taunts of her classmates.

20. *Megiddo Message,* Aug. 28, 1921, 6. "Huldah Eva Goertzen" (obituary), *Megiddo Message,* Mar. 1996, 26.

21. Alice Cummings, interview with author, July 20, 2001.

22. *Megiddo Message,* July 27, 1946, 9. The last part of the quotation paraphrases part of Rev. 21:4.

23. Maud Hembree, "Why Do Not Megiddo Missionaries Go to Foreign Fields?" *Megiddo Message,* Dec. 6, 1941, 6. Nichols, *Treatise on the Coming of Jesus,* 10; L. T. Nichols,

"Paul's Example to Us That Conscience Is Not a True Guide," preached at the tabernacle, Nashville, Tenn., reprinted in the *Megiddo Message,* Apr. 20, 1946, 3; Percy J. Thatcher, "What We Believe," *Megiddo Message,* Mar. 29, 1952.

24. Evidence of Nichols's visit to Swansea includes a letter from "G. G. S." of Swansea in the July 22, 1939, issue the *Megiddo Message* (p. 8), in which the writer reports that while looking for some books, he or she found a sermon delivered by Nichols in Minnesota in 1890. It is impossible to tell how many people have been involved in the Swansea group, but a letter to the mission reprinted in the April 30, 1922, *Megiddo Message* indicates that there were forty people at the Christmas dinner in Swansea that year. "Charlotte Hayward" (obituary), *Megiddo Message,* May 31, 1925, 8.

25. *Megiddo Message,* Nov. 28, 1920.

26. *Megiddo Message,* Nov. 12, 1960, 2.

27. "Our Missionary Effort," *Megiddo Message,* Sept. 10, 1955, 6. *Megiddo Message,* Dec. 31, 1955, verso of cover.

28. *Megiddo Message,* Apr. 15, 1923. According to the article, an advertisement placed in a business magazine brought only three replies.

29. Ruth Sisson, interview with author, Mar. 1996; "Alexander Ploughwright" (obituary), *Megiddo Message,* June 1972, 26; *Megiddo Message,* Feb. 1, 1925. Among the converts of the advertising campaign was Robert W. Switzer, who learned about the Megiddo Church about 1932 when he saw one of the advertisements for Megiddo literature in an issue of *Grit,* a popular family magazine in a newspaper format, which he found while cleaning out a garage. Switzer wrote to the mission faithfully every month for forty years. Other magazines in which advertisements appeared included *Pathfinder, Capper's Weekly,* and *Farm News* (Dallas, Tex.).

8. The Known Bible and Its Defense

1. Wilson, *Sects and Society,* 220. On the evolution of biblical interpretation in nineteenth-century America, see Nathan O. Hatch, "Sola Scriptura and Novus Ordo Seculorum," in *The Bible in America: Essays in Cultural History,* eds. Nathan O. Hatch and Mark A. Noll (New York: Oxford Univ. Press, 1982), 59–78.

2. Lippy, *The Christadelphians,* 100–103; Wilson, *Sects and Society,* 220.

3. Nichols, "Inerrancy," 11; "Questions and Answers: Have Any of Your Members Received the Holy Spirit?" *Megiddo Message,* Apr. 13, 1963, 11. In answer to a question, a Megiddo writer assured a reader that he or she could not have committed the unforgivable sin mentioned in the book of Hebrews, because "the unpardonable sin was against the Holy Spirit and as no one possesses that power today, no one can sin against it" (*Megiddo Message,* Jan. 1969, 22).

4. Ruth Sisson, "The Inerrancy of the Bible: Only in the Autographs," *Megiddo Message,* Jan. 1995, 20.

5. Percy J. Thatcher, "What We Believe," *Megiddo Message,* Apr. 11, 1953, 6.

6. Nichols, "Inerrancy," 10. Maud Hembree did not read either Hebrew or Greek but was considered very adept at using lexicons. Ruth Sisson is the first pastor since Nichols to have studied either language, having studied Greek for two years. She

feels that modern computerized reference tools make it unnecessary to go to the effort of learning Hebrew. Ruth Sisson, interview with author, Oct. 2, 1999. Member Ruth Miller, who worked as a proofreader on the *Message,* had some knowledge of biblical languages. "Marietta Ruth Miller" (obituary), *Megiddo Message,* Feb. 1997, 25.

7. L. T. Nichols, *What Must We Do?* 5, 14–15.

8. "Questions and Answers: Do You Believe the Story of Noah and His Ark Literally?" *Megiddo Message,* Oct. 27, 1962, 11; "Evolution or Creation?" *Megiddo Message,* Dec. 1991, 16. The Megiddos do not believe that Adam was the first man but that he was the first man to enter into a covenant with God. *Megiddo Message,* Aug. 1, 1953, 4–6.

9. In 1938, missionaries traveling through eleven states in the South placed 55 sets of Hembree's *The Known Bible and Its Defense* ("In the Land of Cotton," *Megiddo Message,* Jan. 7, 1939, 8); in 1941, 150 sets were placed during a cross-country trip ("Sowing and Watering," *Megiddo Message,* Feb. 15, 1941, 8); in 1951, travelers to Texas and California placed 35 sets, while others in the Carolinas placed 8 ("Missionaries Return from Trips in the Central, Southwestern, and Southern States," *Megiddo Message,* Nov. 24, 1951, 7). *Megiddo Message,* Oct. 20, 1956, 2. *History of the Megiddo Mission* (1979), 38.

10. *Megiddo Message,* Aug. 27, 1955, 7; Aug. 1999, 1. Kenneth Flowerday is quoted from "Questions and Answers," *Megiddo Message,* July 1968, 23. A statement on Bible quotations on the inside of the front cover of each issue of the *Megiddo Message* reads "Unidentified quotations are from the King James Version" and lists the abbreviations used for other translations that may be used. When asked what translations the church would recommend, Ruth Sisson replied by listing a number of the more popular, "better translations in modern English," as well as two computer Bible programs. "About Translations," *Megiddo Message,* Nov. 1999, 23.

11. L. T. Nichols, "Treatise on Hell" (Rochester, N.Y., n.d.), 32. Maud Hembree also quoted from the Douay version in her writings.

12. Ruth Sisson, E-mail to author, Sept. 12, 2000.

13. Fanella H. Porter, "I Knew a Great Woman," *Megiddo Message,* Sept. 1981, 9.

14. "Clifton H. Fleming, Sr." (obituary), *Megiddo Message,* Oct. 1984, 26; "Margaret B. Owens" (obituary), *Megiddo Message,* December 1978, 27; "Maude E. Frantz" (obituary), *Megiddo Message,* Feb. 1970, 19; "Mrs. Katherine Patten" (obituary), *Megiddo Message,* Mar. 4, 1939, 8–9. *Megiddo Message,* Feb. 1983, 21; Sept. 28, 1930, 9.

15. *Megiddo Message,* Feb. 12, 1922, 7; Oct. 12, 1924, 8.

16. Information about the development of the sound system was provided by Newton H. Payne, Nov. 1999. "The Megiddo Mission Church," *Megiddo Message,* Nov. 21, 1953, 9.

17. *Megiddo Message,* July 23, 1922, 8. Sunday services are occasionally held in the church home, such as when it is exceptionally hot and the air-conditioned meeting room in the home is more comfortable.

18. "Obituary: Maggie Millican, Hattie E. Nichols," *Megiddo Message,* June 1, 1924, 8. The Megiddos generally give gifts to adults for milestone birthdays, such an eightieth or ninetieth or when the recipient is especially esteemed. In its April 30, 1913,

issue, the *Megiddo News* reported that Mrs. Nichols's birthday had been recognized with a special song, a set of dishes, and a stool for her to use while fishing. Since the Megiddos distributed L. T. Nichols's publications for many year after his death, many people wrote to Nichols not knowing that he had died. It is likely that Harriet Nichols answered at least some of these letters.

19. "Publisher and Editor Attend Evolution Trial at Dayton, Tenn.," *Megiddo Message,* July 26, 1925, 7–8; "Rochesterian Scores Darrow on Ignorance," unidentified Rochester, N.Y., newspaper, July 1925, located in scrapbook at Megiddo Church Home. (The text of this article is essentially the same as that of the July 26, 1925, *Megiddo Message* article.) Maud Hembree, "Answers to Some Questions Asked at the Evolution Trial," *Megiddo Message,* Aug. 9, 1925, 4–7; Maud Hembree, "Some Things I Saw and Heard at Dayton, Tenn.," *Megiddo Message,* Aug. 23, 1925, 5–7. The departure of the gospel car on its mission trip was delayed until Flowerday and Thatcher returned from Dayton. The enduring importance of the Scopes trial to Maud Hembree and Ella Skeels is evident from the appearance of a lengthy article, including the text of an article from a Chattanooga newspaper, in an answer to a reader's question that appeared in the *Megiddo Message* of Aug. 30, 1931. Versions of the articles on the Scopes trial also appeared in Hembree, *The Known Bible and Its Defense,* 1:165–81.

20. See *Megiddo Message,* July 12, 1925, to Sept. 6. Quotation is from page 8 of the July 26 issue.

21. Nichols, *Treatise on the Coming of Jesus and Elijah,* 15.

22. The concern about peace negotiations, a frequent theme in articles in the *Megiddo Message* during the 1930s and 1940s, relates to a passage in the prophetic book of Ezekiel in the Bible. In Ezek. 13:10, the Lord condemns false prophets "because they have seduced my people, saying, Peace, and there is no peace."

23. *Megiddo Message,* Mar. 29, 1922, 12–13; Feb. 2, 1930, 7.

24. Ibid., Apr. 2, 1938, 8.

25. Ibid., June 19, 1943, 4. Although the Megiddos saw the world situation as predictive of the approach of the arrival of Elijah, they refused to identify World War II as being specifically mentioned in Scripture. When a reader asked if there were any references to World Wars II and III in the Bible, the answer was that there were none, only references to "wars and rumors of wars" (*Megiddo Message,* Jan. 12, 1957, 11).

26. "Questions and Answers: You Say We Are Living in the Era of Christ's Coming. What Are the Signs to Prove It?" *Megiddo Message,* Nov. 11, 1961, 11. *These Things Shall Be . . .* (Rochester, N.Y.: Megiddo Church, 1983). On nuclear war and prophecy in the post–World II era, see Boyer, *When Time Shall Be No More,* 115–51. While the Megiddos do not focus attention on nuclear war, they do not see themselves as immune from destruction in case of war. In answer to a question regarding whether or not people should build bomb shelters, a Megiddo writer noted, "God does not do for us what we can do for ourselves. He gives us minds that we can use in devising plans for self-protection, and He expects us to use them. If, after using our time profitably we need still more time to perfect our character, only then will He step in and arrange the circumstances to give us added time" (*Megiddo Message,* Nov. 11, 1961, 11).

27. "What does it all mean?" *Megiddo Message,* Nov. 2001, 14–15.

28. *Megiddo Message,* Nov. 5, 1955, 9; Sept. 1969, 23. In an answer to an inquiry from a reader regarding the possible prophetic significance of a recent earthquake in Nicaragua, in the February 1973 *Message* (p. 26), Flowerday cited specific examples of earthquakes that occurred in 1755, 1906, and 1923, in which there was more loss of life than in the Nicaragua earthquake. Flowerday also attributed the appearance of Halley's Comet to "the operation of a fixed law of nature [which] could have nothing to do with Christ's coming or the work He will perform" (*Megiddo Message,* Jan. 1969, 23.)

29. Newton H. Payne, interview with author, Oct. 2, 1999; Ruth Sisson, E-mail to author, July 29, 2001. Ruth Sisson remembers hearing member Fanella Porter say that members hardly knew there was a depression. One of the few possible effects of the depression was the slowing of the influx of new families to the mission, as evidenced by a decline in the enrollment in the mission school, which had fewer than five students by the middle of the 1930s (School records, Megiddo Church Home, Rochester, N.Y.).

30. Ruth Sisson, "About the Antichrist," *Megiddo Message,* Oct. 1997, 20. The concept of an antichrist appears in the Bible in 1 John 2:18, 22, and 2 John 7. On modern popular interest in the antichrist and the number 666, see Boyer, *When Time Shall Be No More,* especially pages 272–90.

31. Ruth Sisson, "666?" *Megiddo Message,* Aug. 1998, 21.

32. A series of three articles in dialogue format, which compared beliefs of the Megiddos with those of the Christadelphians, appeared in the *Megiddo Message* in late 1992. The family of former pastor Newton H. Payne had ties to the Christadelphians, and this may explain some of the persistence of interest in this dialogue.

33. "Spiritualism—Is It True?" by Maude Hembree denounced Spiritualism (*Megiddo Message,* Feb. 16, 1930, 1–8). A version of this article also appeared in Hembree, *The Known Bible and Its Defense,* 2:68–98. L. T. Nichols, *Treatise on the Holy Spirit* (Rochester, N.Y.: Megiddo Mission Band, 1905), 4. "Questions and Answers: Would Somebody Please Give Me Some Light on Revelations [*sic*], Chapter 13?" *Megiddo Message,* Sept. 1, 1962, 11–12. On Christian Science, see Maud Hembree, "What Are Miracles? Is Christian Science Founded on the Bible?" *Megiddo Message,* June 22, 1930, 1–7. A series of articles in the *Megiddo Message* in 1953 entitled "What We Believe" dealt with various theological orientations with which the Megiddos disagree, including Spiritualism, Christian Science, and Jehovah's Witnesses. In the 1960s, the *Megiddo Message* frequently printed the following disclaimer: "The Megiddo Church is an independent organization. We have no affiliation or connection with any other established religious body, whether Adventism, Mormonism, Jehovah's Witnesses" (e.g., *Megiddo Message,* July 1965, 11).

34. *Yamhill County Reporter,* June 14, 1883.

35. On Mormon cosmology and the plurality of worlds, see Erich Robert Paul, *Science, Religion, and Mormon Cosmology* (Urbana: Univ. of Illinois Press, 1992), esp. 75–126.

36. During its history, the movement that became Jehovah's Witnesses comprised several groups known by various names, including Russellism (after founder Charles

Taze Russell), Zion's Watch Tower Tract Society, Millennial Dawn, Dawn Bible Student's Association, and International Bible Student's Association. The first segment of the group to adopt the name Jehovah's Witnesses did so in 1931; in 1956, the entire movement took the name (I. Hexham, "Jehovah's Witnesses," in *Dictionary of Christianity in America* [Downers Grove, Ill.: InterVarsity Press, 1990]).

37. "Timely Topics: Religious Quackery," *Megiddo Message,* Apr. 1973, 7.

38. "Questions and Answers," *Megiddo Message,* Jan. 19, 1963, 11.

39. In more recent years, the Megiddos have added such works as the *New Schaff-Herzog Encyclopedia of Religious Knowledge* and Will Durant's *Caesar and Christ* to the sources of information on church history that they cite in their publications. See *Understanding the Bible, Section 6: Apostasy and Restoration* (Rochester, N.Y.: Megiddo Mission, n.d.). Fanella H. Porter, "I Knew a Great Woman," 8.

40. School registers that list the names of students, their dates of birth, and the names of their parents are located at the Megiddo Church Home, Rochester, N.Y.

41. Newton H. Payne, interview with author, Oct. 2, 1999. *Megiddo Message,* November 1969, 10. Former member, E-mail to author, July 8, 2001.

42. Newton H. Payne, interview with author, July 20, 2001; former member, E-mail to author, July 8, 2001.

43. Nichols, *Fourth Pamphlet,* 253.

9. An Eroding Public Image

1. "The Pastor and Teacher of the Megiddo Mission Peacefully Sleeps in Death," *Megiddo Message,* Dec. 1, 1935, 1–7.

2. "Dedication and Independence Day Services," *Megiddo Message,* June 28, 1936, 6.

3. "Pastor and Teacher Sleeps," 2.

4. Newton H. Payne, interview with author, Aug. 25, 1998. Ruth Sisson, E-mail to author, Dec. 4, 2000. Ella Skeels's husband, H. E. Skeels, whom she married in 1877, died in 1936, shortly after she assumed responsibility for the mission ("Henry Elmer Skeels" (obituary), *Megiddo Message,* May 17, 1936, 6).

5. Jill Watts, *God, Harlem U.S.A.: The Father Divine Story* (Berkeley, Calif.: Univ. of California Press, 1992), 71–72, 97. The Sayville case actually worked to Father Divine's advantage when four days after the verdict was rendered, the judge in the case died of a heart attack. Father Divine was immediately credited with having exacted divine retribution for his treatment in court, enhancing his status among his followers and exciting additional interest from potential converts.

6. Ibid., 149–51. Another object of scandal was Benjamin Purnell, the costumed leader of the House of David, a communal religious organization best known by contemporaries for the amusement park it operated at its Benton Harbor, Michigan, headquarters and for its long-haired, bearded traveling baseball team. In 1923, Purnell was sued by some of his followers who sought to recover property they had surrendered at Purnell's direction. A few years later, Purnell was charged with the statutory rape of several youthful members of his organization.

7. In Shawn Francis Peters's outstanding book on the persecution of the Jehovah's Witnesses during the 1930s and early 1940s, *Judging Jehovah's Witnesses: Religious Persecution and the Dawn of the Rights Revolution* (Lawrence: Univ. Press of Kansas, 2000), he notes that throughout their ordeal the American Civil Liberties Union supported the Witnesses and they were not without other friends. First Lady Eleanor Roosevelt even addressed their problems in her syndicated newspaper column in 1943.

8. The court cases in which the mission and its members were involved were initiated by people outside the mission. While the church believes that in 1 Cor. 6 "Paul . . . condemns the practice of brother going to law with brother. . . . He doesn't lay down any rule about a Christian suing a non-Christian. However, going to law is often more costly than it is worth, and the results usually unsatisfactory" ("Questions and Answers," *Megiddo Message*, Dec. 22, 1962, 11).

9. Megiddo Church Constitution and Bylaws, 5 n. 10.

10. *Rochester (N.Y.) Times-Union*, April 13, 1937.

11. On the Bryant case, see *Rochester (N.Y.) Democrat and Chronicle*, Nov. 1, 1944. This case is also mentioned in the study by seminary students Bristah and Frerichs.

12. Bristah and Frerichs, "A Study of the Megiddo Mission," 37; "Mary Olaevia Greene" (obituary), *Megiddo Message*, Jan. 7, 1939, 7; *Rochester (N.Y.) Evening News*, Jan. 12, 1939; "In the Matter of Awarding Limited Letters of Administration upon the Estate of M. Olaevia Greene," surrogate's court, Monroe County, New York, Jan. 7, 1939; court decision, Jan. 12, 1939.

13. Megiddo Church Constitution and Bylaws, 5.

14. *Rochester (N.Y.) Democrat and Chronicle*, Nov. 13, 1940; Apr. 13, 1941.

15. The first report of Howard Sisson's attendance at services in Rochester appeared in the *Megiddo Message* of March 29, 1931. At that time, it was stated the Sissons were readers of Megiddo literature.

16. Information about the Sisson case is from the *Norwich (N.Y.) Sun*, July 26, 1934, July 28, 1934, and August 13, 1934. The *Rochester (N.Y.) Democrat and Chronicle* reprinted portions of the *Sun* story beginning on the front page of the "City News" section of its July 29, 1934, edition. The case also received coverage in newspapers in Binghamton and Elmira, New York. The two older Megiddo women who appeared in the courtroom were Reverend Hembree and Ella Skeels.

17. *Norwich (N.Y.) Sun*, Aug. 13, 1934.

18. It is not certain what connection Mr. Starr may have had to the case other than as an interested bystander. The Norwich, New York, directory of 1934 lists a Louis Starr who is a clerk at the Maydole Tool Company in Norwich (p. 151). Information on Mr. Starr was provided by Kathryn L. Barton of the Guernsey Memorial Library, Norwich, N.Y.

19. It would be impractical to list all similarities between the Sisson letter and Reverend Hembree's book, but, for example, a sentence in the second column of the Sisson letter reads, "When mankind was turned from the truth to fables (II Tim 4:3–4), the world was made drunk on the pagan idea of a literal devil whom God had created

to tempt man through life and keep the fires burning through eternity." The same sentence, without the Bible verse, appears on page 121 of the second volume of Hembree's *The Known Bible and Its Defense*. The Sisson letter also contains lengthy quotations from such sources as the *Encyclopaedia Britannica* and Andrew Dickson White's *History of the Warfare of Sin*, which also appear in Hembree's book. Materials in the letter that are not from Hembree's *The Known Bible and Its Defense* can be traced to other Megiddo publications. For example, a section on hell is similar in content and organization to an L. T. Nichols tract, *Treatise on Hell*, which has been adapted for articles in the *Megiddo Message* and for tracts published by the mission.

20. *Rochester (N.Y.) Democrat and Chronicle*, Sept. 21, 1934. The paper also printed a response from the mission.

21. *People ex rel. Sisson* v. *Sisson*, 271 N.Y. 285 (New York Court of Appeals, 1936). By the time the case was resolved, public interest had waned to the extent that the court decision merited only a brief article on page 5 of the *Norwich (N.Y.) Sun*, May 27, 1936. In New York State, the court of appeals, rather than the supreme court, is the highest state court.

22. Howard Sisson's missionary trips were reported in the *Megiddo Message*, March 8, 1936; Jan. 5, 10, 1937, 5. The May 1966 issue of the *Message* reported that Howard Sisson conducted a funeral service on behalf of the mission at Fort Johnson, New York. Bristah and Frerichs, "A Study of the Megiddo Mission," 37–38. *Rochester (N.Y.) Democrat and Chronicle*, May 28, 1936; "Howard Sisson" (obituary), *Megiddo Message*, Nov. 1989, 26. Ruth Sisson, E-mail to author, Apr. 15, 2000; Aug. 20, 2001.

23. CPS camps were generally modeled on the Civilian Conservation Corps camps of the depression and worked on forestry and land conservation projects. On the status of conscientious objectors during World War II, see Peter Brock and Nigel Young, *Pacifism in the Twentieth Century* (Syracuse, N.Y.: Syracuse Univ. Press, 1999), 171–80.

24. Kenneth Flowerday, "Questions and Answers," *Megiddo Message*, Aug. 1970, 23.

25. "No Member of Megiddo Mission to Be Drafted for Duty as Combatant," *Megiddo Message*, Feb. 10, 1918. This article appears to have been reprinted from an unidentified outside source. *Rochester (N.Y.) Democrat and Chronicle*, Feb. 7, 1918; Bristah and Frerichs, "A Study of the Megiddo Mission," 35–36; *Rochester (N.Y.) Democrat and Chronicle*, June 12, 1942; "U.S. Drops Sect Member Draft Action," unidentified Rochester, N.Y., newspaper, July 1, 1943, clipping in scrapbook at Megiddo Church Home. While the Megiddos do not believe in taking combat roles in wartime, their patriotism apparently has led a few to accept noncombatant status. After the war, Daigh was active in the mission's outreach, going on several missionary trips. The refusal to engage in combat during wartime is not equated with total nonresistance among the Megiddos. People can legitimately defend themselves against "open attack or assault . . . [because] resistance to such an attack is not resistance to the law but to lawlessness which God never condemned" (*Megiddo Message*, Oct. 1978, 26).

26. On Lew Ayres, see Arthur J. Kaul, "The Conscientious Objection of Lew Ayres," *American Journalism* 12 (summer 1995): 384–92. Ayres was not a member of one of the recognized peace churches.

27. *Megiddo Message,* June 16, 1956, 11. Hembree, *The Known Bible,* 1:307–8. The Megiddos never seem to have been critical of husbands who provided their wives with money to spend on fashionable clothing. The economic and social theorist Thorstein Veblen may have been correct in stating that impractical and even uncomfortable clothing demonstrates that the woman who wears it does not need to, or even cannot, perform useful labor. This not only reflects positively on the status of the woman but also indicates that the husband who supports her is an exceptionally good provider. Thorstein Veblen, *The Theory of the Leisure Class: An Economic Study of Institutions* (New York: Macmillan, 1899; New York: Modern Library, 1934), 134–36.

28. "Timely Topics: Debasing Dress," *Megiddo Message,* May 1971, 18.

29. *Megiddo Message,* Apr. 1968, 15; Aug. 1970, 8–9; Apr. 1972, 23.

30. Among the passages of Scripture that address women's attire is 1 Tim. 2:9, which states that "women should dress themselves modestly, not with their hair braided, or with gold, pearls, or expensive clothes." On the biblical bases for the dress of the Megiddo women, see *Megiddo Message,* Nov. 1965, 23.

31. Ibid.

32. "Synopsis of the Principal Beliefs and Practices of the Megiddo Church" (Rochester, N.Y.: Megiddo Church, 1986), 23–24.

33. "Commemorating Christ's Birth," *Megiddo Message,* May 1, 1948, 7.

34. Clippings of articles from the *Community News* are located in a scrapbook at the Megiddo Church Home. Many of the articles include substantial lists of participants in mission activities.

35. Ella Skeels's role as minister was in many ways largely an honorary position and Brother Thatcher "was her writer/sermon-reader/editor" (Ruth Sisson, E-mail, Dec. 4, 2000). "At the Campfire," *Megiddo Message,* Sept. 26, 1942, 7. *Megiddo Message,* July 1, 1944, 7. "The Pastor and Teacher of the Megiddo Mission Peacefully Sleeps in Death," *Megiddo Message,* Dec. 1, 1945, 1. Accounts of the celebration of the centennial of L. T. Nichols's birth indicate that she was unable to take part in the services and ceremonies.

36. Kenneth E. Flowerday, "Editor and President Succumbs," *Megiddo Message,* Nov. 29, 1958, 3–4.

37. Flowerday, "Editor and President," 3–4; *History of the Megiddo Mission* [1979], 41; "A Service for Parents," *Megiddo Message,* May 7, 1955, verso of cover.

38. "Enlarging the Meeting Room," *Megiddo Message,* May 4, 1946, 5–6.

39. Ibid. "The New Home of the Megiddo Message," *Megiddo Message,* Jan. 21, 1950, 1.

40. *Megiddo Message,* Sept. 20, 1958, 15; Aug. 22, 1959, 2; Jan. 1964, 2. Ruth Sisson, e-mail to the author, Sept. 6, 1999.

41. Minutes Book, Megiddo Church Home, Rochester, N.Y. Bristah and Frerichs, "A Study of the Megiddo Mission," 31. Until at least 1881, L. T. Nichols performed marriage ceremonies. It is not known when marriage ceremonies stopped occurring within the context of the Brethren and marriage began to be discouraged. Joan Marie Salzmann (Meyering) lists three couples married by Nichols and three couples married by his associate H. C. Plummer in her article on the Christadelphians of

Oregon, "Did Your Ancestors Join This Group? The Christadelphians," *Heritage Quest* 68 (March/Apr. 1997): 95.

42. Bristah and Frerichs, "A Study of the Megiddo Mission," 32.

43. *Rochester (N.Y.) Times-Union,* May 26, 1958; Ruth Sisson, interview with author, Oct. 2, 1999; Newton H. Payne, interview with author, Oct. 2, 1999; Donna Ruth Mathias, interview with author, Oct. 2, 1999.

44. Information about people who left and the time and extent of their involvement with the mission are taken from a variety of sources, including letters to the *Megiddo Message,* obituaries in the *Megiddo Message,* "Megiddoites Ponder Fate of Four 'Rebels'" *Rochester (N.Y.) Times-Union,* May 26, 1958, and the author's personal acquaintance with people who left the mission. The Abib dinner in 1958 drew only 195 people, down from nearly 240 in 1954. This may be a sign that there were already problems within the mission congregation ("The Anniversary of Our Lord's Birth . . . at Megiddo," *Megiddo Message,* Apr. 5, 1958, 7). Much information about the events of 1958 was supplied by Ruth Sisson and church member Margaret Tremblay, interview with author, Oct. 2, 1999. Many of the children whose photographs appeared several times in Rochester newspapers in conjunction with the celebration of True Christmas were among those who left.

45. Bristah and Frerichs, "A Study of the Megiddo Mission," 32.

46. Megiddo Church Constitution and Bylaws, 5; Ruth Sisson, E-mail to author, Aug. 20, 2000.

47. Newton H. Payne, letter to author, Oct. 6, 1999.

48. "Eulogy," *Megiddo Message,* Nov. 1985, 8. In what may have been a veiled reference to the events of 1958, in his Abib message in 1959 Reverend Flowerday appealed to his listeners "to surmount or side-step the difficulties and make it a Happy New Year!" ("Memories of Abib," *Megiddo Message,* Apr. 18, 1959, 8).

10. Thy Kingdom Come

1. Ruth Sisson, E-mail to author, Nov. 6, 2000.

2. Ibid.

3. At the time of his death in 1977, Liot Snyder had been a member of the Rochester congregation for fifty-one of his eighty years and was recognized for his contributions to the correspondence ministry and for the "several hundred" poems he had written, many of them composed while he was traveling to and from work. "Liot Snyder" (obituary), *Megiddo Message,* May 1977, 18.

4. On divorce, see "What the Bible Says about Divorce and Remarriage," *Megiddo Message,* Jan. 1979, 17, and "Questions and Answers," Sept. 1971, 25; the occult, "Timely Topics: What about the Occult," July 1974, 7; on the "new morality," see "Timely Topics: No New Morality," Oct. 1970, 7, and "Timely Topics: 'New' Morality," Sept. 1973, 8; on crime, see "Timely Topics: Skyrocketing Crime," June 1970, 8; on alcoholism, see "Timely Topics: Alcoholism," Sept. 1970, 8–10; on drugs, see "Timely Topics: Drugs," April 1971, 11–12, and "LSD—The Mind Drug," Dec. 1966, 16–17 (reprinted from literature of Allied Forces, an advocacy organization); on advertising, see

"Timely Topics: Advertising," Apr. 1972, 8–9; on pollution, see "Timely Topics: Pollution Control," May 1972, 7; on obscenity, see "Signs of the Times: Prevalent Obscenity," Mar. 1969, 10. "Timely Topics: Forgiveness," *Megiddo Message,* Dec. 1974, 12.

5. "Timely Topics: TV—Activated Evil," *Megiddo Message,* June 1973, 8–9. "TV—Blessing or Curse?" *Megiddo Message,* May 1976, 22–23. In another article, the author accused radio, television, and newspapers of having "weakened religion to the point of disrespect" and "destroying the image of religion" ("Signs of the Times: Branded Religion," *Megiddo Message,* Sept. 1972, 7).

6. Ruth Sisson, "Backwash from PTL?" *Megiddo Message,* Sept. 1987, 10.

7. "Timely Topics: Concerning 'Jesus Christ Superstar,'" *Megiddo Message,* Nov. 1971, 8.

8. "Letters," *Megiddo Message,* Dec. 1971, 12; Feb. 1972, 24.

9. *Megiddo Message,* July/Aug. 1980, 17. The two passages of Scripture cited are 1 Tim. 1:3–4, which urges Timothy to instruct "some that they teach no other doctrine, neither give heed to fables and endless genealogies, which minister questions rather than godly edifying," and Titus 3:9: "avoid foolish questions and genealogies and contentions, and strivings about the law; for they are unprofitable and vain." The criticism of genealogy also serves to further distance the Megiddos from Mormons, who are well-known for their interest in genealogy.

10. *Megiddo Message,* Sept. 1969, 22–23.

11. *Megiddo Message,* May 1968, 23. In response to a reader's question regarding racial integration, the writer of the "Your Questions Answered" column in the November 1, 1958, issue of the *Megiddo Message* (p. 11) cited biblical evidence that Christ was "undiscriminating" in his ministry and that the early church "labored unceasingly to break down racial barriers." "A Soldier Rests at Ninety-one," *Megiddo Message,* Feb. 2000, 23–4; Ruth Sisson, E-mail to author, July 5, 2001. Edith Porter, who had been chronically ill for nearly thirty years, died July 30, 1968. "Edith H. Porter" (obituary), *Megiddo Message,* Sept. 1968, 10.

12. "Timely Topics: Violence—On Campus and Off," *Megiddo Message,* July 1970, 8–9.

13. J. Edgar Hoover, "The Interval Between," *Megiddo Message,* July 1970, 15–17. George W. Sewell, "'Quo Vadis?'" *Megiddo Message,* Aug. 1971, 8–9, 26 (reprint from *Pulpit Digest*). The *Lutheran Hour* broadcast appeared under the heading "Hope" in the September 1969 issue of the *Megiddo Message,* pages 15–16.

14. Hembree, *The Known Bible,* 1:376.

15. *Megiddo Message,* Nov. 5, 1955, 9. According to Ruth Sisson, the column appeared at a time when several members were being given the opportunity to respond to readers' questions. The author is unknown.

16. Boyer, *When Time Shall Be No More,* 5, 126–27.

17. *Megiddo Message,* Dec. 1980, 25; *Megiddo Message,* May 1982, 27.

18. R. Chris Connolly, *Millennium Superworld* (Rochester, N.Y.: Megiddo Press, 1997), 11–12.

19. Ibid., 32.

20. James H. Moorhead, *World without End: Mainstream American Protestant Visions of the Last Things, 1880–1925* (Bloomington: Indiana Univ. Press, 1999), 57–58.

21. Sydney E. Ahlstrom, *A Religious History of the American People* (New Haven, Conn.: Yale Univ. Press, 1972), 483.

22. Colleen McDannell and Bernhard Lang, *Heaven: A History* (New Haven, Conn.: Yale Univ. Press, 1988), 194. McDannell and Lang note that Swedenborg was not alone in his view of a more material afterlife, but Swedenborg's vision "is unique in its scope and richness of detail" (199). It would also have been accessible to most Americans, as Swedenborg's writings were translated and made available in the United States throughout the nineteenth century and are still in print in many languages.

23. Helen Sootin Smith, introduction to *The Gates Ajar* by Elizabeth Stuart Phelps (Cambridge, Mass.: Belknap Press of Harvard Univ. Press, 1964), xxv; Moorhead, *World without End,* 60. Phelps's familiarity with Swedenborg's work is indicated by a reference to Swedenborg and a quotation from *Heaven and Hell* that appear in *The Gates Ajar* (113–14). Helen Sootin Smith suggests that Edward Bellamy may have read Phelps's *Beyond the Gates* and that it informed his widely read utopian novel *Looking Backward 2000–1887* (1887).

24. Elizabeth Stuart Phelps, *Beyond the Gates* (Boston: Houghton, Mifflin, 1884), 17–27; Moorhead, *World without End,* 59. It is worth noting that this transition is in marked contrast to that of the Megiddos, who believe that they will enter the millennial kingdom suddenly upon the arrival of Elijah, who will enlist the Megiddos to assist him in preparing for the arrival of Christ.

25. Phelps, *Beyond the Gates,* 126.

26. Connolly, *Millennium Superworld,* 67. In the United States, one branch of Swedenborg's followers, also known as Swedenborgians, was organized as the Church of the New Jerusalem.

27. Nichols, *What Must We Do,* 56.

28. Connolly, *Millennium Superworld,* 31, 37, 39, 40, 109–10. In *Beyond the Gates,* Elizabeth Stuart Phelps envisioned the kingdom of the afterlife as a theocracy and a society with varieties of ranks (140). She also wrote that in the afterlife, "So far from being any diminution in the number and power of the senses in the spiritual life, I found not only an acuter intensity in those which we already possessed, but that the effect of our conditions was to create others of whose character we had never dreamed" (151).

29. Connolly, *Millennium Superworld,* 72–73. Formal education is unusual in Christian afterlife scenarios. In most, those who are saved are already prepared for life in the other world or are taught informally by those already there. One notable exception was the other world of the Spiritualists in the nineteenth century, in which "educational institutions proliferate" (McDannell and Lang, *Heaven,* 297). Elizabeth Stuart Phelps envisioned students in "what we should call below colleges, seminaries, or schools of art, music, or sciences" (Phelps, *Beyond the Gates,* 120).

30. "Angels Glorified Mortals?" *Megiddo Message,* Dec. 1987, 23; *Who Are the Angels?* Although angels are transported from planet to planet, the Megiddos do not believe that they have wings because there is nothing in accounts of angelic visits in Scripture to indicate that they do and they were often mistaken for ordinary men (*Megiddo Message,* Feb. 23, 1957, 11). The ability to see angels was one of the

abilities withdrawn at the end of the Apostolic Age which will return when Jesus comes again, but angels are active in the world, protecting and assisting "those who will be heirs of salvation" *(Who Are the Angels?)*.

31. The Megiddos are adamant that true religion cannot conflict with true science and consequently readily incorporate scientific advances in their view of the world to come. (See "Questions and Answers," *Megiddo Message,* Nov. 1967, 23.)

32. Connolly, *Millennium Superworld,* 79.

33. Ibid., 80–81.

34. Ibid., 91. L. T. Nichols, "In Quarantine," 3–4; *Rochester (N.Y.) Democrat and Chronicle,* Mar. 26, 1906.

35. Connolly, *Millennium Superworld,* 91, 112. In *Beyond the Gates,* Phelps makes frequent references to the beauty and lush vegetation in the world of the afterlife. In her afterlife world, Beethoven creates music that surpasses anything he created when he was alive. Following an afterlife concert, the protagonist Mary states, "What knew we of music, I say, who heard its earthly prototype? It was but the tuning of the instruments before the eternal orchestra shall sound" (157). On this point *Millennium Superworld* differs markedly from Phelps's afterlife in which individuals will be able to indulge in a multitude of pleasures that the Megiddos would find offensive, including novel reading.

36. Connolly, *Millennium Superworld,* 87–88.

37. Ibid., 123, 129.

38. Gerald R. Payne, "The Earth Forever," *Megiddo Message,* Aug. 2000, 16. The Scripture passages cited include Ps. 37:11; Matt. 6:10; and Isa. 45:18.

39. McDannell and Lang, *Heaven,* 198. Like many of the others who speculated on life after death, Lavater considered himself a scientist and is credited with the development of the pseudoscience physiognomics, a system for reading character in the face that competed with phrenology in the nineteenth century. According to McDannell and Lang, Lavater was better known in his day than was Swedenborg. He is unknown to most Americans because little of his work has been translated into English; most works about him are in German.

40. Margaret Converse, "Megiddo Mission: Waiting for the Second Coming on Thurston Road," *Rochester (N.Y.) Democrat and Chronicle,* Dec. 14, 1969. "New Pastor and President Leads On," *Megiddo Message,* Dec. 1985, 11. Newton H. Payne, interview, July 20, 2001. The church has recently improved the health care facility with the addition of a deck and ramp. They have also purchased a motorized wheelchair for Reverend Payne.

41. Ruth Sisson, E-mail to author, July 29, 2001.

42. Ibid., Aug. 20, 2000.

43. "What We Believe: Cross-Examination No. 37," *Megiddo Message,* Aug. 15, 1953, 5.

44. Newton H. Payne, E-mail, Oct. 6, 1999. One may also access a page critical of the Megiddos on a Web site maintained by Watchman Fellowship (www.watchman.org) to provide "a readily accessible Christian response to cults and new religious movements." The article on the site criticizes the Megiddos for their stands on water baptism, the Trinity, hell, the devil, immortality, and annihilation of the unsaved. It

also identifies points on which the Megiddos' beliefs are similar to those of groups with which they are often confused—Mormons, Jehovah's Witnesses, and Seventh-Day Adventists.

45. Ruth Sisson, "Internet Pollution?" *Megiddo Message,* Sept. 1996, 25. An article in the *Message* lists guidelines for safe use of the Internet. It includes a list of programs designed to filter out "pornographic and indecent" Web sites and refers the reader to a Web site with lists of filtering programs ("Browse with Care," *Megiddo Message,* Aug. 1999, 23–24).

46. Alice Cummings, interview with author, Oct. 3, 1999.

47. Ruth Sisson, interview with author, March 24, 1996. The position on jewelry appears to have changed over the years. In "Questions and Answers: Do You Wear Jewelry? Do You Wear Lipstick?" *(Megiddo Message,* Oct. 14, 1961, 11), it states that jewelry is not permitted because it is considered to "come under the head of conformity to the world." In answer to a similar question in the May 1972 issue, it states that the mission does not permit the use of jewelry or makeup because "the Bible defines lawful Christian adornment as exclusive of that which is worn only for show" (25). "Questions and Answers: Do You Believe in Women Bobbing Their Hair?" *Megiddo Message,* Sept. 30, 1961, 11.

48. *Rochester (N.Y.) Democrat and Chronicle,* June 18, 1981. The negotiations center was never used. The church building suffered considerable damage from gunfire. All of the windows on the side of the church opposite the bank were broken and there were numerous bullet holes in the interior of the church.

49. "Questions and Answers: Should Christians Provide for the Future?" *Megiddo Message,* February 1964, 23.

50. Information on the Megiddo Church today was largely provided by Ruth Sisson in interviews conducted in March 1996, May 1998, April 1999, October 1999, and E-mail messages at other times. Other sources include personal observation.

51. Rev. Newton Payne notes that there was some resistance to hiring former members to staff COTE but that the two women have proven to be "the life of the project." The Byers sisters' mother was a member but left the church. However, she retained a high respect for the Megiddos, and when she died a brief obituary for her appeared in the *Message* and her funeral service was conducted by someone from the church. Elva Byers, interview with author, July 19, 2001; "Frances Fern Byers" (obituary), *Megiddo Message,* January 1985, 26.

52. Former member, E-mail to author, June 30, 2001.

53. "George W. Sawyer" (obituary), *Megiddo Message,* June 1980, 21; "Huldah Eva Goertzen" (obituary), *Megiddo Message,* Mar. 1996, 26.

54. A more likely explanation for the late traffic is the fact that in Rochester, which has manufacturing plants and health care facilities, several of which are close to the church, African Americans make up a disproportionately large percentage of second- and third-shift workers.

55. When talking to the Megiddos about the changes in the neighborhood, they invariably speak particularly nostalgically of Merrill's Five and Ten Cent Store, a small

variety store where one "could buy just about anything." The store's owner was obviously a much-beloved figure in the community.

Appendix

1. The original of the diary is located at the Megiddo Church Home in Rochester, New York. This typescript was made from a photocopy provided by the Megiddo Church. The diary is transcribed exactly as written with a few exceptions. Punctuation has been modified for the sake of clarity, and some spellings have been changed to reflect standard spelling. State names have been added in brackets where city and town locations are not obvious. Where necessary, words have been added in brackets to denote missing words, usually due to torn page edges. Dates have been entered in a standard format. In a few places, contents have been summarized in brackets and small portions have been deleted, primarily statements of little substance.

2. "Bro N" refers to L. T. Nichols. Maud Hembree is often referred to as "Sr H."

3. In an untitled memoir, probably written in the 1930s, located at the Megiddo Church Home, Kenneth Flowerday remembered that "Traveling on the Mission Boat was delightful. I can still remember my first ride as Megiddo pulled away from the dock and made a trial run under her own steam."

4. In order to speed the trip downriver, Captain Nichols asked Mrs. James Ogren and Mrs. Rachel Sweet to meet the boat at Quincy, Illinois, instead of Hannibal, Missouri, as originally planned. The two women did as they were directed, but the boat had to stop at Hannibal anyway, as the women had sent some of their belongings on ahead (*Barry [Ill.] Adage,* Nov. 21, 1901).

5. Probably the Loosahatchie River just north of Memphis.

6. G.A.R. stands for Grand Army of the Republic, a Union Civil War veterans organization. According to Kenneth Flowerday's memoir of his life on the *Megiddo,* in addition to the band's playing, L. T. Nichols gave a short talk to the veterans, after which the band, playing "Custer's Funeral March," led a procession of "old veterans" to a nearby cemetery. Flowerday thought the band was well received (Flowerday, "Experiences of Mission Life," 22). Given that the Brethren were conscientious objectors to war and that L. T. Nichols had had a bad personal experience in the Union army in the Civil War, it is interesting that the Megiddo band would play for an encampment of Civil War veterans.

7. The *Fort Madison Morning Republican* reported that the Brethren "speak kindly of their reception in our city, the general good order that prevailed during the meetings and the good attendance and kind attention given during the services." The newspaper reporter wrote, "We can say that they leave with the best wishes of the people. They have conducted themselves like ladies and gentlemen and are entitled to the good and kindly remembrance from our people" (May 31, 1902, reprinted in the *Barry [Ill.] Adage,* June 15, 1902).

8. The *Ravenna* was a steamer that capsized on the Mississippi River during a cyclone on June 12, 1902. According to a *Chicago Tribune* story that was reprinted in the

Davenport (Iowa) Democrat (June 13, 1902), the captain and three members of
the twenty-seven-man crew were drowned in the incident.

9. The sister that Nichols visited was probably Anne Gertrude, who was born in South
    Bend, Indiana, in 1841. She married Nathaniel Blanchard Parmelee, a carpenter and
    shoemaker in Lomira, Wisconsin, in 1862. She died in 1914 and is buried at Iron
    Mountain, Michigan. Information provided by genealogist Owen J. Nichols.

10. Probably Valton, Wisconsin, a small town in Sauk County in the southwestern part
    of the state.

11. The image of the summer land is one that was used by L. T. Nichols. For example, it
    appears in a sermon published as "In Quarantine," 3, and in the sermon he
    preached at the first Abib service in Rochester in 1906 (*Rochester [N.Y.] Democrat
    and Chronicle,* March 26, 1906).

12. *"Millennial Dawn"* was a five-volume work by Charles Taze Russell (1852–1916),
    one of the founders of the movement that became Jehovah's Witnesses.

Bibliography

Primary Sources

Bristah, James, and Margaret Frerichs. "A Study of the Meggido Mission." Student paper. Colgate-Rochester Divinity School [1946].

Constitution and Bylaws of the Megiddo Church Inc. Rochester, N.Y.

Flowerday, Kenneth. "Experiences of Mission Life on Three Rivers: Mississippi—Ohio—Cumberland, Oct. 24, 1901—January, 1904." Memoir. Megiddo Church Home, Rochester, N.Y.

Lee, Mary A. "On the Mississippi on Board the Mission Ship Megiddo." Diary. Megiddo Church Home, Rochester, N.Y.

Minutes of the Christian Brethren (Minneapolis), 1894–1901. Megiddo Church Home, Rochester, N.Y.

Minutes of the Megiddo Mission, 1912–1958. Megiddo Church Home, Rochester, N.Y.

Northwest Colony and Russell Townsite Company, Ledger, 1871–74. Topeka: Manuscript Dept., Kansas State Historical Society.

Publications of L. T. Nichols and the Megiddo Mission/Church

The Coming of Elijah and Jesus and the Kingdom of God. Rochester, N.Y.: Megiddo Church, 1972.

Connolly, R. Chris. Millennium Superworld. Rochester, N.Y.: Megiddo Press, 1997.

Elijah Then Christ. Rochester, N.Y.: Megiddo Press, 1982.

Flowerday, Kenneth. "Recollections." Megiddo Message, Oct. 21, 1944, 3–4.

The Great Apostasy. Rochester, N.Y.: Megiddo Mission, 1975.

Hembree, Maud. "The Faithful and Wise Servant of God Who Gave Meat in Due Season." Megiddo Message, Oct. 7, 1944, 1–4.

———. The Known Bible and Its Defense. 2 vols. Rochester, N.Y.: author, 1933–34.

History of the Megiddo Mission. Various ed. Rochester, N.Y.: Megiddo Mission, 1905–79.

An Honest Man: The Life and Work of L. T. Nichols. 2d ed. Rochester, N.Y.: Megiddo
Press, 1987.
Life and Work of the Rev. L. T. Nichols: Founder of the Megiddo Mission. Rochester, N.Y.:
Megiddo Mission, 1944.
Megiddo Message.
Nichols, L. T. *Adam before He Sinned.* Portland, Ore.: Schwar & Anderson, 1881.
————. *Bible Chronology.* West Concord, Minn.: author, 1899.
————. *Bible Chronology.* Rochester, N.Y.: Megiddo Mission, 1911.
————. *A General Letter to All the Churches.* Memorial ed. Rochester, N.Y.: Megiddo Mis-
sion, 1941.
————. "The Megiddo Mission Boat, Where Built, When and by Whom, Its Object and
Mission." Evansville, Ind.: n.p., [1903].
————. *First Pamphlet of the Condensed Report of the Annual Meeting of the True Chris-*
tadelphians of Oregon Which Commenced May the Twenty-seventh Eighteen Hun-
dred and Eighty-two and Continued over Three Sundays. Holding in All Nineteen
Days and a Half: And an Entire Night. During Which Time, the Author, Publisher
and Printer of This Report: Delivered Fifty-seven Discourses, Which Will Be Sent Out
as Fast as Printed. McMinnville, Ore.: author, 1882.
————. *Second Pamphlet . . .* McMinnville, Ore.: author, 1882.
————. *Third Pamphlet . . .* McMinnville, Ore.: author, 1882.
————. *Fourth Pamphlet . . .* McMinnville, Ore.: author, 1882.
————. *Fifth Pamphlet . . .* McMinnville, Ore.: author, 1882.
————. *Sixth Pamphlet . . .* McMinnville, Ore.: author, 1882.
————. "Told by Himself." *Megiddo Message,* Oct. 4, 1936, 1–9; Oct. 18, 1936, 1–7.
————. *Treatise on Christmas and New Year's.* Rochester, N.Y.: [Megiddo Mission], 1906
————. *Treatise on the Coming of Jesus and Elijah,* 8th ed. Rochester, N.Y.: Megiddo
Mission, n.d.
————. *What Must We Do to Be Saved?* Rochester, N.Y.: author, 1905.
Payne, Gerald. "The Earth Forever." *Megiddo Message,* Aug. 2000, 14–16.
Porter, Fanella. "I Knew a Great Woman." *Megiddo Message,* Sept. 1981, 7–11.
"Reminiscences of the Life of the Rev. L. T. Nichols." *Megiddo Message,* Sept. 29, 1951,
1–4.
"Synopsis of the Principal Beliefs and Practices of the Megiddo Church." Rochester, N.Y.:
Megiddo Church, 1986.
Understanding the Bible: Apostasy and Restoration. Rochester, N.Y.: Megiddo Church,
n.d.
Understanding the Bible: Of Life, Death, and Immortality. Rochester, N.Y.: Megiddo
Church, n.d.
Understanding the Bible: The Mosaic Law—Its Significance. Rochester, N.Y.: Megiddo
Mission, n.d.

Newspapers

Alton (Ill.) Telegraph
Barry (Ill.) Adage
(Boston) Banner of Light

Christadelphian (Birmingham, U.K.)
Christadelphian Advocate
Clinton (Iowa) Advertiser
Davenport (Iowa) Daily Leader
Davenport (Iowa) Daily Republican
Dodge County (Minn.) Republican
Evansville (Ind.) Courier
Mantorville (Minn.) Express
Minneapolis Times
Nashville Banner
Norwich (N.Y.) Sun
Owatonna (Minn.) People's Press
Paducah (Ky.) News-Democrat
Rochester (N.Y.) Democrat and Chronicle
Rochester (N.Y.) Herald
Rochester (N.Y.) Times-Union
Rochester (N.Y.) Union Advertiser
St. Louis Post-Dispatch
St. Paul Dispatch
St. Paul Pioneer Press
West Concord (Minn.) People
Yamhill County (McMinnville, Ore.) Reporter

Books and Articles

Adams, George Worthington. *Doctors in Blue: The Medical History of the Union Army in the Civil War.* New York: Henry Schuman, 1952.

Alexander, Ruth M. "'We Are Engaged as a Band of Sisters': Class and Domesticity in the Washingtonian Temperance Movement, 1840–1850." *Journal of American History* 75 (Dec. 1988): 763–85.

Boyer, Paul S. *When Time Shall Be No More: Prophecy Belief in Modern American Culture.* Cambridge, Mass: Belknap Press of Harvard Univ. Press, 1992.

Brock, Peter, and Nigel Young. *Pacifism in the Twentieth Century.* Syracuse, N.Y.: Syracuse Univ. Press, 1999.

Burke, K. E. "Influence of Thomas and Alexander Campbell in the Oregon Country." *Christian Standard* 69 (May 5, 1934): 5.

Carson, Gerald. *Cornflake Crusade.* New York: Rinehart & Co., 1957.

Chase, Warren. *Forty Years on the Spiritual Rostrum.* Boston: Colby and Rich, 1888.

Cook, Philip L. *Zion City, Illinois: Twentieth-Century Utopia.* Syracuse, N.Y.: Syracuse Univ. Press, 1996.

Cross, Whitney R. *The Burned-Over District: The Social and Intellectual History of Enthusiastic Religion in Western New York, 1800–1850.* Ithaca, N.Y.: Cornell Univ. Press, 1950.

Current, Richard N. *The History of Wisconsin.* Vol. 2, *The Civil War Era, 1848–1873.* Madison: State Historical Society of Wisconsin, 1976.

Dayton, Donald W. *Discovering an Evangelical Heritage*. New York: Harper & Row, 1976.

Hatch, Nathan O. *The Democratization of American Christianity*. New Haven, Conn.: Yale Univ. Press, 1989.

Hayden, Dolores. *Seven American Utopias: The Architecture of Communitarian Socialism, 1790–1975*. Cambridge, Mass.: MIT Press, 1976.

Hughes, Richard T. "Christian Primitivism as Perfectionism: From Anabaptists to Pentecostals." In *Reaching Beyond: Chapters in the History of Perfectionism*, ed. Stanley M. Burgess. Peabody, Mass.: Hendrickson Publishers, 1986.

———. "The Meaning of the Restoration Vision." In *The Primitive Church in the Modern World*, ed. Richard T. Hughes. Urbana: Univ. of Illinois Press, 1995.

Humble, B. J. "The Influence of the Civil War." *Restoration Quarterly* 8 (1965): 233–35.

Jenkins, Philip. *Mystics and Messiahs: Cults and New Religions in American History*. New York: Oxford University Press, 2000.

Jones, Charles Edwin. *Perfectionist Persuasion: The Holiness Movement and American Methodism, 1867–1936*. Metuchen, N.J.: Scarecrow Press, 1974.

Klement, Frank L. *Wisconsin in the Civil War: The Home Front and the Battle Front, 1861–1865*. Madison: State Historical Society of Wisconsin, 1997.

Kostlevy, William. "The Burning Bush Movement: A Wisconsin Utopian Religious Community." *Wisconsin Magazine of History* 83 (summer 2000): 226–57.

Lass, William. *Minnesota: A History*. New York: W. W. Norton, 1977. Reprint, Nashville: American Association for State and Local History, 1983.

Life and Works of Thomas Williams. N.p.: Christadelphian Advocate Committee, 1974.

Lippy, Charles H. *Being Religious, American Style: A History of Popular Religiosity in the United States*. Westport, Conn.: Praeger, 1994.

———. *The Christadelphians in North America*. Lewiston, N.Y.: Edwin Mellen Press, 1989.

———. "Waiting for the End: The Social Context of American Apocalyptic Religion." In *The Apocalyptic Vision in America: Interdisciplinary Essays on Myth and Culture*, ed. Lois Parkinson Zamora, 37–63. Bowling Green, Ohio: Bowling Green Univ. Popular Press, 1982.

Mattern, Carolyn J. *Soldiers When They Go: The Story of Camp Randall, 1861–1865*. Madison: State Historical Society of Wisconsin for the Department of History, Univ. of Wisconsin, 1981.

May, Dean. *Three Frontiers: Family, Land and Society in the American West, 1850–1900*. New York: Cambridge Univ. Press, 1994.

McAllister, Lester G., and William E. Tucker. *Journey in Faith: A History of the Christian Church (Disciples of Christ)*. St. Louis: CBP Press, 1975, 1989.

McDannell, Colleen, and Bernhard Lang. *Heaven: A History*. New Haven, Conn.: Yale Univ. Press, 1988.

McKelvey, Blake. "Water for Rochester." *Rochester History* 34 (July 1972).

Melton, J. Gordon. "Introduction: When Prophets Die: The Succession Crisis in New Religions." In *When Prophets Die: The Postcharismatic Fate of New Religious Movements*, ed. Timothy Miller, 1–12. Albany: State Univ. of New York Press, 1991.

———. "Spiritualization and Reaffirmation: What Really Happens When Prophecy Fails." *American Studies* 26 (fall 1985): 17–29.

Moore, R. Laurence. *Religious Outsiders and the Making of Americans.* New York: Oxford Univ. Press, 1986.

Moorhead, James H. *World without End: Mainstream American Protestant Visions of the Last Things, 1880–1925.* Bloomington: Indiana Univ. Press, 1999.

Peters, Shawn Francis. *Judging Jehovah's Witnesses: Religious Persecution and the Dawn of the Rights Revolution.* Lawrence: Univ. Press of Kansas, 2000.

Phelps, Elizabeth Stuart. *Beyond the Gates.* Boston: Houghton, Mifflin, 1884.

———. *The Gates Ajar,* ed. Helen Sootin Smith. Cambridge, Mass.: Belknap Press of Harvard Univ. Press, 1964.

Pitzer, Donald E., ed. *America's Communal Utopias.* Chapel Hill: Univ. of North Carolina Press, 1997.

Riggle, H. M. *Pioneer Evangelism, or Experiences and Observations at Home and Abroad.* Anderson, Ind.: Gospel Trumpet Co., 1924.

Salzmann, Joan Marie. "Did Your Ancestors Join This Group? The Christadelphians." *Heritage Quest* (March/Apr. 1997): 91–96.

Shuman, L. Herman. "Kiss, Holy." In *Brethren Encyclopedia.* Philadelphia: Brethren Encyclopedia, 1983.

Smith, Helen Sootin. Introduction to *The Gates Ajar* by Elizabeth Stuart Phelps, ed. Helen Sootin Smith, v–xxxiv. Cambridge, Mass.: Belknap Press of Harvard Univ. Press, 1964.

Thomas, John. *Elpis Israel: A Book for the Times, Being an Exposition of the Kingdom of God with Reference to "the Time of the End" and "the Age to Come."* London: author, 1849.

Tyler, Alice Felt. *Freedom's Ferment: Phases of American Social History from the Colonial Period to the Outbreak of the Civil War.* Minneapolis: Univ. of Minnesota Press, 1944. Reprint, New York: Harper & Row, 1962.

Veblen, Thorstein. *The Theory of the Leisure Class: An Economic Study of Institutions.* New York: Macmillan, 1899. Reprint, New York: Modern Library, 1934.

Watson, W. W. *History of Barry.* Barry, Ill.: Barry Advocate, 1903.

Watts, Jill. *God, Harlem U.S.A.: The Father Divine Story.* Berkeley: Univ. of California Press, 1992.

Wiener, Aharon. *The Prophet Elijah in the Development of Judaism: A Depth Psychological Study.* Boston: Routledge and Kegan Paul, 1978.

Wilson, Bryan R. *Sects and Society: A Sociological Study of the Elim Tabernacle, Christian Science, and Christadelphians.* Berkeley: University of California Press, 1961.

Wright, Edward Needles. *Conscientious Objectors in the Civil War.* Philadelphia, Univ. of Pennsylvania Press, 1931.

Wyman, Mark. *The Wisconsin Frontier.* Bloomington: Indiana University Press, 1998.

Index

Waiting for Elijah was designed and typeset on a Macintosh computer system using QuarkXPress software. The text is set in Garamond ITC, and the chapter openings are set in RotisSemiSans. This book was designed by Bill Adams, typeset by Kimberly Scarbrough, and manufactured by Thomson-Shore, Inc.